John Adams

and the Prophets of Progress

JOHN ADAMS

From a portrait painted by Gilbert Stuart in 1798
Published by courtesy of the owner, Mrs. Robert Homans

John Adams

& *The Prophets of Progress*

ZOLTÁN HARASZTI

Harvard University Press

Cambridge, Massachusetts

1952

Preface

The main part of John Adams's library, consisting of over three thousand volumes, is deposited in the Boston Public Library, while a number of other books which once belonged to him are preserved in the Boston Athenaeum and in the Adams Mansion at Quincy. More than a hundred of these volumes contain marginal notes by Adams. Some have only a few scattered sentences; others three to four thousand words each, and two no less than twelve thousand. Most of the books on which Adams commented are by eighteenth-century English and French writers—Bolingbroke, Rousseau, Voltaire, Turgot, and a dozen others. The purpose of the present volume is to bring these notes before the public.

The collection reached the Boston Public Library in a circuitous way. In August 1822, in his eighty-seventh year, John Adams presented his library to the town of Quincy. "I do hereby give, grant, convey and confirm to the inhabitants of the town of Quincy . . . ," he wrote, "the fragments of my library, which still remain in my possession, excepting a few that I shall reserve for my consolation in the few days that remain to me . . ." The books were to be placed in a Greek and Latin School or Academy, for which he made special provision, deeding various pieces of land to the town. Unfortunately, although Adams had even advised the future schoolmasters how to start their pupils on the Greek and Hebrew alphabets, such an academy was never established. After several transfers, the collection was housed in the public library of Quincy in 1882; and eleven years later, to make it more accessible to scholars, it was moved to the Boston Public Library.

No one knows how large Adams's library was at its fullest. It was probably the greatest private collection of its day in America, comparable to that formed by William Byrd of Westover, Virginia, in the first half of the century. John Quincy Adams, too, was an ardent collector; he accumulated even more books than his father, although his library did not possess the same consistently high quality. Furthermore, he brought together a truly magnificent collection of some twelve thousand pamphlets, many of which bear John Adams's signature. The library of John Quincy Adams, with additions made by Charles Francis Adams, is now in the library of the Adams Mansion.

An Adams Manuscript Trust was instituted in 1905 by the three surviving sons of Charles Francis Adams and one of his grandsons. This includes not only the papers of John Adams, but also those of most of his descendants. The Adams Papers are stored in the Adams Room at the Massachusetts Historical Society and are not open to the public. A member of the family is their custodian, and the Massachusetts Historical Society has no control over them.

Portions of Adams's marginal notes were first printed in *More Books*, a monthly bulletin formerly published by the Boston Public Library, and in its successor, *The Boston Public Library Quarterly*. For their appearance in these journals the present writer, who is Keeper of Rare Books and Editor of Publications at the Library, has been responsible. The notes on Rousseau and Condorcet he included in articles published, respectively, in the *Atlantic Monthly* (February 1948) and the *William and Mary Quarterly* (April 1950).

The writer wishes to express his thanks to Mr. Milton E. Lord, Director of the Boston Public Library, for permission to publish Adams's notes in book form. The late Henry Adams (1875–1951) gave similar permission for the notes in those of Adams's books now at the Boston Athenaeum. Thanks are also due to the editors of the above-mentioned magazines for allowing the inclusion of the articles which appeared in their pages.

Adams's marginal notes follow one another so closely that a real dialogue ensues between him and the various authors. The larger part of them are reproduced here precisely in this form—brief excerpts from the texts are given, accompanied by Adams's comments. For the sections on which Adams made few or no comments, connecting paragraphs have been provided in order to give continuity to the discussion.

Adams's comments are printed intact with respect to grammar and syntax. However, the excessive and arbitrary use of capital letters has been abandoned. Many readers are frightened by the archaic appearance of extra capitals; and in any case it seems better to avoid them, for, whereas in the eighteenth century such capitals were normal, today they introduce an element of quaintness and thus considerably distort the effect. The spelling and punctuation have also been modernized, and contractions have been spelled out. In these matters, the present writer has followed the practice adopted by Charles Francis Adams in the editing of Adams's *Works*. Consistency has demanded a similar treatment of quotations from Adams's letters published elsewhere.

More complicated has been the handling of the excerpts from the texts, which occupy about as much space as the comments. These texts fall into three categories: books written in English (Bolingbroke, Mary Wollstonecraft, etc.); printed translations (Rousseau, Condorcet, etc.); and translations made for the present volume (Frederick, Mably, etc.). The treatment has been different for each type. The wording of the excerpts from books written in English is that of the original. Where selections have necessarily been abridged, omissions within excerpts have been indicated by ellipses in the usual way. It was certainly no easy task to reduce the enormous periodic sentences of these eighteenth-century authors to manageable proportions and yet include all the pertinent parts. The printed translations from the French occasionally had to be changed, for they sound stilted today and are at times incorrect. It might have been easier to provide new translations; yet the old ones have been retained, because Adams's comments are often attached to certain phrases. In the fresh translations prepared for the present volume Adams's rendition of words has been followed. For the use of scholars, the excerpts from the texts have been identified, at the beginning of each section, by page references to the volumes which Adams read and also to modern editions.

Omissions in quotations from Adams's published works and letters —and also from the works and letters of Jefferson, Madison, and others —have been marked, except when they occur at the beginning: sentences starting with three dots and a lower case letter are halting to most readers. The words or sentences italicized in the quoted passages are those which Adams underscored in the books. Scholars will welcome this typographical differentiation, and it is hoped that others will not find it troublesome. The italics should, indeed, prove generally helpful, since they draw attention to the words or sentences on which the comments hinge.

It must also be stated that this volume is not intended as a compendium of *all* the notes made by Adams. He was in the habit of repeating in the margins not only names and key words, but sometimes whole sentences, simply as an aid to his memory. These have been omitted, as have been also the repetitious notes and those of little relevance. Further, it should be noted that only those books on which Adams commented at length are discussed; more than a score of other volumes, which he treated fragmentarily, are merely mentioned or are briefly summarized at the end. No attempt has been made to record the innumerable passages which Adams underlined without comment. The student interested in every detail may turn to the books themselves.

The Adams Collection is part of the Rare Book Department of the Boston Public Library, and the writer is glad to record his obligation to many of his present and former associates. Miss Margaret Munsterberg and Miss Honor C. McCusker assisted him in the labor of copying out Adams's notes. They also read the manuscript and prompted innumerable verbal changes, as did Mrs. Alison Bishop, Miss Theresa Coolidge, and Mr. Jesse Zelden. In addition, Miss Harriet Swift, Curator of Americana, Mrs. Julia M. Gurnett, Mrs. Jane Lacy, and Miss Ellen M. Oldham were invariably helpful.

The partial publication of Adams's notes in the magazines mentioned above aroused the attention of a wide circle of scholars, who ever since have urged that all the more important commentaries be printed in a comprehensive volume. The writer remembers with particular gratitude the early interest which Professor Gilbert Chinard, Justice Felix Frankfurter, Professor Samuel Eliot Morison, and the late Harold J. Laski manifested in his work. It was Mrs. Catherine Drinker Bowen who, while engaged in her remarkable book on Adams, persuaded him to complete the task without delay.

Finally, acknowledgment is due to Mr. Thomas J. Wilson, Director of the Harvard University Press. Without his penetrating criticisms and, above all, his expert advice on the revision, the book would not be what it is.

The present writer does not wish to make exaggerated claims for Adams's marginal comments. It is safe to say, however, that since the private printing of Adams's letters to Dr. Benjamin Rush, in 1892, they constitute the most important material brought to light about him. Adams had discussed many of the same questions in his books and letters; however, the comments contain much that is new, and they present his views with fresh emphasis and many valuable details. Out of their searching analysis, the individuality of each author, as well as Adams's reaction, clearly emerges. The notes grow organically as the books themselves unfold.

Above all, the political and social problems with which Adams deals and the opinions he voices have a terrible urgency today.

Zoltán Haraszti

Boston, Massachusetts
July 1951

Contents

Contents

Illustrations

John Adams

and the Prophets of Progress

No Statues or Monuments

Of all illustrious Americans, posterity has perhaps dealt most unjustly with John Adams. He is thought of as a vain, pompous, and ill-tempered man, who had besides some ridiculous notions of royalty. One has to admit, of course, his services to the Revolution; but those were in his early years. Students of his life and work are uniformly fascinated, regarding him as one of the half-dozen greatest men in American history, but their opinion has made little impression on the public. Theodore Parker declared that "with the exception of Dr. Franklin . . . no American politician of the eighteenth century was Adams's intellectual superior"; that, although Hamilton and Jefferson, even Jay and Madison and Marshall surpassed him in some high qualities, "no one of them seems to have been quite his equal on the whole." [1] Yet only recently a popular magazine headed an article about him "The Great Lackluster," smugly reminding its readers that "he has been called the dullest of the Founding Fathers—not without reason, but certainly without enough of it."

Historians have wondered about the causes of Adams's relative obscurity—the indifference, if not animosity, which envelops him. One should remember, however, that he was not popular even in his lifetime. Adams himself knew this best. "Mausoleums, statues, monuments," he wrote to Dr. Benjamin Rush, the Philadelphia scientist and signer of the Declaration of Independence, "will never be erected to me . . . Panegyrical romances will never be written, nor flattering orations spoken to transmit me to posterity in brilliant colors." And he listed a few of the reasons: his defense of the British soldiers who took part in the Boston Massacre had never been forgotten or entirely forgiven; his conduct in the first Continental Congress drew upon him the aversion not only of the Tories but of all the proprietary gentlemen in Pennsylvania; Franklin, Thomas Paine, and many others were alarmed at his advocacy of a government in three branches; the Constitution of Massachusetts acquired for him the reputation of holding notions incompatible with republicanism; his diplomatic success in Holland produced eternal jealousy; and his resistance to the intrigues of the French government during the peace negotiations aroused Franklin's hatred of him, as well as the ineradicable enmity of the French party in America.[2] Two years later when Dr. Rush urged him to compose a farewell address to the nation, to be opened after his death, he was touched but declined the suggestion. He would be charged, he wrote, with the selfish desire of promoting his children: "Washington and Franklin could never do anything but what was imputed to pure, disinterested patriotism; I never could do anything but what was ascribed to sinister motives." Should he recommend religious virtues, he would be accused of attempting the establishment of Presbyterianism; should he inculcate fidelity to the marriage bed, it would be said that he had a malicious desire to hold up Hamilton to the coming ages for his libertinism; should he advise prohibitory taxes on liquor, he would be called "a canting Puritan, a profound hypocrite"; and should he express his abhorrence of the whole banking system, the people of America would think that he died mad. Further, he did not possess the style needed for such an exhortation. Of course, he mused, if he could persuade some eloquent friend, perhaps Jefferson, to write it for him, there is no reason why he could not transcribe it—"as Washington did so often." [3] Rush's letter filled his eyes with tears, but he had to end his reply with mischief.

The feeling of persecution, of the lack of recognition of his services, never entirely left Adams. "From the year 1761, now more than fifty years," he complained, "I have constantly lived in an enemies' country." [4] And thinking of his death, he added: "By the treatment I have received and continue to receive I should expect that a large majority of all parties would cordially rejoice to hear that my head was laid low."

Nor was this merely the suspiciousness and the disillusionment of an old man. In every phase of his long career Adams had made bitter enemies, as innumerable entries in his Diary testify. As a young lawyer he quarreled with Robert Paine ("He called me a numskull and a blunderbuss") and with Eben Thayer ("He called me *a petty lawyer.* This I resented."). Andrew Oliver appeared to him but "a very sagacious trifler"; and about Peter Oliver he emphatically recorded: "I have him in the utmost contempt. I have the utmost contempt of him. I had as lief say it to him as not. I have the utmost contempt of him." Putnam,

with whom he first studied law at Worcester, had "a sneer" and "a
sly look"; and of the Boston bar, Gridley's grandeur was diminished by
"stiffness and affectation" and Thacher was "slow of conception and
communication." Even the patriotism of James Otis, his own idol, was
not unmixed with "cunning." Adams's journal is filled with thumb-
nail portraits, most of them etched in acid. In the Continental Congress,
James Duane had "a very effeminate, feeble voice"; Arthur Middleton's
forte lay "in rudeness and sarcasm"; and John Dickinson, who first
seemed modest, delicate, and agreeable, turned out to be "a great
fortune and piddling genius." During the peace negotiations in Paris he
himself perpetuated the remark made by David Hartley to Sir John
Temple, "Your Mr. Adams, that you represent as a man of such good
sense . . . is the most ungracious man I ever saw." [5] Adams's youthful
determination to examine men's ways of thinking ("Let me search for
the clue which led great Shakespeare into the labyrinth of mental
nature") was made for life.[6] His probing was sharp and relentless.
Past seventy-five, he could still refer to Fisher Ames as "the pretty
little warbling canary bird"; and for her strictures in her book on the
American Revolution, he fought a Homeric duel with Mercy Warren,
roundly denouncing that venerable lady for her "malignancy of
heart." [7]

Adams's jealousy of Washington and Franklin knew no bounds. [2]
"The history of our Revolution," he wrote to Dr. Rush, "will be one
continued lie from one end to the other. The essence of the whole will
be that Dr. Franklin's electrical rod smote the earth and out sprang
General Washington. That Franklin electrified him with his rod—
and thence forward these two conducted all the policy, negotiations,
legislatures, and war." [8] This was during his Vice-Presidency; in his retirement he had still more leisure to meditate about fame, disinterestedness, and similar subjects. To what talents did Washington owe his
"immense elevation" above his fellows? Dr. Rush asked, and Adams
promptly replied: to a handsome face; a tall stature, "like the Hebrew
sovereign chosen because he was taller by the head than the other
Jews"; graceful attitudes and movements; a large, imposing fortune; the
fact that he was a Virginian, as "Virginian geese are all swans"; the gift
of silence, and so on, ending his letter: "Here you see I have made
out ten talents without saying a word about reading, thinking, or
writing . . ." [9] Franklin, he thought, had a great genius, original,
sagacious, and inventive; but his excellence as a legislator, politician, or
negotiator never appeared. From day to day he sat in silence at the
Continental Congress, "a great part of his time fast asleep in his chair";

and in France he was too self-indulgent to attend regularly to the business of the embassy.[10] In Franklin, however, Adams found his match. For the vexations he had to endure during those years in Paris, the old Sage retaliated with a comment which has stuck to Adams and his memory ever since. Adams, Franklin wrote to the secretary of foreign affairs in Congress, "is always an honest man, often a wise one, but sometimes, and in some things, absolutely out of his senses." [11] Volumes of eulogies cannot undo the harm which this dictum has done to Adams's reputation.

This uninhibited use of invective, this delight in finding chinks in the armor of his contemporaries, may be shocking in a great statesman. But Adams, the farmer's son, loved strong language which smelled of the earth; and his temper subsided as quickly as it rose. "There have been·very many times in my life," he confessed, "when I have been so agitated in my own mind as to have no consideration at all of the light in which my words, actions, and even writings, would be considered by others." [12] Perhaps Franklin's saying was literally true; in spite of his strong compact body, there undoubtedly was a deep neurotic strain in Adams. Yet the fact remains that most of his grievances were real. He was vindictive toward Franklin, but it is extremely doubtful that without his angry insistence the rights to the fisheries and the western territories would have been secured for America. He was rude to Mrs. Warren, but it was hardly fair on her part to write that he made his "appearance in the theatre of politics" in 1774, thus suppressing fourteen years of his revolutionary activities; that after his first return from Paris he "continued in his retired and mortified condition for some months," ignoring that in those very months Adams drafted the Constitution of Massachusetts, the model for several other state constitutions and for the Federal Constitution itself. Someone with a greater sense of "decorum" might have kept a resentful silence; Adams made a torrential protest, which was much more sincere and human —and more innocent.

If Adams was ruthless in judging others, he at least analyzed himself with the same unsparing frankness. The young man of Braintree who dreamed of success saw clearly that his "pretensions to wisdom and virtue" had only made people laugh. "It is affectation of learning . . . and it is a weak fondness," he wrote, "to show all that I have, and to be thought to have more than I have. Beside this, I have insensibly fallen into a habit of affecting wit and humor; of shrugging my shoulders and moving and distorting the muscles of my face; my motions are stiff and uneasy, ungraceful; and my attention is unsteady and irregular . . . they are faults, defects, fopperies, and follies, and disadvantages. Can I mend these faults and supply these defects?" And twenty years later as American envoy in Paris he reflected: "There is a feebleness and a languor in my nature. My mind and body both partake of this weakness. By my physical constitution I am but an ordinary man. The times alone have destined me to fame; and even these have not been able to give me much. When I look in the glass, my eye, my forehead, my brow, my cheeks, my lips, all betray this relaxation. Yet some great events, some cutting expressions, some mean hypocrisies, have, at times, thrown this assemblage of sloth, sleep, and littleness into rage a little like a lion." And then he added as an afterthought: "Yet it is not like the lion; there is extravagance and distraction in it that still betray the same weakness." [13]

In spite of his undoubted "pride of talent," Adams was capable of genuine humility. One may fully believe him when he says: "I never could bring myself seriously to consider that I was a great man, or of much importance or consideration in the world. The few traces that remain of me must, I believe, go down to posterity in much confusion and distraction, as my life has been passed." [14] Or when he assures Mrs. Warren, "I never in my life believed that I had any talents beyond mediocrity." [15] And one may forgive much to one who could convincingly write: "I care nothing about this world, except as it is a part of a system of which the remotest fixed star in the galaxy or in Herschel's nebulae, and every satellite about it, is as essential as ours . . . ," even when it is followed by the outrageous remark: "Yet I am as anxious for my children, grandchildren, country, Europe at times as Fisher Ames." [16]

2

The most obvious reason for Adams's eclipse seems to be that he belonged to no party. "I am determined to support," he wrote in 1808, "every administration whenever I think them in the right. I care not whether they call me Federalist, Jacobin or Quid." And a year later he referred to himself as "abjured and abhorred by all parties." The antipathy—the price of his independence—has persisted ever since. Jefferson and Madison on one side and Hamilton and Marshall on the other have become the idols of present-day Democrats and Republicans, to be extolled and exploited for party purposes. But no party has claimed John Adams. [17]

At first a pillar of the Federalists, Adams bolted them by making his French Treaty; and, ten years later, by ~~favoring the embargo against England he antagonized them forever~~. It was not a matter of caprice on his part. "As Hamilton was the Sovereign Pontiff of Federalism," he wrote in 1809, "all his Cardinals no doubt will endeavor to excite the whole Church to excommunicate and anathematize me. Content. It was time for a Protestant Separation." [18] Unafraid, he hit out hard against his enemies: "They spit their venom and hiss like serpents . . . I take no notice of their billingsgate. Let it boil and broil . . . ~~I never hoped for mercy from British Bears and Tory Tigers~~." [19] Nor did he find words strong enough to express his detestation of the banks, which he regarded as "an enormous fraud and oppression," as "the madness of the many for the profit of the few." "There is no honest bank," he insisted, "but a bank of deposit. A bank that issues paper at interest is a pickpocket or a robber . . . An aristocracy is growing out of them that will be as fatal as the feudal barons, if unchecked, in time." [20] In spite of his devotion to a strong executive power and his fight against the sympathizers of the French Revolution, Adams became more and more alienated from the Federalists. "The funding system and banking systems which are the works of the Federalists," he wrote, "have introduced more corruption and injustice . . . than any other cause." [21] As a lover of agriculture, he had more natural affinity with the Republicans, from whom, however, he was irrevocably separated by his political theories.

Adams had many altercations, but of all the people whom he had ever known he really hated only Alexander Hamilton (with the possible addition of Timothy Pickering). [22] It was due to Hamilton's machinations that he received less than half of the electoral votes as Vice-President; it was Hamilton who gave directions to members of his Cabinet; and it was Hamilton who finally crushed his hopes for a second term as President. "In this dark and insidious manner did this intriguer lay schemes in secret against me," Adams wrote, "and, like the worm at the root of the peach, did he labor for twelve years, underground and in darkness, to girdle the root, while all the axes of the Anti-federalists, Democrats, Jacobins, Virginia debtors to English merchants, and French hirelings, chopping as they were for the whole time at the trunk, could not fell the tree." [23]

Infuriated by the conclusion of peace with France and the thwarting of his vast military ambitions, Hamilton published a pamphlet against Adams in the fall of 1800, exposing the "defects" of his character, his "vanity" and "extreme egotism," and condemning his negotiations with the French as "capricious and undignified," in order to show that he was unfit for the Presidency.[24] The attack, exploited in full by the Republican press, ruined both Adams and the Federalist party. With Jefferson's election the rule of the Republicans began, to last uninterruptedly for several decades. Shortly after his retirement, Adams prepared a reply to Hamilton; but it was only in 1809, when both he and John Quincy Adams were assailed by the Federalists for their support of Madison's administration, that he published it in the *Boston Patriot*. He calmly defended his peace mission, excusing Hamilton's errors on the ground that he was "not a native of America" and "never acquired the feelings and principles of the American people." It was only at the end that his indignation reared up. At one place in his letter Hamilton had called him an ordinary man who dreams himself to be a Frederick. "To this," Adams wrote, "I shall make but a short answer. When a Miss of the street shall print a pamphlet in London, and call the Queen of England an ordinary woman who dreams herself a Catherine of Russia, no Englishman will have the less esteem for his queen for that impudent libel." [25] In his correspondence he spoke with complete abandon of Hamilton's "debaucheries in New York and Philadelphia," often referring to him as "the Creole adventurer" and "the Creole bastard." He disputed even Hamilton's talents. "His knowledge of the great subjects of coin and commerce, and their intimate connection with all departments of every government . . .," he maintained, "was very superficial and imperfect." [26]

It is safe to say that, in spite of their political differences and long estrangement, Adams liked and respected Jefferson most of all his contemporaries. Charles Francis Adams did great harm to both him and Jefferson by obscuring the true nature of their relationship. At the end of his biography, he undertook to discuss Jefferson's character, contending that "he did not always speak exactly as he felt towards either friends or enemies," and that consequently "he has left hanging over a part of his public life a vapor of duplicity, or, to say the least, of indirection . . ." As an instance, he related how, on the occasion of the American publication of Thomas Paine's *Rights of Man* in 1791, Jefferson had denounced Adams to Washington, denying at the same time to Adams that he had ever accused him of political heresies. This explains, Charles Francis Adams suggested, why Adams came to believe that Jefferson was "a false and dangerous man," although there is no evidence that he ever learned of Jefferson's letter to Washington.[27] The opprobrium thus cast on Jefferson was more than returned by the latter's biographer, Henry S. Randall. John Adams reminded him, he wrote, of certain enchanted personages in fairy tales: "A part of the time they are glorious warriors, seeking high adventures. The wizard spell falls on them, and they become little, deformed dwarfs . . ." [28] This vengeful 'feeling seems to have persisted ever since among the admirers of Jefferson—and even of Madison.

Charles Francis Adams, of course, had to deal with the controversy between Jefferson and Adams; but his story leaves out the important fact that, from the beginning, there had been an uncommon attachment between the two great men. "He was so prompt, frank, explicit, and decisive . . . that he soon seized upon my heart," wrote Adams, in recalling their first meeting in the Continental Congress.[29] And in discussing the Declaration of Independence, Jefferson said: "No man's confident and fervid addresses, more than Mr. Adams', encouraged and supported us through the difficulties surrounding us, which, like the ceaseless action of gravity, weighed on us by night and by day." [30] The impressions of these early days remained with both all their lives. Jefferson treated Adams with a certain deference, never forgetting that the latter was his "senior." [31] Although recognizing that Adams was "vain and irritable," he wrote to Madison from Paris: "He is as disinterested as the Being who made him; he is profound in his views, and accurate in his judgment except where knowledge of the world is necessary to form a judgment. He is so amiable that I pronounce you will love him if ever you become acquainted with him." [32] Many times afterwards he reminded Madison of Adams's "solid achievements and integrity." [33] And Adams, ever conscious of his own intellectual capacities, respected Jefferson for his learning, talents, and idealism as he respected no one else. Consciously or unconsciously, he regarded him as one of the *philosophes*. The French Revolution kept them apart but did not destroy their fundamental mutual regard.

At dawn on March 4, 1801, Adams left the capital in a huff, not wanting to be present at the inauguration of his successor. But ten years later, when John Quincy Adams was serving as American minister to Russia, he was ready to renew his relationship with Jefferson. To common friends who visited him at Quincy he remarked, "I always loved Jefferson, and still love him." This was enough for Jefferson. He wrote to Dr. Rush, who had been trying to make peace between them, "I only needed this knowledge to revive towards him all the affections of the most cordial moments of our lives." [34] And so their correspondence began, continuing till just before their deaths. In 1823, when his letters to William Cunningham, a distant cousin, written between 1803 and 1810, were treacherously published, Adams was upset, fearing the effect of some of his virulent remarks. But Jefferson allayed his anxiety. "It would be strange indeed," he wrote, "if, at our years, we were to go back an age to hunt up imaginary or forgotten facts, to disturb the repose of affections so sweetening to the evening of our lives. Be assured, my dear Sir, that I am incapable of receiving the slightest impression from the effort now made to plant thorns on the pillow of age, worth and wisdom, and to sow tares between friends who have been such for near half a century." [35] Adams was deeply moved. The letter, he replied, was passed around in his household with a universal cry: "How generous! How noble! How magnanimous! . . . It ought to be printed! . . ." [36] And after John Quincy Adams's election to the Presidency, he wrote to Jefferson about "our" John: "I call him our John, because, when you were at the Cul de sac at Paris, he appeared to me to be almost as much your boy as mine." [37] A few weeks later he signed another letter, ". . . while I breathe I shall be your friend." [38] It is well known that Adams's last words, when he died on the fiftieth anniversary of the Declaration of Independence, were about Jefferson, whom he survived by a few hours.

"The first time that you and I differed in opinion on any material question," Adams wrote to Jefferson following their reconciliation, "was after your arrival from Europe; and that point was the French revolution. You was well persuaded in your own mind that the nation would succeed in establishing a free republican government. I was well persuaded in mine, that a project of such a government . . . was as unnatural, irrational, and impracticable as it would be over the elephants, lions, tigers, panthers, wolves, and bears, in the royal menagerie at Versailles." [00] It was a correct explanation: the French Revolution was the turning point in both their lives.

3

More than for any other reason, Adams is unappreciated because he is the least known of the great Americans. The immense mass of his manuscripts is still locked away. What is known about him is mainly contained in the ten volumes of his *Works*, published a hundred years ago. The first volume is a biography by the editor, Charles Francis Adams, and the other nine include his books and articles, a part of his official correspondence, and some of his private letters. "From the voluminous collection of these, written in the course of more than half a century," the editor stated, "a rigid selection is now made.

Probably not a single leading actor of the revolutionary period has left nearly so many as Mr. Adams. Even if the publication of all were deemed advisable, it could hardly be done within reasonable compass. In the present publication . . . the aim has been to comprise within the space that remains [one volume and a half] all that seem for any reason to present the strongest claims to admission. Of course, much has been rejected." [40]

Charles Francis Adams was a hard-working editor and, according to his son Henry Adams, he had "the only perfectly balanced mind that ever existed in the name." Yet it is doubtful whether, lacking "the sympathetic quality" and being "reserved in nature and repellent in manners"—as noted by another of his sons—he was best suited to sponsor John Adams in all his impetuosity. [41] Bound in black cloth as if for mourning, these ten volumes exude the chill of an ornate mausoleum. Charles Francis Adams's manner of presenting "Mr. Adams"—always Mr. Adams, never just John Adams—is almost funereal in its perfect self-restraint. Turning from his biography to Adams's own Diary is like stepping from dim light into the sunshine—tasting and smelling life on the farm; mingling with men and women in courthouse and drawing room; talking and acting politics from town meeting to Continental Congress, and on to the Revolution and the capitals of Europe. After the cool, precise, and periodic sentences of his grandson, Adams's life suddenly bursts forth with irrepressible energy.

As one would expect, Charles Francis Adams excluded John Adams's letters to Cunningham from the collected *Works* and also disregarded them in his narrative. He did so, he wrote, because these letters had never been intended for the public eye. It is true, of course, that the original publication of the correspondence in 1823 was a vicious betrayal of confidence, intended to hurt John Quincy Adams, then candidate for the Presidency, through exposing the indiscretions of his father. By 1856, however, this was a poor excuse for ignoring the letters; John Adams himself had stipulated reticence only for his own lifetime. [42] Theodore Parker, less squeamish and more incisive than Charles Francis Adams, used the Cunningham letters in his study, although he considered them "not less than wicked." But he also thought that "John Adams possessed such virtues that he can afford to have [his vices] told, and subtracted from his real merit." And, whether virtue or vice, it was a fact that Adams was "*terribly* open, earnest, and direct, and could not keep his mouth shut." [43]

Parker's example may have had a beneficial effect, for in 1878 "two members of the committee acting as the representatives of their

respective families" published Adams's correspondence with Mercy
Warren. Those ten letters in which Adams repudiated the slights made
against him in her history are indeed an extraordinary mixture of events
and personalities, continually pointing to her "malice." Smarting under
his real or alleged injuries, Adams dashed them off, some running to
twenty or thirty pages, between July 11 and August 19, 1807, without
waiting for the answers or taking out time to read them.[44] It was in
vain that Mrs. Warren, gasping at the onslaught, tried to find refuge
behind her sex and age. Not that she needed protection. The aged
authoress of the poetical tragedies *The Sack of Rome* and *The Ladies
of Castile* knew how to return a blow for every blow. It was a good
fight; and it was proper that a few years later the opponents should
remember their "years of endearment" and exchange locks of hair in
token of their friendship.

Adams's letters to Dr. Rush form the most substantial part of the
material that has been published since. They were privately printed in
1892, under the innocuous title *Old Family Letters*, in an edition of fifty
copies, most of which have disappeared. The volume contains nearly
one hundred and fifty letters, mostly written between 1805 and 1813,
only a few of which were included in the collected *Works*. These
letters, indispensable for an understanding of Adams's later period,
have remained practically unknown not only to the public but also to
most scholars.[45] Correa M. Walsh, author of the most penetrating study
of Adams's political science, seems to have overlooked them and thus
not to have fully realized the depth of Adams's hatred of robber capital-
ism.[46] To be sure, Adams was no modern financier; in considering land
as the most desirable form of property, his economic views, like his
political ones, looked back to the seventeenth century. But he was
not altogether blind to the demands of the times. As he himself protested, he was "no enemy to funding systems"; indeed, he regarded
them as "absolutely and indispensably necessary." What he did not
approve of was the American funding system by which the federal
government assumed the state debts at par after the securities had been
bought up by speculators from poor people at a fraction of their face
value. Equally he saw the need of a national bank, with a branch in each
state. What he abhorred was the system of local banks circulating in-
terest-bearing notes to ten times the amount of their capital. Financial
failures were of daily occurrence, while adventurers were building up
huge fortunes.

The two volumes of the *Warren-Adams Letters* (consisting chiefly
of correspondence among John Adams, Samuel Adams, and James

Warren), published in 1917 and in 1925, contain a number of his letters, the most interesting of which were written during the years of the Continental Congress. But these merely make one anxious for more.

The mortmain placed on Adams's papers has been responsible for the scarcity of new works about him. While Washington, Franklin, Jefferson, Madison, and also lesser figures have received their comprehensive biographies extending to several volumes, there has been, since the publication of Charles Francis Adams's book, only one short complete life of John Adams which, although excellent, is no substitute for a "definitive" biography. As for the general public, it cannot very well use even the ten volumes of the collected *Works*, since they are available only in large libraries. None of Adams's books has been reissued for a century, although the Diary would seem certain to command wide interest. How could anyone fail to appreciate the fresh, earthy quality of the work, with its quick changes from action to introspection, its multitude of character sketches, and above all its portrait of a self-made man, or rather a self-made aristocrat? Franklin's Autobiography and Jefferson's Anas were written in old age, but Adams's Diary, however fragmentary, grew with him, mirroring the hopes and despairs of his life as well as the tumults of the times. Adams's style itself is a surprise, with its firm, searching sentences and with words which are clean and sharp like the granite flints on his farm. But there is no need to romanticize the book. It is an American classic about which Americans know next to nothing.

Parrington remarked that "in every responsibility John Adams acquitted himself in a fashion altogether worthy of the notable Adams posterity." [47] The emphasis seems wrong; the point is not that John Adams was worthy of his posterity, but rather that his posterity was worthy of him. For John Adams was a far greater man than any of his descendants. John Quincy Adams was undoubtedly one of the noblest Presidents of America, but, to use Henry Adams's adjectives, his "restless" mind was not the equal of John Adams's "bold" mind. [48] His own monumental memoirs are unique in American letters; but page for page John Adams's Diary is far superior in grasp, insight, and brilliance. Henry Adams has been the darling of the initiated for many years now, and he certainly deserves all their attention. Yet his scholarship, fine irony, and estheticism seem precious compared with John Adams's robust powers. With all due consideration of the differences in time and conditions, he was not of the race of men to which John Adams belonged. James Truslow Adams marveled at the persistence of certain characteristics in the Adams family; it is only another way of saying that John Adams possessed in germ most of the traits which have distinguished his progeny. He was an *aïeul* in the true sense of the word —the grandsire of them all.[49]

Charles Francis Adams, who had published a selection of Adams's correspondence with his wife, regretted that he could not find room for more. "A number of letters," he continued, "addressed to Mr. Adams by distinguished men, which had been prepared, are likewise excluded . . . These materials, however, are not lost. They await a later period, when they may be presented in a shape not less durable than the present, to illustrate the heroic age of the United American States." [50] This was written in 1854. The publication of the Jefferson Papers, planned for over fifty volumes, is now under way, but the Adams Papers are still waiting for "a later period."

"I will not die for nothing. My pen shall go as long as my fingers can hold it," Adams vowed defiantly.[51] And it did. But he has been silenced, after all.[52]

John Adams among His Books

Arriving at Quincy on March 17, 1801, after a journey that had lasted fourteen days, ex-President Adams found his farm neglected, with "a hundred loads of sea-weed" in his barnyard. Recollecting Horace, he thought that he had made "a good exchange . . . of honors and virtues for manure." His greatest fear was the want of employment. "Ennui," he wrote to a friend, "when it rains on a man in large drops, is worse than one of our north-east storms; but the labors of agriculture and amusement of letters will shelter me." [1] He was then sixty-six. For the next twenty-five years—a period nearly as long as his public career since the Continental Congress—he was to live at Quincy, with only occasional visits to Boston. His land needed his attention; but as time went by, he stayed more and more in the house, in the big study upstairs which he had recently added to the building.

His library, the thousands of books which filled the shelves in the hall outside his study, now proved a veritable blessing. As a young lawyer, Adams had recorded in his Diary the collecting of a library, finding that "a great deal of thought and care, as well as money, are necessary to assemble an ample and well chosen assortment of books." He wondered then about the purpose of his enterprise. "Fame, fortune, power, say some, are the ends intended by a library. The service of God, country, clients, fellow men, say others," he wrote; and he asked, "Which of these lie nearest my heart?" He despaired of realizing either. With the rambling, roving life of a lawyer, attending sessions and courts in all parts of the province, what chance did he have for reading and reflection? [2]

He made his most considerable purchases during his ten years' residence abroad, especially in Paris. Hundreds of his volumes bear the date of acquisition, and often the price, in his neat handwriting. When in June 1788 he returned to America, he brought with him so many books that it took three days for John Quincy Adams to unpack them. Presentation copies from American as well as foreign authors came in abundance. However, on moving to New York and Philadelphia, Vice-President—and then President—Adams had little time for reading. A few favorite volumes he took with him, but the library remained at Quincy, to keep him company there for the rest of his life.

It is the library of a statesman—but of an eighteenth-century statesman, whose interest embraced all fields of knowledge. Naturally, law and government make up its larger part. From Coke's *Institutes* to Blackstone's *Commentaries*, and from Acherley's *Brittanic Constitution* to Fortescue's *De laudibus legum Angliae*, there are scores of famous tomes in the collection. In addition, there are the works of Grotius, Pufendorf, Beccaria, Ogilvie, and others, showing Adams's keen interest in the philosophy of law. Social philosophy is the next allied subject, and in this the library is especially rich—probably the richest of its time in America. His legal source books were a great help to Adams, and indeed to the Colony, in the struggle with the royal administration. It was on the authority of John Selden's *State Trials* and *Statutes at Large* that in 1773 he made the astounding recommendation, subsequently adopted by the House of Representatives, of the impeachment of the judges. "My opinion is," Adams recalled the incident forty years later, "that there was not another copy of either of those works in the United States." [8]

History was, of course, indispensable for the study of law and government. Besides the works on English history, which went as far back as Camden's *Annals*, Adams possessed the works of the great French and Italian historians, with many other volumes on the history of Spain, Russia, the Netherlands, Sweden, and even Portugal. But the most impressive group in this field are the Greek and Roman histories. The works of Herodotus, Thucydides, and Xenophon, and of Tacitus, Sallust, and Livy are mostly in huge sixteenth- and seventeenth-century folios. And along with the historians, there is also a large selection of classic poets, philosophers, and orators. The sets of Homer, Plato, Aristotle, Horace, Ovid, Lucretius, Cicero, Epictetus, Marcus Aurelius, etc. are all complete. They are all "Opera omnia quae extant," and not single stray volumes. Greek was "one of the flames" of Adams's youth; and his earliest preserved possession was a small textbook edition of Cicero's *Orationes*, with the note "John Adams Book 1749/50" repeated half a dozen times on the title page. One should also remember that Adams, having made provisions for the creation of a Temple and the establishment of a Greek and Latin Academy at Quincy, later reversed the order. "It is my wish," he wrote in a new deed, "that the building of the Academy and the establishment of a classical master should be provided for before the Temple, of which I see no present necessity . . . and if any descendant of mine should ever presume to call it in question, I hereby pronounce him unworthy of me; and I hereby petition all future Legislators of the Commonwealth to pass a special law to defeat his impious intentions . . ." [4] (In spite of the severe injunction, the Temple was erected in 1828, but the Academy, although a building was raised in 1871, never came into being.)

English literature occupies comparatively few shelves in Adams's library. He had, of course, his Shakespeare, and also his Milton, Pope, Addison, and Swift. He took "incredible delight" in reading romances. He found enchantment in Wieland's *Oberon*, which he read in John Quincy Adams's translation, and even more in the Waverly novels, *The Lady of the Lake*, *The Lay of the Last Minstrel*, and *Marmion*. But Adams could not keep politics out even of his entertainment. "These Scottish and German romances," he told Dr. Rush, "show in a clear light the horrors of the feudal aristocracy as the histories of Genghis Khan and Tamerlane shew the same anarchy in the Asiatic aristocracy." [5] The literatures of other countries are not too abundantly represented in the library either. Adams had the works of Racine, Corneille, Molière, and Voltaire, a small pocket-edition of Rabelais, and an even smaller one of Tasso, but little else. In science the range is wider. It includes not only the works of Euclid, Newton, Buffon, Linnaeus, and others, but also tracts on special subjects in mathematics, optics, and geometry.

Books on religion are, again, a prominent feature of Adams's library. He possessed many Bibles and also quantities of theological works, from the writings of the early Church Fathers to the tracts of contemporary divines. "For more than sixty years," he wrote to Jefferson, "I have been attentive to this great subject. Controversies between Calvinists and Arminians, Trinitarians and Unitarians, Deists and Christians, Atheists and both, have attracted my attention, whenever the singular life I have led would admit, to all these questions." Already at college he was "a mighty metaphysician," and afterwards had many discussions on the subject with Dr. Ezekiel Hersey, a famous physician at Hingham. He doubted Jefferson's interest in the field. "I have been a diligent student for many years in books whose titles you have never seen," he boasted.[6] However, he got a surprise there. It is true that Jefferson did not like to discuss religion, particularly resenting any "inquisition over the rights of conscience, which the laws have so justly proscribed," but he was far from being indifferent to it. He had, in fact, prepared in 1803 a "Syllabus" about the merit of the doctrines of Jesus, which he hoped Dr. Priestley would develop into a larger work.[7] In 1813 he sent a copy to Adams, which the latter returned "with great reluctance" and with the hope that Jefferson himself would produce such a book.[8] In reply, Jefferson outlined what he thought should be done: "We must reduce our volume to the simple Evangelists, select, even from them, the very words only of Jesus . . . I have performed this operation for my own use, by cutting verse by verse out of the printed book, and arranging the matter which is evidently his and which is as easily distinguished as diamonds in a dunghill." [9] He worked on the compilation now and then, finishing it by 1819 under the title "The Life and Morals of Jesus of Nazareth." Adams apparently never saw it.[10]

In his eighty-second year, Adams informed Jefferson that he had read forty-three volumes in one year, twelve of them quartos. Jefferson envied him; half a dozen octavos were his fare in that space of time. But Adams flung more and more new titles at him; he was being overwhelmed, he wrote, with books from all quarters. His "womankind" read to him all those in English, but with the French he was obliged to "excruciate" his own eyes. "And to what purpose?" he asked. "I verily believe I was as wise and good seventy years ago as I am now . . ." [11] But he continued reading just the same.

2

Of all his books, Adams studied the works of the eighteenth-century English and French philosophers with the greatest care. He had purchased them during his embassy in Paris, but he evidently did not have time to read them then. It was during the French Revolution—when he was Vice-President and then President—that he read these books, most of them twice. In his retirement at Quincy he returned to them for the third time.

With pen in hand, Adams carried on discussions with his authors, making notes on the margins and flyleaves. The books which he commented upon form, without any apparent design on his part, a consecutive series, starting with Bolingbroke's *Patriot King* and *Nature of Human Knowledge*, and including Rousseau's *Discourse on Equality* and *Social Compact*, Frederick's correspondence with Voltaire and d'Alembert, the Abbé de Mably's *Legislation*, Turgot's essay on the American constitutions, Condorcet's *Progress of the Human Mind*, Mary Wollstonecraft's *French Revolution*, d'Hauterive's *State of France*, Madame de Staël's *Influence of the Passions*, William Godwin's *Political Justice*, Dr. Priestley's *Heathen Philosophy*, and many more volumes. To be sure, there are gaps. Montesquieu's *Spirit of the Laws* contains no comments, but Adams had fully expressed his opinion about it in his published writings.[12] Nor did he comment on the works of Diderot, or on any of the thirty-eight volumes of the *Encyclopédie*,[13] or on the books of Condillac, Helvétius, Holbach, or lesser luminaries. Yet the picture is fairly complete. Eighteenth-century philosophy was born in England, flourished in France, and then, in some measure, returned to England. All the authors on whom Adams commented were representatives of the Age of Reason. Firm believers in the advantages of civilization, and imbued with boundless optimism in regard to the future of mankind, they were the Prophets of Progress.

The exceptions were Rousseau, Mably, and Godwin, who saw in history nothing more than a continuous process of degeneration. But they, too, shared the most important assumptions of the time, such as the rights of man, freedom of conscience, the evil effects of superstitions, and the desirability of social reforms. Nor did they want to do away with civilization; having diagnosed its ills, they were ready for compromise, preparing projects for the improvement of conditions. Their Utopia lay in the past, but they looked forward to the future. The *philosophes*—the name does not apply to Frenchmen only—were a heterogeneous group of writers, representing many schools of thought yet all having some common characteristics.

In his works and letters Adams made many brief remarks about the eighteenth-century thinkers, and once he discussed the doctrine of perfectibility at some length. He thought that Plato had this idea in mind when he spoke of imitating God, and the Stoics when they described their wise man; and that the Christian Fathers expressed it in stronger terms than any of the modern philosophers. He professed not to understand the latter's meaning, and concluded that most of them merely wanted "to cheat the populace with principles of equality and levelism." [14] But this criticism was general; it was on the margins of their books—the "great books" of the century—that Adams really came to grips with the *philosophes*, stating his own views on countless specific subjects. A caustic and insistent debater, he missed few occasions to show up the weak points of his opponents. These vigorous, often explosive comments constitute the first *critique* of the doctrine of progress (as well as of the doctrine of regress) by an American.

The influence of French political thought in eighteenth-century America has long been a moot question. Some writers have undoubtedly greatly overestimated it, while others unduly minimized it. The contradiction—not to say, confusion—has been largely caused by failure to take into account the fact that American opinion changed with events and to distinguish between the different attitudes which prevailed at various periods: in the years before the Declaration of Independence, during the Revolutionary War, at the time of the formation of the state and federal constitutions, at the outbreak of the French Revolution, and during the reaction aroused by the Terror. Nor has the necessary distinction been made between the influence exercised upon individuals or small groups and that exercised upon the public. To be sure, the field has not been thoroughly explored as yet; but there has been enough investigation to warrant a few conclusions.

The opinions of earlier writers concerning Rousseau's excessive authority in prerevolutionary America can be almost entirely discarded. John Morley could still write, in 1873, "It was from Rousseau's writings that the Americans took the ideas and the phrases of their great charter" [15]; but it was pointed out soon afterwards that the Revolutionary leaders referred only incidentally to Rousseau.[16] The statement in *The Cambridge History of American Literature* that "after 1760 all the important works of Rousseau, Montesquieu, and the Encyclopedists as well as many other French books were advertised for sale in the colonial press" has been too broadly interpreted [17]; an analysis of some of those advertisements has shown that Diderot and d'Alembert did not even figure in the lists, that Rousseau seemed no more important than Le Sage, and that the majority of the imported French books were fiction. Voltaire was eagerly read; but the political writers were in demand only from the eighties on.[18] Franklin and Jefferson sent home copies of the *philosophes'* works [19]; but Montesquieu was the only French writer mentioned in the debates of the Constitutional Convention. Indeed, it has become generally accepted that, up to the time of the establishment of the Republic, Americans were influenced by English thinkers and not at all by the French who followed them. The adoption of the unicameral system by several states seems to disprove this assumption—but only on condition that it was Turgot and his friends who influenced Franklin, and not the other way around. It is generally acknowledged, however, that with the French Revolution the situation suddenly changed and French political ideas swept the country. There was hostile criticism from the beginning, but only a few dared to voice their views openly. John Adams was the first to rise up against them and fight them desperately as a dangerous force.

Adams had known many of the *philosophes* personally. Soon after his arrival in Paris in April 1778, he met Turgot, Condorcet, and the Duc de la Rochefoucauld; sat "very near" to Voltaire in the Comédie Française; witnessed the scene in which Voltaire and Franklin embraced each other at the Académie des Sciences; and heard d'Alembert deliver several eulogies. He and Franklin often dined with Turgot, either in Turgot's home or in their house, the Hotel de Valentinois, at Passy. Marmontel, Condillac, Madame Helvétius, and others were at times present at the parties. As an American Minister, Adams attracted attention, and was cultivated by "high society." Everybody was friendly and hospitable to him, yet he soon became petulant. He testily noted in his Diary that people first mistook him for Samuel Adams, "le fameux Adams"; and when it was settled that he was not the famous Adams, he was regarded as a cipher—"a man who did not understand a word of French; awkward in his figure, awkward in his dress; no abilities; a perfect bigot and fanatic." [20] Of course, he recovered his self-confidence before long; yet there remained a cool reserve between him and the young radicals, the followers of Turgot, who greatly admired "Franklin's Constitution," the unicameral system adopted by Pennsylvania. Adams's own friends belonged to another circle: Chastellux, the Abbés Raynal, Chalut, Arnoux, and later Mably being outstanding among them. On his second visit to Paris, early in 1780, Adams carried with him a copy of the draft of the Massachusetts Constitution, but Turgot and his devotees did not like it at all. [21] It was in answer to the "attacks" of Turgot on the bicameral system adopted by most of the American states that, in 1787 and 1788, he published the three volumes of his *Defence of the Constitutions of America*.

When America was still frantic with enthusiasm over the French Revolution, Adams already had his gloomy forebodings. On February 22, 1790, he congratulated Dr. Rush on the prospect of a new, bicameral constitution for Pennsylvania. "Poor France I fear will bleed for too exactly copying your old one," he wrote to his friend, adding: "When I see such miserable crudities approved by such men as Rochefoucauld and Condorcet I am disposed to think very humbly of human understanding." [22] This was a week before Burke made his famous attack on the French Revolution in the House of Commons, describing it as "an irrational, unprincipled, proscribing, confiscating, plundering, ferocious, bloody, and tyrannical democracy." The Rights of Man, as proclaimed by the Constituent Assembly, appeared to Burke "an institute and digest of anarchy." [23] He had his speech printed and distributed, and was also advertising a more important "public letter" on the subject. The work was to be the *Reflections on the Revolution in France*, published in November 1790. It is not known whether Adams had read Burke's speech and learned about his contemplated book; but it is an interesting coincidence that he began his *Discourses on Davila*, showing the evil effects of unbalanced governments, at precisely the same time as Burke started his own work.

Adams's attitude towards the French Revolution was strikingly similar to that of Burke. The latter accused the *philosophes* of having had a regular plan for the destruction of society and the Christian religion. "These writers," he asserted, ". . . pretended to a great zeal for the poor and the lower orders, whilst in their satires they rendered hateful, by every exaggeration, the faults of courts, of nobility, and of priesthood." The situation was different in England: "We are not the converts of Rousseau; we are not the disciples of Voltaire; Helvétius has made no progress amongst us. Atheists are not our preachers; madmen are not our lawgivers." [24] Adams, too, looked upon the *philosophes* with rancor, holding them chiefly responsible for all the confusion and bloodshed. His marginal notes reflect his emotions. Losing his temper easily, he called Rousseau "a coxcomb" and "a satyr"; Voltaire, "a liar"; and Condorcet, "a quack," "a fool," and "a mathematical charlatan." The gentle d'Alembert, for an irreverent quip about Providence, he upbraided, "Thou Louse, Flea, Tick, Ant, Wasp, or whatever Vermin thou art . . ." Turgot, from whom he could not withhold his respect, was "an enthusiast" and "not a judicious practical statesman." Mably, too, was often "ignorant," and at least once "stark mad." Mary Wollstonecraft he denounced as a "silly woman," "this weak woman," and "a most incongruous creature," apologizing later for having judged her with "too much severity and too little gallantry." Adams berated the *philosophes* for their trust in abstract systems, their lack of experience, and their overweening self-confidence. Their glorification of "genius," particularly, drove him to fury. Yet, on the whole, he was more moderate than Burke; he did not reject indiscriminately all their ideas. Rousseau's advice to entrust the execution of laws to a separate body he found "judicious"; Mably's observations on ambition and avarice were "excellent"; Turgot had great "theoretical knowledge"; Mary Wollstonecraft, usually so wrong, was "correct" in describing the influence of the Parisian populace on the National Assembly; and even Condorcet, now and then, was "sensible." In spite of their bias, these notes were not written by a blind reactionary but by a statesman apprehensive of the consequences of excess, who saw his fears justified.

And what is the "verdict" of history? Depending upon their attitude toward the Revolution, writers have praised or condemned the *philosophes* for their agitation; and others have denied their influence, precisely for the same motives. "Most of the *philosophes*," Chateaubriand wrote in 1796, "are now forgotten; nothing remains of them but the French Revolution." However, years later he changed his opinion: "The French Revolution did not originate with such and such a man, or such and such a book: it was the result of conditions. It was inevitable, although a thousand people will not believe it." According to Taine, "The philosophy of the eighteenth century contained poison, of a kind both strange and powerful . . . Its two principal ingredients have the peculiarity that separately they are salutary but combined they are venomous." Albert Sorel, similarly, affirmed: "Philosophers and men of letters were the major inspiration of the Revolution. It owes them its most generous conceptions, its most disastrous inventions, the humanity of its beginnings, the ferocity of its middle period, its enthusiasm and its fanaticism." This view was challenged by Félix Rocquain, who showed that the Revolution was already on the point of bursting forth before the *philosophes* became active, and that the *cahiers* of the period make no references to them. On the other hand, M. Roustan maintains that it was the *philosophes* who turned discontent, which otherwise would have produced only uprisings, into a revolution. And so the debate still goes on.[25] The leaders of the Revolution, from Danton to Robespierre and from Saint-Just to Babeuf, at any rate, abundantly acknowledged their indebtedness to the *philosophes*.

3

In 1795 the Duc de la Rochefoucauld-Liancourt, a former President of the National Assembly, visited Adams at Quincy. "In the vicinity of Boston," he wrote in the account of his American travels, "I met again Mr. Adams, Vice-President of the United States, a man of merits, ability, and culture rarely equalled, and not generally recognized, in America. He is one of the most estimable characters in the country. No one contributed more to the American Revolution, from the beginning to the end . . ." The Vice-President, the Duke noted, lived "in a small house which a sixth-rate Paris lawyer would disdain to choose for his summer home." But he enjoyed the visit. Mr. Adams's conversation, he wrote, was "extremely agreeable, tinged with barbed friendliness, with a sarcastic yet kindly criticism." [26]

Exasperated though he was with them, Adams did not really hate the *philosophes*. One is, in fact, tempted to say that he had a kind of inverted affection for them. They were idealists, "totally ignorant of the science of government," but still idealists. Knowing the misery of the poor under the old regime, he understood their desire for reforms; joyously contemplating the growth of America, he was no enemy of progress in any other country.[27] He hoped, however, that the changes would come about by orderly development, and not by the sudden overthrowing of all institutions. Above all, he feared a system of government built on the theory of the "natural goodness" of man. Having left behind his native Calvinism, he did not intend to exchange the doctrine of total depravity for that of total innocence. The *philosophes*, who preached the gospel of common sense, appeared to him dreamers; it was he, for whom religion was still entirely metaphysical, who was the realist. After Waterloo, he could not help complimenting himself on the fulfillment of his predictions. But it was not with a vulgar triumph; in writing his notes, he felt the defeat of those great ideals. "Is the Congress of Vienna the sovereign of the world?" he asked, bewildered. "The question now is whether Popes, Jesuits, and Inquisitions shall rule the human race." He had execrated Turgot, Rochefoucauld, and Condorcet through the margins of several volumes, yet he acknowledged at the end that they had "dispositions to equity, humanity, and benevolence toward their country and mankind"; and in a letter to Jefferson he declared that "the eighteenth century, notwithstanding all its errors and vices, has been, of all that are past, the most honorable to human nature." [28]

He could afford now to be magnanimous. Many of his former detractors were apologizing for their behavior, and he was glad to have their testimonials. "And what, perhaps, will be considered more than all," he wrote to one of them, "the learned and scientific President Jefferson has, in letters to me, acknowledged that I was right, and that he was wrong." It was a rather free interpretation of Jefferson's intention.[29] True enough, Jefferson had spoken with disappointment of "the *canaille* of the cities of Europe" which would instantly pervert freedom "to the demolition and destruction of everything public and private"; yet even then, in 1813, he was hoping that "the world will recover from the panic of this first catastrophe." [30] And past eighty, he once more wrote to Adams: "In France, the first effort was defeated by Robespierre, the second by Bonaparte, the third by Louis XVIII and his holy allies: another is yet to come, and all Europe, Russia excepted, has caught the spirit; and all will attain representative government, more or less perfect . . . To attain all this, however, rivers of blood must yet flow, and years of desolation pass over; yet the object is worth rivers of blood, and years of desolation." [31]

To be sure, some of Adams's comments sound peevish and rude. Yet it would be altogether erroneous to look upon them as the reactions of a cranky old man—if for no other reason than that the larger part of them was written when he was still in his fifties. And in some respects, the comments made in his old age are even more important than the earlier ones, since they reflect a new phase in his development, not given sufficient prominence in his collected *Works:* his increasing alarm at the power of the moneyed interests, at the mushrooming of an aristocracy of wealth in the wake of the new banking system. Having read Fisher Ames's essay "On the Dangers of American Liberty," he noted on the margins with the same anxiety which had prompted his pen twenty-five years before, after Shays's Rebellion: "Mr. Ames saw no danger but from one party, the Democracy. There is equal danger from another party, the Aristocracy. Licentiousness is as great in the latter as in the former. The latter has its oligarchy as well as the former. The latter has its demagogues as well as the former. The latter is headed by a faction as well as the former. The latter pants for an alliance with England more than the other with France." In his *Defence* Adams warned against the dangers of democracy, but he was no mere partisan of the rich.

One should also remember that Adams was exceptionally fit even in his old age. He had a "quiveration" of his right hand, but his chief complaint was that he had to resort to glasses in reading! At seventy-eight he took long rides on horseback, and years later he still walked four or five miles a day around his farm. His mind was as fresh and vigorous as ever. These were the years of his eager correspondence with Dr. Rush, and afterwards with Jefferson. When not long ago a selection from the latter appeared—some of it new and the rest reprinted—people were amazed at the octogenarian who could range from Plato to Pythagoras, from Cicero to Lucretius, from Voltaire to Dr. Johnson with such ease, quoting Greek and Latin verse in the most impromptu manner. Adams could not match the magnificence of Jefferson's formal style, but his letters are warmer, more spontaneous, more charged with the feeling of the moment—in short, they are better letters. Copley's full-length painting, done at the time of the peace negotiations with England, caught the truculence of Adams's middle years. But Gilbert Stuart's last picture, with the peering, ageless, still defiant eyes, reveals most his uncanny leonine quality. "He was all the time building theories of society, government, religion, literature, education, conduct," Moses C. Tyler observed, "he was forever piercing with his virile and dauntless intelligence the past, present, and future, the qualities and relationships of all beings in time and eternity, in heaven, and earth, and hell." [32]

The renewal of his friendship with Jefferson especially enriched and warmed Adams's last years. "Esteem" was soon replaced by "affection," and the assurances of "unabated friendship" by "ancient friendly sentiments" in his letters. He called Jefferson the Sage of Monticello, the Man of the Mountain, the celebrated Philosopher and Statesman of Virginia. He also called him Young Man. "When I was of your age, Young Man, that is seven or eight years ago . . . ," he wrote in 1813. There is more and more mellowness and humor as the years advance. To a correspondent engaged on a life of James Otis, he described his service in the militia in the spring of 1770: "I had the honor to be summoned, and attended at the State House with my musket and bayonet, my broadsword and cartridge-box, under the command of the famous Paddock. I know you will laugh at my military figure . . ." [33] It was in the same mood that he argued, on the margin of his book, with Bolingbroke as to whether the instinct of animals were different from man's reason. "My Doves, when they see me," he noted, "alight before me. They remember that I commonly, in that place, have my Pocketts full of Corn. They reason as well in expecting that I shell it to them as I do when I see the Sun in a clear day and conclude that I shall have a pleasant Walk . . ." In a letter Rush described the majority of mankind as "madmen at large," the most prominent among them being "those men who by writing and reasoning attempt to cure them." "Upon honor, now, Rush! You cannot be serious in calling me mad to my face," Adams expostulated.[34] The old lion still emitted an occasional roar; but now he quickly regained his composure. It often happens that strong-willed, violent men become charming in old age, whereas charming men become merely silly.

The John Adams who at the Massachusetts Convention of 1820 proposed equal protection of the laws for "all men, of all religions" was worthy of the John Adams whom Jefferson described as "the Colossus of Independence."

[III]

Adams's Political Philosophy

In order to understand properly Adams's comments on the eighteenth-century thinkers, it is necessary to know the main aspects of his political philosophy—his conception of society as a constant warfare of conflicting economic interests; his unshakable belief in the need for two assemblies and a strong executive; his admiration of the British Constitution; his attitude toward a hereditary senate and monarchy; and his interpretation of the doctrines of the laws of nature and the rights of man. It is the purpose of this chapter to present an outline of Adams's political ideas as expressed in his writings—and notes.

I

"The fundamental article of my political creed is," Adams stated in his old age, "that despotism, or unlimited sovereignity, or absolute power, is the same in a majority of a popular assembly, an aristocratical council, an oligarchical junto, and a single emperor. Equally arbitrary, cruel, bloody, and in every respect diabolical." [1]

His remedy against the evil of despotism was the balance of powers. "A legislative, an executive, and a judicial power," he wrote in November 1775 to Richard Henry Lee, his fellow delegate to the Continental Congress, "comprehend the whole of what is meant and understood by government. It is by balancing each of these powers against the other two, that the efforts in human nature toward tyranny can alone be checked and restrained, and any degree of freedom preserved in the constitution." In the same letter he outlined the ways of accomplishing this balance. "Let a full and free representation of the people be chosen for a house of commons. Let the house choose . . .

a council. Let the house and council . . . choose a governor." And significantly he added: "Let the governor, council, and house be each a distinct and independent branch of the legislature, and have a negative on all laws." [2] This letter, two pages long, contains the foundation of Adams's political philosophy. Charles Francis Adams was right in maintaining: "From first to last, from the year 1775, before the Declaration of Independence, down to the year 1793, when the present constitution had become fully established, the principles upon which he acted and counselled remain substantially the same." [3]

In his remarkable essay *Thoughts on Government*, written two months after his letter to Lee, Adams expressed his views at greater length. His emphasis, even more than before, was on the need for a second assembly as a "mediator" between the house of commons and the executive, and on making the executive an integral part of the legislature. Then in his main work, *A Defence of the Constitutions of Government of the United States of America*, he fully developed his principles. The first volume, begun in October 1786, was published in February 1787 and followed by two more within a year. It is a vast panorama of all the republican systems of antiquity, the middle ages, and modern times, their histories proving that civil wars are the inevitable alternative to balanced government. Adams, then ambassador to England, composed the book to warn his countrymen against the adoption of the unicameral system in their state constitutions, as recommended by Turgot and other *philosophes*. In the three large volumes of the *Defence* he stated his doctrines in many forms, perhaps most clearly in the Preface. "Representations, instead of collections, of the people," he wrote, "a total separation of the executive from the legislative power, and of the judicial from both; and a balance in the legislature by three independent, equal branches, are perhaps the only three discoveries in the constitution of a free government, since the institution of Lycurgus." Conscious of the contradiction between the last two propositions, he described his system as "the tripartite balance, the political trinity in unity, trinity of legislative, and unity of executive power, which in politics is no mystery." [4]

There was, at any rate, no mystery about Adams's intentions. The separation of powers chiefly meant for him the exclusion of the legislature from interference with the executive; otherwise he gave little consideration to the subject. His main concern was with the division of the legislative power among a house of representatives, a senate, and the chief executive. It is important to note that, although Adams was the principal author of the Constitution of Massachusetts, Article

XXX of Section I is not by him. This Article, which is often quoted as the most extreme statement of the principle of the separation of powers, declares: "In the government of this commonwealth, the legislative department shall never exercise the executive and judicial powers, or either of them; the executive shall never exercise the legislative and judicial powers, or either of them; the judicial shall never exercise the legislative and executive powers, or either of them, to the end it may be a government of laws and not of men." The Article says nothing about the division of the legislative power; if anything, it forbids, by implication, such a division, which was certainly not Adams's purpose. In his own draft, the Article read simply: "The judicial department of the state ought to be separate from, and independent of, the legislative and executive powers." [5]

Adams, of course, well knew that a rigid separation of the three powers would inevitably result in a "simple" government. With Locke he believed that "there can be but one supreme power which is the legislative, to which all the rest are and must be subordinate," and also that "the executive power, placed anywhere but in a person that has also a share in the legislative, is visibly subordinate and accountable to it, and may be at pleasure changed and displaced." It was in order to avoid such a fatal weakness in the executive power that Adams insisted on its participation in the legislative power. A share in the legislature would also enable the executive to keep an impartial check upon democracy and aristocracy, each represented in its own house. The best model for a "mixed" government seemed to him the English Constitution, which he extolled as "the most stupendous fabric of human invention." "Not the formation of languages, not the whole art of navigation and ship-building," he wrote, "does more honor to the human understanding than this system of government." [6]

The English Constitution was admired by almost every leader of Revolutionary America as the embodiment of the principle of the separation of powers which alone could secure their liberties. Montesquieu's *Spirit of the Laws*, one of the most widely read political works in the Colonies, corroborated this view, as did, later, Blackstone's *Commentaries*.[7] The chief argument of the opponents of the Federal Constitution, who hoped that the separation of powers would work to the advantage of the legislature, was that the Constitution vitiated Montesquieu's doctrine. The advocates of the Constitution, fearing the excessive predominance of the legislature, contended that it did not.

Thus, in Numbers 47–49 of the *Federalist*, Madison, having affirmed his allegiance to "the oracle who is always consulted and cited on this subject," went on to show that Montesquieu did not mean that the legislative and executive departments "ought to have no *partial agency* in, or no *control* over, the acts of each other." Surprisingly, he did not quote Montesquieu's advice, so much to his point, that "the executive should have a share in the legislative by its power of rejecting, otherwise it would soon be stripped of its prerogatives; however, should the legislature have a share in the executive, the latter would be equally undone."[8] He did however quote Jefferson, who in his *Notes on Virginia* had warned: "All the powers of government, legislative, executive, and judiciary, result to the legislative body. The concentrating these in the same hands, is precisely the definition of despotic government . . . One hundred and seventy-three despots would surely be as oppressive as one . . . An *elective despotism* was not the government we fought for." Both Federalists and Anti-Federalists wanted to have Montesquieu's prestige on their side; and since the French writer was supposed to have described the English Constitution, both had to pretend that they were imitating that model. "The British Constitution was to Montesquieu," Madison remarked, "what Homer has been to the didactic writers on epic poetry."

Unfortunately, Montesquieu's account was sadly out of date by then. "The efficient secret of the English Constitution," Walter Bagehot wrote, "may be described as the close union, the nearly complete fusion, of the executive and legislative powers. No doubt by the traditional theory, as it exists in all the books, the goodness of our English constitution consists in the entire separation of the legislative and executive authorities, but in truth its merit consists in their singular approximation. The connecting link is the *cabinet*. By that new word we mean a committee of the legislative body selected to be the executive body . . ." And he remarked: "The Americans of 1787 thought they were copying the English Constitution, but they were contriving a contrast to it. Just as the American is the type of *composite* governments, in which the supreme power is divided between many bodies and functionaries, so the English is the type of *simple* constitutions, in which the ultimate power upon all questions is in the hands of the same persons. The ultimate authority in the English Constitution is a newly-elected House of Commons . . ."[9] Bagehot's observations were correct on the whole, but they did not apply fully to the eighteenth century, especially to the reign of George III when, through the distribution of pensions and places, the Ministry exercised an exorbitant power. A few more reasons may be suggested to explain the Americans' "failure" to recognize the true nature of the English Constitution:

1. The "separation of powers" meant one thing for the Colonists in regard to their provincial government and something else in regard to the government of Great Britain. The terms "legislative power" and "executive power" were applied by them in the first case to General Assembly and Governor, and in the second to Parliament and King. However, they did not make the distinction clear; they talked of the "English Constitution" while they were really thinking of their own institutions. The habit persisted up to the time of the framing of the new constitutions.[10]

2. It is unlikely that the Colonists were entirely unaware of the new development in England. The denunciations of the town resolutions and pamphlets were all directed against Parliament, but at the same time they expressed loyalty to His beloved Majesty. The disuse of the royal veto since the time of Queen Anne must have been for them an unmistakable indication of the growing importance of Parliament.[11]

3. The English themselves were none too quick to discern the changes. "The 'literary theory of the English Constitution,' " Sir Courtenay Ilbert noted, "was accepted as Gospel on the Continent of Europe. Nor was the theory seriously shaken in England until Bagehot wrote those articles in the *Fortnightly Review* which he afterwards collected in his epoch-making little work." [12] Bagehot's articles and book did not appear until 1867!

After two years' residence in London, Adams, who in his *Novanglus* of 1774 had excoriated Parliament more sharply than had any other American, wrote his *Defence* as if England were still the classic home of the balance of powers. For him it was just that; for it cannot be emphasized enough that what mattered for him was not the separation of the legislative, executive, and judiciary functions but the equilibrium of the democratic, aristocratic, and monarchic elements. He remembered well from Bolingbroke, "It is by the mixture of monarchical, aristocratical, and democratical power, blended together in one system, and by these three estates balancing one another, that our free constitution of government hath been preserved so long inviolate." [13] And, in spite of the changes, the English aristocracy held its own, not only through the House of Lords but in the House of Commons itself, which consisted almost exclusively of representatives of the upper and middle classes. "If instead of a House of Commons and a House of Lords," Jeremy Bentham observed, "there were two Houses of Lords and no House of Commons, the ultimate effect would be just the same." [14]

The *Defence* was written with no thought of the Federal Constitution. In the conclusion of the first volume Adams, in fact, maintained that "the people of America and their delegates in congress were of opinion, that a single assembly was every way adequate to the management of all their federal concerns"; and he saw good reason in this, "because congress is not a legislative assembly, nor a representative assembly, but only a diplomatic assembly." To be sure, eighteen months later he enthusiastically accepted the Constitution. "The new system," he wrote at the end of the third volume, "which seems admirably calculated to unite their [the United States'] interests and affections, and bring them to an uniformity of principles and sentiments, is equally well combined to unite their wills and forces as a single nation." [15] Conceived solely as an apology for the state constitutions, the *Defence* contained nothing about states' rights or federal rights. Yet it exerted an enormous influence on the debates of the Federal Convention. Hamilton, Madison, Gouverneur Morris, and many others reaffirmed Adams's reasonings. Some of the speeches seem to have been taken directly from his work.

Adams's political principles were equally applicable to the Federal Constitution and to the state constitutions. Living in London, he was one of the most vital forces in the Convention at Philadelphia.

2

The belief that the Federal Constitution was the result of purely abstract discussions of moral and political principles has been considerably revised in our time. The purpose was to create a Union, establish an efficient government, and secure liberty; and the accommodation of state and federal sovereignty on the basis that "the supreme, absolute, and uncontrollable power remains in the people" was, indeed, a noble enrichment of the science of government. The work, however, was not done in a vacuum; economic interests played an important part.

The framers of the Constitution, practical statesmen that they were, would have been the first to acknowledge this. In the long and arduous debate on the representation of property Locke's name was not mentioned, but his teaching that "the purpose of civil government is the protection of property" was a constantly recurring theme. James Wilson of Pennsylvania seemed to be the only delegate who questioned the principle, professing that "the cultivation and improvement of the human mind" was the object of government. The proposal that the right of suffrage be given only to freeholders, with the exclusion of servants and mechanics, had many advocates. Madison himself envisaged a future when the majority of the people would have no property at all. He was thinking not so much of the relation between landlords and tenants as of that "between the great capitalists in manufactures and commerce and the members employed by them." People without property, he predicted, "will either combine under the influence of their common situation; in which case, the rights of property and the public liberty, will not be secure in their hands: or which is more probable, they will become the tools of opulence and ambition . . ." Yet he thought that "the mass of citizens should not be without a voice." [16]

In Number 10 of the *Federalist*—one of the most concise and most objective expositions of the class struggle ever made—he undertook to show that the Constitution provided an excellent solution for the problem. "The most common and durable source of factions," he wrote, "has been the various and unequal distribution of property. Those who hold and those who are without property have ever formed distinct interests in society. Those who are creditors, and those who are debtors, fall under a like discrimination. A landed interest, a manufacturing interest, a mercantile interest, a moneyed interest, with many lesser interests, grow up of necessity in civilized nations, and divide them into different classes, actuated by different sentiments and views." When the minority was a faction, the majority could defeat it by a regular vote. The danger arose when the majority became a faction, for "the form of popular government . . . enables it to sacrifice to its ruling passion or interest both the public good and the rights of other citizens." It was here that the Constitution offered remedies. In the first place, because the effect of the representative system was "to refine and enlarge the public views"; and in the second, because the size of the Union would create "a greater variety of parties and interests" and make it thereby less probable that "a majority of the whole will have a common motive to invade the rights of other citizens."

It was mainly the neglect into which the works of the framers of the Constitution had fallen that enabled Story, Bancroft, and other nineteenth-century jurists and historians to make their idealistic interpretations of the Constitution prevail. A letter by Jefferson, written in 1809, discouraging the printer who wished to publish his works, speaks volumes about the intellectual atmosphere of the period. "I say nothing of [the] numerous draughts of reports, resolutions, etc.," Jefferson wrote, ". . . such as the Declaration of Independence . . . the Act of

Religious Freedom, etc., etc. . . . They would no more find readers now, than the journals and statute books in which they are deposited." [17] Story's enormous *Commentaries* gave only a passing glance at the social problems involved. Having said a good deal in favor of the rotten-borough system of England, he would not do more than concede that "the existence of various elements in the composition of the representative body is not necessarily inexpedient, unjust, or insecure." [18] In support he quoted Paley's *Moral Philosophy*, but not Number 10 of the *Federalist*. Bancroft briefly rehearsed the dispute on representation in the Convention, without making any comments of his own. He, too, ignored Number 10 of the *Federalist*, and made no reference to Madison's extensive notes on suffrage.[19]

The focusing of attention on the material forces behind the Constitution has been rightly ascribed to Charles A. Beard, whose *An Economic Interpretation of the Constitution of the United States* created a scandal in 1913. The book may have been prompted by the publication of *The Records of the Federal Convention of 1787* two years before. Yet Professor Beard had his precursors. In his Introduction to Jefferson's *Works*, for instance, Paul Leicester Ford had asserted that "the majority of our great revolutionary leaders never ceased to fear the people." "In the re-building of government," he remarked, "the classes [as against the masses] secured an influence far out of proportion to their numbers. In the State constitutions, they succeeded in somewhat curtailing and limiting the popular control; and later, in the formation of our national constitution they sought still further to wrest powers from the people . . ." In the introduction to a later edition of his work, Professor Beard found it necessary to deny any intention of showing "that the form of government established and powers conferred were 'determined' in every detail by the conflict of economic interests." And in *The Economic Basis of Politics* he again emphasized that "economic explanations pure and simple leave out of the reckoning other aspects of human motivation." [20]

The words "economic interests" and, particularly, "class struggle" still conjure up Marx and communism in the minds of most people. It was so in the time of Marx, who clearly stated: "No credit is due to me for discovering the existence of classes in modern society, nor yet the struggle between them. Long before me bourgeois historians had described the historical development of this class struggle and bourgeois economists the economic anatomy of the classes." [21] He must have included Aristotle, Polybius, and most of the political writers of Greece and Rome among the bourgeois historians and economists.

The consideration of economic interests as the primary factor in society is far from being a revolutionary novelty. On the contrary, to ignore class distinctions, to repudiate any inherent connection between economics and politics—as Rousseau did in his *Contrat social*—was the radical innovation. Having introduced universal suffrage without property qualifications, modern states today, even more than the new American Union in 1787, are confronted with the contradiction between protecting property and observing the principle of equality.

The meaning and significance of Adams's *Defence* is that it is devoted in its entirety to an examination of the warring class interests, and of the means of so harnessing the opposing forces as to assure stability instead of allowing them to destroy society. Adams's reading in politics was immensely wide. Already at twenty-three he had made a resolution: "Aim at an exact knowledge of the nature, end, and means of government; compare the different forms of it with each other, and each of them with their effects on public and private happiness." [22] He was a close student of the science of government—he called it "the divine science"—all his life. His master, however, if one may say that he had any *one* master, was James Harrington, whose *The Commonwealth of Oceana*, first published in 1656, was the earliest comprehensive presentation of the theory that government was determined by the economic structure of the state.

Harrington's conclusion is usually summed up in the single sentence "Empire follows dominion" or, in modern English, "Power follows property." But the doctrine deserves to be quoted in its original form: "Fundamental laws are such as state what it is that a man may call his own, that is to say, property; and what the means be whereby a man may enjoy his own, that is to say, protection. The first is also called dominion, and the second empire or sovereign power, whereof this is the natural product of the former: for such as is the balance of dominion in a nation, such is the nature of its empire." Landed property was the source of all power, and its distribution decided the character of the state. In regarding property as an accumulation of labor-value, and therefore justified by the laws of nature, Harrington clearly anticipated Locke's political philosophy. He agreed with Machiavelli that a nobility overbalancing the popular government was "the utter bane and destruction" of the state; but he also believed that a nobility was "the very life and soul" of the state when it did not surpass the popular elements. A natural aristocracy is diffused throughout the whole body of mankind, and the people have a positive obligation to make use of their guidance. "God has so divided mankind into the few or the natural aristocracy, and the many or the natural democracy," he wrote, "that there can hardly be upon any occasion a meeting of twenty men, wherein it will not be apparent, or in which you may not see all those lines which are requisite to the face of a beautiful commonwealth." And he advised: "An equal commonwealth is a government established upon an equal agrarian [law], arising into the superstructures or three orders, the senate debating and proposing, the people resolving, and the magistracy executing by an equal rotation through the suffrage of the people given by the ballot." [23]

Even these brief quotations are sufficient to show that Adams, although he discussed many writers on government, derived most of his principal ideas from Harrington.[24] There were, of course, modifications. Harrington assigned to the senate the rôle of "debating and proposing" only, while the people had the right of "resolving"; the important point, however, was his insistence that "the supreme authority could not properly be settled in any single assembly whatsoever"— something which Adams never tired of repeating. Harrington's method was historical, the larger part of his works consisting of illustrations drawn from Greek, Roman, and Jewish history. Adams followed him in this, too, substituting the Swiss and Italians for the Jews. There was also another parallel. Harrington's partiality for aristocracy, apart from his own origins, was a reaction against the Levelers' movement. The word "leveling," he explained, is used "when a people rising invades the lands and estates of the richer sort, and divides them equally among themselves." Adams, as he stated many times, was induced to write his book by the news of Shays's rebellion and the other postwar disturbances in America. Much of his later conservatism was caused by his fear of lawlessness, which was fully shared by the framers of the Federal Constitution.

Adams's preoccupation with social strife was too constant to permit the quotation of more than a few examples here. "The controversy between the rich and the poor, the laborious and the idle, the learned and the ignorant," he wrote, "distinctions as old as the creation, and as extensive as the globe . . . will continue, and rivalries will spring out of them." The division of people into aristocrats and democrats was "grounded on unalterable nature," and "human wisdom can do no more than reconcile the parties by equitable establishments and equal laws, securing, as far as possible, to every one his own." [25] He employed many other terms to denote this division, such as patricians and plebeians, upper and lower classes, superiors and inferiors, gentlemen and simplemen, the few and the many, and so on. Like Harrington, he was convinced that its recognition through a bicameral system was absolutely necessary. A senate, he argued, was required for the protection of the people itself. "The rich, the well born, and the able," he suggested, "acquire an influence among the people that will soon be too much for simple honesty and plain sense, in a house of representatives. The most illustrious of them must, therefore, be separated from the mass, and placed by themselves in a senate; this is, to all honest and useful intents, an ostracism." He would not deny, of course, that the upper classes, too, might profit from such an arrangement. "It must be remembered," he observed, "that the rich are *people* as well as the poor; that they have rights as well as others; that they have as clear and as *sacred* a right to their large property as others have to theirs which is smaller; that oppression to them is as possible and as wicked as to others . . ." [26]

This strong sense of the social struggle also runs through Adams's marginal notes. In reading Mary Wollstonecraft's remark about "the magnanimous disinterestedness" which members of the National Assembly affected in the French Revolution, he snorted: "None but an idiot or a madman ever built a government upon a disinterested principle. Such pretensions are false and hollow, all hypocrisy like Franklin's Will and his article in the Pennsylvania Bill of Rights." Condorcet's stricture against the new Amercan constitutions, in his *Progress of the Human Mind*, for introducing the system of balance of powers, "identity of interests rather than equality of rights," made him explode again: "Is it possible that a philosopher, who understood human nature, had read history, and knew anything of government, free or arbitrary, should have written this? What is his idea of an identity of interests? An equality of rights? Is an equality of rights anywhere more explicitly asserted than in the American Constiution?"

Adams has been criticized for not wanting to extend the suffrage to the poorest people.[27] But how many of his contemporaries did? In the French National Assembly only five deputies asked for universal manhood suffrage; and the Constitution of 1793 which enacted it was abolished before the new franchise could go into effect. "Is it not true," Adams asked, "that men in general . . . who are wholly destitute of property, are also too little acquainted with public affairs to form a right judgment, and too dependent upon other men to have a will of their own?" He was afraid that the removal of restrictions might lead to endless controversies, even to a demand by women for the vote! [28] However, he reproved Aristotle for denying the vote to farmers, merchants, and mechanics, virtuously asserting that their "understandings . . . are not always the meanest"; that, indeed, "the most splendid geniuses" may arise among them.[29]

He used the words "the rich and the well born" almost as often as Hamilton. But there was a difference. For Hamilton the "rich" meant primarily the capitalists, whereas Adams hated the banks and paper money and, like Jefferson, hoped that America would remain agrarian for centuries to come. He could see, he wrote to John Taylor, no more impropriety in *well born* "than in the epithets *well bred, well educated, well brought up, well taught*" and so on, pouring out some thirty such combinations. He also told Taylor that by an aristocrat he meant "every man who can command or influence two votes; one besides his own." [30]

It was a modest enough qualification. John Adams, nicknamed at one time "the Duke of Braintree," had enlarged his father's farm and bought a new house; but he had amassed no fortune and during his last twelve years he lived on the annuity for which he had sold his property to his eldest son.[31]

3

More than any of his contemporaries, Adams was attacked and abused for his alleged monarchism. Jefferson, as is well known, firmly believed in the existence of a monarchical party in America—and in it he included Adams.[32] Adams vigorously protested, but the charge persisted during his lifetime, and is heard even today. The question deserves a closer examination.

The debates of the Federal Convention clearly revealed that many of the Federalists had not only aristocratic but monarchist leanings, regarding the Constitution as a mere experiment until something better could be devised. Hamilton was the leader of the group. In his speech of June 18, 1787, he stated that "the British government was the best in the world" and that "he doubted much whether anything short of it would do in America." He recommended that the assembly be elected for three years but the senate and governor serve "during good behavior," which in practice would have meant for life. He denied that this constituted an elective monarchy; it was "a strictly republican system" as long as the senate and the executive remained elective.[33] In the end, five states, Virginia among them, voted for his plan concerning the chief executive.[34]

The "monarchists" found encouragement in Adams's *Defence*, the first volume of which had just arrived in Philadelphia. It took some time before the full import of the bulky volume emerged. "I have read your book," Jefferson complimented Adams from Paris, "with infinite satisfaction and improvement. It will do great good in America. Its learning and its good sense will, I hope, make it an institute for our politicians, old as well as young." [35] As he wrote this shortly after the appearance of the work, it is doubtful that he had had a chance to read it through; and a few months later there were already sharp dissents. "Under the mask of attacking Mr. Turgot," the Reverend James Madison, President of the College of William and Mary, wrote to his famous namesake, "Mr. Adams seems insidiously attempting, notwithstanding now and then a saving clause, to overturn our present constitutions, or at least to sow the seeds of discontent." [36] Soon the work was violently denounced in the press.

The dispute about titles and ceremonies with which Congress opened revived the accusation of monarchism against Adams. Presiding over the Senate as Vice-President, he proposed that, instead of a simple "Excellency," the President should be called "His Highness the President of the United States of America and Protector of the Rights of the Same." [37] The majority of the Senate adopted the title, but the House, under Madison's leadership, promptly rejected it. Through the affair Adams made himself obnoxious to a large section of Congress. "His grasping after titles," Senator Maclay recorded, "has been observed by everybody. Mr. Izard, after describing his air, manner, deportment, and personal figure in the chair, concluded with applying the title of *Rotundity* to him." Maclay's own reaction to Adams's behavior was even more cruel and vindictive. Madison reported the incident to Jefferson, who replied that Adams's proposal was "the most superlatively ridiculous thing" he ever heard of.[38]

In the nation-wide controversy over the French Revolution, Adams came forward as the most bitter critic of events in France. While Jefferson was sanguine with optimism, Adams was filled with despair. To his mind, the adoption of the unicameral system by the National Assembly augured inevitable catastrophe. In April 1790 he began in the *Gazette of the United States* a series of articles under the title *Discourses on Davila*, showing the fatal consequences of an unbalanced government. The articles continued for a year, their language becoming more and more unrestrained. Adams was explaining why "all the nations of the world" had adopted the system of hereditary monarchy. "Mankind," he wrote, "had tried all possible experiment of elections of governors and senates . . . but they had almost unanimously been convinced that hereditary succession was attended with fewer evils than frequent elections." With this, the series abruptly stopped. "The rage and fury of the Jacobinical journals," Adams recorded later, ". . . intimidated the printer, John Fenno, and convinced me that to proceed would do more hurt than good." [39]

But the storm was by no means over. Reissuing Thomas Paine's *Rights of Man*, the publisher prefaced it by a note from Jefferson, then Secretary of State, expressing pleasure that "something is at length to be publicly said against the political heresies which have sprung up" in America. The note was printed without Jefferson's consent; yet in relating the incident to Washington, as well as in letters to Madison and Paine, he admitted that he had "the doctrines of Davila" in mind, and spoke plainly of Adams's "apostasy to hereditary monarchy and nobility." "Those censures," he stated, "I meant for the enemies of the government, to wit those who want to change it into a monarchy." [40] Adams, who knew only of the note printed in the *Rights of Man*, complained to Jefferson of its effect. Unprincipled libelers in the newspapers, he wrote on July 29, 1791, were holding him up "to the ridicule of the world for his meanness, and to their detestation for wishing to subjugate the people to a few nobles." He assured Jefferson that he never had any desire to introduce a hereditary executive or a hereditary senate into the governments of America, and challenged "all mankind" to produce such a passage in his public or private writings.[41]

One of Adams's letters contains a paragraph which might be taken as manifesting such a desire. "I am as much a Republican as I was in 1775," he wrote on June 9, 1789, to Dr. Rush. "I do not 'consider hereditary monarchy or aristocracy as rebellion against Nature.' On the contrary I esteem them both institutions of admirable wisdom and exemplary virtue in a certain stage of society in a great nation. The only institutions that can possibly preserve the laws and liberties of the people, and I am clear that America must resort to them as an asylum against discord, seditions, and civil war, and that at no very distant period of time. I shall not live to see it—but you may. I think it therefore impolitic to cherish prejudices against institutions which must be kept in view as the hope of our posterity. I am by no means for attempting any such thing at present. Our country is not ripe for it in many respects, and it is not yet necessary, but our ship must ultimately land on that shore or be cast away." [42] Evidently Dr. Rush reminded him of the statement, for in the following year Adams heatedly denied "any attachment" to monarchy. After cautioning the Doctor against "a fraudulent use of the words *monarchy* and *republic*," he declared: "I am a mortal and irreconcilable enemy to monarchy. I am no friend to hereditary limited monarchy in America. This I know can never be admitted without an hereditary Senate to control it, and a hereditary nobility or Senate in America I know to be unattainable and impracticable. I should scarcely be for it, if it were. Do not, therefore, my friend, misunderstand me and misrepresent me to posterity." [43]

As the violence of the French Revolution increased, party passions in America similarly rose, reaching their climax in the Presidential election of 1793.[44] But the excitement continued for years. Another letter by Jefferson caused a new flare-up in 1797. Writing to his friend Philip Mazzei, Jefferson again voiced his suspicions of the "monarchists." The main body of the people, he wrote, have remained true to their republican principles; "against us are the executive, the judiciary, two out of three branches of the legislature, all the officers of the government, all who want to be officers . . ." [45] Washington, who often had to listen to Jefferson's denunciations of the "monarchist sect," while protesting that "there were not a half dozen sane men of that kind in all America," became indignant and from then on ceased all contact with him. In his Inaugural Address, Adams declared his determination to support the Constitution "until it shall be altered by the judgments and the wishes of the people, expressed in the mode prescribed in it." [46] But the threat of war with France rekindled animosities, and finally the introduction of the Alien and Sedition Laws in 1798 raised the cries of "despotism." In later years Adams refused responsibility for the panicky legislation, insisting that he had never executed these laws. It is true that he showed no interest in them; Secretary of State Pickering and the federal judges, however, were energetic in their enforcement. A number of aliens left the country, a few went into hiding, and some twenty-five arrests were made.[47]

The charge of monarchism pursued Adams even in his old age. Mercy Warren in her *History of the American Revolution*, published in 1805, made the statement that, unfortunately for himself and his country, Adams during his residence in England, "became so enamored with the British Constitution and the government, manners, and laws of the nation, that a partiality for monarchy appeared, which was inconsistent with his former professions of republicanism." [48] Adams swore, upon his honor and faith, that the accusation was totally unjust. His judgment of the British Constitution, he wrote, was not affected by his years in England, and he never desired a government with a hereditary executive or a hereditary senate in America.[49] But Mrs. Warren stoutly defended her book. "The assertion," she replied, "was not founded on vague rumor, nor was it the result of any scattered and dubious expressions through your Defence of the American Constitutions that might warrant such a suspicion, but from my own judgment and observation soon after your return from Europe in the year 1788. There certainly was then an observable alteration in your whole deportment and conversation. Many of your best friends saw, felt, and regretted it." [50] Adams's reproaches became more and more bitter; he accused Mrs. Warren of having turned against him from personal motives, while at the same time she and her family "cried up" Jefferson as the great republican—"Jefferson," he declared, "who is not half so much of a republican as I am, and whose administration has not been so conformable to republican principles or manners as mine was." [51]

Some writers have accepted the charge of Adams's monarchism, although allowing a distinction between him and the Hamiltonians. Thus Correa M. Walsh remarks that he had looked forward to monarchy and hereditary aristocracy "with pleasurable contemplation," and that, demanding elections only for the House of Representatives, he admitted the coming necessity of the hereditary principle for the other two branches. "Had he lived till the advent of that time, or had that time arrived during his life," the writer concludes, "he would have advocated its actual adoption." More plausible is Charles E. Merriam's opinion that, had Adams been obliged to choose between unlimited democracy and monarchy, "he would have accepted the latter without much hesitation." [52] Yet one is pleased to note that Parrington rejected Madison's imputation that Adams was secretly a monarchist as "absurd." [53]

It is true that Adams praised monarchy just as freely as Hamilton, yet there was enough dissimilarity between the two men to make their phrases sound different. Adams greeted the Federal Constitution as "the greatest single effort of national deliberation that the world has ever seen," while Hamilton called it "a shilly shally thing of mere milk and water" and "a frail and worthless fabric." [54] Adams's flirtation with monarchy—and for a year or two it was conducted with ardor—must be largely ascribed to his habitual lack of caution, his love of shocking people, and his fear that he might not say enough. It would be "weakness, if not a vice," he wrote, if the dread of unpopularity should induce anyone to conceal the possibility of a hereditary magistracy. There was no danger of his ever being guilty of such a weakness or vice. Hamilton told Jefferson that he would not care to publish his opinions "in Dan or Bersheba"; he confided them to close friends only. [55] Adams did the opposite. He trumpeted forth the unpopular doctrine of monarchy while he remained a republican at heart.

It was also a matter of semantics. As Adams explained to Dr. Rush in 1806, the expression "Kings, Lords, and Commons," so freely used at the time of the Federal Convention and after, was susceptible of different interpretations: "Some whom I have heard use them, did not mean titles of King or Lords, nor the quality of hereditary Kings or Lords; they meant no more than that they wished the President, Senate and House of Representatives might be as independent branches of the Legislature as Kings, Lords, and Commons were in England, and as capable of balancing each other." [56] In the same way, the lack of a common agreement on the meaning of "monarchy" and "republic" caused confusion. Thus Adams spoke of "monarchical, aristocratical, and democratical republics"; he defined monarchy as "a sovereignty in one"; and he thought that monarchy "may be hereditary, or it may be for life, or it may be for years or only for one year, or for months or for one month, or for days or only for one day." [57] And, in the course of time, there was undoubtedly a change in his attitude—as in that of every other "monarchist." [58]

In his marginal notes on the French Revolution Adams shows a consistent sympathy with the King; but this was hardly monarchism. It is true, to Mary Wollstonecraft's suggestion that only a second chamber could curb the assembly, he remarked, "An hereditary second chamber is the only effectual check to faction in the first, in opulent nations with great armies, navies, churches, revenues, i.e., a great patronage." He wrote this in 1796. Sixteen years later, on his second reading of the book, he was more cautious. He sarcastically asked Mary Wollstonecraft "if she would reveal to us any way of getting rid of a hereditary senate and a monarch but by substituting greater evils . . ." However, he now significantly added, "in Europe." There are no evidences of secret monarchism in Adams's comments; nor could anyone who really knows him have expected any.

4

The American Revolution had many causes, the most important being the growth of the Colonies, which made their government by a faraway Parliament impossible. The blunders of the Ministry brought the discontent to a crisis, but the break was inevitable. Yet all actions are accompanied by spiritual forces. There is a sense of right and wrong; and even material powers are more efficacious when expressed in an idealistic language. The chief inspiration of the American Revolution was the doctrine of the Laws of Nature.

There was in the Boston of the 1760's a group of lawyers—the whole bar consisted of about a dozen members—who were well versed in the works of Grotius, Pufendorf, Hobbes, Locke, Blackstone, Burlamaqui, and other exponents of the doctrine. One of the first, and certainly the most conspicuous, reference to the Laws of Nature was made by James Otis in 1761 in his speech before the Supreme Court of Massachusetts against the granting of writs of assistance to customs officers. He based his argument on "the inherent and inalienable rights of man to his life, liberty, and property," wrought into the English Constitution as fundamental laws. Adams, who was present and took notes, remarked in his old age that "Otis's oration . . . breathed into this nation the breath of life," and that "American independence was then and there born." [59] In his *Vindication of the House of Representatives of Massachusetts* and *Rights of the British Colonies*, published in 1762 and 1764, Otis further elaborated the principles which quickly spread through America: "Civil government is of God; the administrators of it were originally the whole people; they might have devolved it on whom they pleased; this devolution is fiduciary, for the good of the whole . . ."

Adams, who considered Otis a genius, knew his works as his "alphabet." The spell which the great scholar and orator cast upon him soon showed in his own "Dissertation on the Canon and Feudal Law." In this brief piece Adams cited the rights of man nearly a dozen times. "I say *Rights*, for such they [the people] have," he wrote, "undoubtedly, antecedent to all earthly government,—*Rights*, that cannot be repealed or restrained by human laws,—*Rights*, derived from the great Legislator of the Universe." "Nature and reason," "the inherent rights of mankind," "original rights," and similar expressions follow one another in the essay. The foundations of British laws and government, Adams asserted, were to be sought "in the frame of human nature, in the constitution of the intellectual and moral world." [60]

During the next ten years the doctrine became a household article with the Patriots. The fourteen resolves of the Massachusetts legislature, drafted by Samuel Adams, began with the declaration that "there are certain essential rights of the British Constitution of government, which are founded in the law of God and nature, and are the common rights of mankind." But even more outspoken were the "Rights of Colonists as Men, Christians, and Subjects" adopted at Faneuil Hall on

October 28, 1772, claiming that "all positive and civil laws should conform, as far as possible, to the law of natural reason and equity." At the Continental Congress the two Adamses, Richard Henry Lee, and others strenuously insisted that the doctrine should be invoked in the Declaration of Rights, but on the objections of Rutledge, Duane, and Galloway the idea was dropped. The final text, however, gave prominence to "the immutable laws of nature." [61] In his essay *On the Legislative Authority of the British Parliament*, James Wilson demanded the rights to which the Colonies were entitled "by the supreme and uncontrollable laws of nature," repeatedly referring to "natural rights" and "the dictates of natural justice." [62] And returning to Boston, John Adams, too, again made use of the doctrine. His *Novanglus* papers, which he started in November 1774 in the *Boston Gazette*, bristled with affirmations of "the principle of nature and eternal reason," "the law of nature and nations," "God's general ordinance," etc.[63] "Opposition, nay, open, avowed resistance by arms, against usurpation and lawless violence," he wrote, "is not rebellion by the law of God or the land." And, quoting Grotius: "It is not repugnant to the law of nature, for any one to repel injuries by force." [64] The doctrine was made the cornerstone of the Bill of Rights in Virginia. The Declaration of Independence, with its appeal to "the Laws of Nature and of Nature's God," was the final classic expression of the accumulated principles, every one of which had long been familiar.

The country in which the Laws of Nature, a concept as old as Western civilization, ran an even more vehement course was France. The modern version of the doctrine started with the Reformation, with Calvin, Beza, Duplessis-Mornay, and with Hooker, who, it should be remembered, was a great admirer of Calvin.[65] To the medieval concept of the divine law, the tenets of the consent of the people and the right of rebellion were added. The new theories were first put to the test by the Puritans in the Civil War, producing the *Agreement of the People* on the one hand and Hobbes's absolutist *Leviathan* on the other, with Harrington's republicanism in the middle. They were mellowed and systematized in Locke's philosophy, the perfect expression of the incipient Parliamentary democracy.[66] It was mainly through Locke that eighteenth-century France received them. He was the guide of both Voltaire and Montesquieu, who during their stays in England closely studied his works, and propagandized them afterwards.

All the French thinkers of the century became Locke's disciples. Rousseau, the most influential among them, carried to an extreme Locke's views on the state of nature (in his two *Discours*) and then

Hobbes's views on the state of society (in his *Contrat social*), forcing
the latter into the people's service by his theory of "the general will."
The Laws of Nature had also been called the Laws of Reason; and the
philosophes preferred the latter term. Having divorced the concept
from its theistic connotation, they created a cult of reason, priding
themselves on an enlightenment such as no age had known before.
Reason was their weapon against fanaticism, superstition, all evils.
England had solved her social and political problems, but France was
still living under the structure of the Middle Ages. The contrast between natural rights and actual wrongs was tremendous there—and the
example of the Americans showed that change was not impossible.
"That which had been for nearly two thousand years," James Bryce
remarked, "a harmless maxim, almost a commonplace of morality, became in the end of the eighteenth century a mass of dynamite, which
shattered an ancient monarchy and shook the European Continent." [67]

Adams distrusted the *philosophes* from the beginning. Steeped as he
was in English political thinking, with experience in the workings of
government, their aspirations appeared to him fantastic exaggerations,
their notions of limitless progress "a chimera," and the principles of
liberty, equality, and fraternity "a swindle." Equality, particularly, became his *bête noire*. Not content with a plain denial of the principle,
he built up a whole theory of natural inequality. He still referred to
the Laws of Nature, but the force to which he appealed was very different from that which had inspired him ten or twenty years before.
Now it was the desire for distinction that lay "at the foundation of our
whole moral system in this world"; it was emulation which "nature has
ordained"; "the most universal appetite in human nature" was for honor
—convictions for which he found support in Pope, Hume, and Adam
Smith.[68] His arguments became increasingly psychological. Nature,
which first meant for him God or Heaven, signified more and more
simply human nature. In his early period the Laws of Nature were
vast liberating forces; later they appeared to him as the forces of
restraint.

Yet the doctrine never lost its transcendental meaning for him. It
was a residue of the concept of divine law, which survived much longer
in New England Calvinism than in the Established Church of England.
At the age of twenty, Adams thought that Christianity was encumbered
by "whole cartloads of trumpery," and, through the philosophical
works of Bolingbroke, he came fairly close to the natural religion of the
Deists, emerging finally as one of the earliest Unitarians in America.[69]
Just as he did not come easily by his political convictions, he worked

hard for his faith. Religion and philosophy were intimately linked for him, since he regarded philosophy as "not only the love of wisdom but the science of the universe and its cause." And government, based on the Laws of Nature (or at least on human nature), was a part of philosophy. All of Adams's thoughts and actions had, ultimately, a common origin.

Wisely he confessed that wrangling over philosophy was essentially futile. "I love to read these fluent and flippant metaphysical disquisitions," he commented on one of Frederick's letters, adding, "but I never get any knowledge or satisfaction from them. A song, a romance, a tune is equally instructive and often more so." A man of action, Adams still had in him something of the speculative passion of the New England divines—only, instead of fighting Quakers and Anabaptists, he fought the *philosophes*.

5

In his editorial preface to the *Defence of the Constitutions of America* Charles Francis Adams squarely stated: "The opinions the work expresses must be regarded hereafter as the author's contribution to science, upon which whatever may belong to him of name and fame must ultimately rest." The estimate seems at first startling; yet it was probably shared by Parrington, who concluded his section on Adams: "In spite of his dogmatisms and inconsistencies he remains the most notable political thinker—with the possible exception of John C. Calhoun—among American statesmen." [70] And the present writer remembers the remark made to him once by the late Harold Laski: "John Adams was the greatest political thinker whom America has yet produced."

Histories of political science devote considerable space to Adams, but it must be a determined student indeed who actually wades through his works to get at the substance behind the enormous masses of irrelevant material. The *Defence* is certainly not to be judged by its literary merits. A compilation of fragments taken from fifty-odd chronicles and travel books, it is held together, if at all, by Adams's comments, consisting of interspersed sentences or paragraphs. In addition, there are a few set pieces in the form of introductions and conclusions. Few realize the extent of Adams's borrowings. Usually he merely mentioned his source or spoke of "some writers." Charles Francis Adams, having collated the work with the "original authorities," supplied a large part of the missing quotation marks, but by no means all. A fresh collation with the sources, most of which are preserved in the Adams library, nearly doubles the quantity of borrowed passages.

Thus it appears that nearly three-fourths of the first volume, dealing with modern and ancient republics, is made up of verbatim transcripts from books by Addison, William Coxe, King Stanislaus of Poland, William Mitford, John Gillies, Adam Ferguson, and others, not counting the opinions of historians and philosophers cited under their own names. More than nine-tenths of the second volume and the first half of the third, treating of the Italian republics, were copied from the chronicles of Machiavelli, Guicciardini, Nerli, Varchi, Malavolti, and a dozen others. The most original part is the commentary on the *Excellencie of a Free State* by Marchamont Nedham, the seventeenth-century English journalist.[71] Here Adams let himself go. Nedham's pamphlet, which attempts to prove that the people are the best keepers of their liberties, has forty headings. It was an ideal arrangement for Adams; forty times he could elaborate his fundamental doctrines. The first part of the essay especially interested him, so he smothered its ten thousand words with fifty thousand of his own. The *Discourses on Davila*, which Adams regarded as a supplement to the *Defence*, is similar in nature. Eighteen of its thirty-two chapters are straight translations from the French version of E. C. Davila's *Historia delle guerre civili de Francia*, the remaining fourteen being "useful reflections" on avarice, emulation, ambition, and fame, all based upon one chapter in Adam Smith's *Theory of Moral Sentiments*.

His habit of incorporating unwieldly alien material in his books has been responsible for Adams's reputation as a dull and ponderous writer. It is a pity; for while the description fits the chronicles embodied in his books, his own style was something different. Anyone who has read Adams's essays, and especially his Diary and letters, knows that he wrote a powerful and trenchant English, that he was indeed a master of prose. Writing was as natural to him as talking. He never "copied, corrected, or embellished" anything he wrote.[72] But books, perhaps for this very reason, he could not compose. He lacked the patience to digest his sources and to investigate all aspects of the subject. The control demanded by a larger design was contrary to his nature; his thoughts, in his excitement, had to find their utterance instantly, without waiting for their turn. It is this precipitation that gives freshness and "bite" to the shorter pieces and ruins the longer ones. "My great misfortune, through a pretty long life," Adams himself wrote, "has been, that I have never had time to make my poor productions shorter." And he complained that he had "neither eyes, nor fingers, nor clerks, nor secretaries, nor aids-de-camp, nor amanuenses," any more than time, "to abridge and condense, or arrange and methodize anything." [73] His works are in crying need of just such a revision. By cutting down the borrowed texts to essentials and by eliminating at least some of the repetitious comments, the four volumes of the *Defence* and the *Davila* could be conveniently reduced to a single one. In such a form, after being buried for over a hundred and fifty years, they could still be useful to "young Americans who wish to be masters of the subject."

The fundamental shortcoming of Adams's works, the absence of a logical development of ideas, would still remain. At the moment of their appearance this may even have been an advantage. In times of crisis a book may achieve success either by its brilliance or by its "erudition." Adams's immense cavalcade of authorities could not fail to affect people, while his constant reiteration of the gospel of checks and balances had almost the ring of incantation. But Adams had no form; he was a great political thinker, but not a great political writer. It is in his vision of history, and in his obsessive faith in the rightness of this vision, that the importance of his works lies. It seems wrong, therefore, to consider Adams's writings alone. His activities, his political thinking, and his metaphysical speculations are inseparable from one another. This is what made him a "representative man" of his age.

America added three illustrious figures to the group of the *philosophes*. The first was Franklin, whom the French regarded as one of the most eminent scientists and wisest men; the second was Jefferson, a tougher and more experienced Condorcet, superior even to the great Turgot; and the third, no less genuine than the others—*a philosophe* in spite of himself—was John Adams.

[IV]

Bolingbroke, the Ishmael
of His Age

Three weeks after his graduation from Harvard, in 1755, John Adams began his school-teaching, as Latin master in the grammar school at Worcester. He found that "the principles of deism had made a considerable progress among several persons in that and other towns of the county." He himself had carried with him to Worcester two of the political works of the principal English deist, *The Study and Use of History* and *The Patriot King* of Bolingbroke. He lent these to James Putnam, whose law office he had entered. Putnam was so well pleased with the books that he ordered from London a set of Bolingbroke's works, then recently published.[1]

This gave Adams an opportunity to study Bolingbroke in earnest. In a commonplace book he copied out long passages from his works. "Afternoon wrote Bolingbroke," "wrote in Bolingbroke pretty industriously," he recorded again and again in his Diary. He read all of Bolingbroke's works before he left Worcester; and then began to reread them as a young lawyer. "I arose by the dawning of the day," he noted in Braintree, "and by sunrise had made my fire and read a number of pages in Bolingbroke." He reproached himself for "too much rambling and straggling from one book to another; from the Corpus Juris Canonici to Bolingbroke." In Boston someone flattered him, "You have Lord Bolingbroke by heart!" To be sure, Bolingbroke was no passing interest with John Adams. In his Autobiography he states that he had read him through three times; and in 1813 he wrote to Jefferson that he had read him through "more than five times" in his life, "and once within five years past." [2]

For Jefferson, Bolingbroke had perhaps an even greater fascination. He, too, began to read the Englishman at twenty, filling a notebook with lengthy passages from the *Philosophical Essays,* and at nearly eighty still regarding him as a great advocate of human liberty and a writer of the highest order. "His political tracts," Jefferson wrote to one of his grandnephews, "are safe reading for the most timid religionist, his philosophical, for those who are not afraid to trust their reason with discussions of right and wrong." Professor Chinard, who has published Jefferson's notebook, maintains that Bolingbroke was the strongest and most continuous single influence on Jefferson's development.[3]

Yet Bolingbroke is almost entirely forgotten today, in England as well as in America. Burke once asked, "Who reads now Bolingbroke?" And repeating the question in 1863, Bagehot continued: "Who knows anything about him? Professed students of our history or of our literature may have special knowledge; but out of the general mass of educated men, how many could give an intelligible account of his career? How many could describe even vaguely his character as a statesman?"[4] Of all the cruel things that have been said about Bolingbroke this is the cruelest; and also the truest. Neglected by historians and educators, Henry St. John, first Viscount of Bolingbroke—the most admired and most hated man of his age—has become a hazier figure than Shakespeare's "great Bolingbroke."[5]

A youth of twenty-two, whose dissipations were common gossip, he nevertheless distinguished himself in Parliament, and became at once a leader of the Tories. At twenty-seven he was Secretary of War, the copartner of Marlborough's great victories; and at thirty-two, after a withdrawal of two years, he was appointed Secretary of State. "I think Mr. St. John," Swift wrote to Stella, "the greatest young man I ever knew: wit, capacity, beauty, quickness of apprehension, good learning, and an excellent taste; the best orator in the House of Commons, admirable conversation and good nature, and good manners; generous, and a despiser of money."[6] It was this young man, by then Viscount Bolingbroke, who conceived and negotiated the Treaty of Utrecht. But just as he was on the point of being made Prime Minister, Queen Anne died, and, detested by the Whigs and the new Hanoverian King, he had to flee the country. Declared an outlaw, Bolingbroke served for a while as Secretary of State to the Pretender; after the unsuccessful landing in Scotland, however, he was "dismissed" as a traitor, whereupon he foreswore all further connection with the Jacobites. Nearly ten years went by before he was allowed to return to England, but Parliament was closed to him even then. For the rest of his life— and he lived to be seventy-three—he was compelled to remain in the background. A man thirsting for action, he could exert his influence only through his friends and his writings. This enforced retirement brought out sharply the two sides of his personality: the political thinker and the eclectic philosopher.

He was past forty when he began the serious study of philosophy, also reading deeply in the classics, history, and Biblical literature. At about that time he married the Marquise de Villette, the niece of Madame de Maintenon (his first wife had died two years before in England), and built a home at La Source, near Orleans, where many visitors, among them the young Voltaire, came to see him. Upon his return to England in 1725, he settled at Dawley, fourteen miles from London. Pope, whom he had known since his days in power, lived at neighboring Twickenham, and their friendship soon became firmly established. "Lord Bolingbroke is the most improved mind since you saw him that ever was improved without shifting to a new body or being: *paulo minus ab angelis*," the poet extravagantly reported to Swift.[7] They met almost daily, carrying on innumerable discussions. Their talks formed the basis of Pope's *Essay on Man;* and out of them Bolingbroke later prepared his philosophical essays. A comparison of the prose works with the poem shows that not only Bolingbroke's thoughts but his very expressions had been freely used by Pope.[8]

Bolingbroke was a deist, in the line of Herbert of Cherbury, Shaftesbury, Tindal, Toland, and others. Professing "natural theology or theism, and natural religion or ethics," which he called his "first philosophy," he denounced the "artificial theology" of Christianity. He acknowledged the validity of the Gospels, but abhorred the Old Testament, in which he saw nothing but the biased history of the Jews. He was also an anti-Platonist, and had a positive hatred of Saint Paul. The Fathers of the Church, he claimed, dealt with "wild allegories," and "the pompous jargon of mystery" of the schoolmen was absurd. A thoroughgoing rationalist, he regarded all pretensions to metaphysical knowledge as fantastic; an agnostic, he trusted experience alone, insisting that we may learn something about corporeal but not about spiritual nature.[9] Like all later deists, Bolingbroke profited greatly from Hobbes and Locke, and, through Shaftesbury, from Spinoza, whose doctrine of social altruism he embraced.[10]

But philosophy, no matter how earnestly professed, was only a refuge for Bolingbroke. Bitter over Walpole's determination to prevent his reëntering political life, he began his unrestrained attacks upon the minister. In January 1727 he published the first number of *The Occasional Writer*, a pamphlet which described Walpole's character as a combination of "presumption and distrust, boldness and pusillanimity, indiscretion and cunning, and fifty other contradictions." [11] Walpole hit back with a savage reply: "Though you have not signed your name, I know you. Because a man who is without all principles of honesty, who in no one thing can be relied upon, a betrayer of his friend, a traitor to his prince, an enemy of his country, a perjured, ungrateful, unfaithful rascal, must be you; one who is a composition of all these things, can be only you." [12] With this the war was on. Among the Tories Bolingbroke still had a number of supporters, men like Sir William Wyndham and his friends; he now tried to unite them with the Whigs who followed Pulteney. His *Remarks on the History of England*, a series of articles printed in *The Craftsman*, was filled with allusions to the corruption of the government.[13] The introduction of the Excise Bill, which had stirred up a great deal of antagonism, gave him a fresh chance for assault; in his *Dissertation on Parties* he sounded an alarm, warning against the danger to English liberty.[14] Walpole, however, weathered the storm, and in the new Parliament he had a large majority.

Disappointed, Bolingbroke left England once more, in 1735. This time he took up his residence at Chanteloup, in Touraine, writing his *Study and Use of History*. Three years later he revisited England. Frederick, the Prince of Wales, was the center of the opposition party, and for his guidance he composed *The Patriot King*. His ideal prince was powerful enough to override all political parties, yet derived his authority from the strength of the people itself. But Frederick was no ideal prince; weak and spiteful, he was not even a match for George II. In the next few years Bolingbroke lived alternately in France and England. At last, in 1744, he installed himself on the family estate at Battersea. He was at Pope's deathbed, and, sobbing, he declared that "he never knew a man that had so tender a heart for his particular friends, or a more general friendship for mankind." His sentiments, however, changed when he discovered that Pope, to whom he had entrusted the manuscript of *The Patriot King* with the request that only five or six copies be printed, had ordered fifteen hundred. In a rage, he made a bonfire of the whole edition; and five years later, when he himself published the work, wrote with contempt of "the person" who had betrayed him.[15] He was by then a sick and weary man. After great suffering, he died in 1751.

Bolingbroke's philosophical essays, first published three years after his death, produced a shock. "The wild and pernicious ravings, under the name of Philosophy," Boswell recorded, "gave great offence to all well-principled men." Pope's poem had been celebrated as one of the ethical masterpieces of English literature, but the writings which inspired it were execrated as cynical and blasphemous.[16] Warburton, whom Bolingbroke loathed, was the first to attempt a refutation of them, in a tone so abusive that even his friends found it distasteful.[17] But the excitement did not last long. In view of the well-known licentiousness of his life, Bolingbroke's high moral tone could make no impression; nor could his lofty conception of government make many converts, considering the suspicion which covered all his political actions. The chief reason for the ineffectiveness of his works, however, was that they came too late. The ecclesiastical controversies had been fought out and the political situation was calm; people had little interest either in philosophy or in constitutional theories.

On the other hand, they were most timely in France, where the *philosophes* were just beginning to wage their battle against intolerance. Voltaire recognized at once the arsenal of weapons which Bolingbroke had furnished for them. During his sojourn in England he had been a frequent guest at Dawley, and for the rest of his life he made a cult of Bolingbroke, whose essays he extolled as "the most eloquent, the most profound, and the most powerful writing ever done in the fight against fanaticism." He frequently borrowed Bolingbroke's ideas, and even more frequently used his name to propagate his own doctrines. Thus he palmed off under Bolingbroke's name one of his most violent attacks on Christianity, the *Examen important de Milord Bolingbroke*, making later many references to this fictitious Englishman. His *Défense de Bolingbroke* was, therefore, largely self-defense. Nevertheless, it is safe to say that Bolingbroke's most effective contribution was made through Voltaire, rather than through Pope.[18]

It is painful to rehearse the opprobrium which English critics and historians have heaped upon Bolingbroke. Johnson, who had never read his works, branded him "a scoundrel and a coward"; Macaulay, with his insatiable desire for the pungent phrase, called him "a brilliant knave"; and Leslie Stephen, in his great inventory of eighteenth-century thought, saw in him only "a showy actor" and "a rake and intriguer." Even Lecky condemns him, in his monumental work, as "an eminently Italian character" who combined "recklessness and insincerity" with his "incontestable genius." [19] Disraeli was the one great Victorian who appreciated Bolingbroke, holding him up as "the founder of modern Toryism," who, "with the splendor of an organizing genius, settled the confused and discordant materials of English faction, and reduced them into a clear and systematic order." According to him, Bolingbroke represented a Toryism based on democratic principles and championing the rights of the monarch and the people against the oligarchy.[20]

John Adams thought that many of Bolingbroke's political writings contained "more faction than truth"; yet he was more saturated with Bolingbroke's theories than he himself knew. On reading the *Dissertation upon Parties,* he exclaimed at a passage: "This is a jewel. There is nothing so profound, correct, and perfect on the subject of government in the English or any other language." In Bolingbroke he found the fundamental tenet of his own political philosophy: "Simple forms of governments are governments of arbitrary will, and, therefore, of all imaginable absurdities the most absurd." The Englishman's "abuse of the Christian religion," on the other hand, he considered superficial and impious. But Adams liked an author with whom he could disagree; Bolingbroke's works were just what he wanted to reëxamine in his old age. "His copy of the philosophical writings," Charles Francis Adams noted, "is filled with marginal manuscript annotations, amply sufficient to preserve any reader of that copy from the influence of the fascinating errors with which they abound." [21]

Adams's notes comprise more than twelve thousand words, about half of which are repetitions of names, key words, and short sentences, almost all in the essays on religion.

THE STATESMAN

It was under the pseudonym of Humphry Oldcastle that Bolingbroke wrote his articles, later brought together as *Remarks on the History of England.* The first three pieces were cast in the form of discussions, an ancient venerable gentleman holding forth on the need of constantly defending freedom. The sage voiced Bolingbroke's opinions with undisguised references to Walpole's corrupt practices, and the articles were attacked at once by the "ministerial scribblers." Twenty more letters followed, carrying the study down to Queen Anne's time. When in the last Bolingbroke presented a defense of his conduct, a reply, written perhaps by Walpole himself, appeared. Bolingbroke made a final answer, and with that the series ended.

Adams read the preface, studied closely the first letter, and also made some comments on the second and seventeenth. Bolingbroke's axiom that liberty is in greater danger in a limited monarchy than in a perfect democracy or a mixed republic evoked his violent protests.

And whatever Bolingbroke had to say about factions and parties reminded him of the American scene. His notes date from 1804:

Bolingbroke: If ever à test for the trial of spirits can be necessary, it is now; if ever those of liberty and faction ought to be distinguished from each other, it is now . . .[22]

Adams: The spirit of liberty and of faction ought ever to be distinguished, but amidst the war of gazettes conducted by Freneau, Andrew Brown, Peter Markoe, Callender, Cobbett, Bache, I. Ward, Fenno, and Ben Austin, Anthony Pasquin, Cheetham, Wood,[23] etc. how can the people distinguish them?

B.: Perhaps that time is now; perhaps party-leaders of all kinds are equally in disgrace; and the public may be grown wise enough to judge of the tree by its fruits . . .

A.: Perhaps this time is now in America. But the public is not yet grown wise enough to judge of the tree by its fruits.

B.: This [the reformation of party spirit] can be effected no way so happily as by siding with such . . . who appear to have been really inspired with the genuine spirit of liberty.

A.: Such as have advertised integrity by the common crier. O yes! Integrity to be had cheap! for nothing! enquire of Bonaparte or Mirabeau! or! or! or!

B.: Let but one great, brave, disinterested, active man arise, and he will be received, followed, and almost adored, as the guardian genius of these kingdoms.

A.: Like Bonaparte, or Hamilton, or Burr.

B.: If then there is any one man of sufficient eminence among us, who . . . feels himself to be within this description, let him stand forth.

A.: Bonaparte, Caesar, Cromwell, Robespierre, or Marat would have done this with as much facility as Bolingbroke, and would have deserved credit and confidence as much.

B.: But if modesty should hinder what public necessity makes a duty, let this man endeavour to inspire a few more with the same generous sentiments, and let them divide both the service and the glory. Glory, which . . . is the only thing worth the ambition of the great, and what the voice of the people only can bestow!

A.: Glory and popularity then are synonymous terms! The great, who pretend to aim at glory alone, have always been detected, sooner or later, in schemes for power and wealth. Hypocrisy can assume the pretext of glory among men as easily as that of the glory of God.

Here Bolingbroke's old gentleman takes over. He begins with an encomium on *The Craftsman* which has greatly contributed to "the revival of the true old English spirit." The love of power, he emphasizes, is insatiable, and liberty cannot be long secure unless the people jealously watch over it.

B.: The notion of a perpetual danger to liberty is inseparable from the very notion of government.[24]

A.: In democracies as well as in mixed governments.

B.: In perfect democracies precautions [against this evil] have been taken in the highest degree; and yet even there they have not been always effectual.

A.: What can he mean? When and where did he find his perfect democracies?

B.: They were carried very far in the Athenian form of government; yet one of their magistrates found means to become their tyrant.

A.: Athens was a mixed government as Solon made it. Aristides destroyed the balance. In a democracy one of their magistrates is always their tyrant. France has from 1789 been more of a democracy than Athens, and one of their magistrates is now their Emperor. Algernon Sidney understood this subject better than Bolingbroke.

B.: In mixed governments the danger must still be greater. No history can be more fruitful in such examples . . . than the Roman . . .

A.: In the people as well as in the senate.

B.: In a monarchy like ours liberty would be safer, perhaps, if we inclined a little more than we do to the popular side.

A.: This is very questionable in England.

B.: A spirit of liberty will never destroy a free constitution; a spirit of faction may.

A.: A sacred truth. But the spirit of liberty must flow from an understanding of its system. It must be jealous of encroachment on the judicial as well as on the legislative or executive powers.

B.: The prerogative and power of a prince will never be in any real danger when he invades the liberties of his people . . .

A.: Very questionable. It has not been hitherto, but recent periods may be quoted when the danger was very great. The coalition of North and Fox,[25] and the Conventions and Corresponding Societies in England at the beginning of the French Revolution.[26]

B.: Generally speaking . . . as public liberty is more exposed under mixed governments than under perfect democracies, so is it more exposed under limited monarchies than under any other form of mixed government.

A.: This [is] absolutely erroneous.

B.: Liberty must always be in some degree of danger under every government . . .

A.: True.

B.: . . . and this danger must increase in proportion as the chief powers of the state are intrusted in fewer hands and for longer terms.

A.: But not in exact proportion to the fewness of hands and the length of terms. It is often in danger from the multitude of hands and shortness of periods.

B.: Public liberty cannot be so easily attacked, and may be more easily defended, in a perfect democracy or in a mixed republic than in a limited monarchy . . .

A.: He knew not what a perfect democracy is. There is no possibility of defending liberty in it. The majority is a despotism in the hands of its principal leaders.

B.: No laws, no orders of government can effectually secure liberty any longer than the spirit of liberty prevails and gives them vigor . . .

A.: True. But is there no danger that the spirit of faction will take advantage of the spirit of liberty? The latter must be as jealous of the former as of any other dangers to liberty.

B.: Those who murdered Caesar . . . renewed the civil war in order to restore liberty to a people who had lost the spirit of liberty. Even in the Senate, Octavius had a party, Antony had a party, but the Commonwealth had none.

A.: In 1799 Jefferson had a party, Hamilton had a party, but the Commonwealth had none but Paine and Lawrence.[27]

B.: The spirit of faction may take possession of numbers who meant to entertain no other spirit than that of liberty; for numbers have not the discernment of spirits.

A.: Aye! here is the rub.

B.: Corruption [is] the last deadly symptom of agonizing liberty.

A.: An awful truth!

2

The purpose of the *Dissertation upon Parties*, as the "Dedication" to Walpole states, was to voice the true ideas of the constitution, vindicate the honor of the Revolution of 1688, and unite all parties in support of its principles. Adams made his first comment in the eighth letter, which condemns the "slavish principles of passive obedience" during the reign of James I and his three successors.

B.: They maintained . . . that if the throne was vacant of the father, it must be reputed instantaneously full of the son, upon the foundation of the silly axiom that the king never dies.[28]

A.: Which is the silliest? That the King never dies or that the King can do no wrong? Rather too debonair, my lord. Understood as intended they are both sound maxims of English law. They are misconstrued, perverted, and abused by knaves and fools. So is another more moral, more sacred and eternal maxim that all men are born free and equal . . .

With his thirteenth letter, however, Bolingbroke expiated many of his sins. For such a paper Adams could forgive much! First of all, Bolingbroke asserts that the British Constitution "is in the strictest sense a bargain, a conditional contract between the prince and the people." That is why the supreme power is vested in three estates. "As a bad king," he writes, "must stand in awe of an honest parliament, a corrupt house of commons must stand in awe of an honest people." The peers are properly mediators between the two. Thus, after his flirtation with "perfect democracies" which so irritated Adams in *The Remarks on the History of England*, Bolingbroke declares himself unequivocally for mixed governments in which monarchical, aristocratic, and democratic powers are blended—balanced and checked. He condemns "simple" governments, for they do not only degenerate into tyranny but are tyranny in their very nature. "Absolute monarchy is tyranny," he wrote, "but absolute democracy is tyranny and anarchy both."

Adams, for once, was overflowing with admiration. This is the letter which he called a "Jewel," the finest to be found in any language on the subject of government.

The *Study and Use of History*, Bolingbroke's first work after he settled at Chanteloup, consists of eight letters addressed to Lord Cornbury, the later Baron Hyde, great-grandson of Clarendon. The young lord, then twenty-five and a member of the House of Commons for Oxford, remained all his life a great admirer of Bolingbroke.

Written mainly without recourse to books, the essay contains many inaccuracies; even so, it is one of the author's most brilliant writings. What is the use of history? Bolingbroke asks at the beginning; and he answers with a quotation from Dionysius Halicarnassus: "History is philosophy teaching by examples." This is the theme elaborated in the second letter—the only one on which Adams commented. His notes date from 1811:

B.: When examples are pointed out to us, there is a kind of appeal . . . made to our senses as well as our understandings.[29]

A.: Vanity then is the principle at bottom. This is Tacitus, Rochefoucauld, Swift, Mandeville, but not Butler.[30]

B.: Mitius jubetur exemplo, example teaches more gently, writes Pliny. What pity it is that so few princes have learned this way of commanding . . .

A.: Charles 12th had learned it when he ate the rotten bread and said, it was not good: but it might be eaten.

B.: The citizens of Rome placed the images of their ancestors in the vestibules of their houses; so that . . . these venerable bustoes met their eyes and recalled the glorious actions of the dead . . .

A.: But images of fools and knaves are as easily made as those of patriots and heroes. The images of the Gracchi were made as well as those of Scipio, and the images of Caesar, Antony, and Augustus as well as those of Cicero, Pompey, Brutus, and Cassius. Statues, paintings, panegyrics, in short all the fine arts, even music and dancing, promote virtue while virtue is in fashion. After that they promote luxury, effeminacy, corruption, prostitution, and every species of abandoned depravity.

B.: The virtue of one generation was transfused, by the magic of example, into several; and a spirit of heroism was maintained through many ages of that commonwealth.

A.: The vice too of one generation was transfused into several. And a spirit of usury was maintained through many ages, and at last produced the empire of Augustus.

B.: I admit that the study of history, without experience, is insufficient, but assert that experience itself is so without genius. Genius is preferable to the other two.

A.: Genius! His Lordship seems to have adored genius as a divinity, as much as Condorcet did a century after him.

B.: Mere sons of Earth, if they have experience without any knowledge of the history of the world, are but half scholars in the science of mankind.

A.: How his Lordship looked down with scorn and contempt on these sons of Earth!

B.: The man who has all three is an honour to his country, and a public blessing: and such, I trust, your lordship will be in this century, as your great-grandfather was in the last.

A.: Here it all ends in a panegyric on Toryism. Clarendon, it is true, was a better man than Bolingbroke. But a party man and a tool.

Yet Bolingbroke warns against ascribing an exaggerated importance to the study of history, as many have done from Cicero down to modern pedants. He also makes some slighting remarks on Cicero for his pretensions to military glory, although he did no more than surprise and pillage some wild highlanders. Adams could not let it go without protest: "Middleton," he noted, "who understood better gives a very different account of this matter. So do original documents and even the letters of Caesar." [31] Bolingbroke mentions Cicero's letters to Atticus to show how "impudently" he demanded a conqueror's triumphal reception. "He did no more than all imperators had done," Adams answered, adding: "His Lordship's impudence here is greater than Tully's."

B.: The example of the late Duke of Marlborough shows what genius and experience can do without study. But such examples are very rare; and they would have had fewer blemishes if the views of such men had been enlarged . . . by the study of history . . .

A.: His Lordship and Machiavel and Napoleon make this a little doubtful.

B.: To converse with historians is to keep good company: many of them were excellent men, and those who were not, have taken care to appear such in their writings.

A.: Yet Caesar wrote Anti-Catones: and Machiavel wrote panegyrics on Caesar Borgia. Whom shall we believe? Whom shall we trust? The Gracchi resisted the noble usurers. So did Cataline. Caesar conquered them and they assassinated him.

B.: The examples which history presents to us are generally complete. The villain who has imposed on mankind by his power or cunning, and whom experience could not unmask for a time, is unmasked at length . . .

A.: Not always.

B.: . . . and the honest man is justified before his story ends.

A.: Not always.

B.: Or if this does not happen . . . yet we see the name of the villain branded with infamy and that of the honest man celebrated with panegyrics to succeeding ages.

A.: Tradition and history are radically corrupted.

All this was merely an introduction to an attack on Walpole. Few men foresaw after the Revolution, Bolingbroke points out, how the new taxes would increase the power of the Crown and endanger liberty; the opportunity of amassing immense fortunes was the incentive of those who supported this iniquity. Adams was on his guard. "It is very doubtful," he remarked, "whether the policy of his Lordship and Lord Oxford was any better."

3

The Spirit of Patriotism, also addressed to Lord Cornbury, was commented upon by Adams even earlier, in 1808. He read the essay with great attention, and in his usual caustic mood. At the top of the first page he wrote: "An aigreur d'esprit, a disappointed, mortified, chagrined soul appears in this whole volume, as it does in all the other writings of his Lordship: yet his political and historical knowledge is of great value, and his style is original and inimitable . . . "

The author promises to reason on the basis of principles out of fashion among men whose sole purpose is to feed their avarice, vanity, and luxury. "He begins with the satirical spirit of party, a letter on the Spirit of Patriotism," Adams pounced upon him at once.

B.: Men of superior ability cannot pass unperceived through a country. If they retire from the world, their splendor accompanies them, and enlightens even the obscurity of their retreat.[32]

A.: So his Lordship thought of himself. So Lord Orrery thought of him.[33] But it was the light of a will with a whisp.

B.: They either appear like ministers of divine vengeance . . . or they are the guardian angels of the country they inhabit . . .

A.: Transverse the two members. They either appear the guardian angels, etc. or they are the ministers of divine vengeance, etc. The energy and effect would be greater.

B.: From the misapplication of superior parts to the hurt, no argument can be drawn against this position, that they were given for the good of mankind.

A.: There are strong appearances that they are as often given for the punishment of mankind, all for their good no doubt.

B.: Since men are so apt to act without benevolence to mankind or regard to the divine will, it is the more incumbent on those who have this benevolence and this regard at heart . . . to oppose evil and promote good government.

A.: Submission to the divine will is certainly one principle of the spirit of patriotism, and benevolence to mankind is another. Here then are two ingredients in the composition. And these are all that is directly to the point in the whole piece.

B.: That there is no profusion of the ethereal spirit to be observed among us, and that we do not abound with men of superior genius, I am ready to confess . . .

A.: Why this long though beautiful rhapsody upon the ethereal spirits? Is it because the spirit of patriotism is peculiar to them? or that it is their duty any more than of the common people? A laborer may have this spirit as well as a prince or noble, a soldier as well as a general, a sailor as well as an admiral . . .

Bolingbroke wants to apply these principles to conditions in Britain. But Adams objected: "Patriotism is a virtue in all nations. In treating of its spirit, his Lordship had nothing more to do with England than France."

B.: Not the worst minister could do all the mischief he does by the misapplication of his talents alone . . .

A.: Walpole. There is more of the spirit of envy and resentment against Walpole in this, than of the spirit of patriotism.

B.: Men of the ordinary size of understanding . . . cannot do great and long mischief in a country of liberty, unless men of genius . . . misapply their talents and become their leaders.

A.: Burke, Fox, Pitt, and Sheridan are striking exemplifications of this in modern times. All supported, indigent as they were, by men who were lifted into power by birth.

B.: In such exigencies it is not enough that genius be opposed to genius, spirit must be matched by spirit.

A.: Is genius essential to the spirit of patriotism? Is it any part of it? No, a Dutch traveller may have as much of it as his Lordship, or the most ethereal spirit in the reign of Queen Anne.

B.: In our country many, I fear, undertake opposition not as a duty but as an adventure . . .

A.: There was not a man in England who undertook opposition as an adventure more egregiously than his Lordship.

B.: The service of our country is no chimerical, but a real duty.

A.: But, My Lord, you have omitted the most essential foundation of the duty of patriotism, a belief in a future state of rewards and punishments. Without this faith patriotism can never be anything more than hypocrisy, i.e., ambition, avarice, envy, resentment, lust, or at least the love of fame hidden under a masque. Your other works, in which you have endeavored to destroy or to invalidate and render dubious all the arguments of a future life, have destroyed your whole system of patriotism, the whole spirit of patriotism, and the whole idea of a patriot king, and all confidence in the sincerity of your whole public life and all your political writings. So thinks J. Adams. 1808.

B.: Will it be said that it is hard to exact from some men, in favor of others, that they should renounce all the pleasures of life, and drudge all their days in business, that others may indulge themselves in ease?

A.: These arguments and motives in favor of patriotism are very proper in an essay on its spirit, and very much to the purpose.

B.: The execution [of the schemes of a patriot] is often traversed . . . by the perverseness or treachery of friends and by the power or malice of enemies.

A.: As in the four last years of Queen Anne.

B.: All is little, and low, and mean amongst us!

A.: A bitter philippic against his country!

B.: What passes among us for ambition is an odd mixture of avarice and vanity . . .

A.: What envenomed reproach! How could the nation bear it? They too well deserved it however.

B.: The principal actors are divided, not so much as it has seemed . . . about measures, but about their different ends.

A.: The loaves and fishes.

B.: When his [the Minister's] destruction seemed to approach . . . the reformation of the government was no longer their point of view.

A.: Sir Robert I suppose is meant. He was the Polypheme, whose eye Ulysses always aims to put out. He was the monster who had his Lordship in his den.

Bolingbroke entreats Lord Cornbury and his generation not to let the government of England become absolute. It will be difficult to bring back men from corruption and luxury to honor and liberty, but the task is worthy of the greatest talents. The question is, how to achieve it?

B.: Eloquence . . . gives a nobler superiority than power that every dunce may use, or fraud that every knave may employ . . .

A.: A deaf and dumb man may have the spirit of patriotism.

B.: But eloquence must flow like a stream that is fed by an abundant spring, and not spout forth a little frothy water on some gaudy day and remain dry the rest of the year. The famous orators of Greece and Rome were the statesmen of those commonwealths.

A.: Eloquence is a useful talent, a powerful instrument of a patriot. But it is no ingredient in the spirit of patriotism. Why then all this beautiful rant about eloquence and orators?

B.: A party formed for this purpose [opposition] do not act like good citizens, nor honest men, unless they propose true as well as oppose false measures of government.

A.: It is a more common practice to oppose everything and propose nothing; but his Lordship's idea is more generous, honorable, and patriotic.

B.: Cunning men will . . . object that such conduct would support a weak and even a wicked administration . . .

A.: There are Jesuits in all countries besides the disciples of Loyola. Pharisees among Gentiles and Christians as well as Jews. And Machiavellian cunning, in other countries besides Italy.

In defining the role of the opposition, Bolingbroke in fact forecasts the future development of the British parliament. Adams, however, was skeptical about his performance:

"There is a wonderful magnificence of sound and a splendid exhibition of imagery in this Letter, but very little on the general subject. In truth, what is comprehended in the spirit of patriotism? Piety, or the love and fear of God; general benevolence to mankind; a particular attachment to our own country; a zeal to promote its happiness by reforming its morals, increasing its knowledge, promoting its agriculture, commerce and manufactures, improving its constitution, and securing its liberties: and all this without the prejudices of individuals or parties or factions, without fear, favor, or affection. A great and divine spirit indeed! Alass, how rare! These ingredients may perhaps be all found in this piece: but they are if not confusedly expressed, too much obscured and clouded by the effusions of selfish and party feelings."

THE DEISTIC PHILOSOPHER

Bolingbroke's first Essay is entitled "Concerning the Nature, Extent, and Reality of Human Knowledge." It runs to two hundred and seventy-four pages in the original edition. The author starts out with an argument against Dr. Cudworth, one of the Cambridge Platonists, who in his *Intellectual System of the Universe* [34] had attacked Hobbes on the subject of the divine attributes:

Bolingbroke: Hobbes' opinion . . . carries along with it a more becoming reverence than the learned writer shows when he supposes . . . that intelligence and knowledge in God are the same as intelligence and knowledge in man; that the divine differs from the human in degree, not in kind . . . [35]

Adams: Two and two make four, in the knowledge of God and man. What is the difference?

B.: We pronounce our fellow animals to be automates, or we allow them instinct . . . We scorn to admit them into the same class of intelligence with ourselves, though it is obvious that the first elements of their knowledge and of ours are the same.

A.: Perception, memory, reason, and method, the whole system of our logic are in some degree in beasts, birds, fishes, and insects. Does it follow that they are in the same class of intelligence with us?

B.: Since there must have been something from eternity, because there is something now, the eternal Being must be an intelligent Being, because there is intelligence now . . .

A.: Divine intelligence is here argued from human intelligence. Are they of the same kind, or has my Lord made the same blunder with Cudworth? The eternal intelligence is infinitely different, in degree and manner, no doubt from ours. But we can conceive of none but such as ours.

B.: . . . and such a Being must exist *necessarily* . . .

A.: What is meant by necessarily?

B.: But it is presumptuous to say that your ideas and mine are God's ideas . . . The profound meditations of philosophers have as much regard paid to them as they deserve when they are used as exercise to invigorate the mind . . .

A.: This is good sense.

B.: . . . and prepare it for something more conducive to our happiness:

> "The good, the just, the meet, the wholesome rules
> Of temperance, and aught that may improve
> The moral life."

A.: So far, so good, but Philips' verses are worth more than all his Lordship has yet written.[36]

B.: Have the authors of such systems, from Plato down to that fine writer Malebranche or to that sublime genius and good man, the Bishop of Cloyne, contributed to make us better acquainted with ourselves? I think not.

A.: Why this politeness to Malebranche and Berkeley after so much harsh rudeness to Cudworth?

B.: The nature of [the human mind] is as much unknown as ever.

A.: The nature of matter is equally unknown.

B.: The mind of man is an object of physics as much as the body of man . . . and the distinction that is made between physics and metaphysics is quite arbitrary.

A.: This is as dogmatical as anything in Cudworth and as unfounded.

B.: Let us content ourselves therefore to trace his mind, to observe its growth and the progress it makes from infancy to maturity.

A.: This is sound advice.

Leaving apart the general nature of the mind, Bolingbroke declares himself content to observe some of its phenomena. And he lays down his first rule:

B.: Our ideas are the foundations or the materials of all our knowledge . . .

A.: Ideas, the timber with which knowledge is built. The marble, lime, and clay. The hay, wood, and stubble.

B.: We know that the first ideas are received from without, and are caused by such sensations as the presence of external objects excites in us, according to laws of passion and action which the Creator has established.

A.: The laws of passion and action will not be known till the essences of mind and body are known. Neither our senses or instruments penetrate so far. Incision, knives, and microscopes make no discoveries in this region. Analysis and induction are as useless here as the chemistry of steam, vapor or aether, electricity, magnetism, mesmerism, or galvanism.

B.: What these laws are we know as little . . . as those philosophers who, denying that any such power can belong to body . . . confine all activity to spirit alone.

A.: We must know what spirit is, and matter is, before we can affirm or deny.

B.: Appearances . . . denote plainly one single system, all the parts of which are so intimately connected that the whole begins, proceeds, and ends together . . .

A.: Ends in sleep eternal, does he mean?

B.: This union of a body and soul must be magical indeed, as Doctor Cudworth calls it: so magical that the hypothesis serves to no purpose in philosophy . . .

A.: The hypothesis favors a future state, he means.

B.: . . . and is still less comprehensible than the hypothesis which assumes that . . . the faculty of thinking may have been superadded by omnipotence to certain systems of matter.

A.: This is a dispute about words. Define the terms matter and spirit, and you settle the controversy. But this cannot be done till you know the essence of body and spirit. If you say, one is an active substance and the other an inactive substance, it is a contradiction in terms to say that one can be added to the other, because both will loose their characteristics.

Our second faculty for acquiring knowledge, Bolingbroke goes on, is memory; for as we should have no ideas without perception, we should lose them without the power of retention:

B.: When it was objected to Descartes, that, if thought was the essence of the soul, the soul of the child must think in the mother's womb . . .

A.: Thought an essence!

B.: Descartes maintained that memory consists in certain traces made on the brain by the thoughts that pass through it and that as long as they last we remember . . .

A.: Traces on the brain! Traces on the brain are not souls. They cannot perceive themselves. There must be then some percipient being to read them.

B.: . . . but that the brain of the child in the womb being too moist and too soft to preserve these traces, it is impossible he should remember out of the womb what he thought in it.

A.: The sensorium, the pineal gland, is the palace of the soul, where she resides in great state and gives out her orders like an empress. This is pretty poetry or romance or chivalry or what you will. But alass, we know not whether the soul lodges in the head, the heart, or the heels.

B.: By this faculty, then, whatever it be, our simple ideas are preserved with greater, and our complex ideas with less facility.

A.: What is it, to preserve ideas? Is it as we preserve cucumbers and peppers in vinegar, limes and oranges in sugar, or snakes in spirits? Or grapes in bottles exhausted of air?

B.: Both one and the other require to be frequently raised in the mind, and frequently recalled to it.

A.: The words raised, recalled, revived, preserved signify nothing in this case that can be defined.

B.: The images that are lodged in memory present themselves often to the mind without any fresh sensation . . .

A.: Images again, pictures, emblems. What do these words signify?

B.: We are able . . . to put a sort of force upon memory, to seize as it were the end of some particular line, and to draw back into existence a whole set of ideas . . .

A.: His Lordship's metaphors and figures are happy but give us no information or consolation.

B.: . . . by an act, of which . . . we know nothing more than that the mind performs it.

A.: We know that memory decays by fevers and comes again by age and returns no more. But even these words, decays and returns, are but metaphors; and signify nothing that we can explain.

Bolingbroke disclaims any understanding of substances, modes, and essences, all those things "distinguished by philosophers under a metaphysical mask and called a hard name, ontology or ontosophy." Adams reminded him: "You admit matter, body, my Lord, you cannot deny the existence of substance."

This note occurs in the first section; the next is in the last. Descartes thought that a sensitive soul must be capable of thinking by its nature; however, the perpetual creation and annihilation of so many souls was contrary to the notion of a sensitive soul. "The perpetual creation and annihilation, whether or souls or bodies," Adams remarked, "is very mysterious. As we know nothing about it, but the fact, we had better let it alone." Descartes further affirmed the heterogeneity between the soul and the body, God being the "sole efficient cause" of our sensations.[37]

B.: Shall I believe that it is God who moves the arms of a parricide when he plunges a dagger into his father's heart, or that of some rogue when he picks a pocket?

A.: Some of our divines make no scruple to assert that God is the author of sin, i.e., all moral evil!

B.: According to Leibnitz, every soul has a certain series of perceptions, desires, volitions, etc. . . . we [are] determined by the mechanical dispositions of the machine . . .

A.: Preëstablished harmony of the universe.

B.: This hypothesis gives me no horror; every time it comes into my thoughts, I laugh as if I was at a puppet show.

A.: Laugh on my Lord: but this philosophy is as good as yours, which is absolutely nothing at all.

God shows manifestly, Bolingbroke argues, how repugnant it is to His providence that we should attempt to acquire knowledge about the soul. Reversing his attitude, Adams suddenly became an advocate of experimental psychology: "Why not make experiments and observations on spirit as well as matter? on ideas, and thoughts as well as extension, solidity, colors, or odors?" he asked. Without presuming to penetrate further into the machinery of the universe, Bolingbroke acknowledges that there is a Supreme Being who created, preserves, and governs it. "A theist, and so was Robespierre," Adams, unimpressed, remarked.

2

The second Essay, nearly as long as the first, deals with the "folly and presumption" of the philosophers; who build intellectual and material worlds on "the hypothetical suggestions of imagination"; with the propagation of "error and superstition"; and finally with the discovery of the right use of reason by Bacon. The third Essay, which is comparatively brief, rejects the assumption that the Jews alone knew the one true God and that all other nations were polytheists and idolaters. Monotheism is the fundamental principle of "natural theology or the first philosophy," and its origin goes back to the beginning of the world.

Adams read both pieces carefully, as his copying out of innumerable names proves. However, he made only a few comments. Bolingbroke, to show the perpetual flux of Christianity, points to Arianism, which had nearly prevailed in the Church and which could be extirpated only through wars and persecutions in which millions perished.[38] Adams, not quite relevantly, replied: "Not so many millions as it cost in the last ten years of the 18th century to extirpate sansculottism."

The fourth Essay, "Concerning Authority in Matters of Religion," is the most extensive of all, occupying over five hundred pages in the first edition. Most of Adams's notes occur in the sixteenth, seventeenth, and eighteenth sections:

B.: If we inquire after the *causes* of that strange multiplication of sects which have grown up from the apostolical ages to this, among Christians . . .[39]

A.: What were the causes of that strange multiplication of gods among gentiles? 30,000 at least, some say 300,000? What were the causes of that infinite variety of languages that have grown up in the world? of that infinite variety in the animal, vegetable, and mineral kingdoms? in the sands on the sea shore, and in the stars of heaven? and in the figure, color, intelligence, and animation of the human face?

B.: . . . it seems to me that they are to be found in the metaphysical *madness of philosophers* mixing with the enthusiasm of the first Christians, in the cabalistical practice of giving different senses to the same passages of holy writ, in the uncertainty of tradition . . .

A.: Every tyro knows that heathen philosophy and Jewish ceremonies have been intermixed with Christianity: but what then? . . . If Christianity has been corrupted? What then? What has not?

B.: . . . and in the use that a *distinct order* of men has made, in every Christian state, of these and other circumstances to acquire dominion over private consciences.

A.: Gentiles had a distinct order as well as Christians, Egyptians, Chaldeans, Chinese, Celts, Teutons, even North American Indians. If any "order of men" should ever appear in the world who should not avail themselves of every advantage to increase or preserve dominion, it will be a new phenomenon. Heathen priests of every denomination have been as astute at least as Christian theologians. Increase of power, influence, importance is the constant object of the human mind, discontented with the present and grasping at more.

B.: Though I ascribe so much to the mere influence of philosophy, and believe it to have been the frantic mother of a frantic offspring, I do not mean to exclude absolutely that of *grace* . . .

A.: This is all irony and burlesque.

It was irony indeed. After quoting a passage from Saint Augustine, in which the Saint thanks God for having found the divinity of the Word established in one of Plato's books, Bolingbroke blandly comments: "Thus you see how Plato, in the wanderings of a wild imagination, had discovered one of the greatest mysteries of Christianity . . ."

B.: The sense of no writings, neither sacred nor profane, can be ever fixed if they remain subject to such licentious interpretations.

A.: These, very often, were only figures of rhetoric.

B.: These interpretations have served . . . no other purpose than, that of furnishing the rabbis of both Jews and Christianity with means of giving a color of divine authority to all their own inventions.

A.: Are there not disputes among lawyers and physicians as well as divines? in their interpretations of Hippocrates and Justinian?

B.: They [the Christian Fathers] should have adhered to the word of God: they should have paid no regard to heathen philosophy, Jewish cabala, the sallies of enthusiasm, or the refinements of human ingenuity . . .

A.: Very true! and it is equally true that his Lordship ought to have been a good man, and consistent in his principles and conduct.

B.: If the Council should decree that the system of Christianity would have been incomplete without these adventitious helps, let us make no scruple of saying that the Council would decree blasphemously . . .

A.: Why all this pompous clamor about nothing? His Lordship has been concerned in disputing with as many sectaries about as many absurdities in the construction of the English form of government.

3

The Fragments or Minutes of Essays fill nearly two and a half volumes. Consisting of no less than eighty-one sections, they cover an enormous field. Pope had already published, in 1733–34, his *Essay on Man* when Bolingbroke began to polish up his own four Essays. It was as far as he had progressed at the time of the poet's death; as for the rest of the material, he contented himself "to correct and extend them a little." [40]

Bolingbroke considers Hobbes's doctrine that moral obligations were derived from the laws of society, not from the law of nature, and maintains that the truth lay between the two extremes—that self-love led to sociability. There was such a thing as natural reason; even animals had it:

B.: The difference in reason . . . between some men and some other animals is less than . . . between man and man. [41]

A.: Whether true or not, I neither know nor care. We have not yet discovered a mode of conversing with animals on divine and philosophical subjects. Nor have they yet conveyed to us their ideas and speculations.

B.: Instinct precedes reason in man.

A.: The babe sucks before it understands pneumatics, to be sure. But what is instinct?

B.: That the animals compare ideas, in some degree, is certain. But it seems to be out of doubt that they want totally the great instrument of human knowledge, that is, the wide extended power of generalizing.

A.: If they compare and remember the similitude or dissimilitude, this memory is generalization.

B.: As divines have impudently, and wickedly, assumed . . . that there is a law of right reason common to God and man . . .

A.: This is dogmatically, presumptuously, and arrogantly said! If there is not such a law there is an end of all human reasoning on the moral government of the universe! An end of all arguments from final causes! An end of all proofs of the being of a God.

B.: . . . so lawyers have advanced, most absurdly, that the law of nature is common to man and beast. Is it not plain . . . that the Jews held that beasts are accountable for crimes?

A.: No. No.

B.: The weapons by which a murther had been committed were brought into court, as if they too were liable to punishment.

A.: This was good policy.

B.: There is a sort of genealogy of law, in which nature begets natural law, natural law sociability, sociabiltity union of societies by consent, and this union by consent the obligation of civil laws.

A.: This is not well explained. Butler! Hutchinson! I understand you better and feel you more sensibly upon these subjects. Oratory and logic can never be friends with unlimited confidence. There will and there ought to be a perpetual jealousy between. Bolingbroke was by nature and by study a greater orator than Chatham or Junius. But neither Bolingbroke, Chatham or Junius shall be logicians or philosophers, moralists or divines for me.

B.: Animals all herd with those of their own species, with whom they sympathize more; whose language, perhaps, whether it consists in signs or sounds, they understand better . . .

A.: Benevolence, the sense of beauty, of grace in motion, of elegance, of figure, the wonderful effects of the face, attractions, sympathies of various kinds even before language or love would draw individuals together.

According to Bolingbroke, self-love operates in all stages of sociability: "Like so many different vortices, the center of them all is self-love, and that which is the most distant from it is the weakest." Adams—literary detective—recognized in this the source of a passage in the fourth epistle of *The Essay on Man*, and he neatly jotted down:

> "Self-love but serves the virtuous mind to wake,
> As the small pebble stirs the peaceful lake;
> The center mov'd, a circle strait succeeds,
> Another still, and still another spreads . . ."

Then he added: "But this is not correct in the verse or prose. Self-love is not the mover."

B.: Since the author of our nature . . . has constituted us so that private good depends on the public, and the happiness of every individual on the happiness of society, the practice of all the social virtues is the law of our nature . . .

A: He has not constituted us so. Private good does not always depend on the public. The happiness of every individual does not always depend on the happiness of society.

B.: We say that the law of nature is the law of reason . . .

A.: True, my Lord.

B.: Surely no disquisition can be more vain and needless than that which examines whether actions are lawful or unlawful . . . because they are demanded or forbid by God; or because they are such "per se," and therefore necessarily, "necessario," commanded or forbidden by him.

A.: Search forever and you will not find the meaning of the word "necessario."

B.: Grotius adopts the last of these notions . . . [which] assumes in man a community of reason with God.

A.: If there is any difference between truth and falsehood, it must be in some cases common to all intelligent beings, to God and man.

B.: In creating man, God designed to create not only a rational but a social creature and a moral agent; and he has framed his nature accordingly.

A.: Rational, social, and moral! But the rational part leads us to all the difficulties he had before mentioned.

B.: Therefore, let us be content to know things as God has been pleased to show them to us, and to look no further than our nature for the law of it. In fact, we shall find this law co-eval with our system . . . and as immutable as the system . . .

A.: Sound philosophy.

Pyrrhonians, skeptics, and academicians as well as atheists maintained that there was no immutable law of nature, for "they who doubted God's existence, or who denied it, could not fail to doubt of or to deny the existence of His law." Adams pointed out that "Volney has written a system of the law of nature without any consideration of a God." [42] In speculating about the origin of society, Bolingbroke suggests that "the inhabitants of some other planet may have been from their creation united in one great society, speaking the same language, and living under the same great government." Adams did not like the idea: "This is random supposition. We know nothing about it. We have nothing to do with it; nor is it at all probable, or I believe possible."

4

Through the next three hundred pages, Adams repeated on the margins more than a thousand words, mainly names, covering an enormous range of history, law, and religion, but he made only a few comments. He joined the discussion again in the fiftieth section, where Bolingbroke disputes Wollaston's postulate of rewards and punishments in a future state because many people are "unavoidably both good and evil, and that misfortunes are not so great as they appear at first." Adams this time—a rare occasion—fully agreed with him:

B.: A dancing, drunken, smoking revel makes ample amends to the savage for all the wants he has suffered, and for all the pains and perils to which he had been exposed. Thus the galley slave sings whilst he is chained to an oar . . .[43]

A.: Well done, my Lord! I thank you for putting mankind in good humor with themselves. The real evils of life are more in imagination than reality.

B.: Thus men frequently embrace, by choice, the very evils they complain of . . . sometimes even death itself.

A.: The greatest real misery of life is fear. Reason should conquer this fear.

B.: Let us be convinced, in opposition to atheists and divines, that the general state of mankind . . . is not only tolerable but happy.

A.: My Lord! You need not introduce atheists or divines. Your position is divine, because it is true. I go farther and affirm as my belief that no human being ever suffered more than he enjoyed.

B.: Neither will it avail to say that the desire of life and the fear of death are, one the greatest imperfection and the other the greatest evil of our human state . . .

A.: I agree with his Lordship in all this. In all the gloom of his lingering cancer, I believe he enjoyed more than he suffered. Let his disciples Voltaire and Raynal and his enemy Johnson say what they will. The most detestable of all philosophers are those who represent human terrestrial existence as miserable on the whole.

B.: What hardship is done us [by returning to the earth]? None, unless it be a hardship that we are not immortal, because we wish to be so and flatter ourselves with that expectation.

A.: He allows that we wish and hope.

B.: I should have no reason to complain, though, having tasted existence, I might abhor non-entity.

A.: If you abhor non-entity, how can you be resigned to it?

B.: Let the tranquillity of my mind rest on this immovable rock, that my future as well as my present state are ordered by an almighty and all-wise Creator . . .

A.: It is said that this rock failed him in his last hours. He confessed that his philosophy was not sufficient to support him.

Where Adams got the information, he did not state. Dr. Warburton had spread the rumor that during his last illness Bolingbroke was overheard complaining to himself, "What will my poor soul undergo for all these things?" However, in view of the deadly hatred that existed between Bolingbroke and the future Bishop of Gloucester, the story may be regarded as apocryphal. It is certain, on the other hand, that the dying man refused the ministrations of the clergyman of the parish.[44]

B.: God is the creator and governor of the universe, so that, if there was really *more evil than good* in this part, it would conclude nothing against the whole, wherein there might be still *much more good than evil* . . .

A.: This is Hopkinsian, but irreconcilable to justice or to goodness.[45]

B.: There is even in this world so *much more good than evil* . . .

A.: In this I cordially agree with his Lordship.

The existence of evil, Bolingbroke writes, was used by atheists to show that there was no God and by the divines that there was a future state. He regards this as a proof of their "confederacy":

B.: Having done their best, *in concert with their allies,* to destroy the belief of the goodness of God . . .

A.: Very silly!

B.: . . . they [the professors of theism] endeavour to destroy that of his justice, which is a further article of *their alliance.*

A.: Very silly!

B.: Lest the bare existence of physical and moral evil should not afford . . . the divines a sufficient foundation to erect a heaven and a hell, they pronounce the distribution of evils unjust.

A.: His Lordship appears to have had a terrible apprehension of hell. And well he might.

B.: "Rewards and punishments are necessary to support the honor of God," Clarke claims.[46] Audacious and vain sophist! His whole chain of reasoning . . . is nothing more than one continued application of human ideas to the designs and conduct of God.

A.: Proud and arrogant philosophist! You were but a babe to Clarke, notwithstanding your sounding brass.

Bolingbroke now considers the terms good and bad, happy and unhappy, an analysis which Adams "could not but respect." Tranquillity of mind, Bolingbroke writes in the spirit of the Stoics, is the inseparable companion of virtue; it adds relish to all the comforts and takes off the bitter taste from all the misfortunes of life:

B.: True moral virtue is something very real. It is the cause of our happiness . . .

A.: This is divine and eternal truth. But alass! how shall we define true moral virtue? And where shall we find it? Caesar, Brutus, Cromwell, Pompey, Sulla, Marius, and even Cataline had virtue: but had any of these true moral virtue?

B.: Seneca says . . . that he placed the good things he enjoyed within his reach and yet at such a distance that fortune might take but could not tear them from him.

A.: His Lordship applies this to himself in his Reflections on Exile.[47]

B.: There is a fragment among Plutarch's Miscellanies, where Fortune and Vice are introduced like the contractors who make their offers when any public work is to let out . . .

A.: A beautiful and noble fable.

B.: Men have imagined the Supreme Being best pleased when his temples have glittered with gold and silver . . .

A.: Temples glitter with gold, not for God but the people.

B.: Surely Cotta, when he accused the justice of God for giving prosperity to wicked men, could not have produced a more glaring proof of the contrary.[48]

A.: Who can dispute any part of this with his Lordship? Can we pronounce Napoleon happier than the Emperors and Kings he has beaten? Was Oliver happier than Charles?

5

By insisting on the existence of a general providence, Bolingbroke challenges the belief in "particular providences"—that is, in miracles. "Divines assert the justice of Providence, as clearly as his Lordship," Adams retorted. "If they cannot prove the injustice in this world, he cannot prove the justice of it, without the hypothesis of a future state."

B.: It is impossible to conceive that the course of the sun or the double revolution of the earth should be suspended or altered by a momentary interposition of some particular providence . . . *without violating the mechanical constitution of the material world* and the natural order of causes and effects in it.[49]

A.: Any interposition of providence, general or particular, supposes an interruption of the natural order of causes and effects. He who created the machine can stop it, or annihilate it. So say the theists, Christian as well as infidel.

B.: The world is governed by laws which the Creator imposed on the physical and moral systems. These laws are invariable, but they are general; and from this generality what we call *contingency* arises. The laws of matter and motion *are fixed, no doubt.*

A.: What is contingency? Is it chance? Is it accident? What is the meaning of these words? How do you know that the laws of matter and motion are fixed? How do you know that they are not suspended, altered, and modified as occasion may require? Some rules appear steady, others variable.

B.: All material things, as they partake of the good, partake of the evil which matter and motion cause . . .

A.: Matter can produce neither good nor evil without a power to direct it. Motion cannot exist without a power to excite it. Matter and motion are •esponsible for nothing. The agent that governs them is the author of the good or the evil.

Bolingbroke returns to his favorite pastime of coupling the atheists and divines together: "As little as they approve the natural and moral constitution of the world . . ." Adams interjected: "This is sheer calumny against divines. They approve both the natural and moral constitutions of the world."

B.: Commonsense should have hindered them from assuming that God made the world for the use of man . . .

A.: Atheists do not surely assume that *God* made the world for the sake of man. Nor divines neither.

B.: Without [metaphysics] they would have no pretence to criticize the works of God . . .

A.: Atheists do not criticize the works of God, but the works of chance. The self-existent matter and motion of which they make the universe eternally to exist and consist with all its evils, nonsense, and disorders, as well as its good.

B.: General laws, under the general providence, do not provide sufficiently for human happiness, according to them . . .

A.: This is all a miserable delirious rant. Mortified, disappointed, disgraced, he was dissatisfied with himself and the world and vents his spleen upon imaginary beings, for no such atheists or divines exist.

B.: To keep up a belief of particular providences serves to keep up a belief not only of the efficacy of prayer but of the several rites of external devotion.

A.: His Lordship hates prayer as much as his disciple Tom Paine.

B.: The ministry of a clergy is thought necessary on both these accounts by all.

A.: This hatred of priests is like the hatred of pen and ink men in our American frantics. Voltaire, Frederick, d'Alembert, Diderot, and Tom Paine have been humble followers of his Lordship. Blount, Morgan, etc. were his predecessors.[50]

B.: Though there is little credit to be given to all that lying legends have reported concerning particular acts of providence . . . *yet I will not presume to deny that there have been any such.*

A.: Oh! Strange!

B.: I will say only that they could not be such as must have violated the laws of nature in their production.

A.: This is frivolous nonsense. The Supreme Being may be all perfect in one hypothesis, as in the other.

B.: They become particular by nothing more than the application which *vain superstition* or *pious fraud* makes of them.

.A.: Malice versus religion and the clergy!

B.: I shall suppose them not to have been, and shall rest the cause of God . . . on the unquestionable facts of general providence.

A.: A very ridiculous advocate for the cause of God you are.

B.: "My book," Socrates said, "is the nature of things which is always at hand when I am desirous to read the words of God." What we read in that book is undoubtedly *the word of God* . . .

A.: Had Tom Paine read this? It would mortify his Lordship's vanity to be informed that Tom's eloquence has been more read and been more admired than his in propagating the same sentiments.

Skipping a number of pages, Adams's eyes lighted on the sentence: "However mixed and however moderate the general happiness of mankind may be, it is real, animal happiness; and he who affirms absolute non-existence preferable to existence in such a state as ours . . . scarcely deserves an answer." This again mollified him, and he recollected:

"Will Vassal said to me that a hundred years of pleasure would not compensate for a fit of the gout, stone, gravel, or cholic. One of his neighbors said that if he could be sure of eternal existence he would consent to be pitched about in flames of brimstone by devils upon forks to all eternity.[51] Here are two opinions as opposite as possible. Shakespeare is more philosophical than either. Who would bear the stings, when he could make his quietus with a bodkin? After all, perhaps reason would dictate the preservation of life to the last, even with a certainty of annihilation, though passion, disappointment, diseases, foul weather, etc. would often throw it away. Life on the whole seems to be a blessing."

[V]

Rousseau and the Man of Nature

Adams first read Rousseau in February 1765, in connection with the discussions of the law club—"sodality," as he preferred to call it—which he and his friends had formed. They were reading the Feudal law, marking passages which were taken over by the English law. Adams quoted Rousseau who, in the fifteenth chapter of the *Contrat social*, described the feudal system as "the most iniquitous and absurd form of government." He himself thought that the iniquity and absurdity lay in the fact that nations who lived by commerce and industry had adopted such a system. Gridley, the leader of the club, agreed with Adams, sententiously adding that Rousseau's observation proved his shallowness.[1]

Profiting from his recent studies, Adams couched his protest against the Stamp Act in a criticism of the feudal system in his "Dissertation on the Canon and Feudal Law." One of his authorities was Rousseau, again quoting the opinion which he had submitted to the law club.[2] Thereafter he seems to have forgotten the French writer for at least fifteen years.

He mentioned him again after the framing of the Constitution of Massachusetts, the draft of which he himself had prepared. He was extremely proud of the work. "There never was," he wrote to a friend soon after the ratification, "an example of such precautions as are taken by this wise and jealous people in the formation of their government. None was ever made so perfectly upon the principle of the people's rights and equality. It is Locke, Sidney, and Rousseau and De Mably reduced to practice, in the first instance." [3] In his joy he forgot to mention that the principle of equality had been rather forced upon him.

His draft of the Declaration of Rights began, like the first article of the Virginia Bill of Rights, with "All men are born equally free and independent . . ."—a far more cautious statement than that of the Declaration of Independence. No one knows how the revision was worked out; what, for instance, Samuel Adams had to do with it. At any rate, the Cambridge Convention changed the phrase to "All men are born free and equal." [4]

There was indeed little in John Adams, even in that early period, to dispose him toward Rousseau. To be sure, Rousseau has often been called the Puritan of Geneva; and in a fundamental sense the epithet is deserved. Unfortunately, as readers of his autobiography will remember, grace did not come to him as early as to his fellow Calvinist in Boston: two books more dissimilar than Adams's *Diary* and Rousseau's *Confessions* would be difficult to imagine. It was with the French Revolution that Adams's instinctive aversion turned into positive dislike—Rousseau became for him the symbol of everything that was destructive and dangerous. "The Revolution in France," he wrote to Dr. Price in April 1790, "could not be indifferent to me; but I have learned by awful experience, to rejoice with trembling. I know that encyclopedists and economists, Diderot and d'Alembert, Voltaire and Rousseau, have contributed to this great event more than Sidney, Locke, or Hoadly, perhaps more than the American Revolution; and I own to you, I know not what to make of a republic of thirty million atheists." [5] Twenty-five years later he reflected to Jefferson: "I have never read reasoning more absurd, sophistry more gross, in proof of the Athanasian creed or transubstantiation than the subtle labors of Helvétius and Rousseau to demonstrate the natural equality of mankind." [6]

These, however, were only passing references. It is his marginal notes, totaling nearly twenty-five hundred words, that reveal Adams's complicated reactions to the philosopher. The larger number of his comments he made on the *Discours sur l'inégalité*, which he read in the first English translation. Much of Adams's vexation may be explained by the fact that he went through the book in 1794, during the worst period of the Terror. It would be an exaggeration, however, to say that his later notes, written in 1800, were much milder. [7]

The *Discours sur l'inégalité*, as may be recalled, was composed for a prize offered by the Academy of Dijon in 1753 for an essay on the question, "What is the origin of inequality among mankind, and is such inequality warranted by the law of nature?" Four years earlier, it was for a similar competition arranged by the same Academy that Rousseau had written his *Discours sur les sciences et les arts*, with which he won the contest, and which made him, an altogether obscure person, famous overnight. The new prize was given to someone else; yet the *Discours sur l'inégalité* remains one of Rousseau's masterpieces. With lucidity and eloquence he records in it his ideas about the effects of civilization upon mankind. In the first part he describes man in the state of nature, and in the second, in the state of society. He does not claim that primitive man was happy or virtuous, but merely that he was "not unhappy" and "not vicious." Between the conception of Hobbes and Locke—the one regarding primitive man as *homo homini lupus* and the other as an almost perfect Christian—Rousseau looks upon him as an unthinking animal, weaker than beasts of prey and yet capable of defending himself.[8] It was owing to various accidents that the family, the tribe, and finally society developed. Rousseau's evolutionary view of society, with all its false science, was remarkable for his time; and it is noteworthy that he himself emphasized the hypothetical character of his interpretations. No doubt, a good deal of poetry was mingled with his anthropology, especially in his vision of the Golden Age, that happy period holding a just mean between "the indolence of primitive life and the feverish activity of civilization." However, it was precisely this mysticism which captured the imagination of his contemporaries and, still more, of succeeding generations. The revolt against society and convention, to which the book gave such moving expression, was, as Adams well recognized, one of the prime forces of the Revolution.[9]

It is seldom remembered to what an extent Rousseau's two *Discours* were a protest against the prevailing philosophy of worldliness, propagated by Bayle, Saint-Évremond, Mandeville, Montesquieu, and others. Voltaire especially, in his *Mondain* of 1736, had extolled the pleasures of civilization, drawing at the same time a merciless caricature of the man of nature.[10] Rousseau, in answering the apologists of luxury ("demolishing their pitiful lies"), was leading a new crusade for simplicity and frugality. If his first essay alarmed the encyclopedists, the second revealed him as a dangerous "reactionary." From then on Rousseau, hated by his former friends, has his separate road among the *philosophes*.

The *Discours sur l'inégalité* is preceded by a long dedication to "the magnificent, most honored, and sovereign lords" of the Republic of Geneva. Rousseau wrote the outline in Paris, before he set out to visit his native city in June 1754; and he finished it at Chambéry, near the Swiss border. Unfortunately, his tribute was coldly received. The members of the executive body, the *Petit Conseil*, seem to have resented the fact that it was addressed to the whole body of citizens, the *Conseil Général*. "Since the dedication is already in print," the chief syndic politely replied, "it would be futile to discuss its contents; however, the Council is always gratified when one of its fellow citizens has distinguished himself by works of rare merit and outstanding talent." [11]

Adams thought that the dedication, which represents the government of Geneva as almost perfect, was "extravagant flattery." He challenged most of its statements. "I should have desired to be born in a country," Rousseau wrote, "where the sovereign and the subjects could have but one and the same interests." "Have the majority and the minority in a democracy the same interest?" Adams asked. "I should therefore have desired," Rousseau continued, "that no member of the State be able to boast of being superior to its laws." "In a democracy the majority are always superior to the laws, and that majority is often governed by one man, always by five or six," Adams replied. "Where there are two heads, one national and the other foreign," Rousseau warned, "it is impossible that both should be well obeyed and the State well governed." This made Adams pause. "The American national and state governments should meditate on this," he wrote. Rousseau would have chosen a country where the legislative power was shared by all the citizens; but Adams remarked that "This can only be in a single town." [12]

2

The preliminaries of the *Discours* are long, but the essay itself starts out like a manifesto. "I conceive two kinds of inequality among men," Rousseau announces, "one which I call natural or physical inequality . . . and the other, which may be termed moral or political inequality." It would be absurd, unworthy of free men, to inquire whether there might not be some connection between the two. "This question instead of being absurd is very natural, reasonable, and important. The answer is indeed so obvious and certain that it cannot long be doubted," was Adams's opinion.

How was primitive man to preserve himself and his offspring against the attacks of other animals? Nature intended that we should always enjoy good health; man did not even need to think. "I almost dare to affirm," Rousseau makes his famous dictum, "that a state of reflection is a state against nature, and that the man who meditates is a depraved animal . . ."

Rousseau: There is a very specific quality that distinguishes men from beasts . . . namely *the faculty of self-improvement.*[13]

Adams: The question is concerning the difference between man and man; not man and beast.

R.: Whereas *a beast is at the end of a few months all that it ever will be during the rest of its life* . . .

A.: Dancing dogs, learned pigs, scientific birds had not been educated when this was written. Experiments have not yet been made on the capacity of beasts, birds or fishes, enough to determine the extent of it.

R.: It would be horrible to have to praise for his beneficence the man, whoever he was, who first suggested to the Orinoco Indians the use of those boards which they bind on the temples of their children, and which secure to them at least a part of their natural imbecility and happiness.[14]

A.: Savages are happier than citizens, and brutes are happier than savages! Voilà the sum of J. J. Rousseau's philosophy! A poor atonement for such poisonous stuff is made by all the divinity of his eloquence. His panegyrics on nature, on savages and beasts: his philippics against arts, sciences, society and civilization contributed, however, to make Europe uneasy under their religion and government and promoted the revolution that it begun.

R.: It is through our passions that our reason improves; the passions, in turn, owe their origin to our wants . . . *But savage man knows no goods but food, a female, and rest;* he fears no evils but pain and hunger; I say pain, and not death; for no animal will ever know what it is to die . . .

A.: Death is certainly terrible to all animals. It may be more so to man than to others, from his reflections and his education.

R.: The moderate needs of savages are *so easily supplied* . . .

A.: Not so easily. Savages find it difficult to get food, shelter, covering, physic.

R.: His Soul, which nothing disturbs, gives itself up to the mere consciousness of existence, without any thought of even the nearest future . . .

A.: So far from this, his life is so constantly disturbed that he takes pains to annihilate in sleep as much of it as he possibly can.

Next Rousseau probes into the origin of languages. Man's first speech was "the cry of nature"; but when his ideas began to multiply, the inflections of his voice multiplied too. At first every word had the meaning of an entire proposition; it was only later that the difference between nouns and verbs was perceived, and other long ages had to pass before the adjective was invented. The slight care which nature has taken in promoting the use of speech shows how little she has done towards making men social beings. "So then," Adams remarked, "the distinction between a natural and an artificial society is groundless. Nature never intended any society. All society is art. Nothing will do but a paradox." The compassion lavished on primitive man, Rousseau continues, is altogether gratuitous:

R.: Has any one ever heard of a free savage who ever dreamed of complaining of life and committing suicide?

A.: A daughter has drowned herself to revenge a reproof of her mother. You shall no longer have a daughter. Suicide is said to be common among them.

R.: He had in his instinct alone everything he needed to live in a state of nature; his cultivated reason barely provides him with what is necessary to live in society.

A.: Millions in a state of society are supported with less difficulty than dozens in a state of nature.

R.: There was no kind of moral relation between men in this state; they could not be either good or bad, and had neither vices nor virtues. It is proper, therefore, to suspend judgment about their situation . . . until we have examined *whether there are more virtues or vices among civilized men* . . .

A.: Wonders upon wonders. Paradox upon paradox. What astonishing sagacity had Mr. Rousseau! Yet this eloquent coxcomb has with his affectation of singularity made men discontented with superstition and tyranny.

R.: Above all, let us beware concluding with Hobbes that man must be naturally bad; that, *in virtue of that right which he justly claims to everything he wants, he foolishly looks upon himself as the sole owner of the universe.*

A.: If he thinks of right, he must allow that of his neighbor as well as his own. If his Maker gave him a right, his neighbor's Maker gave him one.

R.: Savages are not bad, precisely because they don't know what it is to be good; for it is neither the development of their understanding, nor the curb of the law, but the *calmness of their passions* and their ignorance of vice that prevents them from doing ill.

A.: Calmness of the passions of savages! ha! ha! ha!

R.: The only natural virtue man has is pity. Even beasts sometimes give evidence of it. An animal never passes unmoved by the carcass of one of his species.

A.: How does this agree with [what he said] about the knowledge of death? Quite inconsistent.

R.: It is reason that engenders self-love, and reflection that strengthens it . . .

A.: Reason begets self-love! Another wonder.

R.: It is *philosophy* that isolates a man from other men . . .

A.: Alias atheism.

R.: It is pity which, instead of that sublime maxim of reasoned justice "Do unto others as you would have others do unto you," inspires all men with that other maxim of natural goodness, a great deal less perfect, but perhaps more useful: "Pursue your happiness with as little harm to others as possible."

A.: A maxim of eternal justice to creatures of the same Creator deriving equal right from him. But a maxim of idiocy or lunacy to atheists.

Finally Rousseau discusses love and the problem of "natural" inequality:

R.: Let us begin by distinguishing between what is moral and what is physical in the passion of love.

A.: There are inequalities in this passion of love, which produce other inequalities in society.

R.: A savage listens solely to the inclinations implanted in him by nature, and not to taste, which he could never acquire; and *any woman answers his purpose.*

A.: This is very questionable: tho' he might not refuse any offered him single; yet if several were offered him, of different figures, colors, beauty, would he have no choice?

R.: As to the inferences which one may draw from the example of animals, we must exclude all those species in which the relative powers of the sexes are different from those existing among us. Thus from the battles of cocks we can form no conclusion about the human race.

A.: In a cage of canary birds, if the sexes are together, the cocks will fight eternally. The Hanoverian Minister in Grosvenor Square showed me his cocks in one cage and his hens in another.

R.: We may see from this picture of the state of nature how much even *natural inequality* falls short of that reality and influence which our writers ascribe to it.

A.: To be sure, if there was but one man in the world, there would be no inequality among mankind.

R.: In fact, among the differences which distinguish men several pass for natural which are merely the results of habit and of the various ways of life adopted by men in society.

A.: If inequalities were not natural but only the necessary effect of association, what then?

R.: If we compare the prodigious variety in the education and manner of living of the different classes in a civil state with the simplicity and uniformity of savage life . . . we shall easily understand *how much smaller the differences between man and man must be in the state of nature than in the state of society.*

A.: It is denied that the difference is greater in society than in nature. On the contrary, there is more equality in society than in nature. Age and childhood are more equal to middle age. The sick are more equal to the well.

R.: But even if nature should exercise so much preference in the distribution of her gifts, what advantage could the most favored derive to the detriment of others? Of what service can beauty be, when there is no love?

A.: Petitio principii. Never was savage insensible to beauty.

R.: What shall cunning avail those, who have *no affairs* to transact?

A.: Savages have food to get.

R.: I hear it constantly repeated that the strong would oppress the weak; that some would rule by violence, and others groan under subjection. But this is precisely what I observe *among us* . . .

A.: He would see as much of it among savages.

3

The second part of the essay begins with the declaration: "The first man who, after enclosing a piece of ground, took it into his head to say, *This is mine,* and found people simple enough to believe him, was the true founder of civil society. How many crimes, wars, murders, miseries, and horrors would that person have saved the human race who, pulling up the stakes or filling up the ditches, had cried to his fellows: Be sure not to listen to this imposter . . ." Adams could hardly wait. Opposite the words *This is mine* he wrote "True"; to the question "How many crimes . . ." he answered "Not one, not one"; and at the end he jotted down in his largest letters: "He would have been a greater impostor." [15]

The idea of property, Rousseau believes, took shape during the last phase of the state of nature. He tries to reconstruct the slow evolution which led up to it:

R.: Among the various appetites of man, there was one that urged him to perpetuate his species; and this blind propensity, *quite void of anything like pure love or affection,* produced only an act that was purely animal.[16]

A.: He must have been worse than the birds and than many beasts.

R.: Their needs satisfied, *the sexes took no further notice of each other* . . .

A.: He must have a perverted head or a cursed heart who could say this.

R.: Such was the condition of infant man . . .

A.: Thou beliest thy species, Satyr. Thou makest him worse than Swift's Yahoo.

R.: But difficulties soon arose . . . He had to learn to surmount the obstacles of nature, to fight if necessary with other animals.

A.: No doubt he was superlatively happy all this time.

R.: Bad harvests, long and severe winters, and scorching summers which parched everything demanded fresh exertions.

A.: He possessed the sovereign good all this time.

R.: The new lights resulting from this development increased his superiority to other animals . . . The first look he took at himself produced the first emotion of pride in him . . .

A.: He was proud long before.

R.: . . . and thus, by attributing first rank to his species, he prepared himself from afar *to pretend to it as an individual among those of his own species.*

A.: What a fool! There is not an ox, nor an horse, nor a cow, nor a sheep, there is not a bird, beast or fish but pretends to it.

R.: My pen . . . flies like an arrow over numberless ages . . .

A.: All this time men were very, very happy.

R.: These first advances enabled man to forge ahead with greater speed. The first epoch of revolution saw the establishment of family, the introduction of something like property, and the building of cabins . . . The habit of living together gave birth to the sweetest sentiments known to man, to *conjugal and paternal love.*

Propenſity, quite void of any thing like *He muſt have*
pure Love or Affection, produced no- *been worſe*
thing but an Act that was merely Ani- *from the Birds*
mal. The preſent Heat once allayed, the *He muſt have*
Sexes took no further Notice of each *a perverted*
other, and even the Child ceaſed to have *head or a curſed*
any Tie in his Mother, the Moment he *heart who could*
ceaſed to want her Aſſiſtance. *ſay this.*

Such was the Condition of Infant Man; *Thou belyeſt*
ſuch was the Life of an Animal confined *thy Species*
at firſt to pure Senſations, and ſo far from *Satyr. Thou*
harbouring any Thought of forcing her *makeſt him*
Gifts from Nature, that he ſcarcely availed *worſe than*
himſelf of thoſe which ſhe offered to him *Swift's Yahoo.*
of her own accord. But Difficulties ſoon
aroſe, and there was a Neceſſity for learning
how to ſurmount them: the Height of
ſome Trees, which prevented his reaching
their Fruits; the Competition of other
Animals equally fond of the ſame
Fruits; the Fierceneſs of many that even
aimed at his Life; theſe were ſo many

H 2   Circum-

A page from Rousseau's *Essay on Inequality*

progrefs, is, from debate in the affembly to dif-
cuffions in print ; from the fearch of truth and
public utility in both, to fophiftry and the fpirit
of party : Evils fo greatly dreaded by the ingenuous " Citizen of New-Heaven," to whom we
have now the honor of paying our firft refpects,
hoping that hereafter we may find an opportunity to make him our more particular compliments.* From fophiftry and party fpirit, the
tranfition is quick and eafy to falfhood, impof-
ture, and every fpecies of artificial evolution and
criminal intrigue. As unbalanced parties of
every defcription, can never tolerate a free enquiry of any kind, when employed againft them-
felves, the licence, and even the moft temperate
freedom of the prefs, foon excites refentment and
revenge. A writer, unpopular with an oppofite
party, becaufe he is too formidable in wit or argument, may firft be burnt in effigy : or a printer
may have his office affaulted : cuffs and kicks,
boxes and cudgels, are heard of, among plebeian
ftatefmen ; challenges and fingle combats among
the ariftocratic legiflators—Riots and feditions
at length break men's bones, or flea off their fkins.
Lives are loft : and when blood is once drawn,
men, like other animals, become outrageous : If
one party has not a fuperiority over the other,
clear enough to decide every thing at its pleafure,
a civil war enfues. When the nation arrives at
this period of the progreffion, every leader, at
the head of his votaries, even if you admit him
to have the beft intentions in the world, will find
himfelf compelled to form them into fome military arrangement, both for offence and defence ; to
build

Marginalia (handwritten): Condorcet It was then my Intention to have examined those Letters at large: but the Rage and fury of the Jacobinical Journals vs these discourses increased as they proceeded, intimidated The Printer John Fenno, and convined me that to proceed would do more hurt than good. I therefore broke off abruptly.

* Alluding to four Letters publifhed about that time, by Condorcet,
who called himfelf a Citizen of New Heaven, in which he recommended
a Government in a Single Affembly, which was accordingly adopted, and
ruined France.

Adams explains why he broke off his *Discourses on Davila*

A.: Had not the female the sweet sentiment of parental love before cabins were invented? It would be hard to deny to woman the feelings of an hen or a robin.

Every family became a little society, Rousseau continues, the women looking after the children and the men rambling abroad in quest of subsistence. At the same time, man began to supply himself with conveniences which were unknown to his ancestors. In this dependence upon conveniences Rousseau saw "the first yoke" of mankind. Adams called his reasoning "Wild, loose, crude talk."

R.: Everything begins to wear a new aspect. Those who hitherto wandered through the woods gradually flock together, and finally form distinct nations in every country . . . Men begin to acquire ideas of merit and *beauty*, which produce feelings of preference.

A.: Beauty would appear to some at first sight.

R.: Jealousy awakens with love; discord triumphs, and the sweetest of passions requires the sacrifice of human blood.

A.: And were there no battles for a female before this improved state? He makes men more stupid than horses or dogs.

R.: He who sings or dances best; the handsomest, the strongest, the most dexterous, the most eloquent comes to be the most respected . . .

A.: These are sources of reputation, influence, and dignity, which in every stage of society surpass merit, in some instances.

R.: . . . and this was *the first* step towards inequality, and at the same time towards vice.

A.: The first step? Agriculture, manufactures, houses were steps to inequality long before.

R.: Men no sooner began to appraise one another and to know what esteem was, than each laid claim to it, and it was no longer possible to refuse it to another with impunity . . .

A.: Love of esteem is much earlier than this. The two first men or women who met felt an affection for each other.

R.: Thus man became blood-thirsty and cruel, whereas nothing could have been more gentle than he was in his primitive state when . . . *natural pity kept him from doing injury to others* . . .

A.: Uncertain, if not improbable.

R.: For according to the axiom of the wise Locke, "Where there is no property, there can be no injury."

A.: To break a man's leg is an injury. Locke must have meant right by the word property.

R.: But we must recognize . . . that the goodness suitable to the pure state of nature by no means suited infant society.

A.: That goodness of heart was probably the goodness of heart of bulls and cows, stallions and mares, boars and sows ready ever to fight to blood for an acorn, and to death for a female.

Though man had become less patient and natural compassion had already lost some of its sweetness, Rousseau goes on, this period must have been the happiest age of mankind. "This natural compassion," Adams rejoined, "was precisely that of cocks and hens, turkeys, geese and ducks, who will not hurt another if he does not stand in their way." Rousseau's insistence that this state was the best for man, that it was the real youth of the world, he shrugged off: "Mad rant!"

R.: The example of the savages, most of whom have been found in this condition, seems to confirm that . . . this age is the real youth of the world.

A.: Credulity! Thou art ready to believe anything but the truth.

R.: As long as men remained satisfied with their rustic cabins; confined themselves to clothes made of the skins of other animals; considered feathers and shells as sufficient oranaments; painted their bodies a variety of colors, improved their bows and arrows, scooped out with sharp-edged stones some little fishing boats, or clumsy instruments of music . . .

A.: Who made their cabins? How much toil and sweat to collect the materials and put them together? How much fatigue and danger in killing the animals to get their skins? How many must perish by the wild beasts? How much labor and study to collect feathers and shells, and how much pains to find the art of painting? How much labor to make their bows and arrows, to scoop out fishing boats, or instruments of music?

R.: But from the moment one man needed the assistance of another, from the moment it appeared useful for one to possess the provisions for two, *all equality vanished* . . .

A.: What equality was there before? Was the child equal to the mother? and the mother to the father? Not in strength, swiftness, understanding or experience.

R.: Metallurgy and agriculture were the two arts whose invention produced this great revolution. For the poet, it is gold and silver, but for the philosopher, it is iron and corn that have civilized men and ruined mankind.

A.: Nonsense. Is it possible this man could believe this?

R.: Perhaps one of the best reasons why Europe has been more thoroughly civilized than other parts of the world is that she is the most abundant in iron and the most fertile in corn.

A.: According to this Asia, Africa, and America have always been happier than Europe.

R.: It is difficult to tell how men came to know and use iron. Mines are formed nowhere but in dry and barren places, as if nature had taken pains to keep this fatal secret from us.

A.: How ignorant! Iron mines are in meadows, swamps, ponds.

R.: As to agriculture, its principle was known long before its practice was established . . . From the tilling of the soil necessarily followed its division; and from property, once recognized, the first rules of justice.

A.: A club, an hatchet of stone, a bow, an arrow was property before land. So was the lion's skin of Hercules.

R.: Things in this state might have remained equal, if men's talents had been equal. But the proportion was soon broken. *The stronger performed a larger amount of work; the more dexterous turned it to better account* . . .

A.: An eternal source of inequality in many stages of society.

R.: . . . the more ingenious found out methods of lessening his labor; the husbandman required more iron, or the smith more corn; and although both worked equally, one earned a great deal, while the other got scarcely enough to live.

A.: Did not the most ingenious find such methods before iron and corn were known? Ingenuity gave him an advantage in taking fish, fowls, and all sorts of game: so it did in climbing trees for fruit: or excavating a tree rotten at the heart for a house.

From now on, man existed in a state marked by inequality of fortunes and the use and abuse of wealth. In political government the rich employed in his own interest the very forces which threatened him—he made allies of his enemies. Already at the time of writing his *Discours*, Rousseau looks upon the establishment of the body politic as "a real contract" between the people and its leaders. He traces the degeneration of legitimate power into despotism, which in turn destroys civil society. How then should one answer the question propounded by the Academy of Dijon? "It is manifestly against the law of nature," Rosseau concludes, "that a child should command an aged man, that an imbecile should lead a sage, and that a handful of people should gorge themselves on superfluities while the hungry multitude lacks even necessities."

Adams read it all, marking almost every paragraph with the word "Note." Here and there he underlined a sentence, but he stopped arguing. He jotted down, instead, his final opinion on a blank page:

"The speculative genius and unequalled eloquence of this writer has pulled down systems; it has invalidated errors; it has undermined impostures: but it has not discovered truth. It remains for others to erect new systems which may be better or may be worse.

"Reasonings from a state of nature are fallacious, because hypothetical. We have not facts. Experiments are wanting. Reasonings from savage life are not much better. Every writer affirms what he pleases.

"The state of nature, the savage life, the Chinese happiness have all been falsely celebrated and cried up, in order to lessen the reverence for the Christian religion and weaken the attachment to monarchical government."

One of the best-known witticisms of Voltaire is his remark about the *Discours sur l'inégalité*. "Never before has so much wit been employed to turn us into beasts," he wrote to Rousseau. "Reading your work, one has the desire to walk on all fours." Voltaire, himself addicted to marginalia, made numerous notes in his own copy. In the privacy of their studies readers are apt to fall into similar moods; it is remarkable how much Voltaire's vocabulary resembles that of Adams. Comments like *ridicule*, *faux*, and *pitoyable* are mixed with exclamations like *quelle chimère* and *tarare* (the French equivalent of "fiddle-sticks"). "*Fou que tu es . . .*," he once intimately addressed his friend. "*Malheureux Jean-Jacques . . .*," he started out another time. At the end he gave it up: "*Tout cela est abominable*."

4

The *Discours sur l'inégalité* was not published until June 1755, and, while still reading the proofs, Rousseau was already preparing his *Économie politique* for the fifth volume of the *Encyclopédie*.

The distance between the two works is great. While the former is a complete expression of Rousseau's individualism, the latter sets forth his ideas about communal living. The first regards property as the cause of all evil, while the second declares it to be the foundation of civil society. Yet the break is not absolute; the *Économie politique* contains many contradictions which show that Rosseau has not renounced his former beliefs. He regards the State as an organized body whose members share the same life and have a common self (*le moi commun au tout*), and praises the law as the essence of the general will (*volonté générale*); he does not, however, maintain his objectivity for long. The State, he emphasizes, is the instrument of the rich for the exploitation of the poor. Thus he summarizes the "social pact" in a sardonic sentence: "You need me because I am rich and you are poor; let us agree therefore: I shall permit you to have the honor of serving me, on condition that you will surrender to me the little that you have for the pains which I take to command you."

Adams was absorbed in the essay, underlining passage after passage.[17] Rousseau's conception of the general will as the source of law for all members of the State especially provoked him. "The French writers have erroneous notions of general will and public opinion," he put down. The assertion that the general will is always the most just, and that the voice of the people is the voice of God, made him to inquire: "If the majority is 51 and the minority 49, is it certainly the voice of God? If tomorrow one should change to 50 vs. 50, where is the voice of God? If two and the minority should become the majority, is the voice of God changed?" Adams well realized the revolutionary character of Rousseau's idea of the general will which, ignoring the rights of property, proclaimed the absolute political equality of all citizens. The majority never could become for Rousseau "a faction"; it was always the equivalent of the general will, which also served the minority. Adopting his philosophy, the National Assembly in August 1789 declared that the law was "the expression of the general will"; yet the Constitution decreed a tax qualification for the right to vote. It remained for the nineteenth and the twentieth centuries to enact universal suffrage, the logical conclusion of Rousseau's doctrine (and to invent new methods for the balancing of interests).[18]

The first part of the treatise is devoted to the observance of the laws:

R.: *It is to law alone that men owe justice and liberty; it is this salutary instrument of the will of all that restores natural equality to its rightful place among men* . . . [19]

A.: But who shall make and who will guard the laws? The guardians of the laws are the desideratum. These can only be something tantamount to King, Lords, and Commons.

R.: If the head of the States wishes others to observe the law, he must do so all the more scrupulously himself. For *his example is of such force* . . .

A.: What gives such force to his example? the oil? his power exciting both fear and gratitude? his pomp? his wealth?

R.: Experience has long taught the people *to prize their chiefs for all the harm that they do not do, and to adore them when they are not hated.*

A.: Is there no medium between adoration and hatred? What is the cause of this adoration? Is this the sin, crime or fault of the chiefs?

R.: The greatest talent of the chiefs is to disguise their power so as to render it less hateful.

A.: Disguise eternally inculcated by demagogues as well as tyrants.

R.: You will ask, *How is one to know the general will* in circumstances in which it has not made itself clear?

A.: A difficult question.

R.: The chiefs understand well enough that the general will is always for the party which is most favorable to the public good . . .

A.: This is not universally true.

R.: . . . that is, the most equitable.

A.: This is not true. The majority is not so fond of justice.

R.: There is no doubt that peoples are in the long run what the government makes out of them: *warriors, citizens, men, when it desires; rabble and canaille if it likes* . . .

A.: The government ought to be what the people make it. Why is it not?

R.: In the ancient governments philosophers gave laws to the people, using their authority to make them wise and happy. Hence *so many sumptuary laws, so many regulations concerning morals* . . .

A.: Sumptuary laws bring all laws into contempt because they are never obeyed.

Rousseau exalts the love of country as a hundred times more keen and more delicious than that of a mistress. "Hyperbole," Adams decided like an expert. Rousseau makes a powerful plea—one of the most original and valuable parts of the essay—for general education: for the bringing up of children in common, for imbuing them with the laws of the State and the precepts of the general will. Adams, however, was skeptical; "This Spartan education is not the thing," he wrote. Rousseau even recommends that retired magistrates devote their old age to teaching: illustrious warriors should preach courage and honest judges should inculcate justice, thus transmitting to succeeding generations their experience and talents. "Very good for what I know," Adams conceded, "but these would be costly schoolmasters."

In some respects the last portion of the *Economie politique* is the most challenging. In it Rousseau advocates the right to work, maintaining that it is the duty of the State to secure the livelihood of its citizens. Adams passed this over in silence. Then, in the discussion of inheritance, he found a passage which he esteemed "worth a volume." It should be the spirit of the laws, Rousseau suggests, that from father to son, and from relative to relative, family property be alienated as little as possible, for nothing is more fatal to morals than the continual shift of fortunes from one hand to another. Adams was pleased with this "deep sense." But soon he had reason to temper his admiration. If the people governed themselves, Rousseau insists, the citizens would only have to tax themselves as occasion demanded, and no abuse could escape their notice. Adams became angry: "It is amazing that eyes so piercing should be so blind! Must not collectors be employed? and would not they be capable of abuse? and with impunity because the same majority who chose them would support them?"

However, it is the *Contrat social* that contains the final embodiment of Rousseau's doctrine of the sovereignty of the State. The existence of civil society being a fact, one should try to do one's best with it. The law of the social order is "sacred," but it does not derive from nature; it is founded on conventions and we have to learn what these conventions are. This is the prelude. Far from giving up his ideas about the origin of society, Rousseau makes the powerful indictment: "Man was born free, yet he is everywhere in chains . . . " [20]

Adams had no less than four copies of the work—two in French and two in English. As has been noted, he first studied the work in 1765; the notes he made during his Presidency. Rousseau's definition of the general will as "something which remains after the contradictory wills are deducted from the aggregate of the individual wills," appeared to him "too mathematical or too witty to be very clear." The allegation that people are worse off when they are ruled by different ranks of superiors than by a single order he found altogether mistaken; and he particularly denied that such a system could guarantee what Rousseau believed to be the two principal objects of government, liberty and equality.

R.: *As regards equality, we are not to understand by this term that the degrees of wealth and power must be absolutely the same; but that power should never be exercised contrary to the laws, and that no citizen should be rich enough to buy another or so poor as to be obliged to sell himself.*[21]

A.: But when or where did such moderation ever exist?—absolutely never, where riches existed.

R.: Do you wish to impart strength to the State? Narrow down the distances between the two extremes as much as possible; tolerate *neither rich persons* nor beggars.

A.: What becomes of the commandment, "Thou shalt not steal"? Must you steal from rich men their property and give it to beggars?— Property, property! that is the difficulty. Without property, there would be no rich men to be sure. But there would not be fewer beggars for that.

Yet Rousseau allows that the institutions should be adapted to the characteristics of the country. Do the waves of the sea lash your inaccessible rocks? Then remain barbarous fish-eaters; you will live more at ease, will be more virtuous perhaps, and certainly happier. But Adams resisted the lure: "The ease is doubted and the virtue and happiness denied."

The laws relating to the body politic Rousseau calls "fundamental"; but a nation can always change its laws, even the best ones, for if it wishes to do itself an injury, who has the right to prevent it? "Who has the right to prevent a madman from hurting himself?" Adams countered.

R.: Every citizen should live in perfect independence of all the others, and in the most complete dependence on the State . . .

A.: An admirable maxim of government and liberty.

R.: . . . *for nothing but the power of the State constitutes the liberty of its members.*

A.: A principle of liberty, not so well relished as his doctrine of equality by the populace.

5

It is a charming picture—John Adams sitting back in an armchair with a copy of the *Nouvelle Héloïse.*

One may doubt, of course, that he read the whole endless series of letters which passed between the passionate yet virtuous Julie and her melancholy lover Saint-Preux; between both of them and her devoted cousin Claire; as well as those by that model husband, M. de Wolmar, and the stern philosopher, Mylord Édouard. His notes are few—but enough to show that he really knew the novel.[22]

In the first volume he repeated the word "honneur" on the margin of a letter from Saint-Preux to Julie, perhaps mocking the man's incessant protestations of his noble sentiments; for that letter was written after the seduction had taken place. At the beginning of the second volume Mylord Édouard tells Claire about the troubled state of affairs between Julie and her lover, owing to the intervention of her cruel father. "Let rank be determined by merit and the union of hearts by their own choice; this is the proper social order," he writes. "Singsong," Adams pronounced. "Those who regulate it by birth or wealth are the real disturbers of this system," the Englishman goes on. Adams added the suggestion *"ou par beauté de visage ou figure,"* continuing in English: "Peoples, nations, not individuals, are guilty of this. Riches and fame are chimaeras too."

There is another comment on the margin of the letter in which Julie informs Saint-Preux of her miscarriage, the death of her heartbroken mother, and her decision to obey her father and marry M. de Wolmar. "We were made for each other, and if the human order had not upset nature's harmony, we should have been happy together," she laments. Adams raised the question: "Is not a human order which is inevitable, to me an order of nature?"

Julie marries the elderly nobleman, and bids farewell to her lover "forever." Saint-Preux contemplates suicide. He tries to justify his plan to his English patron: People say that God has placed us in this world and therefore we have no right to leave it without permission; but he has placed us also in our city and yet we need no permission to leave that. "Excellent sophistry if the word 'excellent' may be used," Adams considered the proposition. Once the weariness of life conquers the horror of death, Saint-Preux meditates, life becomes intolerable. "Rather better," the Old Man at Quincy thought.

In any case, at the persuasion of Mylord Édouard, Saint-Preux decides to live, and with the help of his friend, he procures a commission on an English ship of war and sails the seven seas for years. By the time of his return, Julie has several growing children. At the invitation of her husband, Saint-Preux goes to live with them (even as Rousseau was living, at the time of his writing the novel, with Madame d'Houdetot and Saint-Lambert). From their home, he sends Mylord Édouard a glowing description of the household. It is a great error in domestic as well as in public economy, he argues, to try to combat one evil with another or to create a kind of equilibrium between them . . . Adams was cautious: "This requires explanation, limitation, restriction." He marked several other passages; one occurs in a letter from Julie to her cousin, revealing the fact that M. de Wolmar knew even before their marriage what had passed between her and Saint-Preux.

The *ménage à trois* seemed successful. Saint-Preux achieved a puzzled admiration for M. de Wolmar, whom he represents to Mylord Édouard as cold but without a touch of vice: "He lacks inner feeling, which enables him to resist all other feelings." Adams underlined this. There is no sign of what he thought of the rest of the story—of Saint-Preux's recurring weakness and Julie's own desperate struggle against her love which ends only in her semivoluntary death.

The *Nouvelle Héloïse* exerted an enormous influence upon countless poets and novelists, from Goethe to Byron, and from George Sand to Chateaubriand. Its romantic exaltation started a new era in literature, to last for nearly a century. One may feel certain, however, that John Adams was immune to its raptures. He was well protected by his own wise system of "checks and balances." [23]

[VI]

Frederick, Voltaire, and d'Alembert

"Frederick's works," Adams wrote in July 1815 to Francis Vanderkemp, the Dutch pastor who had come to settle in America, "are in my library over the way. But I have lost my George,[1] who alone could look them up, and I am too indulgent to go in search of them. Indeed, I have no great veneration for the hero,—not more than for Napoleon. He was more 'superficial' than D'Argens." And that, for Adams, meant a great deal of superficiality, for in the same letter he describes the marquis, the author of various memoirs and one of Frederick's closest companions, as a "consummate hypocrite" and "the most frank, candid, impudent, and sincere liar" whom he had ever read.[2] Yet once he had had a more favorable opinion of Frederick, with whom, indirectly, he had an important contact. For it was Adams who, thirty years before, had negotiated the first treaty of commerce with Prussia.

The treaty had a long history, the main points of which are worth reviewing. Upon his arrival in Paris in July 1776, Silas Deane, the first representative of Congress in France, started discussions with the Prussian agent about supplying the Colonies with military stores.[3] Later, in May 1777, Arthur Lee, one of the commissioners serving with Franklin and Deane, himself traveled to Berlin to secure an open port for commerce and obtain permission to fit out armed vessels. He stayed a month but gained only the answer that the King, although well-disposed toward the Colonies, "could not embroil himself with the Court of London."[4] Frederick indeed sympathized with the Americans; or, to be more accurate, he was no well-wisher of the British, who, although his allies, had deserted him during the Seven Years' War. But he was not to be swayed by such sentiments. As he wrote to his brother Henry on June 17, 1777, he wished "to procrastinate in these negotiations and to go over to the side on which fortune should declare herself." Meanwhile he opposed the sending of German troops to America, refusing them permission to march through his lands. Apart from his contempt for the "dirty selfishness" of the German princes who hired out their soldiers to England, he was again motivated by reasons of state. "The King of Prussia," he explained in his Memoirs, "did not like to see the Empire deprived of all its defenders, especially in case of a new war . . . " [5]

Adams, having replaced Deane in Paris, joined heartily in the effort of his colleagues to establish trade relations with Prussia. Not having suffered the earlier rebuffs, he was in fact overoptimistic. On August 4, 1779—immediately after returning to America from his one and a half years' service in France—he addressed a long letter to Congress, submitting "a few remarks" on the general political situation in Europe. "The jealousy between the Emperor and the King of Prussia, and that between the Houses of Bourbon and Austria, are a natural tie between France and Prussia," he wrote. "The rivalry between France and Great Britain is another motive, too natural and too permanent for the former to suffer the King of Prussia to be long the ally of the latter." And he pointed out that Frederick's desire to develop the port of Emden, and to introduce commerce between his state and America, had made the King "most powerfully" interested in American independence. [6]

With the conclusion of peace with Great Britain, the way was open. In February 1784 the Prussian minister, Baron Thulemeier, called upon Adams at The Hague, where the latter was discussing a new loan for America. "He told me," Adams reported to Congress, "that the King, who . . . was acquainted with my character, had directed him to make me a visit, and to say to me, that, as his subjects had occasion for our tobacco and some other things, and as we had occasion for Silesia linens and some other productions of his dominions, he thought an arrangement might be made between his Crown and the United States which would be beneficial to both." [7] Shortly afterwards, the Prussian minister transmitted to Adams a draft of twenty-seven articles, written by the King "with his own hand, in his private cabinet." Adams, before forwarding it to Congress, sent it to Franklin and Jay, his fellow ministers in Paris, who suggested a few minor changes. Instead of the expression "the United States of North America," they wanted simply "the United States of America"; and instead of "respective subjects," they wished to use the word "citizens" for the Americans. Frederick agreed. Congress, however, demanded a number of modifications and introduced two new articles, one of which related to contraband and the other to giving merchants sufficient time to settle their affairs in case of war. The King accepted some of the proposals, and objected to others. It took nearly a year before the treaty, with most of the changes desired by Congress, was signed, and another half year before Congress passed it. For the exchange of ratifications Adams, then Minister to Great Britain, went from London to The Hague. "The Baron Thulemeier," he informed Jay, the Secretary of Foreign Affairs, "had time to transmit the act of Congress to the great prince who first proposed the treaty some days before he expired." [8]

Memories of the old transactions must have returned to Adams as he read Frederick's works—the twenty volumes of the *Œuvres* and *Œuvres posthumes*.[9] But he would have been interested in them anyhow; for Frederick, surrounded all his life by Frenchmen and speaking and writing nothing but French (except to soldiers and servants), was himself one of the *philosophes*.[10] His stormy friendship with Voltaire was known all over the world; and he also carried on an extensive correspondence with other French writers. Adams read some of the King's essays and poems, but he was much more attracted by the letters to Voltaire and d'Alembert. He went through nearly two hundred of these. His comments, totaling over three thousand words, concern Voltaire and d'Alembert almost as much as they do Frederick.[11]

As is well known, in March 1799 President Adams, having decided to send a peace mission to France, suddenly quit the Capital, retiring to Quincy for seven full months. During his absence the Cabinet, swayed by Hamilton, did everything to wreck the mission, until Adams, upon his return to Philadelphia, peremptorily ordered its sailing. The country was wondering, as historians have been ever since, what the President was doing on his farm during that critical period. As the dates of his notes show, a good part of the time he was reading Frederick's works.[12]

2

In 1736 Frederick was established at Rheinsberg, a small garrison town fifty miles north of Berlin. Not yet twenty-five, he had been married for nearly four years to Elizabeth, the homely little daughter of the Duke of Brunswick-Bevern. The marriage was forced upon him, soon after his attempt to flee to his uncle, George II of England, away from his maniacal father, King Frederick William I. His friend Lieutenant Katte, who had been involved in the plot, was beheaded before his eyes; and the young Prince, who had been threatened with the same fate, recognized that there was nothing left for him to do but obey. Throughout his life he hardly ever spoke to his wife.

There were, however, compensations at Rheinsberg. With the permission of the King, an old manor on the edge of the lake was remodeled into a French château, a cheap but still impressive imitation of the Trianon. Here the court of the Crown Prince included several musicians, the Parisian painter Antoine Pesne, the learned Charles Etienne Jordan, secretary and librarian, and the vivacious Count Keyserlingk, whom Frederick affectionately called Caesarion. La Chétardie, the French minister, was a frequent guest. When not visiting in Berlin or on a tour of inspection with the King, Frederick amused himself with concerts and theatricals (or plain drinking parties), and with reading and writing.[13] Anxious for brilliant company, he also invited Fontenelle and Rollin to Rheinsberg, but the philosopher and the historian, both in their seventies, courteously declined. The Prince then turned to a still more remarkable Frenchman. On August 8, 1736, he addressed a letter to Voltaire, heaping lavish praise upon the author of *La Henriade, César,* and *Alzire,* whom, he wrote, the great Corneille would envy if he were to come to life again. Voltaire, "infinitely touched," replied with a long panegyric. With this began their friendship, which lasted till Voltaire's death.

Both Frederick and Voltaire derived enormous pleasure from their correspondence. Each gained precisely what he needed most—Frederick, literary encouragement from the greatest living writer, and Voltaire, snubbed at Versailles, recognition from a royal personage. The mutual admiration which their early letters display was boundless:

Frederick: I place you at the head of all thinking beings; *the Creator would certainly find it difficult to produce a mind more sublime than yours* . . . [14]

Adams: Pitiful!

F.: How different is your way of thinking from that of the priests, those hooded antiquaries! You love truth, they love superstition; *you practice the Christian virtues,* they are content with teaching them.

A.: ! ! ! ? ? ?

F.: My letter is addressed to one who is *an example of virtue* . . .

A.: Oh!

F.: I send you my sincere friendship, and all the esteem which *supreme virtue* and merit may extort even from the envious . . .

A.: Voltaire was too much addicted to lying.

Voltaire, eighteen years older than the Prince, was living in the home of the Marquise du Châtelet at Cirey, and the name of the "sublime Émilie" was soon drawn into the correspondence. Frederick, usually coldly polite if not brutal toward women, was willing to assume an air of devoted interest. He even hinted mysteriously at his own sad experience in love: "I have suffered shipwreck in my life . . . " This was, of course, merely an excuse for writing and talking poetry. Poetry, certainly, plays a prominent part in these letters. In most of them Frederick enclosed "a little ode" (*"une petite ode assez mal tournée et assez insipide"*), asking Voltaire to do him the favor of correcting it. And the poet was only too happy to oblige. He was "drunk with surprise and joy" at the discovery that French verse, "such as only Versailles knew in the days of its glory," was written at Rheinsberg.

Frederick's passion for philosophy was almost as great. He sent Voltaire a dissertation by Christian Wolff, the unhappy professor from Halle whom King Frederick William had ordered to leave Prussia "on pain of the noose," because his doctrine of determinism meant that "no deserter from the army could be punished, since he acted only as was foreordained." What the Prince particularly wanted to discuss with Voltaire was Wolff's theory of "the simple being," a new variety of Leibnitz's "monad," which in turn led to the question whether matter was infinitely divisible or not:

F.: I frankly confess to you that *I have no idea of the infinite* . . .
A.: Ni moi.
F.: Could there be a being finite and infinite at the same time? No, for that implies a contradiction; and since a thing cannot exist and not exist at the same time, matter cannot be infinite, and therefore cannot be endlessly divisible . . . [15]
A.: An infinite surface may be a finite solid. But there is nothing but contradiction in metaphysics relative to infinity, immensity, eternity, etc. Our understandings were not made for them.
F.: I admit that I know only two kinds of numbers, even and odd; now if the infinite, being *a number*, is neither even nor odd, what is it then? [16]
A.: How a number? Number implies limit. If he has no idea of the infinite, how can he call it a number?

Voltaire, while probably loathing Professor Wolff's ponderosities, asked Frederick to send him more. "I love everything that your genius loves," he fulsomely wrote, "although I can hardly touch what you are grasping in your hands." Frederick graciously complied.

F.: Wolff regards extension as the continuity of units. A line, for example, is formed of units which touch each other.

A.: A point has no parts. A point therefore is not matter nor space. How can a continuity of points then make a line?

F.: Space, according to Wolff, is the void between the parts; but a unit, having no parts, and consequently no interstices, cannot contain space.

A.: Molecules, entities, quiddities. All words without meaning.

Half a year later Frederick was still entertaining Voltaire with Wolff's speculations:

> *F.: The first causes will always remain unknown to us . . .*[17]
> *A.:* Why then seek for the Etre Simple, etc.?
> *F.:* But what is sure is that I am matter and that I think . . .
> *A.:* It is not sure that you are matter. If it is sure that there is any matter in you, it is not sure that you are all matter.—This mighty discovery however was stolen from Locke.

Religion and the influence of the Church were other favorite topics. On these Frederick, a militant freethinker, was entirely in accord with Voltaire. Adams, himself no friend of priests, had to defend them against his onslaughts. "There is some virtue, some wisdom and some piety even among the Catholic ecclesiastics," he nobly asserted.

3

On May 30, 1740 Frederick ascended the throne. A few days later he wrote a most cordial letter to his "cher ami" at Cirey. "If I live, I shall see you, and this very year," he announced. Voltaire was overjoyed; in an ode he celebrated the new King as "the Solomon of the North," only more learned and wise and less weak than the one of yore. In August, Frederick traveled incognito to Strassburg, and from there to Clèves, near the Dutch border, where he invited Voltaire to come (with Émilie if necessary, without her if possible).[18] The King was sick with fever, yet the meeting was a success. Two months later the poet set out for Rheinsberg, where he was received with great affection. However, because of news of the Marquise's ill health, he soon left— after he had handed in a huge expense account for the journey. Frederick's mood suddenly changed. "Never did a great lord's jester get such a good wage," he remarked bearishly to his secretary.[19] But they went on writing to each other. The King constantly urged the poet to visit him again, but it was not until the death of Madame du Châtelet in 1750 that Voltaire thought with longing of Frederick's company.

Voltaire's three years' stay in Berlin and Potsdam, with all its drama and comedy, does not need to be told here—it is one of the best-known episodes of literary history. There was his involvement in the Hirsch gambling scandal, his quarrel with Maupertuis, the president of the Berlin Academy, and the publication of his fiendish lampoon, *La diatribe du Docteur Akakia*. Frederick was disgusted, and Voltaire was alternately cringing and arrogant. Before leaving Germany, he was arrested at Frankfort and searched for a manuscript of the King's (an obscene burlesque) which he had supposedly taken with him. The opus was finally located elsewhere, but Voltaire, together with his niece who had come to join him, was kept in prison for six weeks. Ill and dejected, he stayed for a while at Colmar—and soon was making fresh overtures to his Majesty. Frederick, after some show of petulance, assured him that his genius was too great an honor to mankind ever to be forgotten by him.

There are no bickerings in the letters of the last years which Adams read. Voltaire had become "the Patriarch of Ferney," and Frederick himself was by then an old man. They had friendly discussions about religion, the mind and the body, the immortality of the soul. Here are some excerpts, with Adams's reactions:

F.: I believe that the voice of reason . . . *will render future generations more tolerant* than those of our time.[20]

A.: Amen.

F.: I should prefer the colonies of Ferney, whose legislator is Voltaire, to those of Philadelphia, which received their laws from Locke.

A.: How accurate!

F.: We know the·crimes that fanaticism in religion has caused; *let us be careful not to introduce it into philosophy*.

A.: 1799. This was foresight.

F.: Great difficulties will eternally be in the way of those who wish to proclaim a simple and reasonable *religion*.

A.: He is then for some religion!

F.: A society could not exist without laws, but it could without religion. This is confirmed by the experience of the savages found on the Mariana Islands, *who had no metaphysical notions whatever in their heads*.

A.: Problematic.

F.: The Englishman Woolston estimates the survival of the papacy at two centuries. If we destroy the prejudice at the foundation of this structure, it will fall to pieces by itself. This is what Bayle has begun; a number of Englishmen have followed him, and it has remained for you to accomplish the work.

A.: It is poor to praise Voltaire for what he learned from Woolston, Blount, etc., the other English infidels, some of whom preceded Bayle.

The King again raises the question which so much occupied the young pupil of Christian Wolff some forty years before:

F.: I know that I am *a material, animated, and organized animal which thinks.* Hence I conclude that animated matter can think . . .

A.: How confident! He never had considered matter or spirit enough to know that we know nothing of the essence of either.

F.: Sleep confirms this opinion. When it is perfect, the blood circulates so gently that the ideas are as if benumbed, the nerves of the understanding relaxed, and the soul remains as if annihilated.

A.: If this is all badinage, it is well enough.

F.: To my mind the doctrines of empty space and *of spirits without organs are the height of human folly.*

A.: Body and motion with organs are equally incomprehensible.

F.: You have the fire which the Romans called *anima* and which preserves our frail machine . . .

A.: I rather think vanity preserves longer than wit.

Adams owned the 1775 edition of Voltaire's works in forty volumes, besides an eight-volume set of the plays and several single pieces. He made notes in one or two volumes, and there are more substantial comments in a separate edition of the *Philosophie de l'histoire* and the *Traité sur la tolérance,* printed in 1765.[21] However, he never came to close grips with the mighty Frenchman. Voltaire, although he had written about almost everything, was not greatly interested in constitutions. Adams had no high opinion of his morals, but he regarded him as "the greatest literary character of the eighteenth century." He even assured Jefferson of his rejoicing that Voltaire had lived.[22]

4

Frederick had a special esteem for d'Alembert, who in turn revered him. In one of his early works, a treatise on the causes of the winds, the scientist had saluted His Prussian Majesty as one in whom "future centuries will admire alike the sovereign, the sage, and the hero." [23]

D'Alembert, not yet thirty, already had a great reputation. The illegitimate child of Madame de Tencin (the sister of Cardinal de Tencin), who had abandoned him near a church in Paris soon after birth, he was brought up by the wife of a glazier. His father, the Chevalier Destouches, settled a small annuity upon him, and he was sent to Mazarin College. His genius for higher mathematics was apparent early. At twenty-three he was elected to the Académie des Sciences, mainly for his studies on integral calculus; and in a few years his theory of dynamics, applied to the equilibrium and motion of fluids, placed him in the front rank of mathematical physicists. Frederick watched him with interest and in 1752, when Maupertuis fell ill after Voltaire's ruthless ridicule, he offered d'Alembert the presidency of the Berlin Academy. In a long letter—a perfect self-portrait—the French scientist refused. He had only a very moderate income, he wrote, but he enjoyed the tranquillity of his life; was afraid of the harsh climate of Berlin; did not want to leave his friends; was lacking in practical knowledge of men; had just begun a great work with Diderot; and finally, he thought that he owed "something" to his country. Frederick was impressed but did not give up. Seven years later, upon Maupertuis's death, he renewed the invitation, and d'Alembert again declined, just as he had declined, shortly before, an offer of the Empress Elizabeth of Russia to be tutor to her son, the future Tsar Peter III, with a fabulous salary.

D'Alembert, six years younger than the King, was by then an ailing man. In his first letter Frederick tries to cheer him up, and suggests mineral waters for his intestinal troubles. The invitation to Potsdam was an ever-recurrent theme:

F.: If you will not meet me in the valley of Jehoshaphat, decide to meet me here.[24] There is no intermediate choice, and I should be much better pleased to see you in the flesh than I know not how in the guise of a ghost . . .

A.: How much pains he takes to persuade himself that death is an eternal sleep? and how plain it is that he had no success.

F.: I do not know any map on which to find *the valley of Jehoshaphat* . . .

A.: This valley was never out of his head.

D'Alembert's contributions to science were outside of the King's province; most of his letters are on problems of philosophy. Yet in January 1768 Frederick asks the very pertinent question, what good are all the scientific discoveries if morals are neglected? "Is it not true that electricity and its miracles have merely excited our curiosity? Is it not true that the theory of attraction and gravity and the marvels of chemistry have done nothing but astonish our imagination?" Such a distrust of progress was too much even for Adams. "No, no," he protested.

F.: The gospel tells us: do unto others as you would they should do unto you; *this precept is the essence of all morality.*
A.: Good.
F.: I am convinced that if a colony of unbelievers were established, after a few years *superstitions would spring up among them.*
A.: No doubt.
F.: The Reformation effected a great revolution. But what blood and carnage, what wars and devastations followed the rejection of some articles of faith! *What* fury would seize people if all articles were to be suppressed!
A.: In 1799 this question is remarkable.

To his "cher Anaxagoras," Frederick, calling himself a mere "dilettante" and "a sexagenarian pupil," often expounded his belief in an intelligence which presides over the universe. He spoke admiringly of Jesus, "whose religion was pure deism."

F.: Since man is a material, thinking, and moving being, I see no reason why a similar thinking and acting principle could not be joined to universal matter.[25]
A.: What is matter?
F.: If one wants to respect the fundamental axioms of reason, *one is obliged to admit the eternity of the universe.*
A.: This man has his dogmas as well as the Pope of Rome or Geneva.
F.: The idea of Creation leads to absurdities at every step one makes to establish it; it requires the denial of the *ex nihilo nihil est,* which was respected by all the ancient world.
A.: Creation implies no contradiction, any more than motion. Motion of the earth and stars, generation of animals or vegetables, are as incomprehensible to us as creation.
F.: There is but one of these abstract subjects capable of demonstration, that of materialism . . .
A.: Superficial dogmatist.
F.: I am convinced that *a fanatical philosopher is the greatest of all possible monsters, and at the same time the most inconsistent animal that the earth ever produced.*
A.: This is most obvious.

There are many references to Voltaire. The King thought that d'Alembert would perform a useful service by admonishing the poet not to waste his energies in quarrels with literary dwarfs whom he merely rescued from oblivion by such means. "This is very good of Voltaire," Adams noted with relish. Frederick could not refrain, of course, from making jokes at the expense of the *philosophes:*

F.: Helvétius's new book is filled with paradoxes and follies, at the head of which may be placed his notion of a *French Republic.*

A.: 1799.

F.: He maintains that *men are born with very nearly the same talents, and with indelible characters.*

A.: One extreme; another.

F.: I despair of my ability to place my government on the footing which your learned legislators (who have never governed) have prescribed. *Whatever comes out of it . . .*

A.: Enough has arrived.

F.: It is too bad that such fine geniuses should not have at least *some kingdoms to burn—*I mean, to govern.

A.: They have had them.

F.: The mob, which is in the majority everywhere, will always let itself be led by scoundrels . . .

A.: There is too much truth in this.

Allusions to the American Revolution did not escape Adams's attention: "You would like to know what I think of the behavior of the English?" the King writes. "Exactly what the public thinks: that it is a breach of good faith not to keep their pact with the colonies." And again: "It seems as if a mad dog had bitten the English parliament. These people are behaving like madmen. You will surely go to war with these 'gottdams'; the colonies will become independent, and France will regain Canada, of which she has been robbed." Adams marked the passages: "Opinion of the American War, 1777." [26]

"Old Fritz" was reaching seventy by now. A plump youth at the time of his accession, by the end of the Seven Years' War he was a gray old man, and another decade turned him into a shriveled little figure, constantly tortured by gout. Preoccupation with the idea of death becomes more and more evident in his letters:

F.: I have not renounced the hope of seeing you again in this world, *assured as I am that we shall not see each other in another.*

A.: What assurance?

F.: At your age and mine one should find consolation in the thought that we shall not tarry long before *joining those whom we miss.*

A.: i.e. to sleep with them, forever. What comfort is this?

F.: I feel like the tribe in Africa which weeps at the birth of children and feasts at their death, because only those who die are safe from sorrow and countless misfortunes.

A.: Amen! if birth and death were all.

F.: It is embarrassing that all who suffer should be *obliged to give the lie outright to Zeno* . . .

A.: Truth well expressed.

F.: When your heart has received a wound, the Stoic tells you you must not feel pain; but I feel it in spite of myself . . .

A.: True.

It was the loss of his nephew Prince Henry, whom he loved as a son, and who died in 1767 at the age of nineteen, that caused the King such suffering. But he tried to master himself. "I await the moment of my departure without fear of the future and with perfect resignation," he assured d'Alembert, shortly before his death. But Adams wryly remarked: "His resignation was not so perfect at last, according to Zimmerman." [27]

F.: Perhaps *nature* wants us, at the end of our days, to be disgusted with life, so that we may leave this world with less regret.

A.: Why not the parent of nature?

F.: It seems *to me* that man is made *to act rather than to know* . . .

A.: Moi aussi.

F.: . . . *the principles of things elude our most persistent search.*

A.: Very true.

F.: Charles V retired to the convent of St. Just, and the Sorbonne will be the shelter of my old age. Accustomed to being bored with the doctors, I should be prepared to be bored with the patriarchs, and I should be less out of tune in singing hallelujahs . . .

A.: The wit in all these letters is not of the most brilliant kind, the humor is not delicate.

Living modestly in the house of Mlle de Lespinasse, the one great (and innocent) love of his life, d'Alembert had few material demands. Only once did he avail himself of help. Sick from overwork, he was urged to seek rest in Italy, and he asked his royal friend if he would advance him six thousand francs. Frederick complied instantly, and when later d'Alembert, who got no farther than Ferney, wanted to return the unspent part of the money, he would not hear of it. Long after his intended "Italian" journey, the philosopher was still thanking the King for his generosity. His humor not being particularly varied, he repeatedly made some light remarks about Providence. It was this talk which goaded Adams to an outburst of fury, such as has seldom been wasted on a shy and kindly man:

D'Alembert: For the last six months I have lived entirely on Your Majesty's help. I must confess that, seeing how admirably this best of all possible worlds is governed, one is tempted to believe in Providence.

Adams: Providence will not take the trouble to give you money to bribe you to believe it, poor, conceited animalcule!

D.: King Alfonso said, concerning the confusion of the spheres taught by ancient astronomy, that *had he been present when God created the world, he could have given Him some good advice;* and I am sometimes tempted to believe that God was at least as much in need of advice when he created the moral world as when he created the physical.[28]

A.: Thou Louse, Flea, Tick, Ant, Wasp, or whatever Vermin thou art, was this Stupendous Universe made and adjusted to give you Money, Sleep, or Digestion?

D.: My instinctive desire is for peace; but it remains to be seen whether, all things considered, *it is a great benefit for the unhappy human race to prevent it from self-destruction.*

A.: This is modern philosophy.

The letters contain many bits of news from France: the menace of the Jesuits, the plight of literature and philosophy, the death of Louis XV, the good intentions of his successor, Turgot's appointment as Minister of Finance, and so on:

D.: The cohort of Jesuits, should it return to France, will join the madness of revenge to the atrocity of fanaticism . . .

A.: The fury of the philosophers has since been greater than that of Jesuits and their vengeance more savage.

D.: Today literature is hated in France; there is not a man in office who is not its open or secret enemy.

A.: The war began early!

D.: We philosophers exist a little longer on our old literary reputation; but such a precarious life cannot last long, and *we shall end by becoming the fable of Europe.*

A.: Fable tragique!

D.: It will perhaps astonish Your Majesty that during the six weeks that the theaters were closed in Paris *no one regretted them.*
A.: Wonderful!
D.: With good reason has M. Turgot been praised to Your Majesty; he certainly is one of the best informed, most industrious, and most just men in the kingdom.
A.: A very just elogium.

Naturally the letters end with good wishes and compliments to the King—health was an inevitable topic for two old men writing to each other. But Adams could not read even these without censure:

D.: When I feel tempted *to pout at nature for having given me so frail and sad a habitation,* I forgive her, recollecting that she preserved Your Majesty.
A.: Will your pouting have the same effect on nature as your mistress's on you?
D.: But what is really admirable, really worthy of Your Majesty, is the fine inscription which you have put on the Catholic church in Berlin: "Frederick, who does not hate those who serve God differently from him."
A.: Good.

It would be difficult to account for Adams's animosity against d'Alembert, with whom he evidently had no personal contact. He merely heard him speak once at the famous meeting of the Académie des Sciences in which Voltaire and Franklin, in response to the clamorous demands of the members, embraced and kissed each other—a scene which left Adams with singularly unsentimental memories.[29]

5

No one could imagine that Adams read *all* of Frederick's poems. This would have been a feat which probably few people have performed. Nevertheless, he made a valiant effort. He read them as if he were reading the letters, without being the least disturbed by their esthetic shortcomings. And this was precisely the right attitude, for the stuff of Frederick's poetry was the stuff of which good prose is made: thoughts, polemics, the development of ideas. Why the King took so much trouble to put them into rhyme (rhythm he never achieved) is a mystery.

The larger part of Frederick's *Poésies* consists of epistles. He addressed them to Voltaire, Charles Jordan, the Marquis d'Argens; to his sisters, nephews, and other relatives; to the Pope, the Queen of Sweden, and even one to the Emperor of China. Adams made cursory notes on more than a dozen, but one he subjected to a thoroughgoing examination. It was the poem entitled "Sur l'origine du mal," sent to "Monsieur Mitschel," the British ambassador.

Sir Andrew Mitchell was one of the few friends of the King who was not a Frenchman, and certainly one of the few who accompanied him on his campaigns. He was a warm supporter of the alliance between England and Prussia, and the King, greatly in need of the English subsidy, appreciated his services. When weary of politics, they often discussed literature and religion. On these, however, they seldom agreed. The Scot was a partisan of the rising German literature; in contrast to the King, he even liked to speak German. As to metaphysics, he listened to Frederick's arguments, but remained a good Presbyterian.[30]

The epistle on the Origin of Evil reads like a procession of these same arguments. Adams evidently sided with Mitchell:

F.: The Supreme Being is good, and *man is wretched* . . .

A.: Non.

F.: Without their consent, God gave life to his creatures. *We were condemned to live in this abode.*

A.: Is life an evil?

F.: Let us suppose, without touching upon religion, that *both the universe and God are eternal.* The human thinking animal and the crawling reptile are both composed of base matter . . .

A.: What is fate? What is matter? Fate has no more meaning than chance.

F.: If we do not make God the author of this work, *evil is necessary* and becomes my lot. I shall not complain, therefore, when I see insolent crime in its cruel frenzy crushing the weak with unjust triumph.

A.: Is this a solution of the difficulty? What comfort is there in necessity?

F.: Doubtless a Creator should intervene; but God cannot lower himself to our level, *he confines his power to general laws.*

A.: How do you know this?

F.: God is only the preserver of this great whole . . .

A.: Why preserver if not creator? This is all arbitrary assertion. Accounts for nothing.

F.: Perhaps unmanageable matter, a rebel against his plans, *has been able to resist him.*

A.: Then he is not almighty.

F.: People continue to insist that we are happy; alas! I would it were so, but to prove it to me, cease weeping and let me hear no more sighs and moans.

A.: Life may be happy in general, notwithstanding a few sighs and tears.

F.: This is the truth. But some Oxford doctor, anathematizing me, will tell you that I am wrong; that he knows everything, and that, with the aid of science, he can crush the ignorance of a Pyrrhonian king.[31]

A.: Ah! Some shaft against doctors to be sure. But are doctors more ignorant or more dogmatical than philosophers and Pyrrhonian kings?

F.: I admit, I hate a harsh and gloomy doctor, who would have it that God had created mankind to burn in the pit where the evil spirit dwells.

A.: This hatred of doctors is as unjustifiable as my hatred of Pyrrhonian kings and Epicurean philosophers.

The parallel was too tempting to avoid, but Adams realized that he had said more than he intended. To make amends, in his next comment he admonished Frederick in a more respectful tone: "Great King! You should have learned of Pope, to wait the great teacher Death, and God adore." [32]

F.: Lively intemperance, with its curious spirit, believes that it can arrive at evidence by conjecture; but instead of reaching the truth, it goes astray and leads to a hundred absurdities.

A.: His conjectures are not more reasonable than that of the Manicheans.

F.: It is like the story of the poor man overwhelmed by misfortune; to escape want, he searched for riches, for a treasure supposedly hidden under his fireplace; but he was confounded when he found there nothing but rubbish (*fumier*).

A.: Throwing evil upon matter is indeed but fumier.

"Sur l'origine du mal" was dated from Breslau, December 28, 1761 —one of the most critical moments of the Seven Years' War. The Austrians were the masters of Saxony, and the Russians had just captured the Baltic city of Colberg, which placed them in possession of Pomerania. With his exhausted, dwindling army Frederick retired to the Silesian capital for the winter. He saw no hope anywhere. As had happened before, he contemplated suicide, and in this mood he wrote his poem. But soon brighter days followed. The Empress Elizabeth suddenly died, and her successor, Tsar Peter, was an ardent admirer of Frederick. From an enemy, Russia turned into an ally, and at Schweidnitz the Prussians once more defeated the Austrians. Europe was sick of the war, and within a year peace was signed.

To his nephews, the Princes Frederick and William of Brunswick, the King addressed another long poem. "Heaven, in spite of devotees, showers its favors upon the children of Epicurus," run two lines. Adams questioned them: "Is it so certain that devotees have less pleasure than Epicureans?" He liked best the elegy which Frederick wrote to his sister Amelia, the Protestant Abbess of Quedlinburg, wishing to console her for the loss of a friend. Man is born subject to hostile destiny, the King meditated. "No, man is governed by a Friend," Adams protested. "What misfortune have I not suffered! To what disaster, oh Heaven, have you not exposed me! A thousand times have I been drenched in tears . . . ," Frederick lamented. "This is pathetic and amiable," Adams sympathized.

Voltaire, too, found these verses touching. "They come from the soul," he wrote Frederick, "to which I have been attached for these thirty years, and shall remain so till the last moment of my life, in spite of all the harm which Your Majesty has done me . . ."

[VII]

The Communism of the Abbé de Mably

The Abbé de Mably preached communism on the one hand and the sanctity of property on the other. His paradoxical figure is all but forgotten today; yet his name was more often mentioned during the French Revolution than that of any other *philosophe* with the exception of Rousseau and Montesquieu.[1]

He died before the cataclysm began, but the journals of the Constituent and Legislative Assemblies are filled with references to him. In their struggle after the overthrow of the monarchy, Girondists and Jacobins constantly quoted his works, especially *De la législation* and *Des droits et des devoirs d'un citoyen*. However, it was during the Terror that he was most revered. Robespierre's Report of May 7, 1794, on the relation of religious and moral ideas to republican principles, show his complete dependence upon Mably.[2] Curiously enough, his prestige survived even the Thermidorian reaction. In 1795 his literary executors presented a set of the new fifteen-volume edition of his works to the Convention, the President of which expressed the hope that the gratitude of the people would place Mably "among the ranks of the benefactors of mankind." [3] But soon the Directory took over, anxious to finish with the Revolution. Babeuf's conspiracy—the first attempt to translate the communism of the moralists into reality—was quickly suppressed. In his defense before the high court of Vendôme, Babeuf himself described the *Manifeste des égaux* as a "chapter taken from Mably." [4]

Mably believed that equality of wealth was the most natural as well as the happiest state for mankind. His communism, however, was based almost entirely on ethical considerations, and he himself regarded its objectives as desirable but utterly unobtainable. Indeed, he thought it monstrous to trespass upon private property and class distinctions where they already existed. Consulted by the Poles about their new constitution, he advised them to set up a hereditary monarchy. There is a sharp division in Mably between the theorist and the practical man; but in his works this division is often blurred, one mood gliding imperceptibly into the other. This may also explain the fact that he was the favorite author of both Louis XVI and his executioners. Everyone took from Mably's works what suited his own beliefs most. He himself moved from one plane to another without any awareness of inconsistency.[5]

His socialism was certainly not the "scientific" socialism of later days. He speaks of self-interest as the foundation of his doctrine, yet he would have shrunk from a materialistic interpretation of history. He used "materialism" and "atheism" as interchangeable terms; and, convinced that neither public nor private morality was possible without belief in a Supreme Being, he hated atheists more than common malefactors. His communism was mainly derived from Plato,. whose *Republic* and *Laws* he apparently knew by heart; he only regretted that the common ownership of goods these works prescribed for warriors and office holders did not also apply to the whole population. Furthermore, he distrusted the Athenians because of their love of the arts. His ideal way of life was that of the Spartans, and his ideal statesman was Lycurgus; and he blissfully ignored the fact that Greek democracy was based on slavery. He had also learned many useful lessons from Locke and other English philosophers. A Puritan, he shares his isolation with Rousseau; and yet, like Rousseau, he was one of the truest representatives of his age.[6]

The duality of his work may to some extent be accounted for by the contrast between his early and later life. Born in 1709 at Grenoble, the son of a wealthy nobleman, he studied for the priesthood but refused to advance beyond the order of subdeacon. He first attracted notice by a comparative study of the Roman and French governments, and soon became a frequenter of the salon of Madame de Tencin (the mother of d'Alembert), to whom he was related. When in 1741 the Cardinal de Tencin was appointed Minister of State, she persuaded him to take Mably for his secretary. It was common knowledge during the next six years that the Abbé's mind was behind every important action of the Cardinal. He drew up the reports to the King's council, and the treaty with Prussia in 1743; and the negotiations of the Congress of Breda in 1746 were based on his memoranda. Then suddenly this brilliant phase of his career came to an end. He quarreled with the Cardinal and resigned his office at once.

From that time until his death at seventy-six Mably lived in complete retirement. Once the Maréchal de Richelieu, grandnephew of the great Cardinal, offered to secure his election to the Academy. Mably was so frightened that he ran to the Abbé de Condillac—his younger brother—begging him to forestall the calamity. Similarly, when considered for the position of tutor to the Dauphin, he made it clear that he would base the education of the future monarch on the principle that "kings were made for the people and not the people for the king." Naturally he lost the appointment, and with it the opportunity of molding the mind and character of Louis XVI.[7]

During the long years of his retirement Mably devoted himself entirely to the study of history, law, government, and, above all, morals. His first important book, published in 1748, was the *Droit publique de l'Europe*, which, translated into several languages, long served as a textbook in the universities. He wrote a volume on the history of the Greeks and one on that of the Romans; but his greatest historical work was his *Observations sur l'histoire de France*. Then he composed several books on the nature of law, and finally in 1776 *De la législation*, which contains a systematic presentation of his ideas on a righteous and puritan commonwealth. His *Des droits et des devoirs d'un citoyen*, an early work, was not published until the first year of the Revolution.

Adams first met Mably in December. 1782, at a dinner at the house of the Abbé de Chalut. "The Abbé de Mably," he noted in his Diary, "is very agreeable in conversation, polite, good-humored, and sensible; spoke with great indignation against the practice of lying, chicaning, and finessing in negotiations; frankness, candor, and probity were the only means of gaining confidence . . ." Two weeks later they met again: "Had more conversation with De Mably than at any time before," Adams recorded, adding, "He meditates a work upon our American Constitutions."[8] There were many more meetings, and within a year the Abbé published his *Observations sur les États-Unis d'Amérique*, in four letters addressed to Adams.

"I have read, Monsieur, with the greatest attention the various constitutions adopted by the United States; and since you wish it (*puisque vous le désirez*), I shall have the honor of communicating to you my impressions," the first letter, dated July 1783, begins. This introduction gave rise to an obstinate misunderstanding concerning the origin of the work. As Adams later explained, his request was "a mere civility," made after he had heard that Mably was contemplating a book on the American Revolution. When he had presented to the Frenchman his idea of how such a history should be written, the latter excused himself, saying that he would be dead long before he could assemble half the necessary material.[9] The Abbé, therefore, contented himself with a slender volume. Pessimistic over the future of America, he suggested that Congress should issue "a moral and political catechism" for use in schools. Adams actually did request the Abbé to prepare such a work; the latter, however, declined the honor.

Adams differed from Mably on most questions of government. In writing his *Defence of the Constitutions of America* he had him frequently in mind; in the very first sentence he mentioned him, with Turgot and Dr. Price, as one of the three great European writers who had criticized the American constitutions. Yet he respected Mably for his practical experience, placing him in a different category from that of Condorcet or the Duc de la Rochefoucauld. "I love the Abbé and revere his memory . . . ," he wrote shortly after his death.[10] Of all Mably's works, the *De la législation* interested him most. He read it in the original edition, first in 1791 and the second time, some fifteen years later at Quincy. In all, the volume contains no less than three hundred of his notes, and there is hardly a page without underscored passages. As usual, Adams spoke his mind freely. He found most of Mably's ideas fantastic, but was ready to applaud his condemnation of atheism. The chief trouble with Mably, he thought, was that he did not recognize the necessity of a balance between the aristocratic (the rich), democratic (the poor), and monarchical (the executive) forces. So Adams felt sorry for him. "My friend Abby, thou seest not in a true light the distemper nor the remedy," he summed up his opinion.

On the title page of the *Des droits et des devoirs du citoyen*, he wrote in a shaky hand: "Marmontel, at dinner with me, said 'De Mably n'a jamais écrit rien que des choses très communes et en style commun.' " To be sure, Mably's style is not "original." His works are concise and lucid in detached passages, but become rather tiresome with extended reading. Their simplicity was modeled upon Plato's *Dialogues*, without Plato's charm and genius to support the simplicity. He has also been denounced for his gloom; his best friends teased him for being "a prophet of misfortune." Yet he was not a mere visionary. He predicted the Revolution some thirty years in advance, and even prepared the draft of a new constitution.

The literature on Mably is surprisingly meager. His works have never been translated into English, and the *Encyclopaedia Britannica* does not even have a note about him. Yet, with all his shortcomings, he deserves attention. In his passionate criticism of society, he is an ancestor of all modern radicals.

2

An Englishman, a Swedish philosopher, and the author are guests in a château. While walking in the country, they fall into a discussion on government and society, the nature of happiness, and the duty of the legislator to foster the social virtues. On successive promenades they examine such further questions as the equality of goods, the origin of property, the laws needed to suppress avarice and ambition, the regulation of the legislative power, education in a republic, and the necessity of recognizing a Supreme Being. Their conversations fill the five hundred pages of Mably's *De la législation*.

The work, like Rousseau's *Discours sur l'inégalité*, is a sustained attack against those "contemptible philosophers who constantly extol luxury." [11] Of all his contemporaries, Mably hated Voltaire most; however, his main argument is against Bayle, Mandeville, and Melon. It was Bayle who wrote, "Preserve to avarice and ambition all their vivacity, exclude from them only theft and fraud, but otherwise encourage them with compensations: promise a pension to those who invent new manufactures or new means of enlarging commerce." Mandeville, with his doctrine of "private vices, public benefits," taught that the circulation of capital in connection with luxurious living stimulated progress. And Melon was one of the earliest political economists to explain the advantages of commerce.[12] Mably reasons doggedly against their ideas.

The Englishman reproaches the Swede for the decline of his country. Forty years ago Sweden reformed her constitution, and yet she is in no flourishing condition. Her commerce and finances are in ruins, and her administration is unsettled. How is it that Sweden, which for a century has played such an important part in the affairs of Europe, does not enjoy the same prestige today? "Your people should get rich," he advises his friend, "in order to regain their ancient reputation." In reply, the Swede delivers a long lecture on happiness.

The author listened eargerly—and so did Adams. Discovering at once that the Swedish philosopher was merely a literary invention to serve as Mably's mouthpiece, he addressed his remarks directly to the latter.

Mably: What would you think, Milord, if someone proved to you that *good politics are by no means distinguished by good morals?* [13]

Adams: This truth is not incompatible with his Lordship's maxims.

M.: I appeal *to the Spartans*, whom the Swedes would be happy to resemble.

A.: Aux diables!

M.: Proud of their poverty, temperance, their frugality, and their courage, they were happy . . . They *looked with pity* upon the other peoples of Greece . . .

A.: So do the savages of North America.

M.: You remember the story of the philosopher who, on entering the palace of a rich voluptuary, exclaimed, "How many things that I do not need!" *Was he not nearer to happiness than the possessor of these insipid and satiating superfluities?*

A.: Not at all.

M.: There are no good politics and no good laws in society, except those which conform to the intentions of *Providence*, which certainly *has not attached happiness to the injustices of ambition and avarice. Let us try, therefore, to understand these intentions, instead of studying how to satisfy our passions.*

A.: Excellent.

M.: By our poverty we can at least hope to make citizens, whereas you, while increasing your riches, produce only mercenaries; and great riches necessitate even greater, because *avarice is insatiable.*

A.: As passions, are not the love of glory, the love of country, the love of liberty, and the love of law insatiable too?

M.: I am not at all afraid of poverty, because I know that *poor citizens are more disposed to respect justice and law than rich citizens.*

A.: Douteux.

M.: With morals, *it is easy for me to imagine an order and discipline* which would create invincible armies.

A.: "The entire prosperity of every state is in the discipline of armies," said the King of Prussia. But neither morals, nor riches, nor discipline of armies, nor all these together, will do without a constitution.

M.: Besides, what advantage would your treasure be if you encountered a people who had *the courage to love poverty?*

A.: Chimera!

The Swede tries to convince the Englishman that only equality of wealth can preserve our peace of mind, for riches lead to idleness and to the pursuit of harmful pleasures; further, the rich want to usurp public authority, and the State will eventually fall victim to their despotism. The Englishman retorts that nature has endowed us with varying inclinations and unequal talents, and that society implies a subordination which is not compatible with equality:

M.: It is our education which is responsible for the unequal development of our abilities. In the crevices of yonder mountains, misery may be hiding a Horace, a Fersen, a Marlborough, an Aristides, an Epaminondas, or a Lycurgus.[14]

A.: But all men are not Horaces and Marlboroughs.

M.: It is no less easy to see how inequality of strength has helped to banish equality. *Has nature created Briarei,* men with a hundred arms to enthrall mankind?

A.: Yes! Every man of genius has more than an hundred arms! A figure, a face has a thousand arms.

M.: Nature may distribute her blessings unequally, but never in proportion to the monstrous differences which we see in the fortunes of men.

A.: This is giving up the argument

M.: We have not been created equal so that we should remain independent; but we have been born independent in order to be and remain equal.

A.: It is only in point of rights that men are born or created either equal or independent. All that he says upon this head is sophistry.

M.: As to subordination, the magistrates are not our superiors; it is we who *have placed* them in their office, which we might occupy in turn.

A.: Fiction.

M.: Why should *a subordination of that kind be opposed to the most complete equality?*

A.: Because inequality is not equality.

M.: The *Spartans* for six hundred years lived in complete equality . . .

A.: Sparta could not maintain its own population.

M.: We can find happiness only *in the common ownership* of goods . . .

A.: Stark mad.

How much better the poets whom Plato wanted to banish from his republic, the Swede continues, knew the human heart than did the legislators and most of the philosophers: they called those times when property was unknown the Golden Age. Far from regarding common ownership as a delusion, it is difficult to explain how people ever came to establish private property:

M.: One could understand it *if nature had made man avaricious and ambitious* in the same way as she made him sensitive to pity, anger, or friendship.

A.: Has not nature made men ambitious? Is not emulation natural? Man is more sensible to praise than to pity.

M.: Since there was no wealth, there should not have been any avarice.

A.: If avarice followed property, ambition preceded it.

M.: Some philosophers would like us to believe that we are born enemies, and that as soon as they begin to breathe men have the desire to war on one another.

A.: An innate passion for war and an innate passion for distinction are different things.

M.: Nothing was *easier* than to make people contented before the institution of property, for nothing was *easier* than to provide for their needs.

A.: Ask the sachems, ask the Indians.

M.: I could imagine the citizens divided into different classes: *the strongest* destined to cultivate the land, and the others working at useful arts.

A.: Who determines this?

M.: I see everywhere great public storehouses, in which the wealth of the nation is preserved . . .

A.: Poor Abby!

M.: To stop the complaints of the industrious, who would not care to work for useless people, it would be sufficient to accord them compensations and distinctions which would cause them to be looked upon as *the benefactors and fathers of their country*.

A.: This is the greatest of all inequalities.

The Swede, however, hastens to add that he does not dream of constructing a republic more perfect than Plato's, for the simple reason that the needed materials are lacking. His offer of happiness would be rejected with disdain. People have two passions equally masterful and lasting: Is a man only rich? He wants to be great. Is he only great? He wants to be rich. Is he rich and great? He wants to be richer and greater still. "Vrai," "Très vrai," Adams agreed. The legislator, therefore, must employ great tact:

M.: Remember how unhappy some of the ancient republics were, because in them *the rights of property were not held sacred.*[15]

A.: Thou shalt not steal, nor covet. Tho commandments are not sufficient to make property sacred.

M.: Every day people were demanding a new distribution of the land. There were despoiled citizens and enriched citizens . . . *and the State found itself divided into two republics.*

A.: And no arbiter between them.

M.: Monarchies have been exposed to innumerable disasters because the laws lacked force to protect property. Who does not know that most uprisings result from the rapine of princes, their ministers, and their favorites?

A.: The nobility alone in monarchies have made property secure.

M.: Today every law will be good, which will tend to deprive our passions of any means or any pretext for violating, even in the slightest degree, the rights of property.

A.: The balance alone can do this.

M.: It is not enough, my Lord, to restrain avarice; it is necessary to watch every step of ambition; for ambition is born with the inequality of fortune . . .

A.: The Abby has not seen the true source of the passions. Ambition springs from the desire of esteem and from emulation, not from property.

M.: Man's greatest blessing would be to see the multitude of laws with which they are harassed, fall into oblivion and contempt.

A.: Smart but not wise.

3

There follows a discussion of the laws necessary to repress avarice, or at least to prevent some of its evil consequences. The Swede maintains that laws cannot succeed in this respect, unless they begin by reducing the finances of the State. Such was the principle of Lycurgus, who has been blamed by certain "little people." "Grave coxcomb!" Adams retorted.

M.: The two kings, the senators, and the aphors—magistrates of *a rich republic*—would have doubted that it was compatible with their dignity to live in the simplicity prescribed by the laws.[16]

A.: Fire and water may live in peace when wealth and the republic of Sparta can be reconciled.

M.: In Switzerland the office-holders, restrained by sumptuary laws, do not feel the need of *a scandalous fortune.*

A.: Peace and no foreign ministers, no expense.

M.: In Rome, the sight of magnificent public edifices *aroused hitherto unknown desires and needs: a gross avarice which, masquerading as love of glory and country,* introduced an extravagant luxury that despised *both the ancient laws and the new regulations.*

A.: Neither the ancient laws nor the new regulations completed or preserved the balance of government.

M.: If there must be taxes, they should be assessed only on land. It is unjust that . . . the State should take back part of the wages that I have received *for cultivating or defending the lands which I do not own.*

A.: Life and limbs and liberty are to be defended as well as property.

The Swede is convinced that the payment of salaries to magistrates is most harmful. With many references to Roman history he hammers at the idea with all his might:

M.: Since the morality of the officials determines public morality, *I wish* that riches might not be the key to office . . .

A.: And men were different.

M.: Above all, I should want the law to forbid any emoluments attached to such offices.

A.: Franklin's hypocrisy. Marchamont Nedham's nonsense.

M.: Seeing in public offices only trouble, care, and glory, common souls would not dare to aspire to them; this was the strength and greatness of the Romans.

A.: While Rome had no property, their heroes were poor and proud; but as soon as she had property, laurel and oak would not do.

M.: If they had known our fees, pensions, and profits, every citizen would have believed himself worthy of the consulate or censorship. He would have hankered for them and thus made intrigue and corruption fashionable.

A.: Miserable commonplace.

M.: Honest people would have left the administration to seek happiness in retirement; and you know what it means to have officials *without virtue or talent.*

A.: Virtue and talents must have pay where there is property.

M.: People contend that magistrates must live with a certain pomp. But he must be a vile man, for whom valets, dazzling liveries, carriages, a palace, and a sumptuous table *are more important than his duties.*

A.: It is not because pomp touches him more than his duties, but because it touches the people more than his virtues.

M.: An infallible way to degrade our government would be to increase the salaries of our senators.

A.: The people had better pay them than let France pay them.[17]

The needs of the citizens, the Swede insists, should be reduced just as much as those of the State. You don't want me to covet the property of others? Then arrange your laws so that I may be content with a moderate fortune.

M.: There are two kinds of avarice: one is preservative, and the other acquisitive. The legislator will realize much of nature's intention when he has limited this passion to the merely preservative.[18]

A.: Whatever can be done to restrain avarice and encourage generosity with discretion should be done.

M.: People want to be happy "in style," for *they want their happiness to be noticed and possibly envied* . . .

A.: This is the genuine source of the passions.

M.: To remedy the misery of the poor through the folly of the rich is to repair a fault by a fault, that is, to create two faults.

A.: It would be better than that the poor should perish.

M.: The ancients were more sensible than we; in none of their writings will you find the praise of riches or the absurd apology for luxury.

A.: There is no need of elogiums on riches. The New Testament makes no elogium on them. An immoderate thirst of them is a vice, and is not honorable.

M.: When I consider how deadly their charming talents were for the Athenians, how the paintings, statues, and vases of Greece brought injustice, violence, and tyranny to Rome, I ask you what good can an Academy of Painting do for us?

A.: The people would not vote for consuls, praetors or questors who could not or would not entertain them with exhibitions of pictures, statues and vases.

M.: The more austere your regulations will be, the less dangerous will be the inequality of fortunes.

A.: The rich will hoard and the poor will suffer.

M.: Without blaming commerce for the superfluities that it makes necessary to us, is it not true that, being undertaken through cupidity, commerce is essentially contrary to the spirit of good government?

A.: Commerce is more in honor in America than in England or even Holland. Merchants give the tone. Is this a good symptom? Our first magistrates and citizens are merchants.

M.: In a well-governed State the law would dispose of the wealth of the deceased; or if it allowed him *the right to distribute his personal property*, it would be only to acknowledge the zeal and affection of his servants.

A.: The good Abby thought then of his faithful domestic, to whom he finally gave what he had.

A good government would continually break up and distribute the fortunes which ambition and avarice have amassed. This should be done, the Swede contends, through agrarian laws:

M.: Only the agrarian laws can help, *if it is true* that the rich will never believe that the poor have the same right to the administration of affairs.

A.: The people will never believe that a poor man has the same right as a rich one.

M.: It is argued that *agriculture would fall into neglect*. But what does this matter if it saves us from a greater peril? Let the harvests be less abundant, provided that *the republic is not divided into patricians and plebeians*.

A.: Make the harvest as poor as you will, the republic will still be divided into patricians and plebeians.

M.: In a country *where the people are divided into various classes* and enjoy different fortunes and different considerations . . .

A.: Where is the country that is not?

M.: . . . it is impossible to regulate avarice and ambition in the same way as in a democratic government. When Calvin retired to Geneva, he gave to all the citizens the same rights, the same prerogatives, *the same dignity*.

A.: But not the same property.

M.: However, he did not warn them against the lures of avarice, and before people were aware of it, the State *was split into rich and poor citizens*.

A.: And so it was at its establishment.

M.: Examine the laws of Lycurgus, and you will see that *he took the most effective measures to banish from Laconia the vices which were infecting Greece* . . .

A.: . . . and the happiness for which men are born.

4

Next to avarice, ambition is the worst enemy of both the State and the individual. Many revolutions have been brought to nothing, through failure to understand that it is futile to suppress avarice without also suppressing ambition: that saving the one means saving the other as well. But just as a State cannot value riches without encouraging its citizens to do so, the State's ambition also permeates the citizens. The law therefore, the Swedish philosopher continues, should rigorously proscribe this passion:

M.: Suppose the plebeians of Rome who withdrew to the Sacred Mount had allowed themselves to be seduced by the eloquence of Menenius Agrippa; and content with the abolition of debts, the opening of debtors' prisons, and the laws against the usury of the rich, had neglected to demand the election of tribunes? Is it not clear that they would have gained only a passing relief? [19]

A.: It seems impossible that a man who could write this should not understand the whole system of government yet.

M.: We Swedes did not possess the wisdom of the Romans. Having set limits to the royal authority, we thought that we had done enough. And so, for want of laws to restrain the citizens' avarice and ambition, our government received a shock before long.

A.: Faute of a balance to the avarice and ambition of the Senate or Diet.

M.: We diminished the royal prerogative; *we gave the prince very great dignity and very moderate power* . . .

A.: This was absurd. If power is not in proportion to dignity, dignity is only a snare to prince and people.

M.: Why were we not equally cautious regarding ourselves? *If a class had privileges which might incline the government toward aristocracy* . . .

A.: Excellent!

M.: . . . ought we not to remedy the condition? We must stop these abuses *by new laws.*

A.: What new laws?

M.: Let us not permit ourselves to love riches, if we do not want to be victims of ambition.

A.: Madness.

M.: We may be sure that those ambitious men who seek to acquire power through money will amply indemnify themselves for the advance they have made, if they succeed in securing authority . . .

A.: Nothing but balance can restrain these passions.

M.: I will tell you frankly, my Lord, that your constitution seems to me infinitely less secure than ours . . .

A.: What authority has 25 years of time given to this Swedish presumption? [20]

M.: Is it to prevent the King from being ambitious that you grant him *a part of the legislative power?* . . .

A.: This is pitiful ignorance and weakness.

M.: Your laws dealing with commerce are considered the most important ones; and all of them tend to make commerce very lucrative. *Where are your regulations against luxury?*

A.: Have as many regulations against luxury as you will, but without a balance they are idle.

The heroic qualities of Rome, the Swede points out, may also be found in Lacedaemon, which engaged only in defensive wars. "When did Lacedaemon love peace?" Adams wondered. An ambitious nation will acquire a certain harshness which will make its vengeance inhumanly cruel.

M.: What happened in Rome after the Punic Wars and the conquest of Asia Minor? If softness, intrigue, and falsehood do not gain the upper hand, there will arise a Marius, a Sulla, a Caesar, a Pompey, an Octavius; *and these ambitious men will lay the foundations for perpetual tyranny.*

A.: It was not these citizens who laid the foundation. They were laid in the constitution.

M.: From the cradle on, teach children to respect the defenders of their country. Next to justice, let valor be honored more than anything else . . .

A.: These things will excite pride and ambition and love of war in spite of all your philosophy.

M.: Our soldiers dishonor themselves and their victory *by despoiling their beaten enemies, even the corpses on the battlefield* . . .

A.: Vid. our treaty with Prussia.[21]

M.: May it never be permitted to carry war into the enemy's territory, under the pretext of getting a head start on him, or for any other reason whatever . . .

A.: Is it possible the Abby should think all this would do?

M.: Foreign possessions should be strictly forbidden. The experience of the ages teaches us that they are always a source of harm.

A.: I know not what to say to this.

M.: It is to this unfortunate case in carrying war into all parts of Europe that Spain owes her present feebleness and torpor. Would not France have been better off if Italy, the Empire, and the Netherlands had been closed to her forever?

A.: Certainly, if they had been shut also against other powers.

M.: However, the effect of the laws depends largely on the public officials. How will the legislator make sure that they are not abusing their authority? *By dividing the executive power into various portions and entrusting these to different citizens.*

A.: Oh blindness!

M.: One will oversee the other; *all will be warned continually by the presence of their colleagues that their power is limited.*

A.: Opposition, jealousy, rivalry, divisions, seditions, wars.

M.: If a magistrate is not content to be the agent of the law, obstacles on every side should force him to return to his duty.

A.: This rivalry should be between the legislative and executive.

M.: You do not have to fear the ambition of the office holders, if your laws constantly remind them that soon *they will find themselves in the class of ordinary citizens.*

A.: But if they are at the head of a party, that party will support them if the majority.

M.: If the law does not prescribe rigorous tests for the offices, men who have no claim to public esteem will take hold of the government.

A.: This deserves a great consideration.

M.: If the highest offices are filled by schemers and the lower ones by fools, the republic is certain to go to ruin. *Suppose there should then arise a daring man,* capable of profiting from this anarchy . . .

A.: There will always arise a Maelius, a Cassius, or a Manlius in such cases. The people will always look out for such a one and stir him up.

M.: One should have the courage to prefer a good constitution to these great men . . .

A.: What nation ever had such courage?

M.: But how can virtue and talent prevail when we allow avarice and ambition to stifle them?

A.: When was Rome free from these passions?

M.: Sparta never lacked useful talents, because she was poor, *because she loved her poverty* . . .

A.: Because she knew no better.

M.: In the condition in which most of the peoples of Europe are today, Providence would be wasting *a Lycurgus* on us.

A.: Lycurgus was his favorite, but Mahomet might have been with as much reason. Lycurgus had ambition for the blood of Hercules as much as W. Penn had of avarice for land.

The Swede pauses to demonstrate that, just as the vices of government corrupt its citizens, the vices of citizens corrupt the government. "There is a reciprocity here," Adams acknowledged.

M.: Too little attention is given to the interests of the multitude . . .[22]

A.: Ah! melancholy truth.

M.: Why does a legislator addressing the people always adopt the tone of a threatening despot? Why does he not sometimes show the gentleness of an indulgent father?

A.: But my friend Abby, thou seest not in a true light the distemper nor the remedy. This populace is forever seeking a protector against the gentlemen and sooner or later will have him.

M.: *Solon* required that candidates for public office own a certain amount of oil or wheat. It was a poor way to cure the Athenians of their vices—to make riches more necessary than virtue or talent.

A.: The only thing which could preserve Solon's constitution.

M.: I know of only one country where *everything* is for sale, where all the offices are tariffed, and where, nevertheless, one can always find excellent men for all parts of the administration.

A.: The executive in England is not yet so venal.

M.: Intrigue resembles the hydra of mythology—therefore, in filling offices I should prefer the method of the Swiss, who draw their bailiffs by lot.

A.: Is lot better than inheritance?

M.: I fear nothing so much as those ambitious men who, under the cloak of modesty, seem to keep themselves apart, while they fill the republic with their machinations.

A.: Even here there is danger.

M.: I wish our clergy, commons, peasants all might think that *the country belongs to them just as much as to the nobility, and aspire to the same dignities.*

A.: True.

M.: There should be no one who is not included in one of these orders—*a just balance among which is today the only kind of equality that can be established and preserved among men . . .*

A.: Very true.

M.: Despise, if you will, what is called the multitude, the dregs of the people . . .

A.: No. No.

5

The Swedish philosopher makes a thoroughgoing indictment of the English system, where the King has "the ridiculous right" of suspending the activities of the Lords and Commons which are supposed to balance him. "Your parliament, created to watch over the liberty of the nation," he tells the Englishman, "has betrayed it a hundred times, has indeed forged the chains for it." "Has the Diet, the Cortes, or the States General done less?" Adams parried.

M.: It is not because the authority of the Lords and Commons was equal to that of the King that you have shaken off your yoke; but because there was in Holland a Stadtholder, whose ambition was boundless and who had as much courage and spirit as James II had little.[28]

A.: This is not certain, nor probable. The nation would not have acquiesced.

M.: Why don't the English recognize that the unanimity of the three orders required to enact a law is extremely favorable to the King, since it empowers him to reject everything that he does not like, besides having so many means of rallying the Lords and Commons to his side?

A.: These ideas have unhappily prevailed in America, but are not right.

M.: As a result, the King of England cannot be punished if he violates his obligations, and order cannot be re-established except through civil war.

A.: Ministers are responsible.

M.: Unfortunately, laws have almost always been made at random; had they been the work of *reason*, they would have procured our happiness: being *the work of passion*, they have caused our misery.

A.: Law [is] always the work of passions when any passions are unlimited.

M.: Let us laugh at those sublime politicians who credit avarice and ambition with creating happiness, or who flatter themselves that they are making useful reforms by controlling these passions.

A.: Avarice and ambition unchecked will work ruin everywhere. Whether you leave avarice and ambition uncontrolled in the majority of a national assembly or of a senate or in a council or a king, ruin is equally certain.

By now the Englishman sees that all the wrongs of society are due to avarice and ambition. Adams was less convinced. "Has love no evil fruit? Has superstition, enthusiasm, has vanity none?" he asked. In his despair, the Englishman also believes that we are forever destined to be victims of our passions. The Swede does not deceive him by promising that a salutary revolution is as near as the economists think. And yet:

M.: It is comforting to hope that there may appear at last an inflexible and courageous legislator, who, without regard for our vices, will force us to be happy.[24]

A.: Necker, Fayette, Mirabeau, who?

M.: I shall not try to tell you, my Lord, that Gustavus Vasa, occupied with the public welfare, neglected his own interests. However that may be, *this prince combined in a single project his two designs: to restore his country's independence and to raise himself to the throne, assuring it also to his descendants.*[25]

A.: This project was as disinterested as that of Lycurgus or W. Penn.

M.: At the head of the Dalecarlian peasants he looked like one of them. Before appearing powerful, he wanted to be beloved. He knew that if the Swedes yearned for a long time to make him king, his fortune would be the more solidly established.

A.: Gustavus was a favorite character of General Gates, and Washington has read his life.

M.: Had he succeeded in shaking the empire of Christierne? *He still assumes the modest title of Administrator.*

A.: President.

M.: Sweden is a proof that nothing is impossible for a capable legislator; he holds our hearts and spirits in his hands; he can make us new men.

A.: This is more than Parliament can do, according to Coke.

One cannot read the following passage without thinking of World War II: "Let a hostile army land on the coasts of England, and I am convinced that the English would be enslaved beyond redemption. Accustomed only to civil functions, to commerce and agriculture, they would not consider their liberty more precious than their fortune, and after a mild resistance, would come to terms with the conqueror." Adams meditated: "Serious thought."

M.: It is thus that a law which makes us love money will lead us to a hundred vices; and that *the law which induces us to despise it will bring us a hundred virtues.*

A.: Such a law ought never to be made. Money ought never to be despised. Money is good, though honor is better and virtue best of all.

M.: Obstacles which may halt the activities of a bad government are desirable. I ask if the power of opposition which the tribunate introduced into Rome was not beneficial?

A.: Why are not three contrarieties still more beneficial?

M.: I should wish a kind of tribunate to be established in England, too, directed against those offshoots of the royal prerogative, which are incompatible with true liberty.

A.: The Abby mistakes.

M.: I should not even mind that the nobility abused its privileges more grossly, if I could hope that the other classes were wise enough to take effective measures, that is to say, establish perfect *equality*.

A.: This perfect equality can be established only by three branches and no more.

One of the obstacles to good government is the enormous size of modern states. The small republics of antiquity had a great advantage in this respect; their moderate wealth tempered the desires of the officials and citizens. "I deny the fact," Adams cut in, "the desires of the ancients were as immoderate as those of the moderns." The Swedish philosopher is more optimistic than the Englishman. He even thinks that a prince willing to give up some of his power might appear:

M.: Look at the history of Rome; seek the cause of that revolution which brought a new aspect to the republic, and you will find no other than *the love of liberty and law.*

A.: I should rather say than a mutual check of patricians and plebeians. The patricians loved not liberty or law better than before. The plebeians loved not liberty or law better than before, but neither could usurp so easily.

M.: And is the love of liberty and laws extinct in England? If you profit from the balance between an absolute monarchy and an outright republic which prevails among you in normal times *in order to diminish the royal prerogative imperceptibly*, you will see that you will lose those customs which appal you . . .

A.: This is not the secret. Reform the representation, and the prerogatives of the crown will not be too great. A reform of parliament would reform the manners.

M.: To safeguard rights in a large empire, *all that is necessary is to decentralize the State and turn the provinces into so many federated republics.*

A.: Short-sighted legislator.

M.: However, one must remember that laws in small republics have less stability. When all the citizens are assembled, the State has no check any more.

A.: The majority is omnipotent, but not omniscient.

M.: It is not the same in countries where the nation, being too large, meets only through its representatives; these diets are less capricious, because *they have a censor in the mass of the people watching them.*

A.: The majority of the deputies have commonly too much influence over the majority of the nation.

M.: Perhaps if the ancient republics had had a system of representation, *one would have to reproach democracy with fewer vices.*

A.: So thinks the National Assembly in 1791. But it is folly.

The first task of the legislator should be, the Swede maintains, to earn the respect and confidence of the people. However, it would be foolish of the legislator to ignore the fact that men can be moved only by their own advantages. "How is this to be reconciled to the fanatical ideas of love and liberty, country, etc. in other parts of this book?" Adams asked.

M.: The laws should teach the citizen to be content with little; for the less men are occupied with their domestic fortunes, the more interested they are in the public good.

A.: This remark is doubtful.

M.: In Rome the censors continually kept their eyes open for insidious vices. *Light penalties*, such as depriving a knight of *his ring or horse*, closing the door of the senate to a senator, or demoting a citizen to a less honorable class, were sufficient for a long time to save the City from grave misdemeanors.

A.: These were no light punishments. It can only be in times of ignorance that a censor can exist. What would our newspapers make of such an officer?

The Englishman, with the zeal of a neophyte, blames all the ills of society upon kings. Proud of their power and accustomed to despise their subjects, they do not believe that the government of their empire is worth thinking about. "I doubt whether kings deserve all this satire; they are like other men," Adams protested.

Education plays an extremely important part in a republic, the philosopher maintains. Even in their games the young should be taught to be just and generous toward one another. It is our fault if we do not find in the heart of a child that love of glory which nature has planted there. "Is not this love of glory the mother passion?" Adams inquired. The legislator may rightly be afraid of the excesses of youth; but he should also know that young people who are too prudent will later become mediocre men and lax magistrates. "This is a commonplace observation but its truth may be doubted," Adams remarked.

M.: When my blood is boiling with ardor in my veins, do not expect all my steps to be wise and measured; it is for the law to guide me towards prudence.[26]

A.: This idea of boiling blood misled the Abby in his treatise on morals in his latter days, and disgraced him in some degree.[27]

M.: How well did the rules of gymnastics prepare youth for order, obedience, work, and temperance!

A.: Good. Our custom of wrestling ought to be preserved.

M.: It is regrettable that our young men are allowed to travel before they have learned to despise the luxury of our neighbors. How right Lycurgus was in forbidding the Spartans to communicate with other Greeks!

A.: Is it such a felicity to be confined in a cage, den or cave? Is this liberty?

Adams agreed that morals should be no different for the rich and the poor, the great and the small, the magistrate and the simple citizen; that the more the young people know of the causes of revolutions, the more they will detest that ruinous policy which holds that it is useful to be unjust, deceitful, and wicked:

M.: Every society which has not yet reached *the highest degree of perfection*—that is to say, which has not yet established *the most perfect equality among its citizens; or at least among their different classes*—necessarily experiences a thousand agitations . . .

A.: In no sense can this equality be established but by a balanced government.

M.: Citizens have made use of the vices of the government in order to advance their private fortunes; and since the laws imperceptibly lost their authority, the magistrates abused their power and the republic became the prey of despotism and anarchy.

A.: Good and true.

M.: The law should require complete equality in the education of children. When they are convinced *that nature has not made nobles and commoners, rich and poor* . . .

A.: Nature has made some strong, some weak, some handsome, some ugly.

M.: . . . *when they live under the laws of democracy, they will be less tempted to create orders of patricians and plebeians.*

A.: Abby, thou comprehendest not.

M.: I wish the great to be taught that *they lose nothing by making themselves beloved and being considerate toward their inferiors.*

A.: Good.

M.: And I wish the latter to know that it is enough for them to have talent and virtue to be sure of the *esteem* of the public.

A.: But will it be equal to the esteem of those who have virtue and riches too?

The philosopher insists on the necessity of recognizing a Supreme Being—a doctrine which Robespierre later enacted into law. Adams heartily endorsed the Abbé's condemnation of atheism. In a single chapter, he jotted down the words "good" and "true" no less than fifteen times. These are the statements which, checking each separately, he approved: How can the citizens be convinced that the guilty will never escape punishment if they forget that they are under the eye of a Supreme Being? . . . If there is no God, there is no morality . . . The philosophy of atheism, or materialism, produces hypocrites and scoundrels . . . Even the savages will distinguish between lying and speaking the truth, between helping one's neighbor in danger and assassinating him . . . "Between exterminating Rohillas and scaring Americans," Adams contributed.[28]

M.: If I were a prince, I would give one of my provinces to the atheists of the world that they might establish there *Bayle's marvelous republic.*

A.: Very good.

M.: These philosophers will probably prepare *a catechism* setting forth their doctrines. Having read it, *the national assembly* will no doubt pass a law ordering fathers to teach their children that there is no God . . .

A.: The National Assembly has not done this yet.

M.: . . . and that the ignorant have called by this frightful name a certain *movement*, a certain *harmony*, by virtue of which all parts of the universe act together, defend and destroy themselves in turn.

A.: Nonsense certainly.

M.: Providence would then be only an empty word, invented by foolish people to express a chimera which does not exist.

A.: What a catechism!

M.: It will be necessary to repeat again and again to children that *human wisdom consists of avoiding sorrow and finding pleasure;* that the law of nature is no more than self-love, by which *each individual regards himself as the center, object, and end of all things* . . .

A.: This is admirable!

And so the Abbé lashes the atheists with his irony. Today, he writes, they are compelled to conceal their philosophy; in their own republic, however, they will be able to let down the barriers. Let it come then, this republic of atheists! Before the fourth generation, it will pass on to deism. Rather than worship nothing, they will raise altars to Jupiter, Venus, Apollo, to the vegetables in our gardens and the poultry in our farm-yards . . . Adams enjoyed it all hugely.

In some respects, *Des droits et des devoirs du citoyen* is Mably's most remarkable work. Written thirty years before the Revolution, its predictions proved so accurate that there were charges of forgery when his literary executors published it in 1789. Some of the articles of Mably's proposed constitution, which fill the last part of the book, aroused Adams's angry opposition. Thus the "incontestable principle" that public officials should have no part in legislation he branded as "despicable ignorance." Who does not see, the author asks, that their share in the legislative powers makes it possible for the Kings of England to evade the law? "Without this," Adams replied, "the two Houses would soon usurp the executive power. The Commons would soon dismiss lords and judges, and compel Cromwell or Napoleon to send them packing."

[VIII]

Turgot's Attack on the American Constitutions

Of all the French thinkers of the eighteenth century, Adams regarded Turgot as the most dangerous adversary of good government —dangerous precisely because of the respect which his character and achievements justly commanded. It was a letter by the former Comptroller General of Louis XVI to Dr. Richard Price, the English dissenting minister, criticizing the American constitutions, which prompted Adams's *Defence of the Constitutions of America*. The title page itself states that the work was written "against the attack of M. Turgot"; and the name of the French philosopher and statesman appears innumerable times throughout the book. By answering Turgot's objections, Adams wanted to combat his influence which, somewhat rashly, he also connected with the recent disturbances in America.

Adams met Turgot the day after his arrival in Paris. On April 9, 1778, he wrote in his Diary: "Dr. Franklin presented to me the compliments of M. Turgot, lately comptroller of the finances, and his invitation to dine with him. Went with Dr. Franklin and Mr. Lee, and dined in the company of the Duchess d'Enville, the mother of the Duke de la Rochefoucauld, and twenty of the great people of France." One would think that the dinner was at Turgot's home; but "the magnificence of the house, gardens, library, furniture, and the entertainment of the table" which amazed the visitor from Quincy may indicate that it was to the palace of the Duchess, his close friend, that Turgot had invited his guests. In any case, Adams was impressed by him. "M. Turgot has the appearance of a grave, sensible, and amiable man," he thought.[1]

Turgot and his circle were deeply interested in events in America. Some of the latter were contributors to the *Affaires de l'Angleterre et de l'Amérique,* a magazine devoted to information about the war, which Franklin, realizing the importance of public opinion, helped to edit.[2] One of them was the Duc de la Rochefoucauld, who made for the magazine a French translation of the six American state constitutions—those of Pennsylvania, New Jersey, Delaware, Maryland, Virginia, and South Carolina—that had been adopted so far. They were published, in a pirated edition, in the latter part of 1778 in a small volume entitled *Recueil des lois constitutives des colonies angloises.* "These constitutions seem to me the finest monuments of human wisdom, representing the purest democracy that has ever existed," the introduction by "Regnier" began.[3] The *Mercure de France* greeted the book as a landmark in the history of philosophy. "The legislators of Pennsylvania," it wrote, "should be placed as far above Lycurgus and Solon, as our century is above that of Lycurgus and Solon." [4] It should be noted that only the constitutions of Pennsylvania and South Carolina were founded on the unicameral system. The public hardly differentiated between the two kinds of constitutions; the *philosophes* however did, and their dislike of the bicameral system was expressed in Turgot's letter to Dr. Price.[5] The letter was written on March 22, 1778, but it was first published in 1784 in Dr. Price's *Importance of the American Revolution.*

By the spring of 1778 the short but glorious ministry of Turgot was a thing of the past. For thirteen years he had served as intendant of Limousin, establishing a record of public service which could hardly be paralleled in his time. A contributor to the *Encyclopédie,* he was one of the *philosophes,* the most persuasive exponent of the physiocracy of Quesnay and Gournay.[6] The suppression of military requisitions, a more equitable system of taxation, extensive road building, the foundation of boards of charity, and the obligation of landowners to provide for their tenants till the next harvest were among his chief reforms. His circulars to subordinates and his reports to the Cabinet were each one penetrating essays, imbued with warm concern for the welfare of the people. His appointment to the Cabinet in July 1774 caused great excitement among the liberals, while the simple folk of Limousin celebrated masses for his success. With immense effort Turgot undertook the reformation of the economic life of the country. Within a few months he had restored free trade in grain and other foodstuffs, improved communications, given the right of transatlantic commerce to every port, and diminished the deficit to the point where the Dutch bankers were offering loans at four per cent. His measures, however, provoked bitter antagonism. The courtiers hated him for the abolition of their sinecures, the Parliaments for his disregard of their prerogatives, and the clergy for his counsels of religious tolerance. But Turgot went ahead with feverish zeal. In January 1776 he submitted several new edicts to the King, the most important of which were the suppression of the *corvées* (forced labor) and the abrogation of the *jurandes* (monopolies of guilds and trade corporations). In spite of the opposition of the other ministers, Louis accepted the projects. "The more I think of it," he wrote to Turgot, "the more I repeat to myself that you and I are the only ones who really love the people." [7] By an act of *lit de justice* he had the edicts formally registered. [8] Turgot's enemies decided on a showdown. Letters in which he had supposedly disparaged the King and Queen were forged to compromise him. The King vacillated and finally, on May 12, 1776, dismissed him. The *philosophes* were dismayed. "I am terrified," Voltaire wrote, "nothing is left for me but to die now that Turgot has lost his place." And he composed a poem, *L'Épitre à un homme*, exalting him as "the kind philosopher, the citizen-minister who searched for the truth only to do good." [9] "All I wish, Sire," Turgot himself wrote the King, "is that you may always believe my vision was wrong and the dangers I pointed out to you were chimerical . . ." Within three months, the *corvées* and the *jurandes* were reëstablished, the fiscal and commercial measures revoked, and corruption was flourishing more openly than ever. No reform was attempted again until the National Convention took summary action on August 4, 1789. The futility of Turgot's heroic efforts is looked upon today as the most convincing proof that the Revolution was inevitable.

Turgot's letter was confidential, but by 1784, three years after his death, Dr. Price felt free to publish it with his own essay. [10] Adams read the English clergyman's advice to the Americans while still at Auteuil. [11] His acknowledgment of the copy sent him by Dr. Price was a typical Adamsian attempt at graciousness, never entirely free from pugnacity. "I think it may be said in praise of the citizens of the United States," he wrote, "that they are sincere inquirers after truth in matters of government and commerce; at least that there are among them as many, in proportion, of this liberal character, as any other country possesses." [12] He promised to write again. However, it was not Dr. Price's treatise but Turgot's letter which excited him; he made notes only on the financial sections of the first, whereas he discussed the second from beginning to end.

Challenging almost every one of its statements, he made some forty-five comments on the letter. Turgot's chief demand, the collection of all authority into one center, that of the nation (*"ramener toutes les autorités à une seule, celle de la nation"*), appeared to him extremely vague, and the greatest "proof of ignorance." He respected Turgot, yet recognized in the letter that "headlong spirit of system and enthusiasm" which led to his downfall.[13] He insisted upon reading it as meaning that power must be not only vested in but also exercised by a single assembly—something which was far from Turgot's mind.[14] And when the French statesman reproaches the new states for not having separated legislation carefully enough from administration, Adams, instead of trying to understand him, thought that he had caught him in a contradiction. On the other hand, being brought up in the tradition of New England town meetings, he rightly scoffed at Turgot's presuming to give instruction on local assemblies.

So important did he consider these comments that he showed them to Franklin, who had them copied and bound into his own volume. Adams's copy is lost, but Franklin's turned up at an auction in New York in 1856, and was acquired by Charles Francis Adams.[15] In view of Adams's preoccupation with Turgot's ideas, his notes on the famous letter assume special significance.

2

Turgot's letter was provoked by a passage in Dr. Price's *Additional Observations on Civil Liberty*, published in 1777. The Englishman referred to Turgot's administration and, after eulogizing his noble purposes and extraordinary achievements, remarked that his "want of address" was one of the causes of his dismissal from power.[16] Turgot, hurt by the censure, informed the author of the true reasons for his fall. Dr. Price omitted the offending sentence from the second edition of the pamphlet and sent a copy, through Franklin, to the statesman.

It is with thanks for this courtesy that Turgot's letter begins. He reflects further upon his alleged tactlessness (*maladresse*), assuring Dr. Price that the political maturity of the French is fully equal to that of the English—as was proved by the latter's "absurd project" of subjugating America:

Turgot: I might have merited this imputation if you had meant no other want of address than incapacity to unravel the threads of those intrigues that were employed against me, by people much more adroit in such matters than I am, or ever shall be . . .[17]

Adams: The cause of Mr. Turgot's dismission was not merely the want of skill to unravel intrigues: those intrigues were excited, encouraged, and attended with success by that headlong spirit of system and enthusiasm which appears in radiant distinct characters in this Letter. He had an honest heart and great theoretical knowledge; but was not a judicious, practical statesman.

T.: But I thought that you imputed to me the want of address of having deeply offended the public opinion of my nation; and in this respect, I believe, you did justice neither to me nor to my country, where there is much more enlightenment than is generally supposed among you . . .

A.: This is very true. The French character in arts, science, and arms is very much, and very unjustly, as well as illiberally undervalued in England.

T.: I judge thus by the infatuation of your nation on the absurd project of subjugating America, until Burgoyne's adventures began to open their eyes. I judge thus because of the system of monopoly and exclusion which prevails among all your political writers on commerce, except Mr. Adam Smith and Dean Tucker [18]—a system which has been the very reason of your separation from your colonies.

A.: The system of monopoly and exclusion here meant is probably the Navigation Act. This system is not peculiar to England: France, Spain, Portugal, Holland and all other nations practice it, at least with regard to their colonies. It is not to be doubted that the abolition of it in all nations would be a blessing to mankind: but it is a question whether one nation who should abolish it, while the rest maintain it, would not be ruined by their liberality. National pride is as natural as self-love, or family pride, the pride of one city, county, or province, or the esprit de corps of an army, navy, an ecclesiastical order, a body of merchants or tradesmen, farmers, or comedians. It is, at present, the bulwark of defense to all nations. When it is lost, a nation sinks below the character of man.

The French statesman is surprised at the indifference which English authors have shown in the past twenty years toward the science of government; at their treating the question of the rights of nations and individuals as "vain metaphysics." [19] How did this come about? Is it because their condition has not been as bad as that of other nations that they have persuaded themselves it has been perfect?

T.: How is it that you are about the first among your men of letters to expose the fallacy of that notion, harped upon by the most republican writers, that liberty consists in being subject to laws alone, as if a man who is oppressed by an unjust law could be free?

A.: Republican writers contend that liberty consists in being subject to equal laws only. If any have omitted the word *equal,* they have supposed that a free people would make no other but equal laws.

T.: This would not be true even supposing that all laws were the work of the assembled nation; for, beyond all, the individual has also his rights, of which the nation cannot deprive him, except by violence and an unlawful use of the general power.[20]

A.: Laws may be unjust; the public will is not infallible. But personal liberty must be restrained in some cases, so must property.

T.: It is likewise strange that it should not be held a common truth in England that one nation has never any right to govern another nation . . . and that of all tyrannies, the tyranny of a people is the most cruel and the most intolerable, the one which leaves the fewest resources to the oppressed nation. For, after all, a despot is restrained by a sense of his own interest, he is checked by remorse or by public opinion, but the multitude never calculates, is checked by no remorse . . .

A.: This is too general. The multitude in Rome calculated and were checked by remorse, more than 600 years. Multitudes in all free cities and republics, while uncorrupted, calculate and blush. The multitudes in monarchies are no true similitudes of multitudes educated in virtuous republics.

T.: Recent events are a terrible commentary on your book for the English nation! The fate of America is already decided—she is independent now for ever.[21] But will she be free and happy?

A.: Yes.

T.: Can this new people placed so advantageously to give the world the example of a constitution under which man may enjoy all his rights, exercise all his faculties, and be governed only by nature, reason, and justice—can they form such a constitution?

A.: The new Jerusalem, the Kingdom of the Just, if it is to exist upon earth, is not yet to be built. Knowledge and virtue must become more general through the world than they are yet, even in America, before this ravishing scene can be realized or exist anywhere but in imagination.

T.: Can they establish it upon a never-failing foundation, and guard against every source of division and corruption which may gradually undermine and destroy it?

A.: No.

And here begins Turgot's criticism of the new constitutions of the American states, which is the crux of his letter. Turgot found the bicameral system contrary to the principles of democracy. His letter to Dr. Price was confidential, but it is most unlikely that his friends were ignorant of it. They, too, vehemently opposed the division of the legislative power into three branches, and extolled Franklin for having founded the constitution of Pennsylvania upon a single assembly.[22] This was what Adams, who saw nothing but bloodshed and chaos as a resul' of concentrating all power in one authority, set out to combat in his *Defence*.

T.: I confess that I am not satisfied with the constitutions which have been formed by the different states of America up to this time.

A.: This Letter, with all his real merit, demonstrates that he was no judge of a good constitution: it was a subject he had not studied, and he had not practice and experience enough in the rest for such a work as the formation of a government.

T.: It is with reason that you reproach the State of Pennsylvania for exacting a religious test from members of the house of representatives. The case is even worse in other states; there is one (I believe, the Jerseys) which requires a declaration of faith in the divinity of Jesus Christ.[23]

A.: This enmity to test has my most hearty good wishes and prayers. I would try the experiment whether a state can exist without a shadow of a test.

T.: I observe that most of them imitate, without any real necessity, the customs of England. Instead of collecting all authority into one center, that of the nation, they have established different bodies; a body of representatives, a council, and a governor, because there is in England a house of commons, a house of lords, and a king.

A.: Is it possible that the writer of this paragraph should have ever read Plato, Livy, Polybius, Machiavel, Sidney, Harrington; or that he should ever have thought of the nature of man or of a society? What does he mean [by] collecting all authority into one center? What does he mean by the center of a nation? Where would he have the legislation placed? Where the execution? Where the decision of controversies? Emptier piece of declamation I never read: it is impossible to give a greater proof of ignorance.

T.: They endeavor to balance these different powers, as if this equilibrium, which in England may be a necessary check to the enormous influence of royalty, could be of any use in republics founded upon the equality of all the citizens . . .

A.: Is it possible that any good government should exist without an equilibrium?

T.: . . . and as if establishing different orders of men were not a source of divisions and disputes.

A.: Would he have no different orders?

T.: In attempting to prevent imaginary dangers, they create real ones; and in their desire to have nothing to fear from the clergy, they unite them by a common proscription.

A.: He is right. The clergy ought not to be excluded.

T.: The clergy are dangerous only when they exist as a distinct body in the state, and think of themselves as possessing special rights and interests and a religion "established" by law . . . as if men had a right to regulate the conscience of others . . .

A.: The rights of conscience are original rights and cannot be alienated; they are the first rights and prescribe the first duties of man, and should be explicitly reserved out of every social compact.[24]

Next Turgot deprecates the vagueness of state powers and discusses the uses of local assemblies. The views of the statesman who prepared the plan of a new constitution for France based entirely upon the clear definition of the spheres of power of the town, county, and provincial assemblies should have deserved attention. However, in making these comments in 1785, Adams did not know of Turgot's vast project. The French statesman's *Mémoire sur les municipalités*,[25] beginning with the bold statement, "The cause of the trouble, Sire, is that your nation has no Constitution at all . . .," was composed in the fall of 1775, but it was never submitted to the King and was first discussed by Condorcet, in his *Vie de Turgot*, in 1786.[26]

T.: I do not think they have been careful enough to reduce the affairs with which the state governments are charged to the smallest possible number; nor to separate the objects of legislation from those of the general or local administration . . .

A.: This idea is totally repugnant to what he said against the equilibrium.

T.: . . . nor to establish permanent local assemblies . . .

A.: Here he supposed the Americans had no laws but the little volume of constitutions then published. They have town meetings and courts of session enough.

T.: . . . which, by discharging almost all the functions in the detail of government, would relieve the general assemblies from attending to these, and thus deprive their members of every means of abusing a power which should be applied only to general objects.

A.: The legislative assemblies in free governments will always be sought as a school, or as a theater, to learn or to display accomplishments, to acquire the public confidence and a reputation. Administration will look in this place for men to fill offices. You cannot deprive the members of the means, as long as the assembly is respected and has anything to do, nor of the desire of acquiring offices, employment, profits, power, etc. Wherever these desires are, there will be excesses.

T.: I do not find that they have attended to the great distinction . . . between land-holders and those who are not land-holders; to their interests, and consequently to their different rights . . .

A.: These things were all settled by ancient laws in the several states.

T.: No fixed principles of taxation have been established . . . Each state may maintain an interest contrary to that of the other states.

A.: This is a great point and a very knotty one.

T.: They all suppose to have a right to regulate commerce . . . So far are they yet from realizing that the law of complete freedom of commerce is the corollary of the right of property; so deep are they still immersed in the mist of European illusions.

A.: The right of property is here carried a great length. It might as well be said that any exemption from taxes is a corollary from the right of property. Can we say that government had no right to regulate the commerce of individuals? Americans are, no doubt, involved in the mist of many European illusions; but I am not clear that this is so universally an illusion. An enemy to embargoes, prohibitions, exclusions, etc. in general, I cannot swear that they are always unlawful or impolitic.

3

The *Recueil des lois constitutives des colonies angloises* also contained a translation of what purported to be the Articles of Confederation, "resolved upon and signed in Congress, at Philadelphia, on October 4, 1776." It was reprinted from the fifteenth number of the *Affaires de l'Angleterre et de l'Amérique*, where it had been presented as a great "scoop." [27] In a later issue,[28] the correspondent, "un Banquier de Londres," proudly boasted: "I do not know whether the British government was informed of the document which is now spread all over Europe; but it seems to have produced in London the same sensation as everywhere else . . ." [29]

The "Articles" which appeared in the *Affaires* and subsequently in the *Recueil,* was a draft presented to the Committee at Philadelphia on August 20, 1776. Eighty copies were printed originally, one for each member of Congress, all of whom were enjoined not to furnish anyone with information about it.[30] Reading the *Recueil,* Adams of course recognized that what appeared there was not the final Articles of Confederation. "This is false," he noted in his copy, "the Confederation was never signed nor resolved in Congress. But another very different passed in Congress in November 1777." [31]

The defects of the draft of the Articles of Confederation, which he read, were glaring to Turgot, accustomed as he was to a supreme central authority. But he concentrated chiefly on two aspects of the document: a *philosophe,* he admonished the new republics against narrow nationalism, and, an apostle of *laissez faire,* he condemned the setting up of commercial barriers:

T.: In the general union of the states I do not observe a coalition, a fusion of all the parts, to form a homogeneous body. This is only a jumble of communities too discordant, and retaining a constant tendency to separation, because of the diversity in their laws, customs, and opinions . . .

A.: Americans must consider more soberly than Mr. Turgot did what is practicable and what is not. One homogeneous body cannot be made out of such heterogeneous parts scattered over such an immense continent. The parts are too distant as well as unlike.

T.: It is only a copy of the Dutch Republic; and the latter had nothing to fear, as the American Republic has, from the future possible increase of some of her provinces.

A.: The Dutch Republic had infinitely more to fear from the disproportionate grandeur of Holland than the American has from the possible increase of any one of the provinces.

T.: All this edifice has been hitherto supported upon the erroneous foundation of the most ancient and vulgar policy . . .

A.: The Americans had not studied Dr. Quesnay.

T.: . . . upon the prejudice that nations and states, as such, may have an interest distinct from that which individuals have in order to be free . . .; an interest, not in buying foreign merchandise, but in forcing the foreigner to consume their produce and manufactures; an interest in possessing vaster territories . . . in inspiring other nations with awe, and gaining an ascendancy over them in the glory of arts, sciences, and arms.

A.: This policy is so vulgar, that is, so consonant with the feelings of men, that it will be long before it can be fully eradicated. Principles more liberal may become general and they cannot be too much recommended and inculcated. But it is a question whether they can be adopted by one nation without reserve, before they become so general that several nations shall be ripe to adopt them.

T.: Some of these prejudices are fomented in Europe, for the ancient rivalry of nations and the ambition of princes compel every state to keep up an armed force . . .

A.: The ambition of princes is the ambition of nations. They are stimulated by the cries and ardor of the people and are forced away by the public passion and opinion.

T.: America is likely to enjoy, for a long time, the good fortune of having no external enemy to dread, provided she is not divided within herself.

A.: America will have external enemies to dread longer than seems to be here supposed. This may be no harm, for, when she has no enemy, she will be in danger of dividing.

T.: She should appreciate, therefore, at their real value, these presumed interests, these sources of discord which alone are likely to threaten her liberty. By that sacred principle which considers freedom of commerce as a consequence of the right of property, all the presumed interests of national commerce vanish. The desire to possess more or less territory is canceled by the principle that "a territory does not belong to nations, but to the individuals who are proprietors of the lands."

A.: I beg leave to propose that the whole earth should be divided into independent republics of six miles square; that wars should forever cease, commerce be free as light and air, as well as religion; that all men should be wise and virtuous; no more jealousy, envy, avarice or ambition. Amen.

T.: There can be no interest in being feared . . . when one is in a situation in which he cannot be attacked by a considerable force with any hope of success.

A.: When the American states are in a situation not to be attacked, they will have no interest in being feared.

T.: The glory of arms is not worth the happiness of living in peace.

A.: Very true.

T.: The glory of arts and sciences belong to every man who wishes to take part in it. There is ample harvest here for the whole world. The field of discovery is boundless, and all profit by the discoveries of all.

A.: This honor will not prevent men from priding themselves in the glory of a country man.

In advising the American states to form a closer union, the former Comptroller General of France is well aware of the difficulties confronting them:

T.: I imagine that the Americans are not as aware of these truths as they ought to be in order to insure the happiness of their posterity. I do not blame their leaders. They had to provide for the necessity of the moment by a union such as this, against a present and most formidable enemy.

A.: Their leaders were indeed to be pitied: forced on an enterprise against their wills, unprovided in all respects, and the route as unprepared as they.

T.: There was no time to think of correcting the errors of the constitutions and deciding upon the composition of the various states . . .

A.: This is reasonable enough.

T.: . . . but they ought to beware of perpetuating these errors, and ought to endeavor to harmonize the opinions and interests, relating them to uniform principles, in all their provinces.

A.: Uniform principles would be very desirable.

T.: To accomplish this, they have great obstacles to surmount: In Canada, an order of Roman Catholic clergy and a body of nobles.[32] In New England, the still existing spirit of a rigid Puritanism, which is said to have been always somewhat intolerant. In Pennsylvania, a large number of inhabitants holding it as a religious principle that the possession of arms is unlawful . . . In the Southern colonies, a too great inequality of fortune, and particularly the presence of the many blacks, whose slavery is incompatible with a good political constitution, and who even if emancipated would cause great embarrassment by forming a second nation in the same state.

A.: To this may be now added an Order of Cincinnatus which will do us more harm than the Canadian clergy and nobles, the north-east puritanical spirit, the Quakers' pacific principles, or the Negroes in the South. There is too great an inequality of fortune in all the States; but how to find a remedy? The inequality of the Order of Cincinnatus is, however, more pernicious than all this inequality of fortunes.[33]

T.: In all the colonies, they have to surmount various prejudices; a vanity in those which think themselves to be the most powerful; and the wretched symptoms of national pride.

A.: Did Mr. Turgot suppose it possible to eradicate national pride? Or that it would be safe, if practicable, for one nation to eradicate it, unless all did?

Reflecting on the whole section, Adams added:

"In short, liberty has so many enemies to encounter, all at once or one after another, that it is, or at least has been, always overcome. The military spirit, the religious or rather the ecclesiastical spirit, the commercial spirit, the spirit of families, and the spirit of arts and sciences—all these arising from the strength of human passions, imaginations and prejudices, the imperfection of human knowledge, and the weakness of reason—are constantly warring against liberty."

4

It is agriculture, not war, that Turgot recommends to the Americans for their development. They must not neglect the immense territories to the West, otherwise their exiles and fugitives, allying themselves with the savages, will take possession of the land and—lurid fantasy of a European!—"will ravage America as the Barbarians of the North ravaged the Roman Empire." But he hopes for the best:

T.: The colonies close to the frontier will be more inured to war than the others, and this inequality in military strength will prove a terrible spur to ambition.. The remedy for this inequality would be a standing army, to which every state should contribute in proportion to its population.[34]

A.: A standing army, instead of being a remedy, would increase the danger by increasing the inequality.

T.: But the Americans . . . dread nothing so much as a standing army. They are wrong. There should be nothing easier than to combine a standing army with the militia, in such a manner as to improve the militia and gain additional security for liberty.

A.: This Letter is a mass of wild, inconsistent reveries and paradoxes.

T.: There are plenty of difficulties; and perhaps the secret interests of powerful individuals will be joined to the prejudices of the multitude to frustrate the efforts of the truly wise and good citizens.

A.: The Order of Cincinnatus is an horrid proof and instance of this.

T.: It is impossible not to pray that this people may arrive at all the prosperity of which they are capable. They are the hope of mankind. They may become a model to it . . .

A.: Mr. Turgot is very good.

T.: They must prove to the world, by deeds, that men can be free and yet peaceful . . . They must give an example of political, religious, and commercial liberty.

A.: They have exhibited an example of political, religious, and commercial liberty. But Europe will poison them, if she can.

T.: The facility with which the oppressed may escape from bad governments will compel the governments to be just and enlightened; and the rest of the world will perhaps open their eyes upon the empty illusions with which they have been cheated by politicians.

A.: It is a pity, too, but politicians should open their eyes upon the empty illusions with which they have been cheated by soldiers, by priests, by merchants, by mechanics, and even by husbandsmen and shepherds. Politicians are cheated as often as they cheat, and the way to improve society and reform the world is to enlighten men, spread knowledge, and convince the multitude that they have, or may have, sense, knowledge, and virtue. Declamations against the cunning of politicians and the ignorance, folly, inconstancy or effrontery of the multitude will never do it.

T.: All enlightened men, all friends of humanity, should at this moment unite their lights and join their reflections to those of the wise Americans to help their legislation. This, Sir. would be well worthy of you . . .

A.: The enlightened friends to humanity may throw out some hints which may be useful: but, from what is past, I do not flatter myself very much. Their advice will contain bad hints as well as good; and the subject is much better understood in America than by any who have yet given their advice, tho' these are equal probably to any who exist in Europe.

T.: Our two nations are about doing much harm to each other, probably without either of them gaining any real profit. The increase of debts and public burdens (perhaps a national bankruptcy), and the loss of many lives will be the only result.

A.: France had a prospect of real advantages and has obtained them: she has disabled and disarmed her enemy, she has obtained an island, has extended her fishery and her commerce, set Dunkirk free, obtained the friendship of Holland and alienated her from England; she has strengthened her ally Spain, and raised her own character, both in the cabinet and in the field and on the ocean: she has, in short, turned the tide of human affairs in her favor and against her enemy.

At the end Turgot predicts that England will lose the war. Yet this may be the only means to save her from "the gangrene of luxury and corruption" and induce her to amend her constitution. In the final paragraph—ironically enough for one so ready to advise the English about freedom—the statesman begs his correspondent to keep his communication secret and not to answer by mail, for the letter will be opened at the French post offices, and he will be found "much too great a friend of liberty for a minister, even for a discarded minister."

5

During his stay in Paris Adams must have heard that Turgot, when in office, had opposed the French government's taking any action on behalf of America that might lead to hostilities with Great Britain, but he could not know the memorandum which Turgot had submitted to the King on the subject. Spain had tried to ascertain what help she might expect from France in case of war with England, and influential circles advocated a forceful policy, while the Comte de Vergennes, the Minister of Foreign Affairs, was in favor of maintaining peace. Louis, wanting a thorough discussion of the problem, asked for the opinion of his cabinet. Turgot's report, dated April 6, 1776, is the only one which has been preserved. It was discovered during the Revolution in the archives of the King.[35]

"Of all the possible views that one might take of the war," Turgot wrote, "the conquest of the Colonies would offer the perspective of the longest and most solid peace between France and England, for the simple reason that England would be unable to undertake any other enterprise." But he did not believe in the likelihood of English victory; he thought that "the course of events, sooner or later, will inevitably lead to the complete independence of the Colonies," and in the prudence, courage, and intelligence of the Americans he saw proofs that "they intend to give a firm foundation to their government." Like Vergennes, he rejected the idea of a preventive war, which would strain the finances of France to the utmost. Further, he thought, "an attack upon England would lead to a reconciliation with the Colonies and would precipitate the danger which we want to avoid."[36]

To be sure, the *mémoire* was written by the statesman rather than the philosopher; it considered, above everything else, the interests of France. Turgot's apprehensiveness of a quick peace between England and the Colonies seems to justify Charles Francis Adams's remark that his conclusions were "worthy of Machiavel himself." Reading it dispassionately, however, the passage does not show that Turgot was against the reconciliation itself; all that can be said is that he did not want to bring it about by involving France in a war with England. And certainly the document does not bear out Charles Francis Adams's imputation that "the most desirable result he considered to be a long and exhausting contest in America, ending in the victory of Great Britain, but not without the utter ruin of the resources of the refractory colonies." [37] It was Vergennes who envisaged the possibility of the defeat of the Colonies; Turgot, in commenting upon his report, merely pointed out that even such a situation would not be a danger to France, for it would mean the permanent weakening of England.

An ailing middle-aged bachelor, Turgot spent his last years in serene retirement, devoting much of his time to mathematical studies, physical and chemical experiments, translating Virgil, Horace, and Ariosto—and to conversing with his friends, Lavoisier, d'Alembert, Condorcet, and others. His prestige was undiminished. Even contemporary writers, constantly warring with one another, referred to him as "the great Turgot." Frederick, King of Prussia, and Joseph, Emperor of Austria, looked upon him with admiration. His interest in America persisted. Lest the new republics adopt the English system, he prepared a note for Franklin emphasizing the advantages of direct taxation. As Franklin remained doubtful, he worked out the problem in greater detail. Unfortunately, only fragments of the two papers have been preserved. [38] He also began a larger work to be called *Réflexions sur la situation des Américains Unis*, but even his notes are lost. "He hoped to present in it," his disciple Du Pont de Nemours wrote, "all the counsels which that new country might have needed, the institutions which might have been necessary, the reefs which should have been avoided, and the laws and jurisprudence which it has had to establish." [39] Almost all his letters to Du Pont contain comments on the American war—some of them quite pessimistic. [40]

He corresponded with Dr. Price until his death. Sharing Turgot's view of America as a possible asylum for the oppressed of all nations, the Englishman suggested in one of his letters that the American war might be of the greatest service to mankind. "The time probably will come," he wrote, "when a great part of Europe will be flocking to a country where unmolested by spiritual and civil tyranny, they will be able to enjoy in safety the exercise of reason and the rights of man." Turgot, by then, felt less sanguine. "I shall say no more about the Americans," he replied, "for whatever the outcome of the present war, I have lost somewhat the hope of seeing on the earth a nation which is really free and lives without war. This spectacle is reserved for centuries very far away . . ." [41]

IX

The Composition of
Adams's Defence

Earlier in this book Adams's *Defence of the Constitutions of America* has been described as a vast compilation of fragments taken from fifty-odd books, held together by the author's comments. Indeed, apart from the introductions and conclusions, Adams's own writing in the larger part of the work is of precisely the same nature as the notes reproduced in this volume—the comments appearing interwoven with the text instead of jotted on the margins and fly-leaves.[1] The present writer is bold enough to suggest that the *Defence* would benefit enormously by a similar arrangement, that is, by placing the borrowed texts and Adams's comments in dialogue form.

The composition of the *Defence* and Adams's methods of authorship deserve a closer scrutiny than they have received as yet. With neither taste nor time for condensation, Adams seems to have started copying out his extracts before he finished reading his authorities, that is, before he could judge what texts were most to his purpose. In the absence of quotation marks and with only a few buried statements about the sources, readers of the original edition of the *Defence* could hardly have been aware of the character of the work. A careful separation of the comments from the reprinted material is indispensable for revealing Adams's method of composition—or his lack of it. Almost all the volumes which Adams used are still preserved in his library; and by comparing them with the *Defence* the present writer has been able to mark the corresponding page numbers. This new collation nearly doubles the quantity of the borrowed passages identified by Charles Francis Adams. However, it would be impossible to depict here minutely Adams's indebtedness to his sources; only an outline of the relationship will be attempted.

The first volume of the *Defence*, historically the most momentous and influential, deserves special consideration. It is divided into three parts: (1) modern democratic, aristocratic, and monarchical republics; (2) the opinions of philosophers, writers, and historians on government; and (3) ancient democratic, aristocratic, and monarchical republics.

In the first group Adams discusses San Marino, the Swiss cantons, Poland, and other countries. For San Marino he used Addison's *Remarks on Several Parts of Italy*, which devoted six pages to the small state. "Mr. Addison informs us . . . ," he begins the account. Charles Francis Adams puts only a short paragraph in quotation marks, instead of the several pages which were borrowed verbatim. "Let me add," John Adams writes further on, "that the facts relating to the Swiss cantons and their environs . . . are taken from *Quarante tables politiques de la Suisse*, by C. E. Faber, with some additional observations from the beautiful *Sketches* of Mr. Coxe, which are as instructive as they are entertaining." [2] The truth is that out of the thirty-odd pages given to the Swiss republics he copied about twenty from William Coxe's *Sketches of the Natural, Civil, and Political State of Swisserland*. No copy of Faber's book seems to exist in America; the extent of its use, therefore, must be conjectural.

A few more examples of Adams's manner of composing his work may be cited.

The three pages about the canton of Glarus are based almost entirely upon Coxe; only one comment and the last paragraph are by Adams. In Coxe's words Adams relates the heroic stand of the Swiss in the mountain passes of Naesels in 1388, when four hundred men repulsed a large Austrian army. "Such will ever be the character of a people," he exclaims, "who preserve so large a share to themselves in their legislature, while they temper their constitution at the same time with an executive power in a chief magistrate, and an aristocratical power in a wise senate." Coxe thought that the government was entirely democratical, but Adams concludes: "The government here is by no means entirely democratical." [3]

The account of Zurich, too, was literally reprinted from Coxe; Adams's contribution was a single sentence: "Such are commons, as well as nobles and princes, whenever they have power unchecked in their hands!" [4]

Coxe's description of Uri ends with the remark: "Such a diminutive republic, thrown into an obscure corner, must appear unworthy of notice, but the smallest spot of earth on which civil freedom is cultivated and flourishes, cannot fail of being interesting to those who know the true value of liberty and independence." Adams gives a new twist to the statement: "Such a diminutive republic, in an obscure corner, and unknown, is interesting to Americans, not only because every spot of earth on which civil liberty flourishes deserves their esteem; but, particularly, because it shows the impossibility of erecting even the smallest government, among the poorest people, without different orders, councils, and balances." [5]

Of the fourteen pages on Poland, Adams copied twelve from the first volume of William Coxe's *Travels into Poland, Russia, Sweden, and Denmark* and from the third volume of King Stanislaus's *Œuvres du philosophe bienfaisant*. He drew most heavily on Coxe; from King Stanislaus he translated the first few pages only. "The extracts are not made continuously," Charles Francis Adams remarks of the latter, "but only of such paragraphs as are most to the point." [6] Curiously, all such paragraphs seem to occur in the opening parts of the books which Adams used—a fact which arouses the suspicion that he just picked passages until he either ran out of paper or got tired of the book.[7] How can one account otherwise for his habit of first giving the most minute relations of remote historical periods and then, jumping over centuries, summarizing others in a few lines? The narrative is again interrupted with comments like "Such is Polish liberty, and such the blessings of a monarchy elective by a body of nobles," or "Such are the effects of 'collecting all authority into one center,' of neglecting an equilibrium of powers, and of not having three branches in the legislature."

In the section containing the opinions of philosophers, writers, and historians, the six pages taken from Swift's *Contest and Dissensions between the Nobles and Commons of Athens and Rome* have only one paragraph by Adams, assuring the reader that "Dr. Swift weighed the subject much more maturely than M. Turgot." The passages from Machiavelli's *Discourses upon the First Decade of Livy*, Sidney's *Discourses concerning Government*, and Montesquieu's *Spirit of the Laws* are reprinted without comment, and only one page is added to the seven quoted from Harrington's *Oceana*. The sixth book of Polybius's *History*, one of the earliest expositions of the advantages of mixed constitutions, was another favorite source for Adams. The fifteen pages culled from Plato's *Republic* are reinforced only by a few remarks, to point out "how naturally every simple species of government degenerates." [8]

The facts relative to the ancient republics, Adams states, were taken from Robertson, Montagu, Potter, the *Universal History*, and "especially from Mitford, Gillies, and Ferguson, three very valuable and

elegant productions, which deserve to be studied by all America." Of
the whole group, he found the first volume of William Mitford's *History of Greece*, from which he drew his twenty-page account of
Athens, the most serviceable. Even comments which at first seem to be
original turn out to be borrowed. Adams only added observations
like: "Every one of these precautions demonstrated Solon's conviction
of the necessity of balances to such an assembly"; "Is this government,
or the waves of the sea?"; and "Such was Athenian liberty . . ." In
describing the governments of the mythical states of Phaecia and Ithaca,
Mitford used passages from Pope's translation of the *Iliad* and the
Odyssey, remarking that the English translation "will seldom answer
the end of those who desire to know with any precision what Homer
has said." Similarly Adams criticized the English poet for having "departed from the sense of Homer and from the fact." [9] He himself was
very factual. After quoting part of Telemachus's address to the assembly
of Kings, he commented somewhat incongruously: "Neither in Poland
nor in Venice was the aristocratical rage to render weak, unsteady, and
uncertain the royal authority more conspicuous than it was here." [10]

He went on copying with equal freedom from John Gillies's *History of Ancient Greece*, occasionally stopping in order to inquire what
M. Turgot would have thought of such developments. For the chapter
on Rome, the longest in the book, Adam Ferguson's *History of the
Roman Republic* was his chief inspiration. With honesty he stated
that he was giving "an abridgment of the story, very nearly in Ferguson's words." [11] He took passages from the first seventy pages and then,
omitting nearly two hundred, continued at page 253, only to announce
that he had to leave out the rest of the story. Accordingly, to the later
periods of the Roman republic he allotted precisely six lines.

Adams put only about twelve pages of the first volume of the
Defence into quotation marks—three per cent of the book. Charles
Francis Adams used quotation marks for about twenty-five per cent.
He could have extended them to nearly seventy-five.

2

Fully one-half of the *Defence* is occupied by the histories of Italian
republics during the Middle Ages. Adams again disdained the use of
quotation marks; however, he had the names of his Italian chroniclers
printed as running titles.

Nearly one hundred pages of Machiavelli, embedded in the account
of Florence, were borrowed from *The Works of Nicholas Machiavel*,

a translation made by Ellis Farneworth. Adams nowhere mentions the late Vicar from Cheshire, but at least he forbears to cite Machiavelli's work by the original title. It was Charles Francis Adams who supplied the Italian title, *Istorie Fiorentine*, with the remark: "The substance of this work is here given by the author, who now and then translates a passage literally, when he desires to comment on it." [12] However, literal translations occur not "now and then" but continuously. A little later the editor again notes: "This is an error in translation by the author, growing out of a misconception of the office referred to. The words in the original are 'Capitani *di parte*.' " [13] The error—"captains of the arts" for "captains of the districts"—was also copied by John Adams from Farneworth's work. [14] The failure to acknowledge this obligation is especially regrettable since the borrowing extends to Farneworth's glosses, some of which are extensive. Further, Adams was probably indebted for writing his *Discourses on Davila* to the English clergyman, who is described on the title page of his Machiavelli translation as "Translator of the Life of Pope Sixtus V and Davilla's History of the Civil Wars of France."

For the later history of Florence, Adams's main source was Austin Parke Goddard's translation of Guicciardini's *Historia d'Italia*, although he himself translated Piero Soderini's speech before the Council from the Italian. He copied, in all, about fifty pages. The editor is more cautious in this case; commenting on a certain expression, he merely remarks: "This translation does not quite give the sense of the original." [15] The omission of any mention of Goddard, however, makes the reader believe that John Adams was responsible for the translation.

Adams's way of selecting passages from the Italian chronicles was truly remarkable. "We shall not find it tedious," he started the history of Florence, "to consider minutely the affairs of a brave and enlightened people, to whom the world is indebted for a Machiavel, a Guicciardini, and an Americus Vespucius." There are incidents which he regards as "humorous entertainment," but soon he finds it advisable to leave the reader "to amuse himself at his leisure," and finally admits, repeating it a dozen times, that "the details of the errors and disorders is too long to be recited . . ." Once he positively states: "As it is a sketch of the laws, their vicissitudes and variations, that we are attempting, we have nothing to do with wars or disputes between popes and antipopes, the church and the empire . . ." [16] Yet he continually returns to relating— or rather transcribing—the story of the "commotions, altercations, and civil wars" in all its particulars. It is difficult, indeed, to discover any basic difference between the parts which he included in his book and those which he left out. Most of the Italian chronicles were large folios or quartos; he had to leave out some portions and he had to stop somewhere.

"There were in Italy, in the middle ages," Adams wrote, "a hundred or two of cities, all independent republics, and all constituted nearly in the same manner. The history of one is, under different names and various circumstances, the history of all." [17] He chose eight, but why those eight and not others, he did not explain, and apparently nobody asked. Charles Francis Adams notes "an obvious transposition of several pages of the text" at one place, which was faithfully perpetuated in the succeeding editions.[18] Evidently it did not make much difference to anyone. However, in his eight histories Adams found plenty of "lessons." Scattered throughout the narratives, they appear again and again. Even he must have felt at last that the repetition might be too much for the reader; so his phrasing becomes ingenious. He starts out with an air of making a new observation, only to swoop down at the end with another warning about the dire consequences of "collecting all authority into one center."

Adams quarrels with Machiavelli for speaking of the "evil destiny" of Florence. "Why should the people be still deceived with insinuations," he petulantly asks, "that those evils arose from the destiny of a particular city, when we know that destiny is common to all mankind?" —that is, to all states having simple governments or mixtures of two ingredients only. In reproducing the speeches of Soderini and Vespucci, he adds that "Soderini was for 'collecting all authority into one center,' the people; and Vespucci into another, the senate." He finds it astonishing that the Florentines, talented people though they were, "should not have been able to see the causes of their continual misfortunes, and the necessity of different orders, and a balance in their constitution." [19] And what does Sienese history reveal? It shows that "whether the assembly consists of a larger or a smaller number, of nobles or commons, of great people or little, or rich or poor, of substantial men or the rabble, the effects are all the same—no order, no safety, no liberty, because no government of law." The history of Bologna equally demonstrates that "pious exhortations, charitable resolutions, or solemn oaths" are of no avail against "inveterate passions in unbalanced governments." In Pistoia, too, all authority was centered in one assembly, and the results were endless bloodshed and disorder.[20]

Americans, as all these examples show, should be on their guard. Unless they adopt a balanced government, Adams warned, their states will produce families dividing them into two parties which "tear one another to pieces, and rend the vitals of their country with as ferocious animosity, as unrelenting rancor and cruelty, as ever actuated the Cancellieri and the Panciatichi in Pistoia." [21] The argument that America had no distinctions of rank and therefore was not liable to such discords appeared to Adams untenable, for even if titles and privileges were not hereditary in America, the desire for them was as ardent here as anywhere else.

Even Charles Francis Adams thought it difficult "to attach great interest" to the history of the Italian republics.[22] The French translator's explanation of the origin of this half of the *Defence* is worth quoting at length. "After publishing his first volume," he wrote, "Mr. Adams, in order to give still more force to his opinion, had probably had copied or translated (*avait probablement fait copier ou traduire*) from various Italian historians a great number of very diffuse fragments and at times complete chronicles, from which he intended, no doubt, to publish extracts, accompanied with his reflections. It seems however that, pressed by time and the desire to be useful, and not being able to make extracts, he decided to give the printer those same copies which were supposed to have served only as material for him." "It is possible, too," the translator continued, "that the difficulty of procuring the original volumes in America, which could show to Americans the terrible effects of a weak government . . . may have induced Mr. Adams to send them to his countrymen so faithfully transcribed." He ironically added that one may find these books easily in the French libraries, and further that the French public would not tolerate the mere copying of them.[23]

In spite of his sarcasm, the translator's suggestion about Adams's haste may be sound, and so may be his hint that Adams might have hired someone to do the translating for him. In a letter to Jefferson, accompanying a copy of his second volume which had just left the press, Adams spoke of the "trouble and expense" which his search "into Italian ruins and rubbish" had cost him.[24] What expense? A collector of several thousand books, he could hardly have complained of the price of sixteen Italian chronicles. Moreover, with one exception none of these volumes has traces of his working over them, whereas later on the margins of his copy of Davila's *Guerres civiles de France* he regularly indicated the progress of his translation. Nor is it likely that he could in a few months and under the pressure of other duties accomplish such a vast amount of labor—even if his temperament had allowed it.[25]

3

Marchamont Nedham's *The Excellencie of a Free State*—an analysis of which forms the third part of Adams's *Defence*—was originally published as a series of editorials in the weekly *Mercurius Politicus* in 1651–1652, and was first printed in book form in 1656. It was reprinted in 1767 at the expense of Thomas Hollis, whose heir, Thomas Brand, sent a copy to Adams with the inscription: "Mr. Brand Hollis requests the favor of his friend Mr. Adams to accept benevolently this book, to be deposited among his republican tracts, which after the pomp and pageantry of monarchy, 'the trappings of which would maintain a moderate republick,' he will relish well. Chesterfield Street, 19 Jan. 1787."

Undoubtedly it was the receipt of this volume that prompted Adams to write his review.[26] In his *Thoughts on Government* he had mentioned Nedham as one of those English writers whose works "will convince any candid mind that there is no good government but what is republican." [27] In writing the first volume of the *Defence*, however, he seems to have forgotten about him. Then he suddenly rediscovered Nedham's importance and the danger—for it now appeared as such—which his book presented to Americans. "As M. Turgot's idea of a commonwealth," he wrote, "in which 'all authority is to be collected into one center,' and that center the nation, is supposed to be precisely the project of Marchamont Nedham, and probably derived from his book . . . it may be worth while to examine it." [28] With the Italian chronicles off his hands, Adams had more leisure to dissect the English pamphlet. There is certainly no need to complain here of the paucity of his comments. Written in an earnest and dignified style, Nedham's essay contained many illustrations from Greek and Roman history. Adams took them up with pleasure, elaborating them in his own way. His historical passages, too, offered in smaller quantities, are much more effective than those lifted in large blocks from the Italian chronicles. Although he seldom relied here on literal copying, he had, of course, his sources. The tenth volume of *The Universal History* contains many of the originals of his accounts.[29] His main effort was to show that Nedham was refuted by the examples which he himself had quoted. The stories of Cincinnatus and Curius, Camillus and Cassius, and Maelius and Manlius, he wrote, "instead of being an argument for Nedham's inconcinnate system, are full of proof against it." [30] He contends that calumny under Nedham's system "must be more frequent, intolerable, and remediless than under any form of tyranny," because "an accuser who is useful to the majority will rarely be punished, let his accusation be ever so false or malicious." Nedham condemned the "continuation of great powers in any one family"; but Adams thought that "if there are several of a family whose merit is acknowledged, they may be employed without the smallest danger"—an anticipation of the fortunes of his own future dynasty.[31]

But the chief surprise for Adams was Nedham's argument against "a permitting of the legislative and executive powers of a state to rest in one and the same hands and persons." He paused with astonishment. "A person," he exclaimed, "who had read the former part of the book with attention, would think these words a complete refutation of his whole 'Right Constitution of a Commonwealth' "—whereas it was only another proof that Adams had started his commentary before he had read through the pamphlet.[32] His eagerness to give the most damnatory interpretation to Nedham's "supreme representative assembly" led him into the trap. Had he cared to inform himself that neither Nedham nor Turgot thought of having their assembly exercise administrative powers, a considerable part of his trouble could have been saved.

The man to whom Adams paid the compliment of such concentrated attention was one of the most curious characters of his times. Marchamont Nedham began his career as editor of the *Mercurius Britannicus*, an organ of the Parliamentarians. A few years later he turned an ardent royalist and in his paper, now called *Mercurius Pragmaticus*, savagely satirized the Roundheads. With the establishment of the Commonwealth he was committed to Newgate, but three months later, having adopted the cause of the new rulers, he was released and became editor of the *Mercurius Politicus*, one of the two official journals. From then on, in prose and jingling verse, he poured his venom on the Royalists. At the Restoration he fled to Holland, but soon received pardon and returned; his role, however, was ended. Anthony à Wood tells us what his contemporaries thought of Nedham. He was called "Hell's barking cur," "the son of Belial," "Jack of all sides," and similar names; but Wood admits that "he was a person endowed with quick natural parts, was a good humanitian, poet and boon droll; and had he been constant to his cavaleering principles, he would have been beloved by, and admired of, all." [33]

During the first two years of the *Mercurius Politicus* Nedham was closely associated with Milton, then Latin Secretary of the Commonwealth and also censor of the press. The paper started out in the same raucous manner as Nedham's earlier weeklies; then in the sixteenth number it began a series of editorials the tone and learning of which commanded general respect. Could Nedham, who had just boasted of wanting to be clown to the state, have written these high-minded essays? Professor Masson, in his monumental biography of Milton, wondered whether Milton's hand might not be discernible in them. "I have come upon passages of such a Miltonic strain," he wrote, "that I could *suppose* them possibly Milton's. On the other hand, in no complete articles or long continuous passage have I felt positively sure . . . that I was reading Milton." The English scholar also pointed out the stylistic similarity between *The Excellencie of a Free State* and Milton's *The Tenure of Kings and Magistrates.*[34]

It is tempting to identify the pamphlet as Milton's work. Adams's commentary would certainly gain in stature if one had to recognize it as a reply, not to a despised journalist, but to the author of *Paradise Lost.* It would also speak well of his judgment that, under the humble name, he perceived the mind of so great an opponent.

In his final Conclusion, Adams tried to justify the haphazard nature of his book. "The preceding has been produced," he wrote, "upon the spur of a particular occasion, which made it necessary to write and publish with precipitation, or it might have been useless to have published at all. The whole has been done in the midst of other occupations, in so much hurry, that scarce a moment could be spared to correct the style, adjust the method, pare off excrescences, or even obliterate repetitions, in all which respects it stands in need of an apology." [35] But soon he made a virtue of the defects of his performance. To Dr. Price, from whom he received a friendly "approbation," he wrote: "It was not to obtain a name as an author, or a reputation for literary talents, that I undertook the laborious work . . . To accomplish the good I had in view, I thought it would be more useful and effectual to lay facts, principles, examples, and reasonings before my countrymen, from the writings of others, than in my own name." [36] To Jefferson he described his work as containing "long courses of experiments in political philosophy." He liked to refer to it as "The American Boudoir, or a Looking Glass for Monarchists, Aristocrats and Democrats." [37]

Aristotle is said to have examined a hundred and fifty constitutions; Adams, happily, was satisfied with a mere fifty. In any case, he attempted a comprehensive survey, and in his first volume at least he made an excellent selection. Apparently he liked the book just as it was, feeling that it expressed him better than if it had been "contrived with more art."

X

Lessons from the Civil Wars of France

In despair over the news of the French Revolution, in the fall of 1789 Adams turned to Enrico Caterino Davila's *Historia delle guerre civili di Francia,* a work which begins with the outbreak of the wars in 1560 and goes as far as the Edict of Nantes in 1598, telling of innumerable battles, intrigues, assassinations, and treaties made and broken during the reigns of four monarchs—François II, Charles IX, Henri III, and Henri IV. Davila's history of the French civil wars, first published in Venice in 1630, achieved an enormous success; translated into French, English, Spanish, and other languages, it reached more than two hundred editions by the end of the eighteenth century. Modern writers have criticized Davila for not having probed more deeply into the causes of the civil wars; but it was precisely to his freedom from weighty interpretations and to the easy flow and dramatic turns of his narrative that he owed his popularity. In the enormously rich historical literature of the period, which includes the works of De Thou, d'Aubigné, and Popelinière, he still occupies a respectable position.[1]

Adams, although he had a copy of the first English translation, read the 1757 edition of the French version, *Histoire des guerres civiles de France,* published nominally in Amsterdam but actually in Paris. Printed in three large volumes, the work is divided into fifteen books comprising over eighteen hundred pages. Adams read it with great absorption, making notes and underlining many passages. As when writing his *Defence* he had examined the governments of innumerable states of the past and present, he now made a thorough study of the early French revolutions in order to understand better the events of the moment. The conclusion, of course, was ready in his mind: France had to suffer great convulsions in the sixteenth century because of the lack of balance in her government; and the same fate must befall her again, for the same reason, at the end of the eighteenth.[2]

It was not to be expected that Adams would long keep to himself all the wisdom which he had gathered from his explorations. Under the title *Discourses on Davila* he began a series of papers in the *Gazette of the United States*, the Federalist semiweekly published in New York. His first contribution appeared in the issue for April 27, 1790, and the others followed for a full year. There were, in all, thirty-two papers, some of them in three or four installments. In the last Adams discussed the *Servitude volontaire*, that powerful attack upon tyranny by Étienne de la Boëtie, the friend of Montaigne.[3] Adams himself thought the surrender of all sovereign powers to a single individual and his descendants "the most irrational and ridiculous idea imaginable." Yet he tried to find an explanation for the adoption of the system—one which turned out to be a fervent defense of hereditary succession. It was this article, particularly, which aroused the fury of the republicans and led to the discontinuance of the series. The excitement caused by the publication of these papers, Adams's controversy with Jefferson over them, and the charges of monarchism which were to haunt him to the end of his life have already been discussed in an earlier chapter of this volume.[4]

It was not until 1805 that the articles were reprinted in book form. "Since the publication of these Discourses in 1790," the editors remarked, "our observations abroad, and experience at home, have sufficiently taught us the lessons they were intended to inculcate; and the evils they were designed to prevent, have borne testimony to their truth."[5] The volume aroused no particular emotion except in the author himself. Then, in 1813 Adams reread the work. It was the news of Napoleon's return from Moscow that made him remember it. Having seen the report, dated "Paris, December 20, 1812," in the *Columbian Centinel,* he excitedly began to copy it into his volume: "About midnight of the 18th inst. His Majesty the Emperor arrived in the City . . ." After the first fifteen lines he broke off, evidently dismayed by the servile panegyrics of the Presidents of the Senate and Council. The Emperor's speech, however, he found worthy of preservation. Indeed, the whole scene in the Tuileries appeard to him the fulfillment of his own predictions made in the *Discourses on Davila* twenty-two years before. It is most unlikely that Napoleon ever heard of these articles; but Adams, with an excess of imagination, viewed the imperial address as "a Comment" upon them. In his best handwriting he copied on the back flyleaf:

"The contents of the foregoing volume are summarily comprehended in a few sentences in the following Comment by Napoleon, Emperor of France:

"It is to Ideology, to that obscure metaphysics, which, searching with subtlety after first causes, wishes to found upon them the legislation of nations, instead of adapting the laws to the knowledge of the human heart and to the lessons of history, that we are to attribute all the calamities that our beloved France has experienced. Those errors necessarily produced the government of the men of blood. Indeed who proclaimed the principle of insurrection as a duty? Who flattered the people by proclaiming for them a sovereignty, which they were incapable of exercising? Who destroyed the sanctity and the respect to the laws, by making them to depend not upon the sacred principles of justice, upon the nature of things and upon civil justice, but only upon the will of an assembly composed of men strangers to the knowledge of the civil, criminal, administrative, political, and military laws? When we are called to regenerate a state, we must act upon opposite principles. History paints the human heart. It is in history that we are to seek for the advantages and disadvantages of different systems of laws . . ."

It was only natural that Adams should wish to reply to the Emperor. He composed a "Comment on the Comment," which he likewise copied into the volume:

"Napoleon! Mutato nomine, de te fabula narrabatur! This book is a prophecy of your empire before your name was heard.

"The political and literary world are much indebted for the invention of the new word IDEOLOGY. Our English words Ideocy, or Ideotism, express not the force or meaning of it. It is presumed its proper definition is the science of ideocy. And a very profound, abstruse, and mysterious science it is. You must descend deeper than the divers in the Dunciad to make any discoveries, and after all you will find no bottom. It is the bathos, the theory, the art, the skill of diving and sinking in government. It was taught in the school of folly, but alass, Franklin, Turgot, Rochefoucauld and Condorcet, under Tom Paine, were the great masters of that Academy!"

Thereupon he began to reread his book. Since it had received such marked attention from Napoleon, he could not but admire it and express his exuberant approval of the passages which seemed to him to be especially prophetic.

2

Like the *Defence*, the *Discourses on Davila* is a peculiar or, to say the least, unconventional book. The title itself is a misnomer; one would expect it to be a commentary on Davila's *History*. In fact, the book has been regularly described as such; Charles Francis Adams speaks of it as "an analysis" of Davila's work.[6] But it is nothing of the kind. Eighteen of the thirty-two papers—more than two-thirds of the volume—are straight translations from the first five books of Davila, while the remaining fourteen consist of essays on subjects like avarice, emulation, ambition, and fame, with hardly a word about the Italian.

Adams started at the beginning of Davila's *History*, and carried the translation to page 8. Then, impatient to deliver himself of his ideas, he announced: "Before we proceed in our discourses on Davila, it will assist us in comprehending his narration, as well as in making many useful reflections in morals and policy, to turn our thoughts for a few moments to the constitution of the human mind."[7] However, he forgot the promise, and in the next two papers continued the translation down to page 14. After that, he began his "useful reflections"—and poured them out through twelve consecutive issues, extending the "few moments" to more than two months.[8] He then returned to Davila, but progress was slow; by his twentieth paper he had covered only seventy-four pages of the original. So he began to hurry. After the twenty-sixth paper, there are more and more gaps in the translation, bridged by summaries compiled from the marginal guides of the French book. Yet the narrative is fairly complete up to page 215, when it suddenly leaps a hundred pages. Having reached page 383, Adams gave up. "It is not intended at this time," he declared, "to pursue any further this instructive though melancholy history, nor to make any comparisons, in detail, between the state of France in 1791 and the condition it was in two or three centuries ago."[9]

As in the *Defence*, it was Charles Francis Adams who first supplied the quotation marks (although not consistently) for the translations from Davila's *History*. In his articles Adams merely noted on rare occasions, "Davila says," or "as Davila proceeds." Apparently, he trusted the reader to distinguish between Davila's narrative and his own comments, each of which extends only to a few paragraphs or lines and has a most tenuous connection with the text. Nor did he observe any particular method in the division of the articles, which seems to have been determined solely by the space available in the *Gazette*. He evidently did not consult the English translations published in 1647, 1666, and 1758. His own translation is almost literal, although one is likely to pass over his Gallicisms as peculiarities of eighteenth-century prose.[10]

The fourteen essays of "useful reflections" were Adams's most sustained effort as a "moral writer." He was always inclined to hold forth on the subject of human nature, but here his ideas are gathered into a smaller compass and are expressed more cogently than elsewhere. The papers are striking, and reading them one has at first the feeling of having discovered a literary treasure. Unfortunately, a closer examination reveals the fact that the entire group is based upon a single chapter in Adam Smith's *Theory of Moral Sentiments*. The latter's observations on "The Origin of Ambition and the Distinction of Ranks" appeared so important to Adams that he elaborated on them, in varying forms, again and again.[11] However, his own phrasing is often more powerful than Smith's; his passion for stringing together epithets and metaphors makes his presentation particularly vivid. The following examples illustrate his manner of composition:

Adam Smith	*John Adams*
To what purpose is all the toil and bustle of this world? What is the end of avarice and ambition, of the pursuit of wealth, of power, and preëminence? Is it to supply the necessities of nature? The wages of the meanest labourer can supply them. We see that they afford him food and clothing, the comfort of a house, and of a family . . .	The labor and anxiety, the enterprises and adventures, that are voluntarily undertaken in pursuit of gain are out of all proportion to the utility, convenience, or pleasure of riches. A competence to satisfy the wants of nature, food and clothes, a shelter from the seasons, and the comforts of a family, may be had for very little. The daily toil of the million, and of millions of millions, is adequate to a complete supply of these necessities and conveniences . . .
The poor man is ashamed of his poverty. He feels that it places him out of the sight of mankind . . . He goes out and comes in unheeded, and when in the midst of a crowd is in the same obscurity as if shut up in his own hovel . . .	The poor man's conscience is clear; yet he is ashamed . . . Mankind takes no notice of him. He rambles and wanders unheeded. In the midst of a crowd, at church, in the market, at a play, at an execution or coronation, he is in as much obscurity as he would be in a garret or a cellar . . .

Adam Smith	*John Adams*
To become the natural object of the joyous congratulations and sympathetic attentions of mankind is the circumstance which gives to prosperity all its dazzling splendor . . .	Every personal quality, and every blessing of fortune, is cherished in proportion to its capacity of gratifying this universal affection for the esteem, the sympathy, admiration and congratulations of the public.

However, whereas Smith was satisfied to state the point once, Adams returned to this "desire for the attention, consideration, and congratulations of mankind" a dozen times. Finally, as if afraid that he had not made himself clear, he reprinted verbatim the larger part of Smith's chapter! He did not name the Englishman and quoted him only as "a great writer." [12]

Of course, it required art to compose these variations on a single theme. One of his essays Adams embellished with twelve verses from Edward Young's *Love of Fame,* and another with a few well-known lines from *The Tempest* and *Macbeth.* Two of his papers he made up almost entirely from poetic passages: in one he used fifteen lines from the third satire of Juvenal and twenty-eight from Johnson's *London,* and in the other, seventy lines from the first and third acts of Shakespeare's *Troilus and Cressida.*[13] Those last quotations—Achilles on honor, Ulysses on emulation and rank—must have especially pleased him. No wonder that he stressed the lines:

> "The heavens themselves, the planets, and this centre,
>   Observe degree, priority, and place,
>   Insisture, course, proportion, season, form,
>   Office and custom, in all line of order . . ."

He called Shakespeare "the great master of nature," and "the great teacher of morality and politics." When he reread his book, he marked the words on the margin: "Degree" (six times), "Condition," "Rank," "Station," "Situation," "Place." At the end: "The style in these quotations from Shakespear has little of the fluency, and less of that purity which sometimes appear in his writings, but the sense is as immortal as human nature."

A distinctive feature of the *Discourses* are the mottoes which Adams selected for most of the papers. Twenty-three possess such ornaments, and one has two. Ten are in French, nine in English, and five in Latin. In the *Gazette* their sources were not given, but in his copy of the work Adams filled in at least the names of the authors. Again, on closer view the variety is not impressive. Nine are by Voltaire, almost all from the second book of the *Henriade*—that long recital of France's miseries made by Henri IV to Queen Elizabeth of England! Six are by Pope, from the *Essay on Man*, the *Moral Essays*, and the *Essay on Criticism*, all pointing to the fact that "order is Heaven's first law" and that " 'tis from high life high characters are drawn." Johnson contributed three quotations, such as "Slow rises worth, by poverty depressed" from *London*. There is one from Shakespeare, appropriately enough from *Coriolanus*, expressive of the hero's disdain of popular favor. Of the Latin mottoes, one can be identified as from Juvenal, another as from Livy, and a third as a proverb.

3

Davila first gives a bird's eye view of the early history of the Franks, pointing out especially the influence of the Salic laws, which established a hereditary monarchy, while ensuring at the same time the rights of the people. It was at this point, before the real narrative of the civil wars begins, that Adams interpolated his twelve essays. His comments were made mostly on these essays—and, for once, he was in complete agreement with the author. (Those excerpts from the *Discourses on Davila* which are translations from Davila's *Histoire des guerres civiles de France* are placed in quotation marks here.)

Discourses: "Accustomed for many ages to live in the obedience of a Prince, the Franks resolved to choose a King, who should unite in his single person all the authority of the nation." Here perhaps Davila is incautious and incorrect . . .[14]

Adams: Turgot's ideas are equally confused. His "All authority in one centre, the nation" is just as good nonsense.[15]

D.: ". . . but as unlimited authority may easily degenerate into tyranny, the Franks demanded the establishment of certain perpetual and irrevocable laws. These laws, proposed by their priests, have been considered as the primitive regulations and fundamental constitutions of the kingdom."

A.: The priests were the first order of their nobility. See Mr. Walter's review of this work in the *Anthology*. Mr. Walter was "a young man: a forward young man." But he did not know that the first order of nobility among the Franks were priests. It is true, the Salique laws were made by the nobility. It is also true that they were made by their priests: because the nobility and the priests were the same persons. Mr. Walter's criticism therefore might have been spared.[16]

D.: "The rights and prerogatives of the Princes of the Blood to the throne and to the regency were not simply founded upon usage: the States-General of the Kingdom, in whom resides the entire power of the whole nation whom they represent, have frequently confirmed them."

A.: Here again is the French jargon of all authority in one centre, without one clear idea.

Every day, Davila observes, brought fresh occasions of hatred and distrust against the Princes; thus John, Duke of Bourbon, declared himself against Louis XI, and Louis XII was at war with Peter of Bourbon.

D.: Everything was calculated to attract the attention of the people; to attach their hearts to their lawgivers, magistrates, and judges, according to their ranks, stations and importance in the State.

A.: Our mock funerals of Washington, Hamilton, and Ames, our processions, escorts, public dinners, balls, etc. are more expensive, more troublesome, and infinitely less ingenious.

D.: The policy of Rome was exhibited in its highest perfection in the triumph of Paulus Emilius over Perseus. In his speech to the people the victor said, "In the house of Paulus none remains but himself . . ."

A.: Logan. Not one drop of Logan's blood remains. Jefferson's *Notes*.[17]

D.: The connection of honors with lands, offices, and families has been the policy of Europe; and it is to this institution she owes her superiority in war and peace, in legislation and commerce, in agriculture, navigation, arts, sciences, and manufactures, to Asia and Africa. .

A.: This is a truth! But by no means a justification of the systems of nobility in France, nor in other parts of Europe. Not even in England, without a more equitable representation of the commons in the legislature.

D.: It is not the way to obtain a present enthusiastic popularity to tell the people that in a single assembly they will act as arbitrarily and tyrannically as any despot . . .

A.: Witness the quintuple Directory and the triumvirate Consulate.

D.: . . . and if a balance of passions and interests is not scientifically concerted, the present struggle in Europe will be little beneficial to mankind.

A.: Witness France and Europe in 1813.

D.: The principle of alliances is as infallible as the sincerity of interests. With no small degree of vehemence was it urged as an argument for the declaration of independence . . .

A.: By John Adams.

In one of the later moral essays Adams finally asks: "But why all this of emulation and rivalry?" Because, he answers, the whole history of the civil wars of France is no more than an account of rivalries. We are told that the National Assembly of France has abolished all distinctions but, he warned, "miracles must be performed in France before all distinctions can be abolished." In rereading the book he rightly inquired: "How are distinctions abolished now?" There is already a scission, sophistry, and party spirit in the National Assembly: evils so greatly dreaded by the ingenuous "Citizen of New-Heaven . . ." It was here that Adams made his note about "the rage and fury of the Jacobinical journals" which intimidated the printer and induced him to stop the articles.[18]

D.: If one party has not superiority over the other, civil war ensues . . . If this should be the course in France, the poor, deluded, and devoted partisans would be doing anything to increase the power of their commander over themselves.

A.: See Napoleon's speech Dec. 20th 1812 at the end of this book in a blank leaf.

D.: The best apology which can be made for a sovereignty in one assembly is that it is only intended to be momentary. That the subject is considered in this light by the best friends of liberty in Europe, appears by the words of Dr. Price . . .

A.: Oh! That Dr. Price and Dr. Franklin had lived to read the addresses and answers of Dec. 20th 1812, at the end of this volume. Jefferson had lived to see it.

D.: If all decorum, discipline and subordination are to be destroyed, nations will soon . . . follow the standard of the first mad despot.

A.: Napoleon is not all this.

The "useful reflections" end with a great peroration, addressed first to Frenchmen and then to Americans:

D.: Frenchmen! Consider that government is intended to set bounds to passions which nature has not limited . . .

A.: Frenchmen neither saw, heard, or felt or understood this.

D.: Americans! Instead of following any foreign example, to return to the legislation of confusion, contemplate the means of restoring decency, honesty and order in society, by preserving, and completing the balance of your government.

A.: Americans paid no attention or regard to this. And a blind, mad rivalry between the North and the South is destroying all morality and sound policy. God grant that division, civil war, murders, assassinations, and massacres may not soon grow out of these rivalries of states, families, and individuals.

D.: You will find in the statement of the Committee of Correspondence of Boston, appointed on October 28, 1772, the great principles of civil and religious liberty, for which you have contended so successfully . . .

A.: This Boston pamphlet was drawn by the great James Otis.[19]

D.: In your Congress at Philadelphia, on Friday, the 14th day of October, 1774, you laid down the fundamental principles, for which you were about to contend. You declared . . .

A.: This Declaration of Rights was drawn by the little John Adams. The mighty Jefferson, by the Declaration of Independence, 4 July 1776, carried away the glory both of the great and the little. The Declaration of Independence contained nothing but the Boston Declaration of 1772 and the Congress Declaration of 1774. Such are the caprices of fortune.[20]

D.: The various forms of prejudice, superstition, and servility start up, in their true shapes . . . Whatever is loose must be shaken; whatever is corrupt must be lopt away; whatever is not built on the broad basis of public utility, must be thrown to the ground . . .

A.: This was a summary of the language of the world in 1790 in newspapers, pamphlets and conversation. In 1813 we can judge of it, as the author of these *Discourses* judged of it then, to the destruction of his popularity.

D.: Americans, there is reason to fear that France has copied from you errors which have cost you very dear. Assist her, by your example, to rectify them before they involve her in calamities . . . The balance of a well ordered government will alone be able to prevent emulation from degenerating into dangerous ambition, irregular rivalries, destructive factions, wasting seditions, and bloody civil wars.

A.: View France, Europe, and America in 1813, and compare the state of them all with this paragraph written 23 years ago.

D.: A certain duchess of venerable years and masculine understanding said of some of the philosophers of the eighteenth century admirably well, "On ne croit pas dans le Christianisme, mais on croit toutes les sottises possibles."

A.: The Duchesse D'Enville, the mother of the Duke de la Rochefoucauld. The author heard those words from that lady's own lips, with many other striking effusions of the strong and large mind of a great and excellent female character.

4

Reminding his readers once more that kings have the same sentiments as private persons—pride, vanity, jealousy, etc.—Adams continues his translation of Davila's *Histoire:*

D.: "The rivalry between the houses of Guise and Montmorency, or, in other words, the ambition of the Cardinal de Lorraine and the Duke of Guise to outstrip the Montmorency, produced a war."

A.: Voltaire and all other Frenchmen may strive to throw all the blame upon Catherine: but the Guises opposed her to the Bourbons and Montmorencies. Montmorency opposed her and the Guises to the Bourbons. The Bourbons opposed Montmorency to Guises, to the Queen, etc., etc. In short, all four parties in their turns opposed La France à La France. In point of public virtue, sincere religion, and real principle there appears no difference between them.

Suddenly it appeared to Adams that the passage could be applied to America; so he added:

"Compare the conduct of our parties for 24 years, our Federalists and Antis, our Republicans and Federalists. How easily the Federalists united with Clinton and Ingersoll in 1812, and the New England Republicans with Jefferson and Madison in 1800! State rivalries threaten our tranquillity. Virginia, Pennsylvania, New York, and Massachusetts may keep us in hot water as Valois, Bourbons, Montmorencies, and Guises did France."

D.: "The Guises," Davila tells us, "without regard to the general discontent sought the friendship of Diana, Duchess of Valentinois, who soon declared herself openly in their favor. The Constable easily unravelled the intrigues of the Guises, and thought to fortify himself, equally, with the protection of Diana."

A.: With what sacrifices of family pride did those two haughty houses court the aid and influence of an harlot!

At this point Davila introduced sketches of the principal characters, among them Catherine de Medici. Although once in the service of the Queen Mother, he knew well that this "princess of refined genius and masculine courage" had boundless ambition and that, in furthering her designs, "dissimulation was not difficult to her." Adams, however, rose once more to her defense: "The French writers, all endeavour to lay all the blame upon Catherine: but I can see no more selfishness in her than in Montmorency, the Cardinal, the Duke, Navarre, or Condé. Coligny seems to have had religion, but his conscience was very ambitious. The admiral seems to have somewhat of the spirit of martyrdom. But it may be doubted whether Montmorencies, Guises, Bourbons, Chatillons, or Medici believed more than her relation Leo the 10th, who is said to believe 'the fabula Christi' to be only an established political institution."

The New England Puritan gave this summary view of the Massacre of St. Bartholomew:

"Here were four families, the King under the Mother, the Guises, the Montmorencies, and the Bourbons. The coalitions and separations of these four houses all struggling for superiority, all making religion the pretext, deluged France in blood. The King had the crown and the forms of law on his side, which gave him and his Mother an advantage, and produced the Massacre of St. Bartholomew, and others more in number and ferocity than any produced by the other three. The conjunctions and oppositions of these primary planets disturbed the whole solar system."

Then, again remembering the domestic situation, Adams drew an ominous parallel:

"Pray, who at this moment, 12th March 1813, are the four families now in activity? The Higginsons, the Clintons, the Madisons, and the Pinckneys. The Quincys, the Otis's, the Livingstons, the Lees, the Randolphs, the Washingtons, the Rutledges, the Middletons are in the background, or rather completely subordinate. But where are the Winthrops, the Endicotts, the Winslows, the Mayhems, the Skuylers, the Willings, the Shippens, the Penns, the thousand others? Some of these dry bones may resuscitate by and by, rattle and whistle first, and then murder and massacre."

D.: Time must determine whether the continued deliberations of the National Assembly will finally obtain a balance in the government of France.

A.: Napoleon in 1812 and 1813 has determined the question. Indeed he determined it in 1800 or before.

D.: If they fail in this, simple monarchy, or what is more to be dreaded, simple despotism will infallibly return.

A.: What is Napoleon in 1813?

D.: If the wild idea of annihilating the nobility should spread far, the men of letters and the National Assembly, as democratical as they may think themselves, will find no barrier against despotism.

A.: Men of letters! where are ye? Ask La Harpe what barrier they found.[21]

D.: The French, as well as the Creek Indians, at this time our respected guests, have their beloved families, and nothing but despotism ever did or ever can prevent them from being distinguished by the people.

A.: This was written on Richmond Hill or Church Hill, in New York when the author was Vice-President, and when the grandees, the warriors and sachems of the Creek nation with McGillivray at their head were lodged in sight and hearing.[22]

While in this mood, he added:

"A silly review of this work was printed in England, in which it was said that the system of nobility in France was justified. Nothing can be more false. There never has been a system of hereditary nobility rationally digested in any nation. That in England has been accidentally brought the nearest to a rational theory. The nobilities of France and Germany have no more judicious arrangements than those of Wabash or Creek Indians, Tartars, or Arabs or Chinese. Nature produces nobilities in all nations, but those very nobilities will never suffer themselves to be disciplined or modified or methodized but by despots." [23]

5

The rest of the comments are strewn throughout the volume. It would be futile to seek continuity in them; and yet Adams's eagerness to find passages in his book which events had justified gives coherence to his remarks. In a note he expressed the thought uppermost in his mind:

"The haughty, arrogant insolence of aristocracy and the feeble timorous patience and humility of democracy is apparent in this and all other history. But when democracy gets the upper hand it seems to be conscious that its power will be short, and makes haste to glut its vengeance by a plentiful harvest of blood and cruelty, murder, massacre, and devastation. Hence despotism! Hence Napoleon! Hence Caesar! Hence Cromwell! Hence Charles 2d. Hence! hence! hence! etc., etc. Hence Zingis! Hence Tamerlane! Hence Koulican! O man! Art thou a rational, a moral, and social animal?"

D.: "The asylum and the centre of the new sect was Geneva . . . which had shaken off the yoke of its Bishops and Dukes of Savoy, and erected itself into a republic, under the title of a free city, for the sake of liberty and conscience."

A.: Let not Geneva be forgotten or despised. Religious liberty owes it much respect, Servetus notwithstanding.[24]

D.: "The Council of the King agreed that, to maintain the authority of the King and the ministry, the only sure means would be to rid themselves of the chiefs and authors of the conspiracy."

A.: Cut off the heads of the tallest poppies: Tarquin and all other heads of parties; Marat, Charlotte Corday, Robespierre, Danton, etc., etc.

D.: "The Council resolved at length to convoke the assembly of the States-General, in whom resides the whole authority of the Kingdom."

A.: All authority in one centre and that centre the nation! The clergy, the nobility, and the third estate! Neither had a negative on the other. The representation of the third estate was a mere mockery! The King had no negative on the states. They none upon him. All was uncertainty, confusion, and anarchy.

D.: "Kings," says Davila, "never see with pleasure, or indeed voluntarily, these assemblies of the States-General, where their authority seems to be eclipsed by the sovereign power of the nation, whose deputies represent the whole body."

A.: The nation has found a mode of uniting all authority in one centre and that centre Napoleon, who in 1813 thinks he has cured the ideology of the nation: but he has not. Nor his own.

D.: There was always a rivalry between the royal authority and that of the States-General, as there is now between the power of the King and that of the National Assembly . . .

A.: The Constitution of 1789. Ellsworth moved in Senate a vote of approbation of this Constitution. I was obliged to put the question and it stands upon record. Madison moved a vote of admiration in the House and it was recorded there.[25] Washington, Jefferson, and all admired it. John Adams alone detested it. Talleyrand asked me what I thought of the executive power in it? I answered, "The King is Daniel in the lion's den: if he ever gets out alive, it must be by miracle." Talleyrand again asked my opinion of the executive power in a subsequent constitution. I answered, "It is Shadrach, Mecheck, and Abednego in the fiery Furnace.[26] If they escape alive, it must be because fire will not burn. This constitution cannot last longer than the other."

Davila relates that the Queen Mother, although she desired the execution of the Princes, wanted the odium of it to fall upon the Guises.

"What an artful hiena!" Adams indignantly exclaimed, wondering "How deep a dungeon is the human heart!" Diana, Duchess of Valentinois, thought that the true means of her safety would be to allure the Constable into the party of the Catholics. "A harlot preaches popery; not the first either, nor the last," Adams commented.

Having finished reading his *Discourses*, Adams again expressed his approbation of the work:

"This dull, heavy volume still excites the wonder of its author, first that he could find amidst the constant scenes of business and dissipation in which he was enveloped time to write it. Secondly that he had the courage to oppose and publish his own opinions to the universal opinion of all America, and indeed of almost all mankind. Not one man in America then believed him. He knew not one then, and has not heard of one since, who then believed him. The work, however, powerfully operated to destroy his popularity. It was urged as full proof that he was an advocate for monarchy, and laboring to introduce an hereditary President and Senate in America."

But he was not through yet. On December 6, 1814, he made this final entry:

"This volume was returned yesterday from Mr. Colman of Hingham, who has had it almost a year.

"The events in Europe since March 3d, 1813 are remarkable. Napoleon is now in Elba and Talleyrand at Vienna! Let us read Candide and Zadig, and Rasselas, and see if there is anything extravagant in them!

"Have not philosophers been as honest and as mad as popes, Jesuits, priests, emperors, kings, heroes, conquerors? Has the Inquisition been more cruel than Robespierre or Marat or Napoleon? The Inquisition is now revived and the Order of the Jesuits restored. Sic transit gloria philosophiae! Even Gibbon was for restoring the Inquisition! Philosophy is now as distracted as it was at Alexandria, during the siege of Jerusalem!

"And where is our New England bound? To Hartford Convention! And how many Paines and Callenders, Robespierres and Napoleons are to be begotten by that assemblage? Vide Rasselas, Candide, Zadig, Jenni, Scarmontado, Micromegas, the Huron, etc.[27]

"Ridendo dicere verum, quid vetat?" [28]

[XI]

The French Revolution

The first news of the French Revolution was warmly received in England. There were no outbursts of enthusiasm as in America; but it was generally agreed that conditions in France had warranted a change, and it was also felt that the fall of absolutism would lessen the French military threat. Within a short time, however, public opinion had become increasingly divided. Many people were shocked by the violence of the Parisian mob and, while the storming of the Bastille was still comprehensible, the bloody events in the palace of Versailles and the removal of the King to Paris aroused fear and suspicion. At the same time, sympathizers with the Revolution grew louder and louder.

On November 4, 1789, the anniversary of the Revolution of 1688, the Revolution Society held a meeting in London, at which Dr. Richard Price preached a sermon, condemning narrow nationalism and abject submission to authority. "A King is no more than the first servant of the public, created by it, maintained by it, and responsible to it," he said, blandly asserting that the revolution against James II had left much undone. At the end, he thanked God for allowing him to live to see "thirty millions of people spurning at slavery and demanding liberty with an irresistible voice." Like a new Simeon, he asked for his *nunc dimittis*, beholding his salvation in the spreading of freedom all over the world.[1]

It was partly to answer Dr. Price and his group that Edmund Burke began his *Reflections on the French Revolution*. From an argument, the work grew into a review of "the monstrous tragi-comic scene" in France and a complete statement of the ultraconservative view of the nature of government. On its appearance in November 1790, the book created a tremendous impression. Thirty thousand copies were sold, calling forth the most exuberant praises and the sharpest criticisms. The Emperor of Germany, the Empress of Russia, and many more sovereigns sent congratulatory messages to Burke; King George passed out gift copies, saying that "every gentleman should read it." Pitt, Wilberforce, Sir Joshua Reynolds, Edward Gibbon, and Fanny Burney, to name a few, expressed their unqualified approval. George Fox, on the other hand, called it "a libel on all free governments"; and Lord Stanhope, Dr. Priestley, Sir James Mackintosh, and many others attacked it in pamphlets. One of these was *The Rights of Man*, by Thomas Paine.

Perhaps the earliest—and bluntest—of the replies was issued by a then little-known writer, Mary Wollstonecraft. Her *Vindication of the Rights of Men*, a book of one hundred and fifty pages, appeared within a few weeks of the publication of Burke's *Reflections*. The young author took no pains to conceal her indignation at the "contemptible sophistries" of the great orator. Although her style was turgid and repetitious, she assailed Burke's opinions on property, Church, parliamentary representation, unemployment, and many other questions with uncommon force, accusing him of callousness, hypocrisy, and envy. "Had you been a Frenchman," she flung the ultimate insult at him, "you would have been, in spite of your respect for rank and antiquity, a violent revolutionist . . ." [2] The pamphlet aroused attention, and identified Mary Wollstonecraft at once with the radicals—Thomas Paine, Horne Tooke, William Godwin, Thomas Holcroft, and others—many of whom used to meet in the home of Joseph Johnson, the publisher. These men had been her friends since the end of 1787, when she had settled in London, trying to earn a living by literary labors: translations from the French and German, two essays on female education, a novel, a children's book, and numerous articles for Johnson's *Analytical Review*. Her *Original Stories* and her adaptation of G. G. Salzman's *Elements of Morality* were illustrated by another "Revolutionist," William Blake. It was hard work, but she found it infinitely better than teaching school at Newington Green or serving as a governess in Ireland. In London she was independent; she had congenial company, and, what was extremely important to her, she could support her sisters, her shiftless brothers, and even her dissipated father.

Encouraged by the success of her stroke against Burke, she set out to write the book for which she is mainly remembered—*A Vindication of the Rights of Women*. There had already been several champions of woman's education in both England and France, but Mary Wollstonecraft offered, at a time when the new French constitution itself took the subordination of women for granted, the first comprehensive program for their political and intellectual emancipation. A hundred years before Ibsen, she gave eloquent reasons why they should be "companions for men" rather than "pretty dolls." "Would men," she pleaded, "but generously snap our chains, and be content with a rational fellowship instead of slavish obedience, they would find us more observant daughters, more affectionate sisters, more faithful wives, more reasonable mothers—in a word, better citizens." But the book was equally addressed to women. "My own sex, I hope," she wrote, "will excuse me, if I treat them like rational creatures, instead of flattering their fascinating graces, and viewing them as if they were in a state of perpetual childhood, unable to stand alone." Avoiding the question of equality or inferiority, she tried to persuade women "to endeavour to acquire strength, both of mind and body," that "elegance is inferior to virtue," and that their chief ambition should be "to obtain a character as a human being, regardless of the distinction of sex." [3] The book was dedicated to—of all people—Talleyrand, whose Report on Public Instruction struck her as the work of a congenial soul. [4] The *Rights of Women* was avidly read in England, and it was at once translated into French and German. The magazines either hailed or abused it. To some of them, Mrs. Wollstonecraft, as she now called herself, was "the noble champion of a new system"; to others, her work appeared "weak, desultory, and trifling." Among those who felt outraged, women were particularly prominent. Hannah More was "invincibly resolved" not to read the book. "There is something fantastic and absurd in the very title," she wrote to Horace Walpole. The latter could only rejoice at her determination. Mary Wollstonecraft, one of the "philosophizing serpents," he replied, "is excommunicated from the pale of my library." [5]

She was just thirty-two. Enjoying the social and financial rewards of her long struggle, she moved into more comfortable quarters, dressed better, and grew handsomer. At Johnson's she met the talented Swiss painter Henry Füseli, like herself a holder of advanced political views. He was fifty and married, but she became so attached to him that soon their friendship was a torment to her. In the spring of 1792 they planned to go to France together—she, Füseli, and his wife—but the trip was postponed again and again, and finally she went alone in December. Intending to stay for six weeks, she remained for nearly two and a half years.

The *Rights of Women* had ben praised in the French papers, and Miss Wollstonecraft's sympathy with the Revolution was known in Paris. Thomas Paine, who had been elected to the National Assembly, was there; at his retreat in the Faubourg St. Denis (in a palace once occupied by Madame de Pompadour), she met many of the popular leaders, Brissot and General Miranda among them. The English and Americans were all very friendly. There was Thomas Christie, the first editor of the *Analytical Review*, now employed by the National Assembly on an English translation of the new constitution; his wife, the former Miss Thompson, of a wealthy manufacturing family; the poetess Helen Maria Williams; Joel Barlow, the author of *Advice to the Privileged Orders* (and the future poet of *The Columbiad*), who had been elected a citizen of France; his wife, Ruth Baldwin, also from Connecticut, and other celebrities. Mary Wollstonecraft found lodgings in the home of Madame Bregantz, in whose school at Putney, outside of London, her sisters had once taught. A few days after her arrival she saw the King pass by her window as he was being taken to the bar for trial. The streets were empty and silent, except for a few drumbeats which made the stillness even more awful. "The inhabitants flocked to their windows," she wrote to Johnson, "but the casements were all shut. Not a voice was heard, nor did I see anything like an insulting gesture. For the first time since I entered France, I bowed to the majesty of the people, and respected the propriety of behavior, so perfectly in unison with my own feelings." [6] But her sentiments were to change before long. The cruelty and frivolity of the French deeply affected her, and she confessed that "names, not principles" had changed and that "the turn of the tide had left the dregs of the old system to corrupt the new."

To avoid the excitement, she went to Neuilly for a while. Back in Paris, in April 1793, she met at the Christies' Gilbert Imlay, a captain in the American army during the Revolution, whose *Topographical Description of the Western Territory of North America* had recently been published in London. As a collaborator of Brissot, Imlay was then involved in the plot for the French conquest of Louisiana—and in an intrigue of another sort with Miss Williams. [7] Mary Wollstonecraft, not knowing of either, fell in love with him. War had been declared between England and France, and the Convention had ordered the imprisonment of all English people residing in France. Partly to escape persecution, she took Imlay's name and obtained a certificate from the American embassy as his wife. From August on she lived in his house, but Imlay himself was away at Le Hâvre, possibly in flight from Robespierre, after Brissot's execution. Her letters to him, full of devotion and anxiety, reveal her womanly capacity for love and suffering. Toward the end of the year she joined Imlay, and in May 1794 her daughter Fanny was born.

It was in Paris and Le Hâvre that she wrote her *Historical and Moral View of the Origin and Progress of the French Revolution.* "I have just sent off great part of my MS.," she informed her sister Everina on March 10, 1794, "which Miss Williams would fain have had me burn, following her example; and to tell you the truth, my life would not have been worth much if it had been found. It is impossible for you to have any idea of the impression the sad scenes I have been witness to have left on my mind. Death and misery, in every shape of terror, haunt this devoted country . . ." [8] To be sure, not all of her book would have pleased the Committee of Public Safety. Personally, she was more contented than ever before; her love for Imlay and the joys of motherhood gave her a sense of fulfillment. However, the daily horrors began to tell on her. "Of the state of things, and the decree against the English I will not speak," she wrote three months later to Ruth Barlow, then in London. "The French will carry all before them —but, my God, how many victims fall beneath the sword and the guillotine! My blood runs cold, and I sicken at thoughts of a Revolution which costs so much blood and bitter tears." [9]

The French Revolution naturally reflects her bewilderment. She bitterly condemns the ruthless ambition of the leaders, the inadequacies of the constitution, and the degeneration of the French. Yet she hopes that the Revolution has arrived at last at a point where the overthrow of "the tremendous empire of superstition and hypocrisy" is in sight. The tension between her contradictory emotions is present on every page, and makes all her statements intricate and twisted. The book, besides, is full of "desultory disquisitions." Comprising no less than five hundred and twenty-two pages, it reaches only to the fall of 1789. One must remember, however, that it was not intended to be a straightforward narrative of the Revolution, but rather, as the title states, "an historical and moral view" of its origin and progress. Her slow start and heavy tone of philosophizing are fatiguing; as she brooded over the baffling events, she felt a compulsion to make them somehow intelligible. Yet the immense possibilities of the subject could not be spoiled—the work is jammed with picturesque personalities and dramatic incidents. There are the portraits of the King and Queen; the searching characterizations of cabinet ministers like Necker, Calonne, and Brienne, of the sinister figures of the Duke of Orleans and the Count of Artois, and of leaders like Lafayette, Mounier, Sieyes, and Mirabeau; the debates on the King's veto and inviolability; the accounts of the taking of the Bastille, of the "orgy of renunciation" on August 4, of the march of the women to Versailles, and of the removal of the King to Paris. Scores of *vignettes* relieve the strain of her meditations.

The reception of *The French Revolution* was much cooler than that of *The Rights of Women*. This was a time when Thomas Hardy, Horne Tooke, and Thomas Holcroft were tried for high treason,[10] the *habeas corpus* was temporarily suspended, public meetings were forbidden, "Church and King" clubs were formed, and waves of suspicion swept the whole nation. Dr. Priestley, whose house at Birmingham had been burned by the mob, wrote to a friend in America: "I cannot give you an idea of the violence with which every friend of liberty is persecuted in this country; little of the liberty of the press on political subjects is now left." [11] The time was not propitious for the book. Not satisfied with his earlier epithet, Horace Walpole, enraged by the author's treatment of Marie Antoinette, called her a "hyena in petticoats," who had "Alecto's blazing ferocity." [12] The changed situation may have been one reason for the discontinuation of the work. Mary Wollstonecraft had thought to extend her history to two or three more volumes, had announced even that "a considerable part" of these had already been written; but nothing was published beyond the first.[13]

Her circumstances had meanwhile radically changed. Imlay, under pretext of business difficulties, left for England, and she returned to Paris. In April 1795 she went with her child to London, to find that Imlay was living with an actress. Seven weeks later, accompanied by her child and a nurse, she undertook a trip to Sweden, Norway, and Denmark for him, and on her return she found that Imlay had a new mistress. She tried to commit suicide by throwing herself into the Thames but was saved. Her friends rallied around her, and she appeared once more in their society. She renewed her acquaintance with William Godwin, whom she had first met before going to France. The author of *Political Justice* and *Caleb Williams* was now a famous man, surrounded by disciples. In April 1796 she moved into Godwin's neighborhood, and—to quote the latter—gradually "their friendship melted into love." [14] Both had an aversion to marriage, but, on account of her pregnancy, at the end of March 1797 they married and took a house together. She was busy on various literary plans, and intended to do a series of books for children. On August 30 she gave birth to a daughter —Shelley's future wife—but ten days later died.

Mary Wollstonecraft's portrait, painted by John Opie and now in the National Gallery, shows a face of great charm. The features are irregular, but the large eyes and sensitive mouth reveal a generous nature. "Her manners were gentle, easy, and elegant," the *Gentleman's Magazine* wrote in its obituary, "her conversation intelligent and amusing, without the least trace of literary pride or the apparent consciousness of powers above the level of her sex; and, for soundness of understanding, and sensibility of heart, she was, perhaps, rarely equaled." [15] Shelley and his circle naturally cherished her memory. In the dedication of *The Revolt of Islam* he speaks of her

> "Whose life was like a setting planet mild,
>   Which clothed thee in the radiance undefiled
>   Of its departing glory . . ."

Her eclipse during the Victorian era was, in spite of Kegan Paul's warm appreciation, inevitable. But she does not receive her full recognition even today. In many people's minds her figure has become entangled with that of her daughter, the author of *Frankenstein, Valpurga*, and similar novels. Librarians have contributed not a little to the confusion by cataloguing her works under her married name; and that Mary Godwin Shelley is often listed as "Mary Wollstonecraft Shelley" is certainly no help.

Of all his books, Adams commented most profusely on Mary Wollstonecraft's *French Revolution*. He read it first in 1796, and then again in 1812 at Quincy. In going through the first sections, he was unusually calm, making only carping comments about her "indelicate" language and poking fun at her pretensions of philosophy; but later on he became increasingly combative. She uses the word "sacred" fairly often, and Adams tauntingly asked her what she meant by it, unwilling to recognize the fact that she was deeply religious. [16] He took an opposite view on almost every subject. Before going far he noted that Miss Wollstonecraft was "partial to the people and vs the cabinet"; he himself was certainly free from that bias. Miss Wollstonecraft was "too harsh" toward the King; Adams defended him ardently. The Queen he did not like—but that is no surprise. He found excuses for the nobility, and even for such men as the Count of Artois and Calonne. But it was in the analysis of the new constitution that Adams was in his real element; he never missed a chance to point out the dire consequences of having a government without proper balances. All the catastrophes, he insisted, were caused by a single assembly, which in turn had been adopted because of the baneful influence of Franklin, Turgot, and "their blind disciples." The author's praise of the simplicity of the unicameral system drew from him a savage burlesque of the idea.

Adams made notes on more than five hundred passages, jotting down in all some twelve thousand words. They add up to his own version of the Revolution. As to Mary Wollstonecraft, he himself felt that at times he was unjust, and at the end he offered his apologies:

"This is a lady of a masculine masterly understanding. Her style is nervous and clear, often elegant; though sometimes too verbose. With a little experience in public affairs and the reading and reflection which would result from it, she would have produced a history without the defects and blemishes pointed out with too much severity perhaps and too little gallantry in the notes.

"The improvement, the exaltation of the human character, the perfectibility of man, and the perfection of the human faculties are the divine objects which her enthusiasm beholds in beatific vision. Alass, how airy and baseless a fabric!

"Yet she will not admit of the only means that can accomplish any part of her ardent prophecies: forms of government, so mixed, combined and balanced, as to restrain the passions of all orders of men."

TO AUGUST 4, 1789

Intent on tracing the origins of the Revolution, Mary Wollstonecraft goes back as far as the Crusades and the age of chivalry; then she discusses the invention of printing, the administrations of Richelieu and Mazarin, the theater of Molière, Corneille, and Racine, the theories of the *philosophes*, the American Revolution, the characters of Louis XVI and Marie Antoinette, the coalition of clergy and nobility, the activities of the provincial assemblies, and many other subjects. Adams noted the key words in almost every paragraph; and also underlined many sentences, but made only a few comments:

Mary Wollstonecraft: When men once see that *on the general happiness depends their own*, reason will give strength to the fluttering wings of passion, and men will "do unto others, what they wish they should do unto them." [17]
Adams: Heavenly times!
M.W.: We must get entirely clear of all the notions drawn from the *wild traditions* of original sin . . .
A.: i.e. we must get entirely clear of Christianity.

Then, on a single page, Adams twice reproved the author. He found her comparison of the government to a dying wretch prompted by the lust of enjoyment "Indelicate"; and when she spoke of the fair bosom of public opinion, he reminded himself that "A lady is the writer." The people were determined, Miss Wollstonecraft continues, to strike at the root of the combined evils of monarchy, priesthood, and nobility. In a Gargantuan sentence filling nearly a page, she contemplates the right cure:

M.W.: If *the degrading distinctions of rank* be really becoming in the estimation of all sensible people so contemptible that a modest man in the course of fifty years would probably blush at being thus distinguished . . .

A.: Can an army or society move in order without ranks? Are riches to be the only distinction? Is there any distinction more degrading than riches?

M.W.: If the degeneracy of the higher orders of society be such that no remedy less fraught with horror can effect a radical cure, the people are justified in having recourse to coercion.

A.: Is the degeneracy of the higher greater than that of the lower orders?

M.W.: It may be politically just to root out those deleterious plants which poison the better half of human happiness.

A.: Are those plants all rooted out? Are not fresh ones sown?

M.W.: Civilization, by producing inequality of conditions, has so weakened all the organs of the body politic that the strong have always devoured the weak.

A.: It is wealth that produces the inequality of conditions.

For the rest, Adams was calmly amused. "Till men learn mutually to assist without governing each other . . .," the author writes, and he assented, "Very pretty!" She rounds off a poetic sentence: "Men without principle rise like foam during a storm sparkling on the top of the billow . . ." "Beautiful," he applauded. And when Miss Wollstonecraft fervently hopes that perhaps a fairer government may rise from the chaos, "God grant it!" he added. The author describes the inhuman oppressions of feudalism:

M.W.: All lived by plunder . . . and thus *the rich necessarily became robbers, and the poor thieves.*

A.: The edge on these phrases is too sharp to be strong.

M.W.: The lower ranks of the nobility *ill brooked the overbearing insolence of those princes and peers, who haughtily contested every step of honor.*

A.: Nobles must be peers, or envious.

This is a Lady of a masculine masterly Understanding. Her Style is nervous and clear often elegant: though sometimes too verbose. With a little Experience in Public affairs and the Reading and Reflection which would result from it, She would have produced a History without the Defects and Blemishes pointed out with too much Severity perhaps and too little Gallantry in the Notes.

The Improvement, the exaltation of the human Character, the Perfectibility of Man, the Perfection of the human Faculties are the divine Objects which her Enthusiasm beholds in beatific Vision. Alass how airy and baseless a fabrick! Yet she will not admit of the only means that can accomplish any Part of her ardent Prophecies, Forms of Government, So mixed, combined and ballanced as to restrain the Passions of all orders of Men.

Notes on a blank page of Mary Wollstonecraft's *French Revolution i.e to prepare two Sieves ; the flower may be fine.*

Popular Declaimers with a Clapping Gallery and an Obsequious Multitude at their beak, can intimidate Popular assemblies into any Thing far.

Of the same Faction will overawe both assemblies if both are Elective.

hasty decisions ; or the carrying into laws dangerous, impolitic measures, which have been urged by popular declaimers, who are too apt to gain an ascendancy in a numerous assembly. Until the principles of governments become simplified, and a knowledge of them be disseminated, it is to be feared, that popular assemblies will often be influenced by the fascinating charms of eloquence : and as it is possible for a man to be eloquent without being either wise or virtuous, it is but a common precaution of prudence in the framers of a constitution, to provide some check to the evil. *Eloquence is but a Tool. The check must be provided to the Lust of Power & uses ; Tool.*

Besides, it is very probable, in the same state of reason, that a faction may arise, which will control the assembly ; and, acting contrary to the dictates of wisdom, throw the state into the most dangerous convulsions of anarchy : consequently, it ought to form a primary object with a constituting assembly, to prevent, by some salutary contrivance, the mischief flowing from such sources. The obvious preventative is a second chamber, or senate, which would not, it is most likely, be under the influence of the same faction ; and

It will if it is elective.

it is at least certain, that it's decisions would not

an hereditary Second Chamber is the only effectual Check to Faction in the first, in opulent Nations with great Armies Navies Churches Revenues i.e a great Patronage.

Adams for an hereditary second chamber "in opulent nations"

M.W.: Full of the *new notions of independence, which made them spurn at every idea of a distinction of men*, the commons began to rally their forces.

A.: New notions indeed! and very short-lived.

M.W.: To furnish a pretext to introduce a considerable military force, two or three riots were *excited* at Paris . . .

A.: By the court, as the insinuation is; but is there proof?

On May 5 the States-General were opened. In his speech the King asserted that the heavy debts of the country were accumulated "in an honorable cause." Miss Wollstonecraft thought that the cause was "most dishonorable." "Thank you, Miss!" Adams took up the challenge, thinking that she meant the American War; but it was the wasteful luxury at Versailles that she intended to condemn. The fight about the meetings of the States-General—whether they should sit in one house or in three—began at once. In spite of the opposition of the nobles, bishops, and court, the third estate proceeded to business. On June 20, however, they found the entrance to their hall barred; adjourning to a neighboring tennis court, they swore not to disperse until they had framed the constitution:

M.W.: In one of those *instants* of disinterested forgetfulness, all devoted themselves to the promotion of public happiness . . .

A.: When will these instants become hours?

M.W.: The ridiculous pride of the nobles led them to believe that the *purity of their families would be sullied* if they agreed to act in the same sphere with the people.

A.: They were forbid by law to trade.

M.W.: The King exclaimed that he "remained alone in the midst of the nation, occupied with the establishment of concord." Vain words!

A.: Honest words!

Finally, the nobility, pretending to believe that the King would be in danger, decided to attend at the common hall and "bury all rivalry in royalty." "The only way in which nobles ever buried their rivalries; and this only by the compulsion of the people," Adams suggested.

Next, Miss Wollstonecraft presents sharply drawn portraits of Marie Antoinette and Louis XVI:

M.W.: The courtly, dignified politeness of the Queen, with all those complacent graces which dance round flattered beauty, promised all that a sanguine fancy had pictured of future happiness and peace.

A.: Her beauty was chiefly the fiction of flattery.[18]

M.W.: Her *lovely face*, sparkling with vivacity . . .

A.: I never could see it. She was giddy with vivacity.

M.W.: . . . hid the want of intelligence. She happily mingled the most insinuating *voluptuous* softness and affability with an air of grandeur . . .

A.: Miss Wollstonecraft is too fond of such words.

M.W.: She never omitted sending immense *sums to her brother* on every occasion.

A.: What is the evidence of this?

M.W.: During her prosperity, the moments of languor that glide into the interstices of *enjoyment* were passed in the most childish manner . . .

A.: These luscious words might have been avoided by a lady.

M.W.: She acquired unbounded sway over the King . . . *The education of the heir apparent of a crown must necessarily destroy the common sagacity and feelings of a man.*

A.: This is not true. Some thousands of sovereigns in Europe have proved the contrary. But it is the tone to belie princes. Aristocracy is again preparing Barons' Wars, under other names. The people I hope will be gainers by them in the end, but the process is cruel.

M.W.: *Priests* have, in general, contrived to become the preceptors of kings, the more surely to support the church by leaning it against the throne.

A.: It is the tone too to belie priests.

M.W.: The King wanted that *firmness of mind* which constitutes character.

A.: This is probably true.

M.W.: He was extremely fond of seeing those *grimaces made by tortured animals*, which rouse to pleasure sluggish, gross sensations.

A.: I never heard this in France.

M.W.: Taught also to dissemble from his cradle, he daily practiced the despicable shifts of *duplicity*.

A.: This I never heard.

The French nobility Miss Wollstonecraft regards as perhaps "the most corrupt and ignorant set of men in the world." "Corrupt in common with all ranks in Europe; but not more ignorant," was Adams's opinion. They were determined to subvert everything, she goes on, rather than resign their privileges. "They were debarred from more privileges than they enjoyed," Adams thought. A nobleman would never marry a woman of low birth. "This was a restraint hardly recompenced by his privileges," Adams gallantly remarked.

M.W.: Thirty-five· thousand foreign troops were concentrated around Versailles . . . The courtiers vaunted that *the National Assembly would soon be dissolved and the rebellious deputies silenced by imprisonment or death.*

A.: Is it ascertained whether this measure was offensive or defensive? The court suspected that Paris meditated the destruction of the King and royal family. Paris suspected the court to intend the dissolution of the National Assembly. Mutual suspicion is natural and unavoidable in such cases, and rendered incurable by fools on both sides.

M.W.: The firmness of a handful of raw Bostonian militia on Bunker Hill ought to have taught them that *men determined to be free* are always superior to mercenary battalions even of veterans.

A.: I wish this were true: but Alexander and Frederick and Caesar and many others have unhappily proved that freedom is not always superior to discipline.

M.W.: The nobles had no conception that men obeying the impulse of liberty will always be able to resist the attacks of all the enervated mercenaries of the globe.

A.: Alass! this has not been always the case. Russians and Prussians have beat Poles, Alexander Athenians, the Romans Germans, all fighting for liberty. This is youthful and female enthusiasm.

2

A chronicle of the turbulent events of July 13 and 14, including the storming of the Bastille, follows. Lafayette was chosen president of the Assembly, and in submitting a proposal for a Declaration of Rights finished his address with the memorable words: "For a nation to love liberty, it is sufficient that she knows it; and to be free, it is sufficient that she wills it." [19] Adams was impressed: "Very good," he noted.

M.W.: The members of the Assembly reminded each other that, even if they perished, a brave and generous people would erect on their tomb, as an immortal trophy, *a constitution solid as reason, and durable as time* . . .[20]

A.: 1796. The 3d essay is now in operation but it is to be feared that three attempts more will not produce the constitution solid as reason.

M.W.: So *negligent* was the Court that the citizens requested of the committee an order to demand those arms they heard were stored up at the *Hotel des Invalides.*

A.: This negligence is evidence that they intended only self-defence.

M.W.: Various accounts of massacres and assassinations were brought to the *hotel-de-ville* which inflamed the people, though afterwards they proved to be the idle *rumors of fear.*

A.: Perhaps artfully spread.

The account of the taking of the Bastille, and the execution of its commander and of the mayor of Paris, Adams read without comment, merely underscoring sentences and noting the names. Miss Wollstonecraft charges the King with "artful affection" and "cold contempt." Yet the people cheered Louis as he announced the withdrawal of the troops from Versailles:

M.W.: The *transports* of the people and the *sympathy* of the deputies must have formed a highly interesting scene . . .

A.: These transports and sympathies are oftener the destruction of liberty than are its creators or preservers.

M.W.: The old worn-out government fell at the first shock, *never to rise again* . . .

A.: May a better arise!

M.W.: Unhappily, the people have always been governed in their sentiments of men by the most popular anarchists . . .

A.: This is always so till universal ruin, distress, and famine convince the people "We have been all wrong, this will never do. There must be some power that can unite us, that knows more than we do."

M.W.: Sanguine minds, disgusted with the vices and artificial manners produced by the great inequality of conditions in France . . . hailed the dawn of a new day when the Bastille was destroyed.

A.: Can there ever be more equality where there is equal wealth? Or less vice and artificial manners? Wealth is the mischief.

The author makes further "reflections" on the conduct of the Court and the King; meditates on the harmful consequences of complicating laws; and even considers the decline of Aristotelian philosophy and the influence of Descartes and Newton. Adams bravely followed her digressions, often answering before she finished the sentence:

M.W.: The effect produced by the duplicity of courts must be great . . .

A.: The duplicity of democracies, aristocracies, and oligarchies is equally great, where there is equal wealth and power. Mixed governments only can detect these duplicities.

M.W.: The *want of morals in the Court,* and *even in the Assembly,* made a *prevailing mistrust* produce a capriciousness of conduct throughout the empire.

A.: When will this mistrust be remedied? When the morals are better. When will that be? Perhaps when a great part of the nation is depopulated and arts, manufactures, commerce and riches destroyed, and then it is to be feared the rage for introducing them again will produce as bad morals and as much distrust as ever.

M.W.: [The degeneration of morals] has been the cause of the *insincerity*, which has so long disgraced the courts of Europe, and . . . has extended its poison throughout the higher orders of society.

A.: I saw no more sincerity in any class of people than at courts.

M.W.: We ought not to be discouraged from attempting the simplification of laws because no country has yet been able to do it . . .

A.: A complication of laws can never be avoided in a great commercial nation. Plato's commonwealth alone can accomplish it only in part.

M.W.: The laws, made by ambition rather than reason, treated with contempt *the sacred equality of man* . . .

A.: How came the equality of man sacred but by that revelation that Miss W. endeavors to discredit?

M.W.: To what purpose do *semi-philosophers* exultingly show that the vices of one country are not the vices of another . . .

A.: Miss W. is not a whole philosopher.

M.W.: . . . as if this would prove *that morality has no solid foundation.*

A.: Pray on what foundation does Miss W. place morality?

M.W.: Who will dare to assert today that obedience to parents should go one jot beyond the deference due to reason, enforced by affection?

A.: Would you make the child the judge?

M.W.: And who will coolly maintain that it is just to deprive a woman of all the rights of a citizen, because her revolting heart turns from the man whom she can neither love or respect, to find comfort in a more congenial or humane bosom?

A.: Would you divorce her when she pleased? Would you have no women because some are incorrigible prostitutes? Would you have no husbands because some are brutal? Would you have no beauty because it often seduces? Would you have no writers because some like your-self are licentious?

The author maintains that the Greeks and Romans had polished manners but were lacking in "genuine feelings of the soul." Modern times, with all their shortcomings, are better:

M.W.: The cruelties of the half-civilized Romans prove that the progress of the sciences alone can make men wiser and happier.

A.: Witness Marat, Robespierre, Collot, etc.[21]

M.W.: A human being is not now allowed *vainly to call for death,* whilst the flesh is pinched off his quivering limbs.

A.: No. The guillotine is more expeditious; so are the drowning boats.

M.W.: What moral lesson can be drawn from the story of Oedipus? The *gods* impel him on, and, led imperiously by blind fate, though per-fectly innocent, he is fearfully punished for a crime in which his will had no part.

A.: These were heathen gods, Miss W. Thank Moses and Jesus that you have better notions of divinity.

M.W.: At present a man may reasonably expect to be allowed tran-quilly to *follow any scientific pursuit.*

A.: But it is religion and government that have effected this.

M.W.: In the Middle Ages *nothing was founded on philosophical principles . . .*

A.: Now everything is and we see the effect in France.

M.W.: The people were, strictly speaking, slaves; bound by feudal tenures, and still more oppressive ecclesiastical *restraints.*

A.: Now they are to be bound by no tenures and under no restraints. But taxes are almost as bad as tenures, and atheism is worse than even Catholicism, if we judge by its effects.

3

While all Europe was enslaved, the author continues, the Britons alone preserved their early liberty, thanks to their revered constitution. Then she analyzes the nature of freedom and its impediments:

M.W.: Taking for granted that their constitution was the model of perfection, Englishmen never seem to have formed an idea of a system more *simple . . .*[22]

A.: A house 100 foot square all in one room would be more simple than if it had chambers and rooms, garrets and cellars, but would not be so comfortable.

M.W.: The Anglo-Americans having carried with them the principles of their ancestors, liberty appeared in the New World with *renovated charms and sober matron graces.*

A.: I thank you Miss W. May we long enjoy your esteem.

M.W.: Man enjoys freedom in a natural state in its full extent . . .

A.: One man alone would be free, but give him a wife and children and they must all lose a part of their liberty.

M.W.: . . . . but, to unfold his intellectual powers, it becomes necessary to surrender part of his natural privileges; and during the infancy of society it was easy for the *leaders*, by frequent usurpation, to create a despotism.

A.: These leaders were generally as ignorant as their followers, and both leaders and followers are still as ignorant as ever of the form of government which is indispensable to preserve liberty in rich commercial states--and neither will learn.

M.W.: In the progress of knowledge . . . the benefits of civil liberty began to be better understood: and in the same proportion we find the chains of despotism becoming lighter.

A.: It would be quite as correct to say that the progress of navigation and commerce and manufactures necessitated men to agree to fix'd laws of property, and from those laws knowledge and liberty have increased. But in the course, commerce and wealth have destroyed the institutions that preserved morals as well as property; and now all nations and all parties, except a very few individuals, appear to be ignorant of the political organizations and equipoises necessary to preserve liberty, property, life or anything.

M.W.: Still the systematizing of pedants, the ingenious fallacy of priests, and the supercilious meanness of the literary sycophants of courts continued to perplex and confound the understandings of unlettered men.

A.: Pedants, priests and sycophants will flatter the people when supreme, and oligarchy or aristocracy as readily and as successfully as they will a despot. How then will you make and execute law? that is the question.

Miss Wollstonecraft notes the stirrings of freedom in the world of arts and learning. In Germany, especially, the new spirit has invaded even the colleges and courts:

M.W.: It is by *teaching* men from their youth *to think* that they *will* be enabled to *recover* their *liberty*.

A.: I hope so: but they must learn to know the emulation of their own hearts, and how to control it by checks.

M.W.: Though the arbitrary chief judge Mansfield established it as a law precedent that *the greater the truth the greater the libel* . . .[23]

A.: Miss W. did not understand this great subject.

M.W.: . . . yet the clamor which was raised against that *unpopular war* in America is a proof that liberty of thought had not forsaken the island.

A.: Unpopular with one, and very popular with two. With what delight did two-thirds of the nation talk of the vast advantages to the nation in conquering the America! And with what pleasure did they anticipate the ruling America with a rod of iron! And how freely did they express this pleasure in anticipation!

M.W.: It was at this crisis of things that the despotism of France was completely *overturned* . . .

A.: And how many overturns have succeeded?

M.W.: Twenty-five millions of human beings were unloosed from the odious bands which had for centuries *benumbed their faculties*.

A.: Arts, sciences, literature were cultivated in every kind, to greater extent than in any other nation under heaven by those be-numbed faculties.

M.W.: It now remains to observe *the effect* of this important revolution, which may fairly be dated from the taking of the Bastille.

A.: The effect is now observable enough, all over the globe. Napoleon and George 3d have made the effects very striking. [1812.]

4

The destruction of the Bastille filled the Parisians with joy—and where is there such a complete forgetfulness of tomorrow as in Paris? ("Ah! this oblivion of tomorrow will make a strange republic," Adams soberly noted.) Bailly was chosen mayor of Paris,[24] and Lafayette commander in chief of the National Guards. But soon rapture dwindled to suspicion, and the people demanded Necker's recall. The King signified his intention to visit Paris, and accordingly left Versailles on July 16, followed by a hundred deputies:

M.W.: The King saw the Parisians triumphant, moving orderly along, calling out on every side for a *constitution and laws* . . .[25]

A.: A sacred word! but how shall it be made? and what shall it be?

M.W.: Taking the national cockade from the hand of the mayor, the King appeared at the window with his heart in his eyes, as if eager to convince the multitude of his sincerity . . .

A.: This is pathetic. These enthusiasms are contagious, but they must be regulated.

M.W.: Pleasure, now almost mounting to a feverish height, set all Paris quickly in motion . . .

A.: These powers in republics where all should be cool, reasonable, thinking, deliberating, calculating, are deleterious distempers.

M.W.: These sudden transitions from one extreme to another could not be seen in such a strong light anywhere as at Paris . . .

A.: Patience, moderation, reflection, perseverance, firmness are the necessary qualities of republicans. When will the metamorphosis take place? Will atheism and infidelity produce it? Will stage players and romance writers produce it? Such have been for some time legislators in France.

M.W.: The *want of decision* in the character of Louis seems to have been the foundation of all his faults . . .

A.: There is some truth in this.

M.W.: It is difficult to mark any fixt purpose in his actions, excepting *the desire to prevent the shedding of blood* . . .

A.: This is a trait in the character of the family of Bourbon.

Without the Revolution, Miss Wollstonecraft thinks, the Bastille might have remained standing; but even if it had, human misery would not have been increased, for "streams of innocent blood would not have flowed from the guillotine." From a sympathizer of the Revolution, this was a surprising admission. But Adams went further: "The drowning boats of the Loire and the langridge of Lyons and the pikes in the prisons were worse than the guillotine." [26]

M.W.: Even amidst the heroism which distinguished the taking of the Bastille, we are forced to see that *suspicious temper* and *the vain ambition of dazzling* which generated all the succeeding follies and crimes.

A.: Does this weak woman expect that jealousy and envy, ambition and vanity will ever disappear?

M.W.: In the most public-spirited actions, *celebrity seems to have been the spur* and the *glory rather than the happiness of Frenchmen, the end.*

A.: Will a nation all ever act for the happiness of the nation?

M.W.: The morals of the whole nation were destroyed by the manners formed by the government.

A.: Whence is this morality to come? If the Christian religion and all the power of government has never produced it, what will? Yet this mad woman is for destroying the Christian religion.

The reunion of the King and the people frightened the cabal. The Count of Artois, Marshal Broglie, Madame de Polignac, and many others went into exile.[27] Madame de Polignac was a favorite of the Queen, and the author makes a suggestive remark about the latter's "strange predilection for handsome women." "An allusion to disgusting reports which I often heard in Paris," Adams remarked. The *émigrés* met Calonne,[28] the former Comptroller General, who, having heard of Necker's new dismissal, was eager to return to France, hoping that meanwhile the army would destroy the popular forces. Adams doubted the insinuation: "A fact like this is not to be taken on the credit of any historian. The evidence should have been produced." Calonne, Miss Wollstonecraft writes, possessed only showy talents; Mirabeau, on the contrary, had natural dignity, truth, and earnestness. "I shall not take the character of this man upon the authority of Miss W.," Adams rejoined.

Most of the "noble depredators" escaped, but the minister Foulon and his son-in-law were caught and murdered by the mob. The people's vengeance starts the author off on a speculation about the causes of evil:

M.W.: Alas! *It is morals*, not feelings, which distinguish men from the beasts of prey!

A.: But what are morals according to Volney? not even feelings: mere dry rules of convenience.[29]

M.W.: And if it be impossible to e_ase from the memory these foul deeds, it becomes necessary to observe that whilst despotism and superstition exist, the convulsions will always bring forward the vices they have engendered.

A.: Ay! cast all upon despotism and superstition. Are the cruelties of savages owing to despotism and superstition? Allow the truth that all men are ferocious monsters when their passions are unrestrained. Prepare bridles for them.

M.W.: "If the anger of the people be terrible," exclaims Mirabeau, "it is the *sang froid* of despotism that is atrocious."

A.: The Turks say that anarchy does more mischief in one night than tyranny in twenty years. It is perhaps nearer the truth to say that tyranny and anarchy are equally cruel and destructive.

M.W.: "Let us compare," he further adds, "the number of innocents sacrificed by the sanguinary maxims of the courts of criminal judicature and in the cells of the Bastille with the sudden vengeance of the multitude, and then decide on which side barbarity appears."

A.: It was shrewd to throw the blame on the Bastille: but it is curious to compare the cruelties of the last seven years with all the acts of tyranny of Louis 15 and 16 through their whole reigns.[30]

M.W.: In all civil wars, *personal vengeance mixing with public*, has directed the dagger of the assassin.

A.: Rival lovers, authors, artists have often committed murthers. Witness the League and the Fronde.[31]

The news of the conspiracy of the *émigré* princes with foreign powers inflamed the spirit of self-defense; in a single week more than three million men took up arms. Meanwhile, disturbances broke out at Soissons, St. Denis, and elsewhere in the country. On July 23 the Assembly issued a proclamation, requesting all good citizens to maintain order. Mirabeau sounded a warning: "Society would soon be dissolved, if the multitude, accustomed to blood and disorder, placed themselves above the magistrates. Instead of running to meet freedom, the people would soon throw themselves into the abyss of servitude; for in the bosom of anarchy even a despot appears a savior." Adams underlined the whole passage, and noted with satisfaction, "He had then lately read The Defence."

Rumors spread that the English, whom people regarded as natural enemies, wished to avenge the French support of the Americans. Necker was again recalled, but he soon lost his popularity. "The narrow capacity of the minister," the author remarks, "did not allow him to take a determined part in the grand work in which the deputies were engaged." Adams judged him differently: "His capacity was too large to be duped to distraction by either side. He wanted an English constitution which neither king nor nation would agree to."

5

Now came the debate on the Declaration of Rights. Some members of the Assembly argued that it ought to follow, rather than precede, the Constitution, for it might be dangerous "to awaken a somnambulist on the brink of a precipice." Barnave, however, insisted that the declaration would serve as a guide for the formulation of laws.[32] "We need only turn over the page of history," he declaimed, "to lose these vain fears." (The oratory ruffled Adams: "Of how many falsehoods is the page of history cited in proof! The Romans were never more enlightened than in the times of Marius, Sulla and Caesar, and never so unquiet. The French and English were never more enlightened than in these days and never so uneasy.") The majority of the Assembly decided for a declaration. This took place on the morning of August 4. But it was the evening session of that day that has become one of the most memorable events of the Revolution.

A great speech by the Vicomte de Noailles started off the meeting. Patriotism demanded real sacrifices, the Count declared, and he forthwith proposed a series of reforms adding up to the total abolition of feudalism. The motions were accepted with boundless enthusiasm. The spirit of generosity became contagious. The Duc d'Aiguillon was anxious to see the establishment of equal rights. The Bishop of Nancy requested that the ransom of ecclesiastical feudalities should be converted into a fund for the benefit of the lower clergy. The Bishop of Chartres recommended the repeal of the game laws. The Duc du Châtelet wanted tithes eliminated.[33] Not only were all the serfs freed, but the Assembly also thought of liberating the Negroes of West India. Several church dignitaries who had two or more benefices renounced all but one. It was an orgy of self-sacrifice, ending in a resolution, proposed by the Archbishop of Paris, to celebrate the night with a solemn *Te Deum* throughout the country. But Miss Wollstonecraft is skeptical:

M.W.: The *political empirics* have continually *inflamed the foibles of the multitude, by flattering them . . .*[34]

A.: There will always be such in such times.

M.W.: In proportion as this cajolery was more highly seasoned, the power of ruling has descended to *the most desperate and impudent* of the smatterers in politics.

A.: Nations! You have all this to go thro if you will have revolutions.

M.W.: It is very possible that the next morning the different parties could scarcely believe that they had more than the imperfect recollection of a dream in their heads.

A.: The V. de Noailles has said to me, "When I gave up my nobility with one hand, I expected to have received it back again with the other!"

M.W.: But the commons, who had the deepest views, would not let them recede.

A.: The views of the commons were as shallow as those of the nobles or the priests.

M.W.: The steps taken to increase the salaries of the indigent clergy, the most numerous part of the body in the Assembly, secured their influence.

A.: Hear! Read!

M.W.: And by destroying the monopoly of municipal and judicial employments, the support of the cities was obtained.

A.: Hear! Read!

M.W.: Thus the Assembly, without a struggle, found itself omnipotent.

A.: I.e. potent enough to destroy itself and the nation!

M.W.: Almost everything human, however beautiful the superstructure, has hitherto been built on *the vile foundation of selfishness.*

A.: Oh foul confession; Tacitus, Rochefoucauld, Mandeville all agree with Miss W., or rather Miss W. with them.

M.W.: I do not mean to say that there were not any real patriots in the Assembly, men who have studied politics and whose ideas and opinions are reduced to principles.

A.: This is all that can be expected of patriotism. But who were these? Maury or Mounier? [35]

M.W.: But most of the leaders were guided by *a vain desire of applause,* or *deep schemes of emolument.*

A.: What becomes of the perfectibility of man?

M.W.: During the first struggle, the Assembly and the people were divided into republicans and royalists; but soon the higher classes, recruiting from the royalists, formed themselves into a growing aristocracy.

A.: And does this foolish woman expect to get rid of an aristocracy? God Almighty has decreed in the creation of human nature an eternal aristocracy among men. The world is, always has been, and ever will be governed by it. All that policy and legislation can do is to check its force by force. Arm a power above it and another below it; or if you will, one on its right hand, the other on its left: both able to say to it, when it grows mad, "Maniac! keep within your limits."

THE FRAMING OF THE CONSTITUTION

For nearly twenty pages Miss Wollstonecraft analyzes the character of the members of the National Assembly. Considering the despotism of the former government, she writes, it is not extraordinary to find the leading patriots men without principles or political knowledge. But Adams rejected the explanation: "It is artful to impute the morals of France to despotism: but it is sophistry. The truth is 'like people like priest' is as true as 'like rulers like people.' Wealth and commerce have corrupted all Europe nearly alike and governors and governed are all of a piece . . ."

M.W.: It was to be presumed that, *by the improvement of morals, which would necessarily follow,* the evils which the old system produced would vanish before gradual amendments . . .

A.: Morals hitherto have been depraved, rather than improved, and there is cause to fear will grow worse and worse.

M.W.: Reason was tracing out for France the road which leads to virtue, glory, and happiness . . .

A.: Madness was tracing the road to vice, infamy, and misery.

M.W.: . . . yet every debate became a bitter or violent contest, in which the *popular advocates* continued to gain an ascendancy.

A.: Theatrical actors, romance writers, etc.

M.W.: This *want of sincerity,* so generally remarked in the French character . . .

A.: And English too.

M.W.: The coalesced parties were not aware that a watchful, *suspicious multitude* would be as likely to mistrust them in their turn as the court . . .[36]

A.: A suspicious multitude will watch every succession of leaders and set up new rivals to supplant them as long as that multitude have the elections of the executive and senate, while principle is wanting.

M.W.: It appears not a little wonderful that men should not acquire sufficient judgment to adopt the *integrity of conduct,* with which alone people in their senses will ever be satisfied.

A.: Integrity of conduct will be certain ruin to·rulers when their electors are corrupt.

Miss Wollstonecraft particularly deplores that many of the early leaders of the Revolution, disappointed at the turn of events, withdrew or fled abroad:

M.W.: If they find that the current of opinion threatens the destruction of principles the most sacred, the leaders *ought firmly to wait at their post* . . .

A.: And there perish without hope, as every one has done? No. No.

M.W.: But such patriotism is of slow growth, requiring to be *fostered by virtuous emulation.*

A.: Emulation in profligacy, hypocrisy and villainy there will be. Emulation in virtue can only be where virtue is respected.

M.W.: It was by debasing artifices, under the old government, that men obtained favor and consequence.

A.: And by more debasing artifices under the new.

M.W.: Whilst men who were educated and ossified by the ancient regime act on the political stage of France, mankind will be *continually distressed and amused by their tragic and comic exhibitions.*

A.: This I believe unless they adopt a government better balanced. When cunning is balanced against cunning, the most cunning will triumph. When force is balanced against force, the strongest will prevail. When cunning and force united are balanced against cunning and force united, reason must be armed to mediate between them. There must be an armed neutrality.

M.W.: Almost every precipitate event has been the consequence of littleness of mind in the political actors, whilst they were affecting a Roman magnanimity of conduct . . .

A.: It is passing strange that all these things did not convince Miss W. that the French nation were incapable of a republican government.

M.W.: We have first seen Calonne, in order to secure his popularity and place, proposing an equalization of taxes; and, when he found that his consequence and power were lost, abandoning his country in disgust . . .

A.: Condorcet and Rochefoucauld did more harm than Calonne by their idolatry to Franklin, the weak disciple of Nedham.[37] Their simple form of government by causing the murder of hundreds of thousands of innocent heads of families has produced complicated evils to the conviction of mankind. This experiment is nearly blown out.

M.W.: We shall find, likewise, several other declaimers *leaving their posts* . . .

A.: To escape a certain and useless death.

M.W.: The disasters of the nation have arisen from the same miserable source of *vanity* and the wretched struggles of *selfishness* . . .

A.: Alass! poor girl! Vanity and selfishness will never vanish while riches remain at least.

M.W.: And thus it has happened that *ignorance and audacity* have triumphed . . .

A.: Ignorance and audacity would have triumphed and murdered knowledge and modesty if they had stayed.

M.W.: Brilliant talents existed in France; and had they combined and directed their views by a pure love of their country, all the disasters which in overwhelming the empire have destroyed the repose of Europe would not have occurred.

A.: That is if God Almighty had wrought a greater miracle for the delivery of France than he ever did for the preservation of the Hebrews. The best talents in France were blind disciples of Franklin and Turgot and led the blind to destruction. I mean Rochefoucauld and Condorcet. [1796.] All that astōnished me in the whole Revolution was that all the disasters which overwhelmed the empire and destroyed the repose of Europe were not foreseen and foretold by every man of sense in Europe. [1812.]

The author regrets that there was no "systematic management" in the introduction of reforms. Above all, "the moderation and reciprocity of concessions," which are a prerequisite of peaceful progress, were lacking:

M.W.: It is true that in a nation chiefly celebrated for wit so much prudence could scarcely be expected; yet that is not a sufficient reason for *condemning all the principles* that produced the Revolution.

A.: She has condemned them more universally than any other historian that I have read. Selfish principles, love of glory are not absolutely and universally to be condemned. They are to be condemned when they do wrong but not when they do right. But there were generous and benevolent principles in this business.

M.W.: It would have been prudent then for men who agreed in the main objects to have overlooked trifling differences of opinion: and of this several members seem to have been aware. Lally-Tollendal, in particular . . .[38]

A.: Ah! Tollendal! Thy filial piety is immortal! I have eaten and drunk in thine apartments. I am proud to say thou were my disciple and convert to the doctrine of branches. But if Guy Fawkes had put a spark to his powder, it would have been too late for the Speaker to call the House to order.

M.W.: . . . said: "It is not doubtful at present that a single chamber is preferable. There is so much to destroy and almost all to create anew . . ."

A.: Joel Barlow in his History, no doubt on this principle will record Tom Paine as the greatest politician of the Revolution.

M.W.: But *designing knaves* conceived the plan of rising to eminence *by the accumulating foibles of the multitude* . . .

A.: The envy and rancor of the multitude against the rich is universal and restrained only by fear or necessity. A beggar can never comprehend the reason why another should ride in a coach while he has no bread.

The Revolution, the author points out, was not solely the concern of Frenchmen; the passions and prejudices of all Europe were set adrift:

M.W.: Having *overcome those formidable obstacles to the happiness of her citizens*, society seems to have arrived at that point of civilization when it becomes necessary for governments to meliorate its condition.

A.: Under color of destroying unnatural distinctions and veteran prejudices they have destroyed all the institutions to which they owe their superiority to Asia and Africa.

M.W.: This is a truth which the parasites of courts and the *advocates* for despotism have not been willing to believe.

A.: Such parasites and advocates have no doubt done much wrong: but the parasites and advocates of the mob have not done less.

Miss Wollstonecraft suggests that man in his savage state was especially warlike. Adams, however, believed: "Nations in every stage of society from savages to the most civilized are too much addicted to war, and the freer they are, the greater their pride, the stronger their resentment and the more prone to war." Rereading the book, he added: "Governments are not more disposed to quarrels than people: witness the Peloponnesian War and all others. England the free has not been less disposed to war than France, Spain, Germany, Prussia, and Russia the despotic." As man's ferocity wore away, the author goes on, the right of property grew sacred. "As the respect for property wears away, his ferocity will return," Adams predicted.

Once more, Miss Wollstonecraft paints a picture of French customs and manners. It would be a mistake to think, she writes, that there was no such thing as domestic happiness in France, or "even" in Paris:

M.W.: All that could be done by *a body of manners, without a soul of morals*, to improve mankind, has been tried in France.

A.: Where was there ever a better body or soul with so much riches?

M.W.: The result was polished slavery; and such an inordinate love of pleasure *as led the majority to search only for enjoyment*.

A.: Wealth, wealth, how shall we prevent thee from producing this effect? Many are like Indians; when rum is to be had they will get intoxicated. The cup of Circe is irresistible to many. How can we take it away if property is sacred and the cup is one's own?

M.W.: Many French families exhibited an affectional urbanity of behavior to each other, seldom to be met with where a certain easy gaiety does not soften the difference of age and condition.

A.: It would require a volume to make a comparison between the moral characters of the two nations, the French and the English. And after all, which to choose would be difficult for me to decide.

M.W.: Mothers were also to be found who, after suckling their children, paid a degree of attention to their education, not thought compatible with the levity of character attributed to them.

A.: This is a true picture. [1796.] I shall be thought a visionary, no doubt; but is not the predominant interest of agriculture, and the consequent perpetual demand of the nobility of an increase of the army in France, and the predominant interest of commerce and the consequent continued demand of an augmentation of a navy in England, the true secret of the policy of the two nations? Is not this the secret of the conduct and history of Holland? And is not this the secret of the inscrutable conduct of our American Congress? Commerce has vitiated morals in England more than agriculture in France. If there is any inferiority of morals in France, has it not sprung from the power of pardon and absolution in the priests? Religion has corrupted France, more than England. [1812.]

2

The resolutions of August 4 aroused wild jubilation, but also sarcastic disparagement. The Assembly had long been reproached for dwelling on trifling subjects; then suddenly, in a single night, more than twenty basic laws were established in an uproar. ("Every word of all these reproaches is true and well founded," Adams thought.) Some of the nobles and clergy of the provinces felt particularly aggrieved; and as for the people, the very concessions of the nobility seemed to increase their thirst for vengeance. Disturbances occurred in every part of the country, and the Assembly appealed to the militia to quell them.

Necker proposed to raise a loan of thirty million livres. Mirabeau, however, opposed the project. With pretended disinterestedness he recommended that the deputies offer their individual credits, rather than depart from their instructions. ("Nothing so infallibly gulls the people and nothing more universally deceives them in the end than this pretended disinterestedness," Adams remarked.) The debate on the Declaration of Rights still went on. In describing it, Miss Wollstonecraft separates the character of the philosopher, who wishes to promote the welfare of mankind and is not bound by consideration of time, from that of the politician, whose duty is to attend to the interests of his own day. ("A curious distinction between a philosopher and a politician! and not without sense," Adams noted.) The Declaration was introduced by a solemn exordium asserting the natural, inalienable, and sacred rights of man. ("What did they mean by sacred?" Adams importuned.)

Finally, the drafting of the Constitution began. The first question was what share of power the King ought to be allowed in the legislature. The debate was heated, "rudely personal and loudly uncivil," modest men having no chance to be heard:

M.W.: The blind zealots for the rights of kings eulogized the royal prerogatives, and made vapid *remarks* on the British constitution.[39]

A.: These remarks were the most judicious that were made.

M.W.: Mirabeau, with Mounier and Lally-Tollendal, argued for the absolute veto. "The possession of this power," he said, "is the only way to render a king *useful,* and to enable him to act as *a check* on the legislative body."

A.: He had read the Defence. Pity he had not adopted more of it.

M.W.: "The majority," he went on, "*might tyrannize in the most despotic manner*, to the very *expulsion* of the members who dared to thwart the measures they could not approve."

A.: They have guillotined them as well as expelled them.

M.W.: "The veto," Mirabeau maintained, "is but another right confided to the king by the people, because he and they are equally interested to prevent the establishment of an aristocracy."

A.: He and they under that Constitution of 1789 were equally interested to establish an hereditary aristocracy: for only such could defend the people against king, or king against people as was soon found.

M.W.: However, it became a mark of patriotism to oppose the veto. The public would scarcely allow it to be mentioned; and the Assembly, to steer a middle course, adopted the suspensive veto.

A.: The veto was useless in that constitution; so was the royal office. It could resist nothing.

M.W.: One of the deputies maintained that a suspensive veto would force the King to execute a law of which he disapproves, thus making him *a blind and passive instrument.*

A.: A blind and passive instrument he must be, under that constitution whether with or without a veto, or be guillotined, as we shall see he was.

M.W.: From the commencement of the Revolution, the misery of France has originated from the folly or art of men who have *spurred the people on too fast.*

A.: The people will be spurred on too fast by the folly or art of some, to the end of time without a check.

M.W.: An absolute veto would have given the King at least a semblance of his former authority which would have *gratified him.*

A.: Nothing should be instituted for the gratification of any one, all should be for the public good.

M.W.: The King was thus set up as an idol, merely to receive *the mock respect of the legislative body, till they were quite sure of the people.*

A.: This is very exact.

It would have been better, Miss Wollstonecraft believes, to retire the King than to "shuffle him off the throne" and make him appear as a "theatrical King," thus giving the despots of Europe a pretext to interfere:

M.W.: The liberating an imprisoned monarch was a plausible motive, though the real one was *to stop the progress of principles* . . .

A.: No doubt.

M.W.: . . . which, once permitted to extend themselves, would ultimately *overturn all the courts in Europe.*

A.: And what governments are to succeed? I fear they will be despotisms instead of monarchies, Turkish republics, Algerine or Morocco republics. Tyrants cutting off heads at will—without law or judge.

M.W.: The Assembly seems to have been influenced by *a ridiculous pride, not being willing to take the British constitution,* so far as it respected the prerogative, for their model.

A.: According to Necker this pride or ignorance prevented the King from agreeing to a constitution like the British. They have since, in 1795, adopted three branches: but still unbalanced and undigested. They must come nearer to a balance or still wade on in blood.

M.W.: That party that opposed the junction of the three orders still opposed, with rancorous heat and wily stratagems, every measure proposed by the really patriotic members.

A.: Who were the patriots?

M.W.: They were seconded by the insincere and the wavering, who always took the side best calculated to gratify the wishes of the multitude. This *unyoked multitude* . . .

A.: Not swinish.[40]

M.W.: . . . *all become consummate politicians*, began to control the decisions of a divided assembly.

A.: One party in an assembly will ever form an alliance with the multitude out of doors.

3

Prudence and resolution were needed to restrain the torrent of opinions. But there were no such influences anywhere. The intrigues of the nobility as well as demagoguery made the people greedy for power, and, instead of adopting the British constitution as a model, the Assembly followed the dreams of philosophers. Adams's comments crowded over the margins, until he was forced to scribble between the lines:

M.W.: So much wisdom would scarcely have been expected from the depraved and volatile French, who *proudly*, or *ignorantly*, seem to have fixed on *a system proper* only *for a people in the highest stage of oivilization*.[41]

A.: A system the most improper of all. The vanity of invention and original genius was ridiculously paraded, because all their system is a servile imitation of Nedham's.

M.W.: This political plan, *ever considered as utopian by all men who had not traced the progress of reason, or calculated the degree of perfectibility the human faculties are capable of attaining*, was the most unsuitable for the degenerate society of France.

A.: The Proteus Nedham who changed sides like an Arnold had, no doubt, traced the progress of reason, and calculated the perfectibility of the human faculties.

M.W.: *The men termed experienced believed it physically impossible.*

A.: With infallible truth and reason.

M.W.: Thus a fresh odium has been thrown on *principles*, which, notwithstanding, *are gaining ground*.

A.: What principles?

M.W.: The *accelerating progress of truth* promises to demonstrate what no arguments have hitherto been able to prove.

A.: Wild enthusiast! The progress of anarchy has nearly convinced the world that her system for the highest stage of civilization is a perfect Golgotha.

M.W.: The first article of the Declaration of Rights, establishing the equality of man, *strikes at the root of all useless distinctions*.

A.: With great propriety and justice.

M.W.: The second secures his right against oppression, and the third confirms the authority of the people. These are the essential points of a good government; and it is only necessary *to provide against the abuse of the executive part*.

A.: Provisions against the abuse of the legislative part are equally necessary. The efficiency of the executive cannot be secured but by its independence, and its independence cannot be maintained without a negative.

M.W.: The opposers of two chambers ridiculed the idea of a balance of power, and instanced the abuses of the English government to give force to their objections.

A.: Their unbalanced power has made sad havoc.

M.W.: The plan of a senate, proposed by the constitutional committee, only excited fresh apprehensions that *the ancient hydra would again rear its head.*

A.: This hydra has not only 100 heads but millions of millions. They will sprout to all eternity. As long as there are three men left, one at least will be an aristocrat.

M.W.: They represented this senate as *a dangerous counterpoise to popular violence* . . .

A.: There must be some counterpoise.

M.W.: . . . and to show their entire disinterestedness, they unanimously voted that *for each legislature* a total change of the deputies would take place.

A.: Robespierre made a curious use of his exclusion from the legislature. They have since voted that two-thirds should be reëlected whether the voters would or no.

M.W.: An indivisible assembly was adopted by a great majority, to *the entire satisfaction of the public*.[42]

A.: That public has been since converted. 1796.

M.W.: The deputies who opposed the upper chamber did it from a belief that it would be *the asylum of a new aristocracy*.

A.: So it ought to be.

Miss Wollstonecraft makes it clear that she is no blind devotee of the absolute veto, which may give one man the power to counteract the will of a whole people. "The veto is given as a weapon of defence to prevent the executive from being run down by the legislative," Adams enlightened her. On the other hand, the author remarks, the dignity of the crown may prevent an overweening aristocracy from concentrating all authority in themselves. With this Adams agreed. But Miss Wollstonecraft's vacillations annoyed him, and he angrily concluded: "This ignorant woman knows nothing of the matter. She seems to have half a mind to be an English woman; yet more inclined to be an American. Perhaps her lover gave her lessons."

M.W.: The veto seems to have been expedient, likewise, as long as the manners of barbarians remained: as *savages are naturally pleased with glass and beads* . . .

A.: The independence of the executive power is not a bauble, nor glass, nor beads. Without it there can be no government, no security for life, liberty or property.

M.W.: In the progressive influence of knowledge on manners, both *dress and governments* appear to be acquiring simplicity.

A.: Dress and government are very properly studied together by a lady; but not by a philosopher or statesman.

M.W.: As they grow wiser, the people will look for the solid advantages of society; and watching their own interest, the veto of the executive branch of the government would become *perfectly useless*, though in the hand of an unprincipled chief magistrate it might prove a dangerous instrument.

A.: She who thinks a veto useless knows not the disposition of popular assemblies to usurp and encroach. An unprincipled chief must be *felo de se* to use his veto but in self-defense.

M.W.: A representative government should be so constructed as to prevent *hasty decisions*; or the carrying into laws *dangerous, impolitic measures which have been urged by popular declaimers, who are too apt to gain an ascendancy in a numerous assembly*.

A.: I.e. to prepare two sieves that the flour may be fine. Popular declaimers with a clapping gallery and an obsequious multitude at their beck can intimidate popular assemblies into anything from fear.

M.W.: It is to be feared that popular assemblies will often be influenced by the *fascinating charms of eloquence* . . .

A.: Eloquence is but a tool. The check must be provided to the lust of power that uses the tool.

M.W.: It is very probable . . . that a faction may arise which will *control the assembly*, and . . . *throw the state into the most dangerous convulsions of anarchy*.

A.: The same faction will overcome both assemblies if both are elective.

The obvious preventative, Miss Wollstonecraft thinks, was a second chamber which would not be under the influence of the same faction. Adams, however, had no trust at this point in an elective senate: "An hereditary second chamber," he commented, "is the only effectual check to faction in the first, in opulent nations with great armies, navies, churches, revenues, i.e. a great patronage."

M.W.: It is at least certain that the decisions of a second chamber would not be directed by the same orators.

A.: The orators in both houses will address themselves to the same prejudices, passions, and feelings among the people, i.e. to the same popularity, as France will soon see.

M.W.: The minds of young men generally having more fire, activity, and invention, it would be politically wise to restrict the age of senators to *thirty-five or forty years* . . .

A.: But age is as susceptible of fear as youth, and popular clamors and applauding or reprobating galleries are as dangerous to an election of old men as young.

M.W.: . . . at which period of life they would have become more sage and steady.

A.: But not more courageous and self-denying perhaps.

M.W.: They would be better calculated to decide respecting the policy of the chamber of representatives.

A.: There is wisdom in this.

M.W.: The Assembly should have remained indivisible, and as the members became acquainted with legislative business, they would have prepared senators for the upper chamber.

A.: Something like this has been done in 1795 and a great improvement it is, but not yet well matured.

M.W.: It has been a common remark of moralists that we are the least acquainted with our own characters.

A.: This is sound sense.

M.W.: No people stand in such great need of a check as the French; and it must have been clear to all men of sound understanding that some such plan alone would have enabled them to avoid many fatal errors.

A.: Why did not all men foresee this? How could Mr. Burke say that the Constitution of the States General was a good constitution? He certainly understood not the Constitution of the States General; nor had he considered the history of France as connected with, and springing out of, that constitution. A Ligue and a Fronde should have convinced Mr. Burke that an undefined sovereignty could not be a good constitution. The question never was decided whether the sovereignty was in the King or in the States General. Besides, it was never decided in the States General whether the concurrence of the three branches, i.e. the nobles, the clergy, and the commons or tiers état was necessary to a sovereign act, i.e. a legislative act. [1812.] [43]

4

The first efforts of the Assembly, Miss Wollstonecraft insists, were truly magnanimous; but the character of the men was too light to maintain the same level of heroism, too giddy to support with grave dignity the splendor of sudden glory. "This rhapsody is full of sense and nonsense," Adams growled. "It is true of France, to whom she thinks it peculiar, and it would be equally true of England, and every other nation of Europe. What shall I say of America? Oh! my country!"

M.W.: Men are most easily led away by the ingenious arguments that dwell on *the equality of man.*[44]

A.: The only equality of man that is true was taught by Jesus: "Do as you would be done by." The same Jesus taught "Render to Caesar the things that are Caesar's."

M.W.: When the members of a state are not directed by practical knowledge, the nation plunges into wretchedness, pursuing the schemes of those philosophers of genius who, advancing before their age, have *sketched the model of a perfect system of government.*

A.: It is provoking to see Nedham's model called a perfect system of government.

M.W.: Thus it happened in France that Hume's idea of a perfect commonwealth . . .

A.: It was not Hume's.

M.W.: . . . the adoption of which would be eligible only when civilization has arrived at a much greater degree of perfection, was chosen as the model of their new government.

A.: Civilization may advance to all eternity and Hume's commonwealth will remain a monument of a greater blockhead than he pronounced Mr. Locke to be. [1796.] If ever there existed a wise fool, a learned idiot, a profound deep-thinking coxcomb, it was David Hume. As much worse than Voltaire and Rousseau as a sober decent libertine is worse than a rake. [1812.] [45]

M.W.: Some of the members, it is true, alluded to the improvements made by the *Americans* on the plan of the English constitution . . .

A.: What Americans? Not Franklin; for they adopted his system. Not the first Constitution of Pennsylvania; for they adopted it. Not the Constitution of Massachusetts, New York or the United States, for they rejected them all for Franklin's, Turgot's, i.e. Nedham's.

M.W.: Even the system of the British constitution was considered, by some of the most *enlightened ancients*, as the sublimest theory the human mind was able to conceive . . .

A.: She had read The Defence too, but to little purpose.

The argument that a single chamber represented a simpler and therefore more desirable form of government galled Adams particularly. Rereading the book in 1812, he delivered himself of a long soliloquy:

"The clock would be more simple if you destroyed all the wheels and left only the weights or the spring, but it would not tell the time of day. A farmer's barn would be more simple if without apartments and he turned in all together his horses, cattle, sheep and hogs: yet his haymows would be wasted and his stock killed and gored. A ship would be more simple without a rudder, with but one mast and but one sail. A city would be more simple if you built it all in one house or barrack without departments and turned all the people in together. The solar system would be more simple if all the planets were destroyed and you left only the sun. The universe would be more simple if it were all in one globe. The earth would be more simple if it were all fire, water, air or earth, but its inhabitants must perish in either case. The laws would be more simple if all reduced to one 'Be it enacted that every man, woman and child shall do their duty.' It is silly to be eternally harping upon simplicity in a form of government. The simplest of all possible governments is a despotism in one. Simplicity is not the summum bonum."

There must have been some feeling that a single chamber, renewed every five years, was impolitic, but the moderates reassured themselves with the idea that the suspensive veto provided a sufficient counterpoise:

M.W.: So easy is it for men to frame arguments, to cover the homely features of their own folly—so dangerous is it to follow a refined theory . . .

A.: It is provoking to see a legislature, a sovereign, in one house called refined theory. It is a savage theory. A barbarous theory. Indians, Negroes, Tartars, Hottentots would have refined it more.

M.W.: The Assembly had not enough courage to take a decided part. They justly *dreaded* the depravity and influence of the nobles . . .

A.: They dreaded too the loyalty of the people, and their habitual affection for the King, and their superstitious reverence for the Lord's anointed. The Holy Phial at Rheims was still worshipped. That ampoule brought down from heaven by the Holy Ghost in the form of a pigeon.[46]

M.W.: . . . but *they had not the sagacity to model the government in such a manner as would have defeated their future conspiracies, and rendered their power nugatory.*

A.: This mischievous power of the nobility would have been rendered nugatory by three branches.

M.W.: But no; *the regeneration of France must lead to the regeneration of the whole globe. Vive La liberté!* was the only cry . . .

A.: It has regenerated poor Geneva and poor Holland, and had like to have regenerated America.[47]

M.W.: The women too came forward to sacrifice their ornaments for the good of the country. They were the wives and daughters of artisans who first renounced their female pride—or rather made *one kind of vanity take place of another.*

A.: There was in France much real patriotism in nobles, clergy, commons, citizens and countrymen, and in women as well as men.

M.W.: However, the offering was made with theatrical grace.

A.: Gallantry, grace, theatrical pride, vanity comprehend most of the patriotism I fear in France, and I fear in most other nations.

The proposition that the person of the King was sacred and inviolable and that the crown was hereditary in the male line was unanimously accepted by the Assembly. But meanwhile, the reactionary nobles and the clergy were intriguing to prevent the King from sanctioning the resolutions of August 4. As a result, Louis sent a memoir to the Assembly approving "their spirit" but recommending changes in nearly every article. The Assembly, however, insisted on immediate sanction, and the King complied:

M.W.: The King's object was secretly to favor the efforts of the counter-revolutionists and, if possible, effect his own escape.

A.: His escape was the only way to save his life.

M.W.: It is difficult to determine which was the most reprehensible, *the folly of the Assembly, or the duplicity of the King.*

A.: The duplicity of the Assembly was greater than that of the King.

M.W.: The occasions of remarking that the Frenchmen are the vainest men living often occur . . .

A.: Whether the French are the vainest men or not, English melancholy pride would behave as ill or worse in a revolution.

M.W.: . . . yet France is highly indebted to the Assembly for establishing many constitutional principles of liberty, which must ultimately *produce the perfect government.*

A.: God grant it!

M.W.: The consideration of several other articles of the constitution was continually interrupted by want of a proper procedure.

A.: And does this great lady suppose that such interruptions can be prevented or avoided in any great assembly?

The loan still failing, several persons made magnificent gifts to the nation, sacrificing their jewels and plate. The King, in spite of the remonstrances of the Assembly, sent his rich service to the mint. However, the donations barely afforded temporary relief:

M.W.: Necker, therefore, *incapable of forming any great design,* for the good of the nation, proposed that the citizens contribute one-fourth of their income.

A.: The malice of this lady against Necker is unworthy of her.

M.W.: Mirabeau prevailed on the Assembly to adopt the plan . . .

A.: The famous Mr. Wilkes told me in London that Mirabeau affected to be ignorant of his own eloquence and to value himself on his depth of thought. But, says Wilkes, he is a very eloquent man and has no depth of thought at all. Wilkes however seems to have mismeasured him.[48]

M.W.: "From the throne has emanated the most striking example," he declared. "O thou, so justly the dearly beloved of thy people—King —citizen—man of worth! . . ."

A.: How soon was this adulation followed by the guillotine?

M.W.: "Think of the price which has been paid for liberty by other nations," he went on. "For this, rivers of blood have streamed; long years of woe and horrid civil wars have everywhere preceded the glorious birth! . . ."

A.: This was to be the fate of France too. May liberty at length have the glorious birth!

5

Miss Wollstonecraft criticizes Necker for attempting to supply the needs of the government by vague measures. It is true, she writes, that no government has yet established a just system of taxation, and perhaps the only way to do it would be "by laying all the taxes on land, the mother of every production." ("She had been among the economists, who may be right," Adams admitted.) Yet an able and bold minister might have recommended that the Assembly take the national property under its direct management; and if he had pointed out that this property was worth nearly five billion livres, moneyed men would have come forward with help:

M.W.: Deficits are dangerous; every state ought to take every just measure to render the interest secure, and *to fund the principal.*[49]

A.: Her American husband then has not taught her to condemn a funding system. But the question is, what is the principal? In paper money, is it the nominal value or the real value? In bank bills, is it the real or the current nominal value?

M.W.: The precious metals are the standards of exchange. Paper is a dangerous expedient, except under *a well established government.*

A.: Paper is always a dangerous expedient. It will soon make a well-established government an ill-established government.

M.W.: Its extent should be consistent with the commerce of the country; but it is *the spirit of commerce to stretch credit too far.*

A.: Paper money never was and never will be conducted with any moderation or any sagacity. Neither the monarchy nor the democracy of France, nor the limited monarchy of England, nor the representative democracy of the U.S. have ever discovered either moderation or sagacity on this subject.

M.W.: These are considerations which ought to have occurred to the French minister and have led him to take decided measures.

A.: Did this silly woman think it possible for any minister or any king or any national assembly to take decided measures? No! They had ignorantly and madly introduced the despotism of old Anarck and Old Chaos; and must leave it to fate, fortune or providence to create order out of this confusion. If there had been moderation or sagacity among them, they must have seen that a military power alone could effect it. [1812.]

M.W.: The credit of every government *greatly* depends on the regulation of its finances.

A.: Why not wholly?

M.W.: The most certain way to have given stability to the new system would have been by making such *arrangements* as would have insured promptitude of payment.

A.: And who could make such arrangements? The Angel Gabriel could not have taken such measures, in such an assembly with such a court, clergy, nobility and mob about it.

M.W.: The line in which Necker had been accustomed to move, by restraining what *little energy* his mind was capable of exerting, precluded his seeing the faint lines marked on an expansive scale . . .

A.: No man appeared in France with half his energy unless we except Robespierre, till Napoleon.

M.W.: The nation, confiding to him the direction of a business *for which he had not sufficient talents* . . .

A.: No talents were sufficient.

M.W.: . . . seems to have contemplated a prospect which had *not yet been realized.*

A.: And never will be.

After this, the author turns again to the more familiar subjects of morals and philosophy, complaining that improvements in these fields have been extremely slow. "I know of no improvements in morals since the days of Jesus," Adams commented. In 1812, he added: "Improvements in physical and metaphysical philosophy have made none in the science of politics. This is still the sport of passions and prejudices, of ambition, avarice, intrigue, faction, caprice and gallantry as much as ever. Jealousy, envy and revenge govern with as absolute a sway as ever. Enthusiasm and superstition have lost but little of their power."

Depressed though she was, Miss Wollstonecraft did not give up hope:

M.W.: Our ancestors have *labored* for us; and we, in our turn, *must* labor for posterity . . .

A.: They did, and we do. But they labored to transmit their prejudices, and we to propagate and transmit ours.

M.W.: In spite of adversities, we may contemplate *the approximation of the glorious era* when the appellations of fool and tyrant will be synonymous.

A.: Amen and Amen! Glorious Era come quickly!

Then Adams set down his own more modest expectations, and the ways in which they may be accomplished:

"Men must search their own hearts and confess the emulation that is there: and provide checks to it. The gentlemen must be compelled to agree. They never will from reason and free will. Nothing short of an independent power above them able to check their majorities ever can keep them within bounds. It is the interest and the policy of the people for their own safety always to erect and maintain such a power over the gentlemen: and such another under them. [1796.] Power must be opposed to power, force to force, strength to strength, interest to interest, as well as reason to reason, eloquence to eloquence, and passion to passion." [1812.]

THE REMOVAL OF THE KING TO PARIS

Miss Wollstonecraft deplores the delay of the Assembly in forming a new constitution, something which the American states had accomplished "within a month" after the declaration of their independence. Adams thanked her for her "complaisance to America," even if she was not quite correct about the dates:

M.W.: The French nation had already ascertained the most important political truths . . .[50]

A.: How were these truths ascertained? Forty-nine fiftieths of the nation knew no more about them than the King's menagerie. Among the remaining fiftieth part, there were ten thousand different opinions about the meaning, limitations, restrictions and exceptions with which they were to be understood. Besides, very few of them appear to have had any idea of one of the most essential truths of all, the drunkenness of absolute power in any assembly of nobles, commons or mixture of both as well as in an emperor or king.

M.W.: Moderate men would have been satisfied with what had been gained, allowing the rest to follow progressively. France had to contend with the prejudices of half Europe at least, and to counteract the influence of insidious intriguers . . .

A.: The National Assembly had to contend against the prejudice of nine-tenths of the nation, their own people, their own constituents.

M.W.: Such is the difference between men acting from a practical knowledge and men who are governed entirely by theory, or no principle whatever.

A.: There was no practical knowledge. There was no theory in which a tenth part of the nation could agree. I believe there was more principle than there was practice or theory.

M.W.: The leading men of America knew that there was a necessity of having some kind of government . . .

A.: They were men of experience in popular assemblies as well as theorists.

M.W.: The members of the Assembly, on the contrary, *aiming at a state of perfection* for which the minds of the people were not sufficiently mature . . .

A.: Aims at perfection will always fall short.

M.W.: . . . affecting likewise to be directed by a *magnanimous disinterestedness*, they not only planted the germ of the most dangerous and licentious spirit, but they continued to irritate the desperate courtiers.

A.: None but an idiot or a madman ever built a government upon a disinterested principle. Such pretensions are false and hollow, all hypocrisy, like Franklin's Will and his article in the Pennsylvania Bill of Rights.

The freedom of the press quickly degenerated; it became an engine employed against the Assembly itself. "Is it not astonishing," Adams asked, "that the National Assembly did not foresee that the press would be employed against them? that their own creatures would uncreate their creators? that their own tools would cut their own throats? That their own devils would become their tempters first and tormentors afterwards?"

M.W.: The simplicity of some of the members, their awkward figures and rustic gait, afforded an excellent subject for satire and caricature. The most respectable decrees were twisted into jests, which divided the people into two distinct parties . . .

A.: The jests, epigrams and caricatures did not produce the divisions. The divisions were deep and ineradicable. The divisions produced the jests. Jests and libels were thick and terrible from all parties.

M.W.: It would have been easy for the Assembly to have passed a decree respecting libels . . .

A.: A decree against libels would not have restrained the temper of the times. Libels would have been multiplied by it. Such a decree would have been epigrammatized more than rustic gaits.

M.W.: But so ardent was become their passion for liberty that they were unable to discriminate between a licentious use of that important invention and its real utility.

A.: Is there any nation that will distinguish between the license and the freedom of the press? Not the English. Nor the Americans most certainly. Neither government can do it, and the people will not.

After the wreck of a government, the author contends, the plan of a new constitution should be immediately formed and presented for acceptance to the citizens. Adams agreed: "I had preached this doctrine a whole year in Congress in 1775 and 1776 before I could prevail upon that body to pass my resolution of the 15th of May 1776 recommending that measure to the people of the States."

M.W.: A constitution is a standard for the people to rally round.

A.: How was it possible to bring twenty-five millions of Frenchmen who had never known or thought of any law but the King's will to rally round any free constitution at all?

M.W.: It is the pillar of a government, the bond of all social unity and order . . .

A.: A constitution is a standard, a pillar and a bond when it is understood, approved and beloved. But without this intelligence and attachment, it might as well be a kite or balloon, flying in the air.

M.W.: And whenever the wheels of government, like the wheels of any other machine, are found clogged, they equally require alteration and improvement.

A.: These machines called constitutions are not to be taken to pieces and cleaned or mended so easily as a watch.

M.W.: The authority of the Assembly had been acknowledged nearly three months without their having taken any decided steps to secure these important ends.

A.: Did this lady think three months time enough to form a free constitution for twenty-five millions of Frenchmen? 300 years would be well spent in procuring so great a blessing, but I doubt whether it will be accomplished in 3000. Not one of the projects of the Sage of La Mancha was more absurd, ridiculous or delirious than this of a revolution in France, per saltum from a monarchy to a democracy. I thought so in 1785 when it was first talked of. I thought so in all the intermediate time, and I think so in 1812.

M.W.: It is to be presumed that, the liberty of Frenchmen having been previously secured by the Declaration of Rights . . .

A.: How was liberty secured by the Declaration of Rights? No more than their innocence and obedience by the Ten Commandments. Besides there were not two men in fifty who believed in those rights. There were in France twenty times as many who believed in the King's divine right.

M.W.: . . . if the Assembly had formed some kind of a constitution, the dispute between the people and the court would have been brought to a speedy issue.

A.: The disputes were between the people and the people, more than between the people and the court. Those who were called the people were for butchering king, court, nobility, clergy and all the rich: even the National Assembly itself.

M.W.: The natural, civil, and political rights of man are the main pillars of all social happiness . . .

A.: I would rather call the natural, civil, and political rights of man the foundations, than the pillars. If they are pillars they must stand upon a firm foundation. Is a Declaration then a foundation? No more than a heap of sand or a pool of water. They stand as firmly without a Declaration as with, if nothing more is done. Laws and guardians of laws must be made, and guardians to watch one another.

2

The decree of September 15 which made the King inviolable, the author writes, was both "idle" and "dangerous." Louis' earlier life exhibited a series of follies, and it was likely that if the doctrine "kings can do no wrong" were enacted into law, he would use it to cover his contempt for the national sovereignty. Adams called this "Plausible trash."

M.W.: When kings are considered by the government of a country merely as ciphers, it is very just and proper that their ministers should be responsible for their political conduct . . .[51]

A.: The supreme head of the executive of a great nation must be inviolable or the laws will never be executed. If such heads are liable to civil actions and criminal prosecutions and impeachments, the government will easily be ruined.

M.W.: . . . but at the moment when a state is about to establish a constitution on the basis of reason, to undermine that foundation by a masterpiece of absurdity appears a solecism as glaring as the doctrine itself is laughable.

A.: The absurdity consisted in establishing an hereditary executive as a balance to a vast legislature in one national assembly. You might as well constitute an army, to determine every movement by a vote of an 100,000 men and give the general a veto upon each vote. A gladiator in a pit without arms to defend himself against an hundred lions.

M.W.: Whilst Mirabeau contended for the *infallibility* of the King, he seems to have had no right from reason to deride those who respected that of the Church; for if the government must necessarily be supported by a pious fraud, one was as respectable as the other.

A.: No infallibility is implied in the maxim, and Mirabeau had more sense than Miss W. The maxim means no more than that the laws will not impute blame to the king but to his ministers, because he can do nothing but by ministers.

M.W.: Louis, whose bestiality had been carefully pampered by the Queen and Count d'Artois, was made in his person and conduct sacred and unimpeachable.

A.: It was not for the person but the office that this policy was adopted.

M.W.: This was the extreme folly of weakness . . .

A.: The evils arising from exposing a king to prosecutions civil and criminal are infinitely greater than any that can spring from their inviolability.

M.W.: But when it is also kept in view that, at the very period when he was declared inviolable, he was suspected *to be actually meditating his flight*, there seems to be a *pusillanimity* in it as contemptible as the pretended dignity of the Assembly was ridiculous."

A.: The constitution was not made for Louis 16 but for the nation; for future king and people.

M.W.: Mistaken lenity in politics is not more dangerous than a false magnanimity is palpable littleness . . .

A.: It was not mistaken lenity in Mirabeau. He saw that absolute power in the Assembly would be abused: and meant to give the King a bridle to it, not considering that that bridle was but a silken thread or rather a rope of sand, or a cord of burnt tow. Nothing less than a numerous body of rich, powerful, able and hereditary senators placed between that Assembly and the King could have saved him or the constitution. It is indeed very doubtful whether that could have done it.

The secret cause that induced the Assembly to preserve the shadow of monarchy, the author believes, was the fear of intervention on the part of the courts of Europe. "This is wicked misrepresentation," Adams thought, "the nation could do nothing at this time but in the name of the King." She considers therefore the external and internal dangers which revolutionary France had to face, while the parasites of the old regime continued their machinations:

M.W.: Machiavellian cunning directed the movements of all the courts of Europe. Their agents had private instructions to promote the escape of Louis. Their continual theme was the ignominious state to which the most mild of the Bourbons was reduced . . .

A.: All the ages of the world and all the history of courts cannot show more impudent and more bloody and cruel and perfidious examples of Machiavellian cunning than the successive leaders of the French conventions and assemblies for the last seven years.

M.W.: Restraining the authority of the throne was an alarming signal to a certain class of men, to the drones and mirmidons who live on the spoil and blood of industry and innocence.

A.: Meaning the clergy and armies. But are the drones diminished? and are not the mirmidons increased threefold?

M.W.: A general sorrow was expressed by all the minions of the courts of Europe . . .

A.: Her enmity to monarchy and hierarchy is as strong as that of the republicans who beheaded Charles the first. It would be laudable if she would reveal to us any way of getting rid of them but by substituting greater evils, in Europe.

M.W.: Hope began to animate them when the King was prevailed on to *concert his escape* . . .

A.: The great advocates for the right of expatriation ought not to deny it to a king any more than a subject.

M.W.: The court still persisted to cherish the belief that the public opinion was changed only for the moment . . .

A.: The court misjudged the character of the nation as much as the Assembly did. Both were the dupes of their hopes and their credulity.

M.W.: The court projected an entertainment to seduce the military, while famine was at the very gates of Paris. But previously the old French guards began to manifest some symptoms of discontent . . .

A.: The army was become revolutionist. The Rights of Man had been insinuated into them by their officers as well as by citizens. They had a horror of opposing the nation in a struggle for liberty. They thought it impious against fraternity to fire upon their brothers.

M.W.: The cabinet had not sufficient discernment to perceive that the people were now to be led, not driven . . .

A.: Nor had the Assembly discernment to perceive that the people were neither to be led nor driven.

M.W.: While one party seemed to be endeavoring to rivet on the people the chains of servitude, the other lifted them above the law with vainglorious notions of their sovereignty.

A.: Court and Assembly equally deceived.

M.W.: And this sovereignty of the people, the perfection of the science of government, only to be attained when a nation is truly enlightened . . .

A.: There is great truth in this.

M.W.: . . . consisted in making them tyrants; nay the worst of tyrants, because the instruments of mischief of the men who pretended to be subordinate to their will, though acting the very part of the ministers whom they execrated.

A.: Tyrants they will ever be made to be, while they exert their sovereignty by simple majorities, whether collectively or by representation.

3

On the first of October, the chief officers of the bodyguards gave a magnificent festival in the opera of the Palace at Versailles. The dragoons, whose attachment to the popular cause was well known, were excluded. The aim of the promoters, as the mingling of the officers with the lower ranks showed, was to strengthen the loyalty of the troops. The drinking and banqueting culminated in a chivalric scene: the Queen, carrying the Dauphin in her arms and accompanied by the King, appeared before the crowd. Their presence was intoxicating. "Vive le roi! vive la reine!" resounded from all sides, while the music played the air "O Richard, O mon roi, l'univers t'abandonne!" [52] The national cockade was torn to pieces and stamped underfoot. The revel was repeated two days later, and there were preparations for a third. Adams made the following comment:

"How correct this history is, I cannot say. It was very ill-judged. But no body of men judges right in such times. It seems as if nothing could be right but flight and that secretly. Had the King resigned his crown, the Assembly would not and could not have accepted it. Had he asked leave to retire out of the kingdom and taken an oath never to return, they would not have consented. They could not. It would have ruined them.

"They had instilled into the soldiers such ideas of liberty, equality, fraternity, humanity and tenderness of blood that I do not believe there was a regiment in the army that would have fired upon the people in obedience to their officers; no not even to defend the King's castle or life."

Rumor even exaggerated the happenings at Versailles, which were looked upon as the beginning of fresh hostilities on the part of the court. The cry was that the stunned aristocracy had again reared its head. ("Such cries in such cases come out of the ground, nobody knows where or by whom conjured up. Like the wind they blow where they list. None knows whence they come nor whither they go," Adams remarked.) The story spread, seemingly confirmed by the appearance of white and black cockades, that thirty thousand officers had signed up for the King, and that the Queen was at the head of the conspiracy. The scarcity of bread aggravated the fears and made the people so desperate that it was easy to incite them to any enterprise. Liberty was the constant watchword, Miss Wollstonecraft relates, though few knew of what it consisted. This drew forth a new tirade from Adams:

" 'Few knew.' There was not one of the poissonières, not one of the mob of women, who did not know in what liberty consisted as well as Miss Wollstonecraft, Mr. Condorcet, the Duke de la Rochefoucauld, Mr. Turgot or Dr. Franklin. This is said ore rotundo! I know it. But the mask must be torn off from these imposing visages. And I am stark mad, or every one of these was an idiot in the science of government.

"Equality, a more fascinating watchword, and fraternity, a more enchanting watchword still, were equally constant. Liberty flattered the natural savage; equality flattered all the pride and vanity of civil life; but fraternity added the moral, the Christian feelings, and melted all into tears. Here is a miniature of human nature. This fraternity was set up by men who at the same time annihilated marriage and thereby destroyed the relations of father, son, and brother. And this Madame Wollstonecraft was as good a sister as any of those philosophers was a brother."

In one of her most masterly passages, the author describes the events of October 5—the march of women to Versailles. Early in the day, a number of women banded together and, hurrying to the City Hall, forced every female they met to join them. Many men, armed with pikes, bludgeons, and hatchets, were also in the caravan. It was a mob, very different from the honest crowd which took the Bastille. The national guards, forming a hedge of bayonets, tried to prevent them from entering the building, but the women hurled a volly of stones at them. Unwilling or ashamed to fire on women, Miss Wollstonecraft writes, the soldiers retreated into the building and left the passage free. ("This was," Adams commented, "an universal sentiment among the soldiers as well as the people. A horror of firing at brothers. Nay, the doctrine among the people was, to my certain knowledge, if you were attacked by an highwayman who demanded your purse with a pistol at your breast, rather than knock him down or blow his brains out or run him through, you ought to deliver him your purse.")

The women broke open the magazines and, taking possession of all the arms and ammunition, chose a commander to lead them to Versailles. Dragging cannons along, they pushed ahead, some four thousand strong, accompanied by four or five hundred men. The author is convinced that this was no spontaneous revolt, but a plot, organized by the Duke of Orleans, who wanted to avenge himself on the royal family, especially the Queen. "There is no calculating the mischief which may be produced by a revengeful, cunning knave," she writes. ("The Bastille used to be a precaution against such a character," Adams replied.)

While the procession was advancing toward Versailles, the Assembly was debating the King's answer to the Declaration of Rights. It was a vague statement, acknowledging that the document contained excellent principles, but insisting that the meaning of these should be determined by laws. The dissatisfaction was general, and one of the deputies—Robespierre—claimed that it was not an approval but a censure, and therefore an attack on the rights of the people. ("Robespierre begins his career, a more remarkable one than that of Orleans or the King," Adams took note.)

The rabble arrived at Versailles, and a few women entered the hall of the Assembly, voicing their grievances. The King, with great affability, received another group. Unfortunately, some of the women returning to Paris were roughly handled by the guards, which led to violent outbursts. The court became alarmed and urged the King to set out for Metz. A loaded coach actually left, but the national troops forced it to turn back. The King declared that he would rather perish than see the blood of Frenchmen flowing—a profession which Miss Wollstonecraft regards as another proof of his duplicity. ("His whole life was a proof of his sincerity in this declaration," was Adams's opinion.)

The arrival of Lafayette calmed both the King and the multitude. The General assured the people that provisions were to be speedily distributed; that the King had announced his resolution to remain among them. The crowd shouted with joy and began to fraternize with the soldiers. Thereupon, about five o'clock in the morning, Lafayette retired, hoping that the situation was well in hand; but scarcely an hour later the mob began to prowl about in the galleries of the Assembly. ("Prowl. This is not the style of a democratic lady," Adams censured her.) Many of them rushed upon the Palace. A guard killed one of the intruders, and then the riot began in earnest. Lafayette was roused from his sleep, and with the help of the national guards restored order.

The Duke of Orleans stayed away in England, returning only after the danger had passed. Appearing in the Assembly, he protested his innocence, and the "mock patriots" were glad to have him on their side. The villains were permitted to escape, and the Assembly submitted to the demand of the multitude that the King should reside in Paris. ("Ay. The multitude at Paris was the real government, the ruling power at that time," Adams added.) By exciting and humoring the people, a minority of the Assembly directed the majority. (Adams, usually so jealous of the rights of the minority, agreed: "The minority by crying out for more freedom will always gain the people and undermine the majority.")

Miss Wollstonecraft reflects that, changing from despotism to freedom, probably every nation must struggle with various forms of tyranny before it can consolidate its new system. In spite of what has happened in France, she believes that consulting the public mind will be not only necessary but also extremely fruitful in the future. "The public mind should always be consulted, but not always followed; it should be informed and conducted by rational and honest means," Adams corrected her.

4

On the morning of the sixth of October, the King, with the Queen and the Dauphin, appeared before the people. "My children," he said, "you wish me to be in Paris. I will go, but on condition that my wife and family accompany me." Mad cheering received his words. The Assembly decided at once that they too should go, for Mirabeau and others wanted to keep a hold on the court.

M.W.: That the representatives of the nation should have surrendered their authority and thrown themselves headlong into the heart of a city almost surpasses belief.[53]

A.: They wanted to shine in the eyes of the ladies of Paris, as well as of the multitude.

M.W.: Independent of the additional incense of praise, with which Mirabeau wished to be continually regaled in the metropolis, he frequently asserted that it was the only place where society was truly desirable.

A.: I suspected in the former page the motives of Mirabeau and others.

But even Miss Wollstonecraft had to acknowledge that Paris was "a superb monument of human ingenuity." The entrance to the city was magnificent; the roads, lined with lofty trees, were beautiful, and the stately ramparts were truly picturesque. ("Built since I left Paris," [54] Adams noted.) Nature and art combined to charm the senses. But how quickly all this delight vanishes at the thought of the guillotine! Remembering the horrors of the recent past, the author seeks consolation in the future:

M.W.: As the world is growing wiser, it must become happier . . .

A.: This is the burthen of her song. If the world grows wiser, it will grow more sensible of the emulation of the human heart and provide checks to it.

M.W.: The improvement of the understanding will prevent those baneful excesses of passion which poison the heart.

A.: The understanding will only make rivalries more subtle and scientific, but the passions will never be prevented, they can only be balanced.

The Assembly continued to sit at Versailles until the nineteenth. After some debate, the title of the monarch was changed from "King of France" to "King of the French," because Rousseau had once remarked that the title ought to express the chief of the people rather than the master of the soil. "That will with a whisp has led them into many a bloody bog. Now De Mably with his plural executive is doing the same," Adams, writing at the time of the Directory, remarked.

M.W.: The intended removal of the Assembly to Paris excited apprehension in some of the deputies, relative to their *personal safety.*

A.: It was no doubt intended to get the members into the power of the popular party, and Brissot and the other delegates of great cities such as Bordeaux, Lyons, Marseilles, Nantes, etc., not foreseeing the rivalry of cities to which they afterwards fell a sacrifice, were at this time for removing to Paris.[55]

M.W.: The president, Mounier, pleading his bad state of health, begged to be dismissed; and Lally-Tollendal, thinking that he could not stem the torrent, retired from public business at the same time.

A.: Bicamerists, despairing of their cause from the terror of a Paris mob, most probably.

M.W.: Mirabeau, who so earnestly desired to be at Paris, ridiculed every opposition made to the removal.

A.: Mirabeau, if he was not a single assembly man, was a dupe of his love of the pleasures of Paris and his passion to be admired.

M.W.: Several members gave an account of the gross insults they had received in Paris. One of them proposed that a decree respecting libels should instantly be passed.

A.: The removal to Paris surrendered the sovereignty to libels and riots.

Before its departure for Paris, the Assembly resolved that leave could be granted to deputies only for urgent business. ("This was a tyranny as absolute as that they complained of," Adams thought.) The entire conduct of the Assembly, according to the author, showed an affectation of the virtues of the Romans, with the degenerate minds of their posterity. Here Adams gave his full consent: "Nothing better than this has yet appeared," he commented. Nevertheless, Miss Wollstonecraft believes that the Assembly could not help laying the foundation of useful plans, considering that the science of government had lately been so ably studied by many writers:

M.W.: It is only in the progress of governments that hereditary distinctions, cruelly abridging rational liberty, have prevented man from rising to his just point of elevation by his improvable faculties.

A.: Hereditary distinctions among the Greeks and Romans, and in all Europe since their times, have been essential to the liberty that has been enjoyed.

M.W.: It is a palpable error to suppose that men of every class are not equally susceptible of common improvement . . .

A.: The distinction of property will have more influence than all the rest in commercial countries, if it is not rivalled by some other distinction.

M.W.: If, therefore, it be the contrivance of any government to preclude from a chance of improvement the greater part of the citizens of the state, it can be considered in no other light than as a monstrous tyranny.

A.: No part of the citizens ought ever to be precluded from a chance of improvement.

M.W.: To the Assembly it is that France is indebted for having prepared a simple *code* of instruction, containing all the truths necessary to give a comprehensive perception of political science.

A.: This code will make knowledge more general, but how much more general is still a problem.[56]

M.W.: From the Declaration of Rights . . . men may learn that they have the power of doing whatever does not injure another, and that this power has no limits which are not determined by *law*.

A.: But the question is who shall be the guardian of the law? and what shall secure its efficacy and energy?

M.W.: These principles had not been recognized by any senate or government in Europe; and it was an honor worthy to be reserved for the representatives of twenty-five millions of men to be the first to dare to *ratify* such sacred and beneficial truths . . .

A.: After America had first adopted them.

M.W.: . . . truths which have been fostered by the genius of philosophy, whilst *hereditary wealth* and the bayonet of despotism have continually been opposed to their establishment.

A.: Yet hereditary wealth first began to demand them. Witness the barons who demanded Magna Charta.

M.W.: Wars and their calamitous effects will become less frequent *in proportion* as the people are consulted respecting their necessity and consequences.

A.: This is much doubted.

M.W.: The mysteries of courts have continually deluged Europe with the blood of its most worthy and heroic citizens . . .

A.: This is commonplace cant: but very probably vulgar error.

M.W.: If it were only for abolishing the sway of the court of Versailles, *Europe ought to be thankful for a change* . . .

A.: Will Europe be more safe from a French republic than from a French monarchy?

M.W.: . . . that must ultimately lead to universal freedom, virtue, and happiness.

A.: So be it.

M.W.: It is to be presumed that governments in future will make it their principal object to counteract the tendency of tyranny, by restraining within just bounds the ambition of individuals . . .

A.: So may it be: and so it may be.

5

Men in a primitive state preserve their independence and adopt no regular system of policy, the author begins her last chapter. "This is not true; they have all a system of policy," Adams contradicted. Later on, she continues, absolute governments were tolerated by the most enlightened part of the people in order to prevent confusion during changes. "If confusion cannot be otherwise avoided, absolute governments will always be resorted to, for confusion is more intolerable. Let Sam Adams say what he will," Adams declared.[57] From then on he challenged almost every one of Miss Wollstonecraft's statements:

M.W.: It has been one of the advantages of the large cities of Europe to light up the sparks of reason and extend the principles of truth.[58]

A.: Cities have advanced liberty and knowledge by setting up kings to control nobles.

M.W.: Hence it has happened that the despots of the world have found it necessary to maintain large standing *armies*, in order to counteract the effects of truth and reason.

A.: And the cities have enabled them to do it, as a security against their own mobs as well as against the nobility.

M.W.: The economists showed that the prosperity of a state depends on the *freedom of industry:* that *talents should* be permitted to *find their level;* and that the *unshackling of commerce* is the only secret to render it flourishing . . .

A.: Freedom of talents, industry, and commerce infallibly produce inequalities as great as any that have existed.

M.W.: It might have been supposed that Frenchmen would become as passionate for liberty as a man restrained by some idle religious vow is to *possess a mistress*, to whose charms the imagination has lent all its own world of graces.

A.: This woman's head forever runs on love.

The author now expatiates upon the role of Paris. She thinks that its rise and splendor were due chiefly to the old system, and that if a republican government were to be consolidated the city would rapidly fall into decay. Adams had even less faith in its future: "Paris will perish before a Republican government can be established in France."

M.W.: Since the existence of courts, the convenience and comfort of men have been sacrificed to the ostentatious display of pomp and pageantry.

A.: Since the existence of courts, the barons have been humbled and the people liberated from villainage.

M.W.: The prevailing custom of living beyond their income has had the most baneful effect on the independence of individuals of every class in England as well as in France . . .

A.: It is wealth and commerce, not courts that has done this. Courts are not more splendid now in proportion than the courts of the barons were in the times of deadly feuds.

M.W.: The destructive influence of commerce, it is true, carried on by men who are eager by overgrown riches to partake of the respect paid to nobility, is felt in a variety of ways.

A.: Now you come to something to the purpose.

M.W.: The most pernicious, perhaps, is its producing an aristocracy of wealth which degrades mankind . . .

A.: This aristocracy of wealth is now destroying the aristocracy of birth. That is all, unless it should destroy the aristocracy of genius, talents, and merit too.

M.W.: The acquiring of a fortune is likewise the least arduous road to preëminence, and the most sure.

A.: Thus, money is getting the better both of birth and merit.

M.W.: It may admit of a doubt whether large work-shops do not contain men who impede the gradual process of improvement . . .

A.: Ay! destroy all arts and manufactures as well as commerce, and build Plato's republic.

M.W.: The only excuse that can be made for the ferocity of the Parisians is to observe that they had not any confidence in the laws. When had they seen the execution of a noble or priest, though convicted of crimes beyond the daring of vulgar minds?

A.: They saw the execution on the wheel of two officers for crimes.

M.W.: A barbarian, considered as a moral being, *is an angel*, compared with the refined villain of artificial life.

A.: This you learn from Rousseau, but it is not true.

M.W.: Then let us coolly and impartially contemplate the *improvements* which are gaining ground in the formation of principles of policy.

A.: I hope improvements are making, but I wish to see the fruits of them before I depend too much upon them.

M.W.: It will be allowed by every humane and considerate being that a political system *more simple* than has hitherto existed would effectually check those aspiring follies, which have banished from governments the very shadow of justice and magnanimity.

A.: There can be none more simple than despotism. The triple complication, not simplicity is to be sought for.

In her last long peroration Miss Wollstonecraft compares France to a diseased body. As in medicine, she writes, there is a species of illness of the bowels which works its own cure, so there is in politics: the "excrementitious humours" exuding from the body may arouse a general dislike for the nation, but the philosophical eye will discern the cause which has produced the dreadful effects. Adams was disgusted: "This nasty rhetoric could be learned only in France. By an English lady it could be only written in the temple of Cloacina, at her devotions to the goddess." Then returning to the theme of simplicity, he added a few final arguments:

"The word 'simplicity' in the course of seven years has murdered its millions—and produced more horrors than monarchy did in a century. A woman would be more simple if she had but one eye or one breast; yet nature chose she should have two as more convenient as well as ornamental. A man would be more simple with but one ear, one arm, one leg. Shall a legislature have but one chamber then, merely because it is more simple? A wagon would be more simple if it went upon one wheel: yet no art could prevent it from oversetting at every step." [59]

[XII]

Condorcet and the Idea
of Progress

Among the guests whom Adams met at the Duchésse d'Enville's soon after his arrival in Paris was the Marquis de Condorcet. In the original entry of his Diary Adams mentions only the presence of "dukes, abbots, etc." Thirty years later, however, reminiscing in his study at Quincy, he recalled among the unnamed company "M. Condorcet, a philosopher, with a face as pale, or rather as white, as a sheet of paper . . ."[1]

Eight years Adams's junior, the Marquis de Condorcet was thirty-five at the time. A brilliant mathematician and secretary of the Académie des Sciences, he had a great reputation, increased by his well-known connection with Voltaire and, above all, by his friendship with Turgot. When Comptroller General, the latter made Condorcet Inspector of the Mint, a post which he kept—upon the insistence of Necker—even after Turgot's fall. At the same time, he was working on a book of commentaries on Pascal and carrying on a controversy about Negro slavery. He stood out among the new generation of radicals as the youngest and last of the *philosophes*.

Voltaire and Rousseau died in 1778, Turgot in 1781, d'Alembert in 1783, and Diderot and Mably in 1784; in the decade preceding the revolution, Condorcet was increasingly conscious of the position he had to uphold. Like everyone else in Turgot's circle, he was deeply interested in the American war, and afterwards in the governments of the new states. In 1786 he published an essay, *L'Influence de la Révolution d'Amérique sur l'Europe*, dedicated to the Marquis de Lafayette, in which he had many flattering things to say about the Americans. "They are the only people," he wrote, "among whom the teachings of Machiavellianism are not erected into political doctrines, and whose leaders do not profess the impossibility of so perfecting the social order as to harmonize prosperity and justice." [2] Because of the respect American laws showed for the natural rights of mankind, Condorcet felt that every man was certain to find asylum there, regardless of his religion or political principles. By their example, he thought, Americans would help to maintain peace in Europe and would contribute greatly to the perfecting of the human race.

In a *Supplément*, which he added a few months later, he discussed Shays's Rebellion, the news of which, magnified and distorted, had just reached Europe. "The mutineers in Massachusetts," he argued, "did not insult anyone, caused harm to nobody, and paid just prices for everything they needed. But even more striking was the conduct of those who wanted to stop the riots . . . Where else could one find companies of volunteers ready to rush to the defense of their government? The uprising is perhaps the most convincing proof that the preservation of order should be entrusted to the nation itself." [3] The larger part of the paper, however, was devoted to the Federal Constitution, the draft of which had just been sent to the thirteen states. Condorcet sharply criticized the provision for two legislative chambers, insisting that "the legislative power may reside, without any danger, in a single assembly." [4] His mind was much less flexible than that of Franklin, who as chief delegate from Pennsylvania signed the document even though most of his recommendations had been rejected.

When Adams published his *Defence of the Constitutions of America*, ostensibly "against the attack of M. Turgot," it was Condorcet who undertook to refute him. His *Lettres d'un bourgeois de New-Heaven* was inserted in the first volume of Philip Mazzei's *Recherches historiques et politiques sur les États-Unis de l'Amérique septentrionale*, published in 1788.[5] Condorcet wrote under the guise of an American, but it was not for a mere whim that he signed himself (with a misspelling) "a Citizen of New-Heaven"; together with La Rochefoucauld, the jurist Target, and other Frenchmen, he had shortly before been made an honorary citizen of the Connecticut town. The *Lettres* were addressed to "a Citizen of Virginia," who might well have been Jefferson; and their purpose was to prove "the unprofitableness of the division of legislative powers into several bodies." Adams read them soon after their appearance, and noted that he intended to examine them "at large," but the rising antagonism over the French Revolution prevented his plan.[6]

Condorcet was by then playing a role in the Revolution itself. Although not a member, he regularly attended the meetings of the

Constituent Assembly and published some forty articles advising on its course. Fearing that the third estate was more interested in establishing "a bourgeois aristocracy" than in emancipating the people, he fought for "the poorest and most numerous class." In September 1791 he was elected to the Legislative Assembly and a year later to the Convention. As secretary of the Assembly, he composed most of the addresses sent to foreign powers as well as the proclamations addressed to the people of France. Until the attempted flight of the King he advocated constitutional monarchy, but after that he turned republican. Breaking away from Lafayette and La Rochefoucauld, his closest friends, he moved farther to the left.

Lafayette fled the country in August 1792, while La Rochefoucauld was killed in the country a month later. Condorcet, suppressing his private emotions, immersed himself in still more work. In October he was made chairman of the committee entrusted with the drafting of a new constitution, thereby incurring the jealousy of Robespierre. Helped by Thomas Paine, he set himself to the task with enormous industry, submitting the document to the Convention on February 15, 1793. The debate, however, was put off for two months, and then took the form of personal abuse. Condorcet had questioned the Convention's right to judge the King, and later voted against the death sentence. This was enough to class him with the Girondists. His draft was attacked as designed in the interests of the propertied classes, and a committee was appointed to prepare another constitution. The new draft, made by Hérault de Séchelles, was rapidly adopted. While it was under referendum, Condorcet published a letter attacking it. "The first plan was made for the nation," he wrote, "and the second for assuring the power of a particular group . . . Everything that is good in the second was copied from the first; and what pretends to be an improvement, is merely its perversion and corruption." [7] A week later he was denounced for treason, and the Convention ordered his arrest. He went into hiding, which made him guilty of contumacy. On October 3, together with Brissot, Vergniaud, and forty other deputies, he was condemned to the guillotine.

The story of Condorcet's proscription and death is well known. Outlawed, he found refuge in the home of the widow of the sculptor Louis-François Vernet, while the horrors of the Terror were steadily mounting. It was during these months, in constant danger, that he wrote his *Esquisse d'un tableau historique des progrès de l'esprit humain*, unrivaled for its limitless confidence in the future of mankind. Having finished the book, he began at once to work on a larger history, going

ahead at top speed, until he received word that his hiding place was discovered. Fearful of endangering his hostess' life, he decided to leave. He
wrote a farewell letter to his little daughter, and on April 5, 1794, an
hour after Danton's execution, stole out of the house. Two days later,
starved and exhausted, he entered a tavern in a near-by village. His appearance having aroused suspicion, he was taken to Bourg-la-Reine and
thrown into prison, where on the following day he was found dead. A
rumor has long persisted that he poisoned himself.[8]

2

Less than a year after Condorcet's death, the Committee of Public
Instruction warmly recommended the publication of the *Esquisse*.
"This is a classic work, offered to your republican schools by an unfortunate philosopher," the Committee wrote to the Convention. "It
shows the improvement of social conditions as the most worthy purpose
of the human mind; and your children, studying from it the history of
the arts and sciences, will learn above all to cherish liberty, and to detest and vanquish tyranny." [9] People would read Condorcet's book, the
report predicted, when nobody could recall the insults which Robespierre had heaped upon him. It also emphasized the fact that Condorcet
had written his work without any recrimination, taking his personal
tragedy as one of the calamities which are almost inevitable in a great
upheaval.[10]

The frenzy of the Terror was over and, in spite of renewed Jacobin
uprisings, the Convention tried to steer a middle course. The surviving
Girondists had returned from exile, and Condorcet's name was grate-
fully remembered. The Convention at once approved the Committee's
recommendation, and upon its order three thousand copies of the work
were printed and distributed.

The *Esquisse* consists of ten chapters. The first nine are devoted to
the past, the tenth to the future. According to Condorcet, mankind has
gone through nine great epochs. First, men were united into hordes and
lived by fishing and hunting; the pastoral stage followed, and then the
agricultural. The fourth and fifth epochs were those of Greece, Rome,
and Alexandria. The Middle Ages occupied the sixth and seventh
epochs. The eighth extended to Descartes, while the French Revolution
marked the end of the ninth. As to the future, Condorcet had three
great hopes: the destruction of inequality among nations; the progress
of equality within each nation; and lastly, the real improvement of man.

He wanted to show that nature set no bounds to the development of human faculties; that the perfectibility of man was limitless. "The day will come," he prophesied, "when the sun will shine on an earth of none but free men, with no master save reason; for tyrants and slaves, priests and their stupid and treacherous tools, will all have disappeared." [11]

The work has been severely criticized for its errors and omissions—the arbitrariness of its divisions, its failure to explain the causes of the epochal changes, its misunderstanding of the Middle Ages, its lack of appreciation of the part which institutions play in history, and so on. But considering the circumstances of the book's composition, mistakes were inevitable.[12] Condorcet's abstract treatment of history was intentional; and, with all his Voltairean bias, he was at least forthright. A fanatical believer in reason, he regarded tyranny and religion as the most vicious enemies of mankind, and conceived progress as a fight against them. Despite its shortcomings, the *Esquisse* has been recognized as one of the great works of the century. Saint-Simon regarded it as "the first history of the past and future of the human spirit," and Comte, who looked upon him as his chief precursor, declared: "After Montesquieu, the only important step in the basic conception of sociology was made by the unfortunate Condorcet . . . For the first time, the scientific—the truly fundamental—idea of the social progress of mankind was at last clearly and definitely announced." [13]

What critics generally ignore is that the *Esquisse* was only a preliminary study for a larger work. Condorcet himself called it a "prospectus" for his detailed history—to which he referred as the "ouvrage" and of which he composed the accounts of the first, fourth, fifth, and tenth epochs. A part of the latter was printed in 1804; but the whole work, together with Condorcet's preface to the *Esquisse*, was published for the first time in 1847. As if anticipating later strictures, the *philosophe* protests that his short treatise was not intended to sketch the history of the governments, laws, morals, and customs of the various peoples, but was limited to general traits.[14]

Condorcet's forecast of the future in particular has been decried as utopian, and even absurd. It is astonishing to see, therefore, how many of his ideas have proved practical. To be sure, most colonies are not yet free, and the ruthless exploitation of primitive peoples continues; but equal rights for women, free public education, old age pensions, mutual aid societies, life insurance for the masses, and support of widows and orphans have been enacted in most civilized countries. Condorcet's belief that "some day no time limit will be assignable to the average human life," [15] still sounds chimerical, yet hygiene and preventive medicine have certainly produced a considerable prolongation of the average life-span. And science and technology have progressed more rapidly than even Condorcet dared to imagine. It is the moral improvement, which he expected would accompany greater prosperity, that is conspicuously lacking.

This is precisely the terrifying problem of our time: what the immense advance in science without any corresponding advance in morality may do to humanity. The question apparently never crossed Condorcet's mind. "Is it not in the order of nature," he blithely asked, "that the progress of the moral and political sciences will exercise the same influence upon our actions and sentiments as do the mathematical and physical sciences upon the arts employed for our needs?" Enlightened people, he was sure, will "gradually learn to regard war as the greatest of crimes." Condorcet saw no reason why Descartes's axiom concerning the immutability of the general laws of the universe should not apply to the moral development of man just as much as to other operations of nature. [16] In this, he merely carried the idea of progress, the common belief of most of the *philosophes*, to its ultimate conclusion. The *Esquisse*—to use Benedetto Croce's happy phrase— was "the last will and testament of the eighteenth century." [17]

Adams read the *Esquisse* in the English translation, entitled *Outlines of an Historical View of the Progress of the Human Mind*, which was published in 1795 in London. He read it at least twice, in 1798 and 1811. This is one of the books which he annotated most copiously; his comments total over four thousand words. It was on the margins of this volume that he really replied to "the ingenuous citizen of New-Heaven."

His notes, from first to last, show his intense irritation with the philosopher. He finds fault with almost everything. Condorcet had an unbounded faith in genius; he thought, indeed, that men of genius were the chief moving force of progress. Adams was enraged by the idea. "Oh vanity of genius what mischiefs have you not done!" he exclaimed. He could not see the word without an angry protest. It became for him the symbol of all the "pretensions" of the philosophers, men who had no practical experience, and even boasted of it. "He was as mere a monk as Loyola," he exclaimed with exasperation. Condorcet's attribution of certain features of the American Constitution to "prejudices of education" was more than galling. "Fool! Fool!" he exploded. Condorcet believed that the French Revolution had opened the gates to a better future and wrote consistently from that point of view; and

Adams, who regarded the Revolution as a catastrophe, attacked him with equal consistency. Looking back upon all the bloodshed, and reviled at home for his very action of averting war with France,[18] he found in the *Esquisse* a convenient scapegoat. Condorcet, the only one of the *philosophes* who lived to take part in the Revolution, stood in his eyes for the entire group. And when after the Napoleonic wars he turned once more to Condorcet's book, it was still the "rashness" and "conceit" of the philosophers which he remembered with the greatest bitterness.

Yet with all his thunder, Adams was far from being insensible to Condorcet's character. In 1809 he wrote to a friend: "I was personally acquainted with M. Turgot, the Duke de la Rochefoucauld, and Mr. Condorcet. They were as amiable, as learned, and as honest men as any in France." [19] And eight years later he repeated to James Madison: "I was personally treated with great kindness by these three great and good men. But I lamented and deplored, notwithstanding their profound science and learning, what appeared to me their blind infatuation to a chimera." [20] In the same spirit he noted his copy of the *Outlines*, on the first page which offered a blank space:

"As a writer he would have done little harm, tho extremely erroneous in many things: but as an active legislator he contributed to destroy all the good he aimed at. He might and probably did mean well, but his ignorance and inexperience in the nature of free government, like his friends Turgot's and Rochefoucauld's, ruined his country.

"These three are memorable examples of the profoundest science, most extensive literature, united with total ignorance and palpable darkness in the science of government, with dispositions too to equity, humanity, and benevolence toward their country and mankind."

3

"Man is born with the faculty of receiving sensations . . . He can retain, recognize, compare them," Condorcet begins his introductory survey. It is this faculty which enables man to advance; and if we consider the development of all individuals in a certain place, following it from generation to generation, we have a picture of the progress of the human mind:

Condorcet: This picture . . . will present the order in which the changes have taken place and show, by the modifications which the human species has experienced in its incessant renewal through the immensity of ages, the course which it has pursued.[21]

Adams: Immensity of ages. Eternity I suppose he means, for I presume he was no believer in creation.

C.: My work will prove, by fact and reasoning, that no bounds have been fixed to the improvement of the human faculties; that *the perfectibility of man is truly limitless* . . .

A.: Agreed. What then? Will man ever be free from disease, vice, and death?

C.: The course of this progress may doubtless be more or less rapid, but *it can never be retrograde* . . .

A.: This is more than can be proved.

C.: The first state of civilization was that of a society of men, few in number, subsisting by hunting and fishing, and having *a rude form of government* . . .

A.: A better form than yours and Turgot's and Rochefoucauld's, in one assembly.

Man later tamed animals and slowly learned rudimentary agriculture. Property began to include more and more objects; industry and art awakened; and even the dawn of science appeared:

C.: Some men of genius, the eternal benefactors of the human race, noticed that all the words of a language were only combinations of a very limited number of syllables, and conceived the idea of representing them by visible signs . . .

A.: Genius is now deified and substituted for heathen gods and Roman Catholic saints. Genius is now the mythology of French philosophers. Because men of genius want to be worshipped.

From this point on, Condorcet shows that there is an unbroken chain of development. If there be an art of foreseeing, directing, and accelerating the progress of mankind, it must be based upon a knowledge of the progress already made. "Everything tells us," he asserts, "that we are approaching one of the grand revolutions of the human race." "Grand indeed! but will it be for better or worse?" Adams, less confidently, asked. In any case, "history is our surest guide"; the future will be happy, but only if we know how to help ourselves, and also know what obstacles are to be feared and surmounted. "Aye, Sir," Adams ironically approved.

And now the main discussion begins. The story of the first epoch is brief. In considering the influence of teachers and priests, Condorcet describes the formation of a powerful class of men:

C.: The human race became divided into two portions: one destined to teach, the other to believe; one wishing to raise itself above reason, the other debasing itself below humanity . . .[22]

A.: Are not the pretensions of genius, set up by this visionary, as dangerous and indeed in the end a worse system?

C.: The distinction is too widespread not to have a foundation in nature; and the state of the human faculties at this early period may explain the credulity of the first dupes as well as the rude cunning of the *first impostors*.

A.: These were your men of genius, the ethereal spirits of Boling-broke, Condorcet. There was never a more flagrant one among them all than yourself, nor one who opened wider the box of Pandora. The credulity of dupes and the cunning of impostors was never more gross or glaring than in the French Revolution.

The account of the second epoch is equally short. As the flocks of each family, Condorcet writes, could not multiply in the same proportion, a difference in wealth arose. Adams disagreed: "This difference existed equally in the hunting and fishing life. One man had more and better bows and nets and greater skill in using them."

C.: We observe advancing at the same time the art of deceiving men in order to rob them . . . Ideas about supernatural powers become more refined; and with this we see the appearance of pontiff princes, sacerdotal families, colleges of priests—a class of persons assuming insolent prerogatives.

A.: Man is by nature a religious animal, a religious man will say: and that the philosophers have taught the people atheism and irreligion in order to rob them. Invisible powers that produce sun, moon and stars, animals, vegetables, fruits, flowers and blossoms force themselves on the human mind as soon as it can think. A sense of his own weakness, wants and dependence forces him to think whence he came, and what produced him and all things.

Some peoples remained primitive, because of climate, habit, and the "sweets of independence." The transition to a state of civilization, however, implies no degeneration; it is a necessary crisis in mankind's advance toward perfection. Condorcet's doctrine was different indeed from Rousseau's. Adams noted it with pleasure: "Civilization a benefit."

The third epoch receives much more detailed treatment. Adams read it with close attention: "Husbandry attaches men to the soil. Surplus produce. Separation, merchants . . . Colonies, serfs, villains. Feudal system . . ." Then came the inevitable flare-up:

C.: The people who have not yet experienced the misfortune of conquering or being conquered show the simple but strong virtues of agricultural nations, the morals of heroic times made so attractive by a mixture of greatness and ferocity, of generosity and barbarism.[23]

A.: When? Where was such a people? Where is their history, their tradition, or fable? This is all fiction.

C.: In contrast, the empires founded by conquerors present all the shades of abasement and corruption. It is there that we see taxes upon industry and commerce, exactions compelling a man to purchase the right of employing his own abilities as he pleases . . .

A.: All this we see in every commercial nation, however founded— and shall see it.

C.: . . . in short, all those acts of arbitrary power, legalized tyranny, and superstitious wickedness that contempt for human nature could invent.

A.: And that wickedness like yours, Condorcet, has excused if not justified.

C.: The habit of using alcohol, opium, tobacco, and betel, which has proved an obstacle to the progress of ignorant and enslaved nations, prevents the diffusion of truth through all classes in more civilized countries as well.

A.: I doubt. Some are said to owe all their genius to them. Churchill,[24] Tom Paine and others.

The improvement of the arts and sciences, Condorcet writes, would have been slower if certain families had not made them the foundation of their power. "Ay! Families promote arts and sciences," Adams gladly recorded.

C.: The knowledge they possessed, with the seeming austerity of their lives, gave weight *to their impostures* . . .

A.: And to their honest communication of useful knowledge too.

C.: The members of these castes pursued two different objects with equal ardor: the acquisition of new information, and the use of such as they already had to *deceive* the people.

A.: You omit all the good and take only the evil.

C.: Their wise men devoted themselves particularly to astronomy, learning by continued observation a good deal about the movements of the stars. These empirical laws did not lead to the discovery of general laws, but were sufficient . . . to enhance the credit of these *usurpers* of the right of instructing man.

A.: There never was one of them more arrogant or more mischievous than thyself, Condorcet, or more empirical.

C.: It seems that we owe them the ingenious idea of arithmetical scales . . .

A.: These were benefactors indeed to man.

C.: Their chemistry, on the other hand, consisted of making certain nostrums calculated *to dazzle an ignorant multitude, subjected to chiefs not less ignorant than itself* . . .

A.: In this they resembled thee and thy Parisian philosophers.

C.: They sought truth only in order to disseminate errors; and it is not to be wondered at that they so seldom found it.

A.: This is as applicable to thee as to them.

C.: Since their purpose was not to enlighten but to govern . . .

A.: This also was thy view, and that of thy associates and colleagues.

C.: . . . they did not communicate anything to the people without adding something supernatural, sacred, celestial, which led them to be regarded as superior to humanity.

A.: Just as you pretend to illuminations and inspirations of genius, superior to other men.

Condorcet saw a connection between the origins of language and religion. In the earliest language almost every word was a metaphor and every phrase an allegory:

C.: Little by little the priests forgot some of the truths hidden behind their allegories, and at last became themselves *the dupes of their own fables.*

A.: Just as you and yours have become the dupes of your own atheism and profligacy, your nonsensical notions of liberty, equality, and fraternity . . .

C.: All progress of the sciences came to a halt; and the human mind, a prey to ignorance and prejudice, was condemned to that shameful stagnation which has so long disgraced Asia.

A.: God grant that your extravagances may not introduce another such Age of Darkness.

C.: The Asiatic nations are the only ones where one may still observe this state of civilization and this decadence.

A.: All Europe will be another if your plans are pursued.

C.: Then alphabetical writing was introduced into Greece, among . . . a people which fate had decreed to be the benefactor of all nations and all ages . . .

A.: As much as I love, esteem, and admire the Greeks, I believe the Hebrews have done more to enlighten and civilize the world. Moses did more than all their legislators and philosophers.

C.: Only one other nation has since conceived the idea of leading a revolution new in the destiny of mankind . . . But let us not seek to penetrate what an uncertain future as yet conceals from us.

A.: Ah! Let us cast a veil over this awful scene.

4

The fourth epoch begins with the fall of the tyrants and the establishment of republics in Greece. The Greeks had acquired their knowledge, as well as their errors, from the East; the sciences, therefore, could not become among them the patrimony of a particular caste. Their sages, who soon took the more modest name of philosophers, tried to combine in a single rule the duties of morality and the secret of happiness. Thus, instead of revealing truths, they only created systems. Yet the doctrines of Democritus and Pythagoras, Condorcet thought, foreshadowed the discoveries of Descartes and Newton. Socrates's death was the first crime committed in the war between philosophy and superstition.

C.: This war will continue to be waged as long as there shall exist *priests or kings* upon the earth.[25]

A.: Your philosophy, Condorcet, has waged a more cruel war against truth than was ever attempted by king or priest.

C.: Frightened hypocrisy hastened to bring accusations of impiety against the philosophers. Socrates could not escape their fury. There was no longer in Athens a Pericles to watch over the safety of genius and virtue.

A.: Pericles, no doubt, was a good Sansculotte, since he protected the God Genius.

The enchanting style of Plato's *Dialogues,* Condorcet continues, makes us forget that they are based upon philosophical dreams, upon that abuse of words which Socrates himself had so often castigated. However, the academies contributed greatly to the spread of knowledge. The philosophers exerted considerable influence upon the laws and government, but chiefly because they did not have, or even want to have, a political existence. "Very different from the French philosophers who aspire at the government of the world," Adams could not resist saying.

C.: The philosophers could not aspire as yet to found the *super-structure* of a society of equal and free men upon reason, upon the maxims of universal justice.

A.: All authority in one center and that center the nation. Fool!

C.: To guard against change, such institutions were sought for as cherished the love of country, including the love of its legislation and even customs.

A.: What fault do you find in this?

C.: The rich, who alone were in a position to acquire knowledge . . .

A.: Will not knowledge always be confined chiefly to the rich?

C.: . . . could, by seizing the reins of authority, oppress the poor and compel them to throw themselves into the arms of a tyrant.

A.: This is stupid and wicked.

C.: The ignorance and fickleness of the people, and its jealousy of powerful citizens, might suggest to the latter the desire of establishing aristocratic despotism . . .

A.: He knows that nature has ordained an aristocracy, and he wishes only that his men of genius might have the aristocratic despotism.

C.: Modern republics have hardly an institution with which the Greeks were unacquainted. The Amphictyonic League, as well as those of the Aetolians, Arcadians, and Achaeans, present examples of federal constitutions and unions more or less close; and there were established more liberal rules of commerce between these different nations.

A.: There is not among them all a form of government which could hold together any modern commercial nation.

C.: A study of existing governments alone was not enough to convert politics into an extensive science. Thus even in the writings of the philosophers it appears to be *a science rather of facts* than a true theory founded upon general principles . . .

A.: Is there any science, not of facts? Newton's science is empirical. Principles drawn from nature are drawn from facts. What is nature but facts? How can reason acknowledge anything but facts and inferences from facts? Behmen and Swedenborg were not more mystical and unintelligible than this philosophical and mathematical charlatan.

In this epoch—the dawn of philosophy and science—the fine arts, Condorcet points out, reached a perfection such as they had not known before and have hardly known since. Homer lived about the time of the establishment of the republics; and the great dramatists, historians, and sculptors were contemporaries of Socrates:

C.: Liberty, the arts, and knowledge have contributed to the refinement of manners. The vices of the Greeks, so often ascribed to their civilization, were those of ruder ages.

A.: In this paragraph I am inclined to agree with him rather than Rousseau.

C.: We shall demonstrate that *the progress of virtue has always accompanied that of knowledge,* just as the progress of corruption has always followed or announced its decline.

A.: This is capable of much discussion: many distinctions, limitations, and explanations.

The fifth epoch includes the history of Greece from Aristotle to her final decadence, as well as that of Rome and Alexandria. Condorcet did not idolize Aristotle, who, on the basis of hypothetical data, tried to explain everything with "too great readiness." But it was Aristotle who first perceived the need of separating the sciences. Subsequently, great progress was made in mathematics and geometry, as also in astronomy and medicine. Archimedes may be considered the father of theoretical mechanics. Meanwhile, several schools of philosophy flourished, those of Epicurus and Zeno being the most influential. The skeptics had a passion for whimsical opinions. "A modern, no less than an ancient passion," Adams added.

In arts and sciences, as well as in philosophy, the Romans were purely imitative. In jurisprudence, however, they excelled, and they bestowed their laws upon the countries which they had conquered:

C.: We behold in Rome *the origin of hereditary patrician rank,* and the artful means that were adopted to give it greater stability and force, by making it less odious.

A.: Such a rank exists in every nation under the sun, and will exist forever.

C.: We see there a people accustomed to arms, but never employing them in domestic dissensions . . .

A.: Never drew blood, till the Gracchi.

C.: . . . a great nation, which for four centuries was the patient dupe of an absurd but consecrated mode of voting.

A.: Saved, however, by this mode.

C.: The avarice of the conquerors covered Italy with the masterpieces of Greece, taken by violence from the temples and cities which they had adorned.

A.: The French have lately imitated them in spoiling Italy of all its glories.

In religion, the Romans had many ceremonies but no metaphysical doctrines; their priests directed public worship, without interfering with private life. With the union of so many nations under the empire, it became more and more evident that all their worship was directed to one god. ("The Hebrews knew this long before," Adams inserted.) The religions of the Gauls and the Jews, in which the priests were arbiters of morality, were bound to wound the Romans' pride, and at the end both nations were destroyed. Conquered peoples usually turn to metaphysical consolations; and thus twenty Egyptian and Jewish sects, uniting against the religion of the empire while furiously fighting one another, produced the religion of Jesus.

Alexandria had many scientists and scholars. Its library was crowded with grammarians who, Condorcet writes, "measured their admiration for a book by its antiquity and the difficulty of understanding and procuring it." [26] These curators of rare books, credulous to the point of absurdity, were responsible for the decline of the human spirit.

5

The sixth epoch, the first part of the Middle Ages, Condorcet regarded as "disastrous." Europe was crushed between sacerdotal tyranny and military despotism, although slavery at least gave way to serfdom, a milder form of servitude. The pontiffs of Rome wanted to rule every aspect of life, using treason and perfidy, assassination and parricide, to realize their ambition. ("This picture is very like," Adams agreed.) Under the triple oppression of kings, warriors, and priests, feudal anarchy extended to every village. Whenever tyranny wishes to reduce a people to the will of one of its portions, Condorcet holds, it counts upon the ignorance and prejudices of the victims themselves. "Is there any nation of Indians, Negroes, Tartars or Hottentots, in which the mass is not guided by one of its portions?" Adams asked.

In the East the decline was slower. Theological disputes occupied the learned, yet intolerance was no less savage than in the West. The Greek language had lost its purity, but Homer and Sophocles were still read in Constantinople. Meanwhile, a new force appeared in the East in the Empire of the Arabs, welded together by Mahomet. The Arabs studied Aristotle, and cultivated astronomy, optics, medicine, and other sciences; their light, however, owing to the despotism of their religion, shone for only a few moments.

C.: Thus we see, for the second time, *genius* abandoning nations which it had enlightened . . .[27]

A.: What a pity that this man of genius cannot be king and priest for the whole human race!

C.: Born in the cradle of a fanatical religion, it furnished only a fleeting exception to the laws of nature, which condemn superstitious nations to brutality and ignorance.

A.: But was there no genius among the Hebrews? None among the Christians, nor Mahometans? I understand you, Condorcet. It is atheistical genius alone that you would honor or tolerate.

C.: But this second example should not frighten us concerning the future: it should serve only as a warning not to neglect any *means of preserving and augmenting knowledge.*

A.: Right. What would you say to the 4 Sept. 1797 and its consequences? [28]

The Crusades, by bringing the West into closer touch with the East, broadened the horizon. In the ensuing seventh epoch, the common people profited from the rivalry of the kings and nobles, and slowly republics were formed in Italy, in the northern cities of Germany, and in Switzerland. The revival of the study of Aristotle led to scholasticism, which sharpened men's minds. Unfortunately, it also retarded the progress of natural science. Two important inventions were to exert enormous influence: the compass, by making navigation more secure, and gunpowder, by ending the superiority of brute force. "Thus the invention," Condorcet significantly remarks, "which seemed to threaten mankind with annihilation, has brought about its real equality." The awakening was particularly vigorous in Italy, where Dante, Petrarch, and Boccaccio perfected the language of the people. Works of art were produced there which justified the hope that genius was again about to adorn the spirit of man. "Genius," Adams wryly commented, "is still his Moses and the Prophets. Inspiration is his system as much as that of a Jew or a Christian. The inspiration of genius. Oh vanity of genius, what mischief have you not done?"

The eighth epoch comprised all the great events which ushered in the new age: the Renaissance, the Reformation, and the geographical and astronomical discoveries. It is astonishing how long a time elapsed between the first making of woodcuts and the invention of printing from movable type:

C.: However, this was fortunate, for *priests and kings* would have united to stifle, from its birth, the invention that was to unmask their hypocrisy and hurl them from their thrones.

A.: You must have your malicious strokes against kings and priests. I see no probability of such a union.

C.: Knowledge has become the staple of an active and universal trade. A new kind of authority is established, from which is exercised a less tyrannical empire over the passions, but a more firm and lasting power over reason . . .

A.: The empire of the press, over the passions, in the hands of Marat and others was more tyrannical than the government of Caesar Borgia.

C.: A *public opinion* is formed, powerful by the number of those who shared it . . .

A.: This public opinion is at times as great a tyrant as Marat.

C.: A tribunal is erected in favor of *reason* and *justice*, independent of all human power . . .

A.: As often in favor of error, absurdity, and vice as of reason and justice.

C.: Every *new error* is resisted from its birth: frequently attacked before it has been propagated.

A.: There has been more new error propagated by the press in the last ten years than in an hundred years before. 1798.

The press, Condorcet claims, frees the education of the people from all political and religious chains. ("Oh! that it had!" Adams wished.) How can one amidst such a multitude of books shut the doors so tightly that truth will be unable to enter? ("Ask Barras and Co. 1798. Ask Napoleon in 1811," Adams suggested.) But even if inquisitors could suppress those palpable truths which wound their interests directly, could they prevent the dissemination of such as include the proscribed truths? Could they do it without abandoning their mask of hypocrisy? "This mask can be worn by Talleyrand as well as by Tartuffe, or Condorcet," Adams riposted.

The fall of Constantinople and the discovery of America, the author continues, greatly stimulated the progress of knowledge. The Greek literati who fled to Italy brought manuscripts with them which helped to break the Aristotelian yoke. Unfortunately, the geographical discoveries were attended by brutality and avarice. But up to this epoch the crimes of priestcraft had escaped punishment. Then Luther challenged the despotism of the Popes. The deists concealed their views for fear of persecution, and even thought that it was desirable to deceive the multitude in its own interest:

C.: If the *natural equality* of mankind be the foundation of all morality, what could it hope from a philosophy, one of whose maxims was an open contempt for this equality?

A.: There is no such thing without a supposition of a God. There is no right or wrong in the universe without the supposition of a moral government and an intellectual and moral governor.

C.: Yet in some countries toleration became established—liberty of thought, not for men in general but for Christians. With the exception of *France*, it exists to this day only for Christians.

A.: In France it exists not for Christians or anything else. 1798.

Meanwhile some courageous minds questioned the basis of royal power. Others, more timid, were satisfied to assert a reciprocity of rights and duties between kings and people:

C.: This doctrine struck rather at the individual invested with sovereignty than at sovereignty itself. It was, therefore, almost always embraced by reformists, and adopted as a principle in all political dissensions and revolutions.

A.: The people have a right to change their rulers from day to day, from hour to hour, from minute to minute. What then? Who are the people? The whole nation, not every individual or town or county or province. How shall you know when the whole nation wishes to change?

Brighter hopes were dawning. Copernicus revived the true system of the world, Kepler calculated the orbits of the planets, Galileo discovered the laws of the descent of bodies, and chemistry and medicine also made astonishing progress. Painting, sculpture, literature arrived at perfection. The critical spirit awakened as the use of the vernacular tongues made learning accessible to larger numbers of people. Thus the contest between reason and authority began. Philosophy was opposed even more stubbornly than political inquiry, the improvement of which was dangerous only to the authority of kings and aristocratic assemblies. "Yes! it was dangerous to your and Turgot's system of government in one centre, which deluged France and Europe in blood," Adams helped to complete the picture.

6

Finally, progress produced a revolution in the entire mass of certain nations: a sure pledge of the revolution which will some day engulf all mankind. Condorcet's account of the ninth epoch—especially his version of the American and French revolutions—excited Adams more than any other part of the book. His comments are faster and angrier—his words tumble over one another:

C.: After ages of error, political writers at last discerned the true rights of men. It was no longer practicable to divide people into two races, one destined to govern and the other to obey. It was necessary to acknowledge that everybody has the same right to be enlightened about his interests, to know all truths, and that no authority can be entitled to retain him in ignorance.[29]

A.: Here are profound truths of philosophy and politics delivered in the slang of party newspapers. His great model of infidelity, Bolingbroke, however, in his *Patriot King* thinks that a few ethereal spirits are ordained by God to do all the good and all the evil in society. All the rest are Dutch travellers. How shall we decide when such great doctors as Bolingbroke and Condorcet disagree? No authority has a right to retain the people in ignorance. Agreed. But twenty-four million and a half in France will retain themselves in ignorance, and if left to themselves will soon extinguish the remaining half of a million who can read and write. They would soon exterminate the pen and ink men as aristocrats, oligarchs, priests, and tyrants.

C.: Those principles, for which the generous Sidney paid with his blood,[30] and to which Locke gave the prestige of his name, were developed later with more force and precision by Rousseau, whose glory it is to have placed them among those truths which cannot henceforth be forgotten or disputed.

A.: I do not believe that he ever read Sidney or Locke. Rousseau had not half the glory of Tom Paine who carried the theory of liberty much farther and asserted that no compact, no constitution, no oaths were binding on mankind.

C.: These principles once acknowledged, there still remain duties for the authorities to perform. It is for them to set up regulations determining the weight, bulk, length, and quantity of articles of commerce.

A.: Is it not for this authority to forbid murder, theft, adultery, perjury, etc.? Has it nothing to do but regulate weights, yoke hogs, and govern alewives?

Political economy, Condorcet continues, was explored by John de Witt,[31] Adam Smith, and the French economists. But, next to Descartes, it was Locke who through his study of the human mind most fruitfully influenced philosophy and the sciences. By analyzing the experience of pain and pleasure, men arrived at their notions of morality:

C.: The abasement of reason before the frenzy of supernatural faith disappeared in *society* as well as in philosophy . . .

A.: "Society," i.e. in the company he kept, Rochefoucauld, Franklin, d'Alembert, Diderot, La Lande. He knew very little of the world. He was as mere a monk as Loyola.

C.: Soon a class of men formed in Europe, less occupied with the discovery and deepening of truth than with its dissemination.

A.: Voltaire, Diderot, Hume, Gibbon, Rousseau, Raynal, T. Paine.

C.: In England, Collins and Bolingbroke, and in France, Bayle, Fontenelle, Voltaire, Montesquieu, and their disciples fought on the side of truth with all the weapons that learning, wit, philosophy, and literary ability could furnish . . . artfully caressing prejudice, the more easily to strangle it . . .

A.: According to Condorcet, the writers mentioned in this page adopted all the maxims and practiced all the arts of the Pharisees, the ancient priests of all countries, the Jesuits, the Machiavels, etc., etc. to overthrow the institutions that such arts had established.

C.: . . . sometimes soothing the enemies of reason by pretending not to desire more than partial toleration in religion and partial freedom in politics . . .

A.: This new philosophy was, by his own account, as insidious, fraudulent, and cruel as the old policy of priests, nobles, and kings.

C.: . . . siding with despotism when they were combating religious absurdities and with the clergy when they wanted to unmask tyranny . . .

A.: Precious confessions!

C.: . . . uniformly vindicating freedom of thought and writing as the right and salvation of mankind . . .

A.: How did they tolerate this freedom when they possessed power?

C.: . . . commanding kings, soldiers, magistrates, and priests to respect, in the name of nature, the blood of mankind.

A.: How did these writers respect the blood of mankind when they obtained power in 1792, 3, 4, 5, etc.?

C.: Such was this new philosophy, the common object of hatred for all the classes that exist by prejudice and live upon error.

A.: This is too true.

The principles of the new philosophy, strengthened by the doctrines of the economists, Condorcet goes on, rapidly spread to all classes and penetrated into most countries. The thinkers espoused the interests of all humanity, without distinction of nation, race, or creed. It was obvious that change had to come—either by revolution or by reform. The corruption and ignorance of the governments favored the first. Common sense had taught the people of the British colonies that Englishmen born on the other side of the Atlantic received from nature the same rights as the Englishmen born under the meridian of Greenwich.

C.: The British government, however, pretended to believe that God had created America, as well as Asia, for the pleasure of the inhabitants of London . . .

A.: Too true!

C.: Then could be observed, for the first time, a great people, freed from all chains, peaceably framing for itself constitutions which it judged most conducive to its happiness.

A.: But if this example is followed too closely by European nations, they will repent, as France has done.

C.: If we examine these constitutions, we shall discover what they owe to the progress of political science, and what are the old errors which prejudices of education succeeded in injecting into them . . .

A.: Fool! Fool!

C.: . . . why, for instance, the system of *a balance of powers* disfigures their simplicity; and why identity of interests rather than equality of rights is their principle.

A.: Is it possible that a philosopher, who understood human nature, had read history, and knew anything of government, free or arbitrary, should have written this? What is his idea of an identity of interests? An equality of rights? Is an equality of rights anywhere more explicitly asserted than in the American Constitution?

C.: At the same time, these American republics realized the necessity, then almost new even in theory, of establishing a peaceful method of amending the constitutions . . .

A.: New indeed! But France and America, too, have found it difficult to practice.

C.: The American Revolution soon had to extend to Europe. And if there was a people among whom the writings and principles of the Americans were more widely diffused than elsewhere, was this people not destined to give the first impulse to the revolution which the friends of humanity expected with such hope and impatience?

A.: How have these friends been disappointed!

C.: The French Revolution . . . was more complete than that of America. The Americans restricted themselves to setting up new powers in place of those exercised by the British. Nothing in their innovations touched the mass of the people, or changed the relations between individuals. In France, on the other hand, the Revolution embraced the entire economic system, changing every social relation . . .

A.: This and several pages before are to trumpet his hobby of a new heaven, i.e. a government in one democratical representative assembly; in one centre and that centre, the nation, which he learned from Franklin, Turgot, and Rochefoucauld. His majorities in France would always consist of Jacobins and sansculots, gorgons, hydras and chimeras dire.

C.: We shall see how much more pure, accurate, and profound are the principles upon which the constitution of France has been founded than those which directed the Americans . . .

A.: Pure! accurate! profound! indeed!

C.: . . . how limitations of power have been put in the place of that specious balance which has so long been admired . . .

A.: Where is the specious balance now? in 1811.

C.: . . . that we were the first to dare to preserve for the people its rights of sovereignty, the right of obeying no laws but those which have received their last sanction from the nation itself.

A.: Condorcet! Thou wert as superficial in legislation as abstruse in geometry.

The rest of the chapter outlines the tremendous progress of all the sciences. They used to be the heritage of a few, but the time is approaching, Condorcet predicts, when their application will be of universal benefit. The arts have been sterile for a long time, but this must have been due to changes in politics and manners, and not to exhaustion. ("The mythology of the Greeks and the theology of Christian Rome have been the great encouragers and rewarders of painters, statuaries, and architects," Adams reflected.) The art of printing has made possible the circulation of literature among an incomparably larger public than before. Having learned how to weigh authorities, scholarship itself has become more useful.

None of the sciences will deteriorate; nor will the principles of freedom and the rights of man ever again sink into oblivion, Condorcet confidently affirms. Adams was less certain: "A pleasing hope!" he wrote.

7

Condorcet himself was most interested in the tenth epoch—the future. Unfortunately, Adams made few specific comments on his pro-

compulfory taxation. This injuftice, fhe conceived, authorifed her to diffolve every tie of
connection, and fhe declared her independence.

Then was obferved, for the firft time, the
example of a great people throwing off at once
every fpecies of chains, and peaceably framing
for itfelf the form of government and the laws
which it judged would be moft conducive to
its happinefs; and as, from its geographical
pofition, and its former political ftate, it was
obliged to become a federal nation, thirteen
republican conftitutions were feen to grow up
in its bofom, having for their bafis a folemn
recognition of the natural rights of man, and
for their firft object the prefervation of thofe
rights through every department of the union.

If we examine the nature of thefe conftitutions, we fhall difcover in what refpect they
were indebted to the progrefs of the political
fciences, and what was the portion of error,
refulting from the prejudices of education,
which formed its way into them: why, for
inftance, the fimplicity of thefe conftitutions
is disfigured by the fyftem of a balance of
powers; and why an identity of interefts

S 4   rather

[Handwritten marginalia:]
But, if this example is followed too closely by European Nations, they will repent as France has done.

I God !
Fool !

Is it possible that a Philosopher, who understood human Nature, had read History, and knew any Thing of Government, free or arbitrary; Should have written this? what is his Idea of an identity of Interests? and an Equality of Rights. Is an Equality of Rights, any where more explicitly afserted than in the American Constitution blèrent croire que l'or ne circulait dans leurs États que pour enrichir le fisc, et que la nature ne produisait des hommes que pour qu'on en fît des soldats. La thésaurisation et le recrutement devinrent la double manie de tous les gouvernemens. Dans les mains de la plupart des ministres, la thésaurisation ne fut que la chimère des Danaïdes ; mais le recrutement fut une réalité ruineuse qui surchargea tous les États de l'Europe, violenta les ressorts de toutes les administrations , rendit insupportable à toutes les nations le joug des autorités qui pesaient sur elles, multiplia les prétextes de faire la guerre , disposa les princes à en rechercher les occasions, leur donna des facilités pour les rendre plus générales, plus durables, plus sanglantes, et prépara enfin la désorganisation politique, dont la guerre de la révolution a été le dernier et un des plus déplorables résultats.

Il me reste à indiquer les conséquences du troisième événement que je me suis proposé de développer. Mais avant d'entrer dans l'examen de ses effets, je crois devoir prévenir l'interprétation trop étendue qu'on pourrait donner aux expressions que j'ai

Thesaurisation.

Recruits.

How fortunate and how wise in the United States to have avoided this System of Thesaurisation & Recruitment. In 1800 Hamilton & Co. would have swallowed it whole. Adams prevented it at the Risque of his Reputation and his office. Forget it Americans and bless it.

The *State of France* reminds Adams of his struggle with Hamilton gram. It is significant, however, that he found the destruction of inequality among nations "hopeless," and the advance of equality within one nation and the real improvement of man, "not quite hopeless." To the question whether there is a single country whose inhabitants are condemned by nature never to enjoy liberty, he answered, "Not that I know of." He expressed horror at the treatment of the natives in Asia and Africa, and doubted that European settlements there would ever become examples of enlightenment. But with that he stopped. Condorcet's prognostications were not for him.

Yet he was far from dismissing the chapter as unimportant. It was with the future in mind that he covered the flyleaf with a long meditation, dated 1811:

"The rapid progress of the mind to perfection has been the commonplace topic of declamation for half a century. But I can see no other end they have in view as their ultimate object than to bring men back to the state of mind so frankly avowed by Tacitus and Quintilian—absolute doubt whether chance or fate governs the world. But it will be found that men must be governed as well as cultivated. Without government, there is not a more savage beast of the forest.

"The philosophers of France were too rash and hasty. They were as artful as selfish and as hypocritical as the priests and politicians of Babylon, Persia, Egypt, India, Greece, Rome, Turkey, Germany, Wales, Scotland, Ireland, France, Spain, Italy or England. They understood not what they were about. They miscalculated their forces and resources: and were consequently overwhelmed in destruction with all their theories.

"The precipitation and temerity of philosophers has, I fear, retarded the progress of improvement and amelioration in the condition of mankind for at least an hundred years.

"The public mind was improving in knowledge and the public heart in humanity, equity, and benevolence; the fragments of feudality, the inquisition, the rack, the cruelty of punishments, Negro slavery were giving way, etc. But the philosophers must arrive at perfection per saltum. Ten times more furious than Jack in the Tale of a Tub, they rent and tore the whole garment to pieces and left not one whole thread in it. They have even been compelled to resort to Napoleon, and Gibbon himself became an advocate for the Inquisition. What an amiable and glorious Equality, Fraternity, and Liberty they have now established in Europe!"

There was still all the empty space on the half-title page. Unable to resist the temptation, Adams made another attack from a fresh angle:

"This book is more learned and entertaining than the Sophiometer of John Stewart, the pedestrian traveller,[32] which I received from him from England three days ago: but not much more solid.

"The logos of Plato, the ratio of Manilius,[33] and the mind of Condorcet, all plausible and specious as they are, will be three thousand years longer more delusive than useful. Not one of them takes human nature as it is for his foundation. Equality is one of those equivocal words which the philosophy of the 18th century has made fraudulent. The word as it is used is a swindler. In the last twenty-five years it has cheated millions out of their lives and tens of millions out of their property."

Four years later, as news reached him of Napoleon's escape from Elba and the declaration of the Congress of Vienna, Adams turned once more to Condorcet's work, and, at the bottom of the last page, ended the dispute:

"Quincy, May 2ᵈ 1815. Napoleon has been exiled to Elba; Popes, Jesuits, and Inquisitions restored and revived, conformably to the advice of Gibbon to the Portuguese. Napoleon has returned in triumph to France: and now it is said the Congress of Vienna has declared war against him. Is the Congress of Vienna the sovereign of the world? The question now is whether Popes, Jesuits, and Inquisitions shall rule the human race?"

"Nations will know," Condorcet wrote, "that they cannot become conquerors without losing their freedom; that perpetual confederations are the only means of maintaining their independence; that their object should be security, and not power . . . Institutions, better organized than those plans for permanent peace which have occupied the leisure and consoled the hearts of certain philosophers, will accelerate the progress of the brotherhood of nations."[34] All this Adams regarded as wild optimism. But his idea that the world could go muddling along for the next three thousand years shows him, in spite of his forebodings, a far greater optimist than Condorcet ever was.[35]

[XIII]

Napoleon's Bid for a Continental Alliance

In October 1800 a volume appeared in Paris which, in spite of its modest title—*L'État de la France à la fin de l'an VIII*—created a great stir in the capitals of Europe. The censorship of the press, which the First Consul had established six months before and which had silenced sixty-two of the seventy-three political newspapers of Paris, made it obvious that the book was an official document. It was a manifesto addressed to the neutral and belligerent powers maintaining that their interest lay with France and that their common enemy was England. It urged that, instead of continuing the war, all countries should unite with France to throw off English domination. In a glowing picture of the future, the work projected an inspiring program—the adoption of a universal navigation act which would ensure equal privileges to all nations. Although published anonymously, everybody knew that it had been written by Alexandre d'Hauterive, Under Secretary of the Ministry of Foreign Affairs. The book was Napoleon's bid for a continental alliance.[1]

In order to understand the general European situation, the author argues, one must go back to 1648, the year of the Treaty of Westphalia. During the century and a half since the conclusion of the Thirty Years' War a new Europe has come into being. Three great events have occurred during this period: the emergence of the Russian Empire in the North; the rise of Prussia to the rank of a great power; and the prodigious development of the colonial and maritime system of England. As to Russia and Prussia, Hauterive readily acknowledges that their roles had been inevitable; England's mastery of the seas, however, was a usurpation, and it was the duty of all the European countries to defend their rights against her. France, as ever, will be on their side.

The book appeared—as was intended—at a critical moment. There had been a change in the air. Tsar Paul, feeling betrayed by Austria, had ordered home Suvaroff's army, and blamed England for the failure of their joint campaign in Holland. The overthrow of the Directory and the rapidity with which the First Consul was consolidating his power excited his interest; and after the victory of Marengo and the triumphs of the French armies in southern Germany he became a fervent admirer of Napoleon. And the latter knew how to play upon the sympathies of the Tsar; he offered the self-styled Grand Master of the Order of St. John the possession of Malta, then ready to capitulate to the English. England, less generous, wanted to keep the island for herself, meanwhile continuing her ruthless policy in the Baltic.[2]

Indeed, British control of the seas had long been a source of irritation in European politics. It was during the American Revolution that, in order to protect their commerce from the interference of the British navy, Russia, Sweden, and Denmark had concluded a pact of armed neutrality. France and Spain, at war with England, were naturally enthusiastic about the alliance, and gradually Holland, Prussia, Austria, and other countries also joined the league. Yet when England, in reply, declared war upon Holland, they remained silent and let their small ally be severely beaten. Thus the pact of 1780 became a dead letter. More than this, at the beginning of the First Coalition the same powers signed a convention with England not to lend any protection to the commerce of France. Denmark was the only country which continued to hold out for the rights of neutrals. In December 1799 a Danish frigate, off Gibraltar, fired upon the British boat which tried to search a vessel in her charge, and half a year later another Danish cruiser fought a British squadron in the Channel until she was captured with the six vessels under her escort. The Danish Government demanded satisfaction, whereupon England sent a punitive fleet to the Sound. Tsar Paul, hardly normal under the best of circumstances, raged at the news. He ordered the sequestration of all British property in Russia and, when England refused to surrender Malta to the Order of St. John, placed an embargo on British vessels in Russian ports. At the same time, he sent a representative to Napoleon, and called upon the Kings of Prussia, Sweden, and Denmark to reëstablish the armed neutrality.

It was during this ferment of the Northern countries that Napoleon ordered his Under Secretary of Foreign Affairs to publish an indictment of the maritime supremacy of England. The result was the *État*

de la France, composed and printed in six weeks. Written with eloquence and logic, the book served its purpose well. It was a masterpiece
of propaganda, provoking discussion everywhere. Certainly Napoleon
was well pleased, for he made a present of 25,000 francs to the author.[3]
Adding force to the argument, he announced that the French Government, "appreciating the truly patriotic zeal of the Emperor of Russia
for the common cause of all Continental Powers," would not treat for
peace with England until the Russian, Danish, Swedish, American, and
Prussian flags were respected on the sea as the armies of these Powers
are respected on land. Significantly enough, the treaties of the Second
Armed Neutrality, making the principles of the First even more strin-
gent, were concluded ten days later.

The first two months of 1801 were filled with vast schemes in both
Paris and St. Petersburg. The Tsar was feverish with excitement and
proposed to his new ally a joint invasion of India by way of Bokhara
and Khiva. Napoleon, who had already been as far as Egypt, was cool
to the suggestion, but he let the Tsar rave on. The Northern League
was becoming more and more determined. After some vacillation, Prussia also joined it. And Napoleon, having just forced the "terrible"
Treaty of Lunéville—worse even than the Treaty of Campo Formio—
upon Austria, was leading the fanfare.[4] "The Powers of the North,"
he declared to the Senate, "may rightly count on France. The French
Government will avenge with them an injury common to all nations,
without losing sight of the fact that it fights only for peace and the welfare of the world . . ." England was more isolated than ever before;
and, with almost all her former enemies behind her, France stood forth
as the champion of freedom. Then events took a new turn. On March
23, 1801, Tsar Paul was murdered, and on April 2 Nelson destroyed
the Danish fleet in the battle of Copenhagen. The new Tsar, Alexander
I, started negotiations with England at once, and by June 19 the friendship between the two countries was restored. Within half a year, all
the other powers had signed a convention of compromise with England.[5]

Able and unassuming, Alexandre d'Hauterive was the ideal type of
the "permanent" official. For thirty years he worked as Under Secretary of Foreign Affairs, composing innumerable state papers and editing
no less than sixty-two political and commercial treaties. Four times he
served as Acting Foreign Minister, but never as Minister in his own
right.

Born in 1754, the son of a poor farmer, Hauterive was teaching in
a college at Tours when, in 1780, the Duc de Choiseul, governor of the

province, paid a visit there with his wife. The young professor, whose address of salutation moved the Duchess to tears, was invited to the ducal estate at Chanteloup, where he met many celebrities. When the Duke's nephew was appointed Ambassador to Turkey, Hauterive accompanied him, remaining in the East for several years, for some time as secretary to the *hospodar* of Moldavia. After the Revolution he applied for a position in the consular service, and in the summer of 1792 he was appointed Consul for New York. Upon Genêt's recall, however, he too lost his post. He was bitter against the *Conseil Éxecutif*. "There was no need," he wrote to a friend, "to include me in Genêt's disgrace: I have not been known in this country as one of the instruments but rather as one of the foils of the man whose conduct the Council wanted to censure." [6] Feeling no temptation to go back to France, he rented a few acres outside New York, bought some seed on credit, and settled down as a gardener. By the following summer he was selling his vegetables in the market. Finally in 1797 the way was at last open for his return. In the winter of that year he sailed for France.

Talleyrand, whom he had first met at Chanteloup and whom he had seen again in New York, was now Minister of Foreign Affairs; but Hauterive did not ask for employment. It was Charles Reinhard, replacing Talleyrand temporarily, who appointed him chief of the political division. However, Talleyrand was glad to retain his services, and it was under him that Hauterive found his true vocation. Since the Minister, attending every important social function, spent little time in his office, his assistant had a chance to labor to his heart's content. Through a memorandum on the reorganization of the diplomatic service he attracted the attention of Napoleon; and soon afterwards he was asked to write his book against England—the book with which he made history.[7]

Adams read the *État de la France* in the summer of 1801, soon after his retirement from the Presidency. He was aware of its authorship and recognized its purpose; across the title page of his copy he wrote: "By Citizen Hauterive, first clerk in the office of foreign affairs." [8]

His interest was keen from beginning to end. How could it be otherwise? France had been connected with the most dramatic events of his administration—the contemptuous treatment of the American commissioners in Paris; Talleyrand's alleged attempt to extort a bribe for the members of the Directory and a "loan" for the government; [9] the preparations for war, with the fitting out of naval vessels and the creation of cadres for an army; Washington's appointment as Lieutenant General, with Hamilton as his second in command; the conciliatory attitude of the French, and the sending of a new peace mission to France, with the ensuing fury of the Hamiltonians; and finally the Treaty of Morfontaine. He had acted in opposition to his Cabinet, and was abused for averting the war with France as acrimoniously as he had been for his opinions about the French Revolution. A letter by Hamilton, designed to circulate only among party leaders, was published in October 1800, denouncing him for his "extreme egotism of temper" and declaring him "unfit for the office of Chief Magistrate." [10] Noah Webster, William Pinckney, Uzal Ogden, and others defended Adams, but he himself thought it undignified to reply during his Presidency. [11] It was not until 1809, after a Baltimore newspaper had printed a grossly insulting article about him, that Adams published his reply to Hamilton in the Boston *Patriot*, and afterwards also in book form. Proudly he stated that there was no danger for the country in the negotiation with France: "To me only it was dangerous. To me, as a public man, it was fatal, and that only because Alexander Hamilton was pleased to wield it as a poisoned weapon with the express purpose of destroying." [12] And in 1815 he wrote the memorable words to James Lloyd, Senator from Massachusetts: "I will defend my missions to France, as long as I have an eye to direct my hand, or a finger to hold my pen. They were the most disinterested and meritorious actions of my life. I reflect upon them with so much satisfaction that I desire no other inscription over my gravestone than: 'Here lies John Adams, who took upon himself the responsibility of the peace with France in the year 1800.' " [13]

Yet, as his comments in the *État de la France* show, Adams had little confidence in the French. His answer to the repeated charge of arrogance against England was that France was no better, settling the matter with the comment: "Perhaps the truth will warrant us in saying that the two nations are equally selfish." Toward the end, Hauterive asserts that the recently adopted constitution is the one best suited to the character of France, being republican in both principles and origin; but Adams, as if anticipating future events, remained doubtful. [14] Reading the author's panegyric on Napoleon, however, he had to admit that the First Consul might justly be compared to Caesar. In spite of his animosity, he was dazzled by the great Corsican.

2

Adams's close watch over the argument began at the discussion of the position of Prussia, as he was reminded of recent events at home.

Under the rule of the German Elector, the author writes, Prussia became the rallying point for all the Germanic countries, thus supplanting the influence of France. Gold and soldiers were the Great Elector's chief means of strengthening his country, and, following his example, these have been a mania with every government.

Hauterive: In the hands of most ministers the hoarding of treasure was nothing but a dream of the Danaides; recruiting, however, was a reality which ruined every state in Europe . . . and brought about the political disorder which resulted in the Revolutionary War.[15]

Adams: How fortunate and how wise is the United States to have avoided this system of thesaurisation and recruitement. In 1800 Hamilton & Co. would have swallowed it, whole. Adams prevented it at the risque of his reputation and his office. Forget it, Americans and belie it.[16]

H.: The confusion which followed these events could have been prevented; and the blame rests with those who have allowed themselves to be surprized into a career in which everything depends on competition.

A.: The blame would most justly have been imputable to Hamilton & Co. if they had been surprized into this career, and to Adams if he had permitted them.

H.: The source of the trouble was want of discernment in the statesmen, who did not realize that laws already in existence provided states with sufficient means of preventing any expansion which might impair their relations.

A.: When and where were the statesmen who acted or could act upon foresight so distant and obscure?

H.: These statesmen thought that force was better than policy, that courage was above wisdom.

A.: People, nations always believe that force is more to be admired than policy, courage than wisdom.

H.: They listened only to the voice of mistrust, jealousy, and vanity; and, to come to the true source of the evil, they conceived a monstrous idea of the preëminence of France.

A.: France has made to herself a more monstrous idea of her preëminence than any nation of Europe had, and acted with proportional presumption.

H.: Then, when the powers whose expansion they had fostered by their lack of foresight became dangerous, they blamed France.

A.: There is more of patriotism than of impartiality in this Frenchman.

H.: Whoever examines the history of Europe since the break-up of her political ties will see that France has always unveiled to her friends, in season, the secret designs of princes against them.

A.: They will also see whether England has not always unveiled in season the secret views of France.

At the time of the Treaty of Westphalia, Hauterive continues, no one was interested in maritime affairs except England. Cromwell's Navigation Act boldly claimed the rule of the seas and, concurrently, welded the power of the State to its commercial interests.[17] Since then England has profited from all the discord in Europe. It would require a larger book to depict satisfactorily the restlessness which has agitated Europe for the last hundred and fifty years. ("Barons' wars and Catholic wars agitated Europe as much 500 years before, and Crusades before them. Mankind must always have some source of inquietude," Adams interjected.)

H.: What has been the ambition of France since the War of the Succession? Her security and the gain of a few advantages which but slightly affected her enemies.

A.: Partiality here is too gross.

H.: Had France won in the wars of Louis XIV, maritime power would have been subordinated longer to continental politics; Holland and Portugal would have preserved their independence toward England; England would not have changed her government, and the Stuarts would have been reëstablished.

A.: Rather too much imagination, speculation, and conjecture here.

H.: All Europe seemed to unite then to protect a revolution in England . . .

A.: Europe acted wisely.

H.: In our times, we have seen Europe united to prevent a revolution in France.

A.: Europe acted wisely again.

H.: The stability as well as the adequacy of a political system depend on the *federative system* of each power . . .

A.: I suppose he means the system of foreign affairs of each power. The fate of the U.S. seems likely to be decided in future entirely by the conduct of their foreign affairs.

H.: The proper principles of the federative system may be reduced to two: every alliance ought to guarantee the permanence of existing relations; and every alliance ought to guarantee the political interests of the Continent against the ascendancy of the maritime interests.

A.: These principles may be good for France.

H.: Spain, Holland, Italy, Germany, and England entered into a common war against France; Denmark, Sweden, and the United States were invited to join in . . .

A.: The U.S. did not associate. How soon they may unite with France is now uncertain. 1801.

H.: Never before had the world witnessed so gigantic a combination . . .

A.: There never was so gigantic a danger.

H.: Can it be said that the forgers of this alliance had the general interest in view, that they desired to separate the rights of the continental nations from those of the maritime?

A.: This separation is ideal and chimerical. It is impossible. Power is power whether derived from sea or land.

H.: Can it be supposed that connections so hurriedly formed are likely to be permanent?

A.: We have seen that they were not susceptible of permanence.

H.: I think that there can be no doubt about these questions. To raise them is to state their answer—and their condemnation.

A.: The truth is that oppression from France made all Europe mad.

H.: Instead of "coalition," posterity will distinguish this league by the name of "conspiracy" against a single nation, and will call it a solemn abjuration of all the rules of international law.

A.: Not so fast, Citizen! Who began the abjuration?

H.: France has returned to her traditional system of alliances, and accomplished a task that has never yet been imposed upon any nation.

A.: England can say the same thing.

H.: She has been compelled to rescue her allies from engagements that were contrary to their interests. She could have overthrown Spain, invaded Holland, and seized Genoa; but she preferred friendship to conquests. She has understood that *without a federative system there is neither justice, nor guarantee, nor lasting hope in mere power.*

A.: This is unhappily a maxim too universally true.

H.: The aim of this system does not lose itself in an indefinite expanse of conquests.

A.: What unblushing heads these folk have!

H.: Its only purpose is order, justice, and stability.

A.: With how much naïveté this is said!

H.: It is for the maritime nations of Europe to choose between their present situation and the advantages and disadvantages of the *federative system* of France.

A.: Rather "système dominatif."

H.: This appeal is directed in the first place to Turkey, Barbary, Naples, and Portugal, and in the second, to Denmark, Sweden, and the United States.

A.: Dit en maître.

H.: France has laid the foundation of her continental system; the rest depends upon the chances of war and fortune. As long as this uncertainty lasts, she will find, by sustaining the energy of her warfare and by strengthening her maritime relations, sufficient means to avert every danger.

A.: The energy of her system of war cannot be sustained. It depends on the present First Consul. 1801.

H.: And if she cannot otherwise extend her federative system, she will employ military rather than federative aid. If the princes ignore the voice of their own interests, France will ally herself with their countries which they are unable to defend.

A.: This is unqualified revolutionary impudence. It is worthy of Robespierre or Barras.[18]

3

In considering France's situation with regard to her enemies, Hauterive ponders over the impulses which drive states to make war on one another. They are almost always unknown to the governments themselves, and the hidden springs are scarcely ever in accord with the avowed motives. La Bruyère has observed that in time of peace it is impossible to imagine a cause strong enough to disturb the calm of a people, while in wartime it is difficult to imagine one powerful enough to restore it. ("La Bruyère was in the right," Adams thought.) A blind fatalism holds the will power of most governments captive during the war, and the end usually comes through an unexpected event:

H.: After the Thirty Years' War peace was concluded when it was most despaired of, and for reasons which no one could anticipate.[19]

A.: The Constitution of U. S. of 1787 was concluded in the same manner by the arrival of a ship with the first volume of the Defence.[20]

H.: Even after the Peace of Utrecht, the quarrels about the Spanish Succession disturbed Europe for twenty years more; and it was only the death of Alexander Farnese, the least important prince of his time, bringing about the union of the principal powers, that compelled the Emperor to conclude the Peace of Vienna.[21]

A.: A curious group of haphazards.

Yet the author hopes that it will not be left forever to chance—the death of a prince or minister, the success or failure of a court intrigue —to establish a true balance in Europe. What a spectacle France presented only a year before, and how different her present situation was![22]

H.: France has placed her destinies in the hands of a man who himself has a great destiny to fulfil.

A.: Destinies precarious enough.

H.: One might say of the sudden consolidation of our forces what a famous poet said of the emergence of the earth from chaos·

"Spiritus intus alit, totamque infusa per artus
  Mens agitat molem, et magno se corpore miscet."[23]

A.: How flattering to Bonaparte! Yet how true! for the present.

H.: It is easy to unfold the principles upon which the French system of warfare is based. France does not recognize "natural" enemies.

A.: She is however a natural enemy and has several natural enemies.

H.: France does not wish to force her enemies into partnership with her. Without allies, she repelled the attacks of all Europe; and, with very few allies, she resisted the hostility of Europe, Asia, Africa, and America.

A.: There is too much French forehead in this.

H.: There is, or ought to be, an equilibrium in Europe . . .

A.: I am glad to see the necessity of an equilibrium acknowledged. It may however conclude against the views of our author.

H.: The alliances of France are natural relationships inherent in her position and essential to her dominance . . .

A.: Dominance and predonderance are so familiar in the language of Frenchmen that they think they have a right to both. By land they have more than they ought, by sea it ought not to be permitted them.

H.: It is for the powers which are trying to control various regional balances to seek the aid of France.

A.: What hauteur!

Turkey, the author continues, has most to fear from losing her affiliation with France. If Turkey is anxious to keep her European possessions, she should seek admission to the federative system of France —the only country which has a stake in her independence. As to Russia, she should endeavor to civilize her vast domains rather than make new conquests.

H.: Let Russia open her ports to all nations. She should discharge the debt for her civilization; having imitated Europe in the arts, she ought now to set her an example of wisdom, moderation, and justice.[24]

A.: Ah! Wisdom, moderation and justice! All is extravagance and injustice: and France is the most extravagant and unjust in Europe.

H.: Russia should maintain the balance of the North, while France guarantees that of the South; their accord will then ensure the peace of the world.

A.: Paul was captivated and converted by this pretty declamation.

H.: Russia thus will take her place in the front rank of the founders of international law and the benefactors of humanity.

A.: This may be yet. The death of Paul makes it more probable.

The author then turns to France's relations with Austria. The Treaty of Campo Formio, negotiated "by the first general of the republic, now its first magistrate," is the basis of the federative system of France. It is unjust to accuse her of boundless ambition:

H.: France has conquered Belgium, the left bank of the Rhine, Savoy, and Nice, but she has reserved for herself only Belgium and the Venetian Islands.[25]

A.: Reserving Belgium and the Venetian Islands was proof enough of her ambition.

H.: The power of the Austrian Emperor has even increased; he has acquired the richest stretch of navigable riverway that exists.

A.: To be sure, that overpaid the Emperor for Belgium. But making Austria a maritime power is as dangerous to Europe as giving France the preponderance at present at sea.

H.: France agreed, even wished, that Austria should become a maritime power . . .

A.: A great truth. But will Prussia, Russia, Sweden, Denmark or Holland, not to name England, be content?

Hauterive paints a sinister picture of England's influence on every continent. All the nations of Europe have suffered from her supremacy; yet France, with her long history of sacrifices, is willing to reconcile her interests with those of England.

H.: Europe is condemned to eternal disturbance unless the power of England can be harmonized with the preponderance of France.

A.: How can he reconcile his pretences to an equilibrium with his continual claim of preponderance for France?

H.: I wish to discuss only the barriers which the common interest of the maritime powers demands against the indefinite extension of England's designs.

A.: This indefinite extension is only applicable to France. England is confined to her island by nature.

H.: The ships of England cover every sea . . .

A.: If France has a preponderance at land, England ought to have it at sea. All the rest of Europe would be slaves if either had both preponderances.

H.: In Southern Asia England has possessions superior in extent and equal in riches to the largest countries of Europe. In Eastern Asia her agents impose her commerce on every nation along the coast. We have seen the English government send a gaudy embassy to China, to create the impression there that every work of art in Europe was produced by English industry.[26]

A.: This may be truth or it may be mere French envy and jealousy.

H.: The doctrines which have disorganized the French islands in America were imported from England . . .

A.: This is intolerable.

H.: She has even offered alliances to chiefs whom she would have put to death had they attempted in her domains the crime to which she incited them.

A.: In the French legislature the liberty of Negroes has been asserted and propagated more than in Parliament.[27]

H.: On the continent of America she now possesses only Acadia and Canada. But these provinces enable her, by their location, to monopolize the commerce of the fishery and the game.

A.: England does not envy thus the conquests and military superiority of France in Europe.

H.: In Europe we behold the same conditions. In time of peace, England is the leading market; in time of war, she is almost the only one for the exchange of the world's products.

A.: Suppose all this were true of France as it is of England, what would become of Europe?

H.: There is more than one way to deliver Europe from these fetters . . . However, most European governments have chosen England as a guide in all their affairs.

A.: One part of Europe takes France and the other England for guide.

The governments of Europe, the author argues, ignore the fact that nations with the greatest share of trade necessarily rise above other nations; they check rather than foster the natural tendencies of their industries. England has profited immensely from these mistakes.

H.: If the policy of every state were similarly calculated to secure a legitimate share of the advantages of commerce, all would be proportionately powerful. And such a result would gratify us, who *do not wish to oppress* any country . . .

A.: None will avow a desire to oppress. But has any nation ever oppressed more than France?

H.: To achieve this end, first of all the war should be terminated. Is it so difficult for Russia, Austria, Naples, Turkey, etc. to understand that the present war, into which England has forced them, is shamefully opposed to the elementary interests of their wealth, power, and dignity?

A.: If no triumvirate could ever long agree, is it possible that Russia, Austria, and Turkey should?

H.: The problem of Europe's independence can easily be solved: the countries at war with France should realize that the regeneration of their power depends entirely on a quick and honorable peace.

A.: It seems that all the littoral powers must have a regeneration like that of France.

H.: All the efforts of France are directed toward the establishment of a federative system. She does not aim at any aggrandizement or prosperity which she is not willing to share with every other nation.

A.: How sincerely this fellow lies!

4

Until lately it was commonly believed, Hauterive writes, that to ruin a rival and to enrich oneself were the same thing. ("This error or distemper is too deeply rooted in the human constitution to be curable," Adams commented.) It is becoming more and more fully understood, however, that commerce cannot be injured in any part without damage to its entire body. Thus the maritime hegemony of England also impairs the welfare of the neutrals:

H.: A universal maritime law would allow neutrals complete freedom of trade and navigation.[28]

A.: A lie.

H.: French policy is instinctively allied to the independence and prosperity of every nation.

A.: This is very ridiculous.

H.: England, however, put a different practice into law. In every war she has arrogated to herself the right of tormenting neutral commerce.

A.: Has France tormented it less?

H.: A letter from the king of England to his admirals is sufficient to overthrow in a moment the entire law of the sea.

A.: Or of Sonthonax or Victor Hugues.[29]

Because of the tyranny of England, Hauterive goes on, commerce seeks safety in stratagems: the forgery of bills of lading and invoices has become a legitimate industry. "Awfully true," Adams conceded.

H.: The regulation of France's marine, the agreements which she is about to conclude with the United States,[30] and finally her adherence to that fundamental principle of the sovereignty of neutral states according to which every commercial vessel navigating under armed naval escort is exempt from inspection, will prove France's respect for nations engaged in trade.

A.: The bait of the hook.

H.: What government, excepting that of England, could regard such dispositions as contrary to its interest? What publicist would dare to declare that they are neither politic nor just?

A.: I fear there is no argument to prove those dispositions politic or just which will not equally prove all wars to be impolitic and unjust.

H.: France had modified the laws of privateering (*les lois de la course*); she will never cease to desire their abolition.

A.: Until she had ruined England. Then she would revive la *course*.

H.: The navigation of nations connected by alliance should be authorized, welcomed, and protected in their respective ports. I except from this law of reciprocity only the navigation between the colonies and the mother country . . .

A.: Monopoly of colonies to continue.

H.: Thus the ideas of coöperation will produce, by degrees, a general system of association and the abolition of all prohibitory laws.

A.: Chimerical!

Finally, the author answers at length the propagandists for England —Friedrich von Gentz and François d'Ivernois—who have been harping on the weakness of the French armies and finances compared with English finances and the armies of the Coalition.[31] The real picture is different; France, after six years of revolution and eight years of war, is stronger than ever:

H.: Has not France repelled the efforts of all her enemies? Has she not twice penetrated into the heart of Germany? Has she not concluded peace with Prussia, Spain, and Holland? Has she not twice conquered Italy?

A.: This is shrewd. Indeed it is very good. It is unanswerable.

H.: Two causes, more than any other, have contributed to the success of France: the French have in late years perfected the art of war; and they have always placed the theater of the war in their neighbors' territory.

A.: Vengeance may one day be demanded for this.

H.: Thus we have witnessed the constant superiority of a ruined Republic over enemies who possess all the riches of the world and could arm against it all the states of the Continent.

A.: Unlimited violence at home and abroad has hitherto answered the end.

H.: Can the difference between the military history of France and that of her enemies be explained otherwise than by their respective practice of the art of war—the one, obsolete, the other, bold and progressive?

A.: Desperation moral and political is the great principle of French success.

H.: In the only period when France suffered reverses, the greatest of our generals was far away from the scene of the European war.

A.: Bonaparte.

H.: With the same army this general of everlasting fame dispersed in a few months five successive armies. He was never numerically inferior in a single battle. Accelerating the march of his troops, in the moment of action he was certain of beating the enemy, over whom he had acquired the advantage of numbers.

A.: Celerity has been the principal cause of French success. Attack and surprise have been added to celerity.

H.: Of all the countries of Europe, France is the most favorably situated, surrounded on almost every side by seas and mountains.

A.: This is true and of great importance.

H.: She is accessible only on the northern frontiers; and long experience of danger has there led to a multiplication of all the means of defense that tactics has invented.[32]

A.: This was done by the monarchy.

H.: Against the deficit upon which the writers of the Coalition base their hopes for a new crisis in France, I could set the indemnities that France has been able to collect beyond her borders, not only for the maintenance of her armies but also for the needs of her administration.

A.: This is an exulting history of French tyranny.

Hauterive now turns to the internal situation of France. Apologists for England would have it that every country has benefited from the war, except France. But it is a well-known fact that the burden of war falls most heavily on an exporting country; therefore, the population and industry of England must have suffered most. To be sure, England has adopted a clever system of taxation, and her "moneyed men" support the government with generous credits; in appraising her financial problems, however, one has to consider that the workers who have produced the goods accumulated in the past few years have already received their wages:

H.: Those classes in England which get their living from trade must have increased either the list of the dead or the list of those who live on the five or six million sterling just voted by Parliament for the maintenance of the poor.

A.: There is some color of good sense in the foregoing observations. But they show that all our knowledge of this subject is ignorance.

What is now pompously called "the science of political economy," the author continues, lacks that mass of small facts upon which calculations must be based. The only means of ascertaining the national revenue is by learning the details of local production and consumption, and the government which instituted such a survey would accomplish more in a few years than all the theorists have done in centuries. Meanwhile, the national revenue may best be estimated by multiplying the annual expenditures of one individual by the total of the population; and there are nearly three times as many Frenchmen as Englishmen. It will be said, of course, that the standard of living in England is two or three times higher than in France:

H.: I do not believe that observations have yet been made sufficiently precise for us to form a reliable opinion about the relative subsistence of Frenchmen and Englishmen.

A.: Can these precise observations ever be made without an inquisition into the families and affairs of individuals, inconsistent with their comfort, their liberty, their peace?

H.: At the same time, the social organization of France is less subject to vicissitudes, and her property, industry, and income are less exposed to unforesen events that may occur through either war or the fear and effects of revolution.

A.: Revolution will be an épouvantail in future to all governments for some time.

H.: The more a nation has developed the art of production, the more it will suffer when political disturbances destroy its bonds with other nations.

A.: This prophecy may experience the fate of so many others.

H.: The campaign of the year VIII has shown that France needs only an object to fix the wandering public attention, a rallying point to unite the general confidence, a steady hand to guide the reins of government . . .

A.: i.e. a monarch.

H.: Why did not the ravages of war affect the fabric of France perceptibly? Agriculture has expanded during the Revolution; and the war has given scope to an infinite variety of speculation which has provided employment for capital.

A.: When soldiers return to their former professions and capitals to their usual speculation, the military will languish.

H.: The first magistrate has never ceased to offer peace . . . All Frenchmen know that their government demands only security, the preservation of the glory of eight years of victory, the establishment of the *boundaries* of the Republic.

A.: Ay! there is the rub.

5

The last chapter is a defense of the new constitution and a tribute to Napoleon.

Are the new laws in accord with the character of France? The author's answer is enthusiastically in the affirmative. After years of disorder, the real inclinations of men gradually asserted themselves, and the laws made during the period of violence became proportionately untenable—until the time arrived when the ultra-revolutionary system was overtaken by the same catastrophe which had destroyed the monarchy ten years before. The new constitution, which is neither democratic nor monarchical, combines the elements of good government:

H.: In all that I am to say about the laws, I shall consider the political establishment, the civil institutions, and that social hierarchy which springs from inequality of natural talent . . .[33]

A.: The political establishment means the constitution. A social hierarchy is it seems admitted.

H.: . . . and which, at a time when the abolition of titles and privileged classes has secured for everybody the chance for a good life, nevertheless admits differences owing to education, personal merit, and even wealth.

A.: The title of general, admiral, colonel and captain are as legal as those of duke, marquis, and count. Admitting distinction of education is admitting generally distinctions of birth.

In examining the essentials of good laws, Hauterive suggests twelve principles: the laws must correspond to customs; the stability of a government depends upon its power to change the laws in accordance with variations in customs; legal distinctions between classes can exist only when the classes have different customs; no political regime can become permanent unless the lure of prestige attracts men to the new institutions, and so on. "These twelve observations are curious, some of them profound," Adams remarked. However, he made specific comments only on two:

H.: Even when there are no classes, there are qualifications proper to the various professions. Two kinds of moral subordination must be established—one based upon the position of employer and employee . . .

A.: At length subordination is admitted. How could it be denied?

H.: . . . and the other, upon the superiority of talents, virtues, and knowledge.

A.: Here is the source of eternal controversy. Who shall be judge of the talents, virtues and information?

H.: In modern times, the heroism of a few famous men has taken the place of mythological ideas . . .

A.: Washington seems to be alluded to, and Bonaparte is, I suppose, to be a Washington.

Certain writers, the author complains, are possessed by a mania for finding analogies to the French Revolution. They ransack both ancient and modern times for examples, hoping that they may thus predict a counterrevolution and the probable course of events. But their efforts are futile. The revolution in England ended with the return of the monarchy and in Holland with the founding of a republic:

H.: The revolutions in Switzerland and the United States have given birth to two republican constitutions, one of which is remarkable for its firmness and the other for the wisdom, simplicity, and excellence of its institutions.

A.: Thanks for the compliment and more for the prophecy. But! Prophecies like Burnet's panegyrics ought always to have a "but" in them.[34]

H.: The comparison to the English revolution is especially meaningless. Cromwell left England as he had found her, not having wisdom enough to know that only new institutions can secure a new form of government. It did not require much discernment for his son to see that an English republic had never existed . . .

A.: In this sense, has the Republic of France ever existed?

H.: All superficial comparisons of the French republic to other republics deserve only contempt . . .

A.: Bravo! Ay despise them all!

H.: However, I confess that as to genius and moral qualities the First Consul and Caesar may justly be compared.

A.: This I believe.

H.: But while Caesar had to fight only barbarians and warriors of no great renown, it has been the destiny of Bonaparte to vanquish the most warlike nations, the most disciplined armies, and the most capable generals of Europe.

A.: This is all correct.

H.: But what similarity is there between Rome and the French republic, the latter *well organized* . . .

A.: Indeed?

H.: . . . neither oppressed by castes *nor tormented by party factions* . . .

A.: Indeed?

H.: . . . with citizens who have *just and enlightened ideas of liberty and laws?*

A.: Indeed?

In a brilliant historical summary, the author argues that the most important cause of the French Revolution was the impact of the new industrial and commercial system upon the social structure of the country. Colbert was the man who broke the power of the nobility by creating a merchant marine, awakening and encouraging manufacture, and establishing a financial system which provided Louis XIV with the means of realizing his *gloire.*[35] At last, there was only one difference left—that between men of the world and men of the people; and it was in vain that the laws tried to perpetuate class distinctions:

H.: The commercial system *has created the power of riches,* placing it in perpetual opposition to the power of dignities and titles . . .

A.: It would be more correct to say it has created a monied interest and placed it in opposition to the landed interest. But as avarice is a meaner passion than ambition, is there not danger of corruption, depravation and ruin from the change?

H.: It has introduced, instead, an inequality due to varying degrees of wealth, an inequality which increased as the influence of rank diminished.

A.: These are curious observations.

H.: It has favored the spread of knowledge, the flowering of talents, and the realization of success in the arts and sciences.

A.: The invention of academies, too, which is modern has eclipsed the universities and brought into fashion an infidel philosophy.

A final close view of the excesses of the Revolution brings into clearer relief the distinguishing marks of the new constitution:

H.: Founded upon abuse, upon exaggeration of principle, and reared upon supports incapable of bending, the ultra-revolutionary system was incompatible with the national character . . .

A.: Note well!

H.: In the monarchical constitution, as well as those which followed after, pride, ignorance, and passion encompassed all the contradictions that can exist between the character and the political institutions of a nation.

A.: This is true!

H.: The constitution of the year VIII is *republican* not only in its principles but also in its origin . . .

A.: It is here impossible to know his meaning.

H.: No one could question that it is representative. I might even say that it is the most *representative* that there is . . .

A.: Here again a vague word is employed.

H.: The laws of France have been made by men who, chosen at first by force of circumstances, were confirmed later by the will of the people.

A.: The monarchs were in by the force of circumstances and were confirmed by a general acceptation.

One of the earliest acts of the First Consul was the lifting of the proscription against the *çi-devant* nobles. It seemed as if he might wish to restore the monarchy. This is what the Comte de Provence, brother of Louis XVI and now Louis XVIII for the *émigrés*, hoped, and he sent an inquiry to Napoleon. The reply he received—six months later

—was chilling. "Your return," Napoleon wrote, "is not a thing to be wished for; it could only be accomplished over a hundred thousand corpses." To eliminate further doubts, he took a strong hand against the royalist bands which were terrorizing the provinces; and then, using the attempt on his life as a pretext, he suppressed the Jacobins.

In his last pages Hauterive expresses his confidence that, whereas England is facing an uncertain future, France has the right to expect progress in every field. Adams made no prophecy.

There were constant changes in the kaleidoscope. What France lost with the assassination of Tsar Paul, she gained with the resignation of Pitt and the formation of the Addington ministry.[86] Peace negotiations started at once, and on March 27, 1802, the Treaty of Amiens was signed. There was great rejoicing in both Paris and London, but the enthusiasm of the English soon gave way to irritation on learning that they had to renounce most of their maritime conquests and that the Continent remained closed to their commerce. "I was persuaded," Napoleon said wistfully at St. Helena, "that both the future of France and my own were settled at Amiens. It was my intention to devote myself entirely to the administration of the country, and I believe that I should have worked wonders. . . ."

[XIV]

Dr. Priestley and Other
English Divines

Dr. Joseph Priestley was a puzzling figure, such as only the England of the eighteenth century could produce. He was a great scientist, the discoverer of oxygen and nearly a dozen other "gaseous bodies"; but he was an even greater expert on the prophecies of the Book of Daniel, and he literally believed that the ten toes in the image of Nebuchadnezzar and the ten horns of the Fourth Beast in the Apocalypse referred to the monarchies of Europe.[1] A known radical, whose house at Birmingham was burned down by the mob, revolutionary France conferred upon him the honor of French citizenship, inviting him also to sit in the National Assembly; and he actually contemplated going to France—to preach the Gospel there. Luckily for him, he decided to come to America instead. In June 1794, aged sixty-one, he arrived at New York and soon afterwards settled in Northumberland on the Susquehanna, a village of a hundred houses five days' journey from Philadelphia. It was there that he died ten years later.

Adams knew Priestley very well. Among the friendships which he formed in London, that with the remarkable scientist and theologian occupied an important place. To be sure, the chemical experiments of the Doctor, however epoch-making, aroused little curiosity in him; it was Priestley the expounder of new religious ideas that interested Adams. In his Diary he jotted down the day—April 19, 1786—when he first met Priestley; and the following Sunday he went to hear him in Essex Street, in the first avowedly Unitarian chapel. Ten years later in Philadelphia, then Vice-President, Adams was a regular attendant at Priestley's lectures on the Evidences of Revealed Religion. The lectures, in two bulky volumes, were printed in 1796–97, with a long dedication to Adams. "The happiness I have had of your acquaintance and correspondence ever since your embassy to England," the author begins, ". . . your steady attachment to the cause of Christianity, the favourable attention you gave to the following Discourses when they were delivered, and the wish you expressed that they might be published, induce me to take the liberty to dedicate them to you." Unfortunately, by this time Adams felt a trifle uneasy about the compliment. "It will get me the character of a heretic, I fear," he wrote to his wife. "I presume, however," he added, "that dedicating a book to a man will not imply that he approves everything in it." [2]

Significantly enough, only the first volume of Adams's copy of *The Evidences of Revealed Religion* bears Priestley's inscription; the second is not a presentation copy. The friendship of the two men, indeed, rapidly cooled, ending in complete estrangement. "When my lectures were less popular, and he was near his presidentship," Priestley explained, "he left me, making a kind of apology, the members of the principal Presbyterian church having offered him a pew there." And further: "That any statesman should risk his popularity on account of religion, is not to be expected. He would have been the first in any similar situation if he had done it. I suppose too, he was not pleased that I did not adopt his dislike of the French." [3]

This was undoubtedly the crux of the matter. With the threat of war between France and the United States, Adams's administration looked with increasing animosity upon all French sympathizers, especially upon the immigrants, finally putting into the law books the Alien and Sedition Acts of 1798. Priestley was bitter. On July 26 of that year, he wrote to a member of Congress: "I find I am at the mercy of one man, who, if he pleases, may, even without giving me a hearing, or a minute's warning, either confine me, or send me out of the country." [4] Accustomed to giving free expression to his sentiments, he soon got into trouble. His friend Thomas Cooper, a capable chemist who had preceded him in coming to America, published some scathing attacks on Adams in the *Northumberland Gazette* for June 29, 1799, and it was rumored that Priestley had done what he could to have the article printed in handbills and distributed. The case was reported to Secretary of State Pickering, who notified Adams at once, with unequivocal observations on "the Doctor's want of decency . . . his discontented and turbulent spirit, that will never be quiet under the freest government on earth." And the Doctor was not even—never intended to be— naturalized. "Cooper has taken care to get himself admitted to citizenship," Pickering continued. "I am sorry for it; for those who are desirous of maintaining our internal tranquillity must wish them both removed from the United States." [5] But Adams preserved his calm. "I do not think it wise," he replied, "to execute the alien law against poor Priestley at present. He is as weak as water, as unstable as Reuben, or the wind. His influence is not an atom in the world." [6] At the same time he intimated to Priestley that he wished he would abstain from politics.[7] Toward Cooper, however, he felt no sentimental obligations. Cooper was brought to trial for libel, and was sentenced to six months' imprisonment.[8]

Things were more pleasant for Priestley under Jefferson's administration. A few days after his inauguration, the new President addressed a long letter to him condemning "the bigotry and reaction of the barbarians" and extolling him as "the great apostle of science and honesty." "It is with heartfelt satisfaction," Jefferson declared, "that, in the first moments of my public action, I can hail you with welcome to our land, tender to you the homage of its respect and esteem, cover you under the protection of those laws which were made for the wise and good like you, and disdain the legitimacy of that libel on legislation, which, under the form of a law, was for some time placed among them." [9] Two years later he wrote again, on religion and ethical questions, signing himself with "high veneration and affectionate attachment." [10]

A dozen years passed. Dr. Priestley was dead, and Adams and Jefferson were exchanging friendly letters in their retirement. Then unexpectedly, and much to the writer's annoyance, Jefferson's two letters to Priestley were published.[11] Adams was nettled by the obvious references to himself. "As your name is subscribed to that law, as Vice-President, and mine as President, I know not why you are not as responsible for it as I am," he reproached Jefferson, justifying the law by the swarms of French spies, some of whom were "intolerably impudent, turbulent, and seditious." [12] To explain his remarks certainly called for ingenuity on Jefferson's part; but Adams, happy to have found an invaluable correspondent, tried to quiet his alarm; his own reputation, he consoled Jefferson, had been so much the sport of the public that he regarded it "a bubble, a gossamer, that idles in the wanton summer air." [13] The indiscretion brought Priestley and his doctrines forcibly into their correspondence, providing an inexhaustible topic for Adams. "What does Priestley mean by an unbeliever, when he applies it to you?" he asked Jefferson. "How much did he unbelieve himself? . . . We are to understand, no doubt, that he believed in the resurrection of Jesus, some of his miracles, his inspiration; but in what degree? He did not believe in the inspiration of the writings that contain his history. Yet he believed in the Apocalyptic beast, and he believed as much as he pleased in the writings of Daniel and John." Then this sentence: "This great and extraordinary man, whom I sincerely loved, esteemed, and respected, was really a phenomenon; a comet in the system, like Voltaire, Bolingbroke, and Hume. Had Bolingbroke or Voltaire taken him in hand, what would they have made of him and his creed?" [14]

In the same letter he challenged Jefferson. "I do not believe," he stated, "you have read much of Priestley's *Corruptions of Christianity*, his *Early Opinions Concerning Jesus Christ*, his predestination, his no soul system, or his controversy with Horsley." He told his friend of his own deep reading in the writings of Priestley, Lindsey, Farmer, Cappe, Tucker, Search, Edwards, and Hopkins; and that he was not uninformed of the controversies in Germany and of the research of universities about the Bible. "What is all this to you? No more than if I should tell you that I read Dr. Clarke, and Dr. Waterland, and Emlyn, and Leland's View or Review of the deistical writers more than fifty years ago." [15] Jefferson made no pretensions to similar learning, but Priestley's works he read "over and over again." "I rest on them," he wrote, "and on Middleton's writings, especially his letters from Rome and to Waterland, as the basis of my own faith." And he sent Adams a copy of Priestley's *Doctrines of Heathen Philosophy*. [16]

Although a center of controversy through most of his life, Dr. Priestley was an innocent and gentle man. He was bold, even arrogant, only over the causes which he championed. His scientific discoveries never made him proud; he declared, with rare honesty, that they were the results of lucky chance. In his beliefs concerning the Scriptures, however, he felt the power of direct and infallible inspiration. And it was the Scriptures that mattered most to him. Of the twenty-five large volumes of his *Collected Works* only six are on experiments, while the rest deal with religious problems. "How insignificant are all subjects, compared to those which relate to religion!" he exclaimed in a letter. And he added: "And yet I am persuaded I have more pleasure in my philosophical pursuits than any of my unchristian brethren. My views of these subjects give a dignity and importance to them, which in the eye of an unbeliever, it is impossible they should have." [17] He tried to evolve a "rational religion" and did not think that science would interfere with it at all. His effort was not new either. Sir Isaac Newton was a diligent student of the Prophets; and so were Robert Boyle and many of the greatest English physicists. Priestley, though somewhat belatedly, was in their tradition.

To some, of course, his preoccupation with the Bible seemed paradoxical. Cuvier, especially, regarded the division of Priestley's interests as both strange and lamentable. In his *Éloge* before the Institut de France, the great French naturalist quoted Priestley's last words to his small grandchildren, "I am going to sleep like you, for death is only a good, long, sound sleep in the grave . . . ," and then made the final reflection: "Such was the end of a man whom his enemies long accused of planning the destruction of all religion and morality, and whose greatest error was in forgetting his vocation, and in attaching too much importance to particular opinions on subjects concerning which the most important of all sentiments is the love of peace." [18]

2

The bitter misunderstanding with Priestley left but a faint memory in Adams. "If Priestley had lived I should certainly have corresponded with him," he confided to Jefferson. He assured the latter that he was ready to "forgive" Priestley entirely, though he had "great complaints against him for personal injuries and persecutions"; and that he even prayed that Priestley "may be pardoned for it all above." [19] This was, however, not pure magnanimity on his part. What a delight it would have been for him to correspond with Priestley in those years, to ply that great expert with questions like "What is matter?" "What is soul?" But Priestley was gone, and Adams could make his inquiries only on the margins of his books.

The largest number of comments occur in the *Early Opinions Concerning Jesus Christ.* Since his *Corruptions of Christianity* had been attacked for its lack of thoroughness, Priestley wanted to produce here as many proofs for his Unitarian principles as he could. He examined all his sources in the original—the list fills five pages—"without even looking into any modern author whatever." Priestley was convinced that the first followers of Christ were pure Unitarians, and so he assails not only the dogma of the Trinity but also those of Gnosticism and Arianism. Adams was on the whole in sympathy with him, yet he grew weary of the endless hairsplitting and speculation, and gave up the struggle at the end of the first book.

Priestley: It certainly requires no small degree of patience, as well as judgment and sagacity, to trace the real estate of the unitarian Christians in early times, from the writings of their enemies only. For all their own writings are grossly interpolated, or have perished, except the *Clementines*.[20]

Adams: The destruction of ancient books has not been accidental. The lost classics, the lost infidels, and the lost heretics were probably all destroyed by design, either of civil despots or ecclesiastical craft and fraud.

P.: The great objection to the doctrine of the Trinity is, that it is an infringement of the doctrine of the unity of God. Any modification of this doctrine ought to be regarded with suspicion, in proportion as it makes a multiplicity of objects of worship, for that is to introduce idolatry.

A.: Priestley's zeal to expose his antagonists to the odium and terror of idolatry has led him into much sophistry. Neither Arians nor Trinitarians are idolaters.

P.: According to some Arians, Christ made this solar system only. There must, therefore, have been other beings, of equal rank with him, to whom the creation of the other systems was assigned; and observation shows, that there are millions and millions of systems. The probability is, that they fill the whole extent of infinite space.

A.: The Universe is infinite then. Price said to me that he was inclined to believe it infinite and eternal. So thought Frederick and d'Alembert.

P.: I might have urged another kind of argument against both the divinity and pre-existence of Christ, viz. from the doctrine of the *materiality of man.*

A.: "God is a Spirit." Will Priestley assert the materiality of God?

P.: The doctrine of a soul as a substance distinct from the body was borrowed from pagan philosophy; it is totally repugnant to the system of revelation, and unknown in the Scriptures which speak of no reward for the righteous or punishment for the wicked . . .

A.: It was borrowed from Indians, Negroes, Caffrarians, Hindoos, Chinese. All nations have believed it as much as philosophers and Christians.

Priestley states that the first writer in whose works the doctrines of divinity and preëxistence of Christ are found is Justin Martyr, who wrote about A.D. 140. The writings of the Apostolic Fathers, however, are almost entirely spurious. The doctrine of the deification of Christ was preceded by Gnosticism, which was derived from the East:

P.: Simon Magus is represented in the Clementine homilies as saying to Peter, "Since you acknowledge, from the Scriptures, that there is an evil being, tell me how he was made, if he was made, and by whom, and for what purpose."

A.: Very sagacious questions.

P.: The Gnostics concluded that . . . matter only had been eternal, and that its nature was such as that nothing perfectly good could be made out of it; so that, however it might be modified by the Supreme Being, every system into which it entered must necessarily contain within itself the seeds of evil.

A.: This is more ingenious than the great Frederick's essay on the Origin of Evil.

P.: Many persons who had been addicted to philosophy would consider Christianity as a new and improved species of philosophy.

A.: What is philosophy but the study of the world and its cause? Man is a riddle to himself. The world is a riddle to him. He puzzles to find a key, and this puzzle is called philosophy.

The chief source of "orthodox Christianity" after the Council of Nicaea, Priestley argues, was Plato. The name of the great Greek philosopher moved Adams to the unphilosophical comment: "Plato, Rousseau, Zinzendorph, Swedenborg, Towers, Wesley, Faber, Priestley, Nimrod Hughes, etc., etc. some of them immensely learned, some divinely eloquent, some ignorant as horses, and crazy as Bedlamites. Yet I would implicitly believe in one as soon as in any other." [21]

P.: There is a manifest confusion in Plato's account of the ideas of the divine mind; so that he sometimes makes them to be a second principle of things, and the world itself, which was produced from those ideas, a third principle.

A.: Idea, agent, effect: Trinity.

P.: The Demiurgus, or immediate maker of the world, was evidently the Supreme Being himself, and not any subordinate agent, or principle, whatever.

A.: Demiurgus: a strange name for the Supreme Being!

P.: It is evident that the *logos* here spoken of, as that by which God made the universe, was, in Plato's ideas, synonymous with *dianoia* and *episteme*, or his understanding, and by no means any other proper person or agent.

A.: If nature produced all things, nature is the Supreme Being: the first cause. If with intelligence, nature is God. If without intelligence, nature is self-existent and the same as eternal fate, which according to Virgil ruled Jupiter with as inflexible a rod of iron as it did all the other gods, as well as men, animals, and the material world celestial and terrestrial.

P.: That, in Plato's idea, it was the Supreme Being who himself accomplished the work of Creation, is evident from his representation of him as rejoicing at the conclusion of it.

A.: "And he saw that it was good."

P.: According to Plato, *logos* has only two acceptations, viz. those of speech and of reason.

A.: Logos is sometimes speech, sometimes thought!

P.: The term *nous* is another denomination of the *logos*. One of Plato's definitions of it is: "*Nous* is either the same thing with truth, or exceedingly like to it."

A.: Who can understand this oratory without meaning?

P.: There is by no means any personification in it, and Plato makes no difference between the mind of man and that of God in this respect.

A.: Ratio the same in God and man! Bolingbroke! thou were not much more mad than Plato. Presumption indeed to compare the intelligence of foxes, dogs, and elephants to that which pervades Herschel's universe!

P.: Asserting that understanding and right opinion are two species of things, Plato says, "Of one of these (meaning right opinion) all men are capable; but of the former (viz. *nous* or understanding) only the gods, and a few men are capable."

A.: Gods and a few men! Who were these few men? I am not one. I understand nothing of this gallimauphry!

> "In pride, in reasoning pride, our error lies:
> All quit their spheres and rush into the skies." [22]

P.: Plato makes the good and the idea of the good to be synonymous. This, I hope, may serve as a specimen of his metaphysical acumen.

A.: The auricular acumen of Plato appears in the harmony of his diction: his rhetorical acumen in the beauty of his images: but his metaphysical acumen is as blunt as a beetle.

The Platonists, Priestley writes, did not proceed beyond a figurative personification of the divine intellect. Philo used the term *logos* much more frequently. Although he did not make it a fixed intelligent person, as did the platonizing Christians, he made it the visible medium of all the communications of God to man—that is, of the creation of the world and of God's contact with the patriarchs of the Old Testament. Adams made his summary: "Philo's system," he wrote, "seems to be, 1. God, the good, the Supreme Being; 2. God's ideas, intelligence,

thoughts, reason, logos; 3. The world made by the logos of God."
Then he gave his own creed:

"Such is Philo's Trinity. But what do we mean by the ideas, the
thoughts, the reason, the intelligence, or the speech of God? His intelligence is a subject too vast, too incomprehensible for Plato, Philo,
Paul or Peter, Jews, Gentiles or Christians. Let us adore, not presume
nor dogmatize. Even the great Teacher may not reveal this subject.
There never was, is not, and never will be more than one Being in the
universe capable of comprehending it. At least this is the humble
adoring opinion of the writer of this note.

"Moses says, God spoke the world into being. He said 'Let there be
Light' and there was Light. Plato and Philo seem to teach that God
thought the world into existence. Which is the most sublime? Which
the most incomprehensible? But if God's idea was of itself almighty
and produced a world, the world must be eternal because God must
have had an idea of it from eternity. These are all the effects of great
minds grasping at ideas too vast for their comprehension. The will of
God must come into consideration. Moses seems to have understood it
best. God had the idea from eternity. At length he willed the existence
of the world, expressed his will by a word, and it was done. The world
existed and stood fast. Thinking, or willing a world into existence is as
sublime as speaking it. A thought is more simple than a word! But
these are incorrect figures, to express inadequate ideas.

"Admire and adore the Author of the telescopic universe, love and
esteem the work, do all in your power to lessen ill, and increase good:
but never assume to comprehend."

3

In his *Institutions of Moses*, printed at Northumberland in 1799,
Priestley wanted to prove that the religion of even the most enlightened
of the heathens was "absurd and despicable," while that of revelation
was "rational and respectable." Adams read the first chapters carefully,
making notes on every page. It was Priestley's assertion that the Hindu
religion, with its abstruse metaphysics, could not have been completed
at a very early period that first roused him to contradiction. "This conclusion is loose, like the reasoning from which it is drawn," he objected.
Priestley maintained that the Books of Moses were free of such superstitions as may be found in the Vedas, and wondered why.

P.: Why should the Israelites be more free from such observances than other nations, when they were equally ignorant; and *superstition has always prevailed in proportion to ignorance?*

A.: Is this exact?

P.: The Hindus go far beyond the rest of mankind in voluntary restrictions and mortifications.[23]

A.: Far beyond the Romish Christians?

P.: Restrictions with respect to eating and drinking are numerous with the Hindus. Among other things, *all fermented or spirituous liquors are forbidden.*

A.: Not much amiss.

P.: In the laws of Moses the use of wine is only forbidden to the priests during their attendance in the sanctuary.

A.: Wine maddens men in some climates.

Next, Priestley turned to the Greek philosophers. The result was *The Doctrines of Heathen Philosophy Compared with those of Revelation,* which he completed in January 1804. "I could not have closed my life with more satisfaction than after a work of this kind," he wrote in the preface. Shortly afterwards he died; the work was published posthumously.

Adams, as has been mentioned, received his copy from Jefferson. Of the eight chapters discussing Pythagoras, Socrates, Plato, Aristotle, the Stoics, and the Epicureans, he made marginal comments on the one on Platonism. But he must have read more of the book, for on Christmas Day of 1813 he sent Jefferson a thorough analysis of it. "Why has Priestley not given us a more satisfactory account of the Pythagorean philosophy and theology?" he asked, and forthwith discussed the works of Ocellus and Timaeus. "I wish I owned Ocellus's treatise," he added, "and one hundred thousand more that I want every day, now when I am almost incapable of making any use of them." [24] He wanted more information on Archytus, Zaleucus, Charondas, and the religions of Zoroaster, Sanchoniathon, and Confucius. Writing in his seventy-ninth year, he had a boy's eagerness to show off. But the volume itself has few notes:

P.: From the Eastern part of the world, in which it is said he travelled in the disguise of a merchant, Plato seems to have gained some knowledge of the system that generally prevailed there.[25]

A.: Why this mystery? or obscurity? Why not say he travelled to Indostan and conversed with the Bramins?

P.: Plato acknowledges that "what the Greeks knew concerning the gods and their worship was derived from the barbarians."

A.: There is more in this than meets the eye!

P.: But in his opinion, the Greeks had divine instruction as well as human.

A.: Was there ever a popular religion that did not pretend to divine instruction?

P.: The notions of the vulgar about the marriage of gods and goddesses were rejected by all who pretended to philosophy or superior knowledge, from long before the time of Socrates.

A.: Was there ever a country, in which philosophers, politicians, and theologians believed what they taught to the vulgar?

P.: The being of a god or gods, Plato generally takes for granted. Occasionally, however, he introduces arguments from the consideration of the structure of the earth, the sun, the stars, and the whole universe.

A.: Strange mixture of wisdom and absurdity, derived from India and Egypt. Greece made it more elegant, tasty, and classical: but not more rational than Egyptians, Persians, Tartars, Chaldeans or Hindoos.

It was for the flyleaf that Adams reserved his final judgment:

"This is the work of a dying man of extraordinary application and research. But Enfield's *History of Philosophy* will show its glaring imperfections.[26] Enfield is but an abridgment of Brucker's *Historia Critica Philosophiae*, in five volumes folio or large octavo.[27] Of this work there is probably but one copy in America. That was brought from Europe by Mr. Buckminster, and sold at a great price at his auction, when Mr. Shaw in behalf of the Athenaeum was outbidden by the deeper purse of Harvard College.[28] It would be more useful in the Athenaeum than in the Cambridge library."

4

In all likelihood, it was Jefferson's admiration for Conyers Middleton that prompted Adams to make a thorough study of the latter's works, which in turn led him to John Disney's biography of Arthur Sykes, Middleton's inveterate antagonist. Had he read only these two writers, he would already have gained sufficient insight into the theological disputes of the period—the half-century extending from Locke to Hume—in which the battles between the Low Church and High Church parties were fought out, with the skirmish over Deism thrown in for good measure.

His talent for clear, forceful—and vituperative—prose sets Middleton apart from the ordinary writing divines. He had no new system to teach, but he was a pioneer in the use of the historical, rather than dogmatic method. Clashing with orthodox, latitudinarian, and deist alike, he opposed the literal interpretation of the Bible and denied the credibility of miracles after the earliest age of the Church. His first real quarrel started in 1731. Matthew Tindal, the Oxford freethinker, had published his *Christianity as Old as the Creation*, declaring that revelation is superfluous because the religion of nature is perfect in itself. The book drew forth some thirty answers, among them one by Daniel Waterland, vice-chancellor of Cambridge University. Middleton stepped into the controversy with his *Letter to Dr. Waterland*, showing how Tindal should have been answered.[29] The *Letter*, of course, made the fray even more violent, starting a separate tussle with Zachary Pearce, the future Bishop of Rochester. Adams seemed satisfied with Middleton's position. The latter charges that Waterland, instead of vindicating the Scriptures, had himself furnished matter for new scandal. ("No revelation can contain anything false, irrational or immoral," Adams asserted.) Middleton accuses Tindal of attempting to abolish Christianity and set up reason as a national religion. ("Abolish Christianity! Set up reason!" Adams snapped: "The authority of reason is not stern enough to keep rebellious appetites and passions in subjection.") Tindal, Middleton contends, betrayed his ignorance of antiquity by magnifying the moderation of pagan governments. ("Deistical cant," Adams reinforced him, adding, "Atheists are the most cruel persecutors.") The intolerance of this "rational Protestant," Middleton jeers, is even worse than Romish popery. ("Deistical popery," Adams chimed in.)

Himself accused of atheism, Middleton was threatened with expulsion from Cambridge, where he was Librarian. He composed five or six more essays of similar nature, but wisely decided to keep them in his desk. They were first published in his *Works*, in 1752, two years after his death.

In his *Reflections on the Variations in the Four Evangelists* [30] Middleton discusses the genealogies given by St. Matthew and St. Luke, the former naming forty-two and the latter twenty-eight generations between David and Jesus. He agrees with Grotius's suggestion that Matthew probably divided the genealogy into three equal periods of fourteen generations "for the sake of assisting the memory." ("Huzza!" Adams exclaimed, "Grotius, you are as dexterous as Chrysostom or Jerome!") Another example of contradiction is Matthew's attribution of the prophecy about the thirty pieces of silver to Jeremiah, whereas it occurs in Zechariah. Augustine thought that "Matthew was directed by the Holy Spirit to make this mistake." (Adams was incredulous: "The Holy Spirit committed this blunder, on purpose?!") But Augustine also observed that Jeremiah spoke of buying a field from his uncle's son, and that there might have been a mystical reason for omitting mention of the thirty pieces of silver. ("Is this not making the Evangelists and Christ too as arrant sophists and punsters as the holy Father was himself?" Adams asked.)

The Gift of Tongues [31] questions St. Luke's claim concerning the marvelous linguistic abilities of the Apostles. This "sign of God," Middleton contests, could not have lasted long; the Apostles' Greek not only could not have been ascribed to God but was scarcely worthy of man. He further remarks that the Apostles must have been helped by Greeks born in Syria. (Adams busily jotted down: "Greek current in Judea in Jerusalem"; "A great number of the first converts in Jerusalem were Greek"; "Greek honored by the Doctors as much as Hebrew.") In his *Creation and Fall of Man* [32] Middleton lines up a large amount of testimony in support of the allegorical interpretation of the Bible. How could any man in his senses, Origen asked, believe that the first three days of the world passed without sun, moon, and stars? ("Bravo!" Adams was delighted.) The strangest conceits have been invented about Paradise, the location of which no one has ever known. (Adams noted: "Brandanus, a Briton, sailed around the world in search of it.") The narrative of the fall of man, Middleton concludes, is a moral fable. ("Like Aesop, Phedrus, La Fontaine, Gay or More," Adams added on his own.)

In 1747 Middleton published an "introductory discourse" on miracles, followed by his *Free Inquiry into the Miraculous Powers*. Hume, whose *Enquiry Concerning Human Understanding* containing his essay on miracles had just appeared, recorded in his autobiography: "On my return from Italy, I had the mortification to find all England in a ferment, on account of Dr. Middleton's *Free Enquiry* while my performance was entirely overlooked and neglected." [33]

Middleton's treatises on miracles constitute his most important work. Reading them, Adams sprinkled the margins with the names of innumerable Fathers. To discredit Justin Martyr, Middleton derides his doctrine that God committed the care of the world to angels, who fell in love with women and begot children on them. ("Is this from Enoch or Indostan Brama?" Adams learnedly inquired.) Irenaeus was no better than Justin. A believer in the millennium, he presented it as Jesus's own prediction that some day vineyards should grow each having ten thousand vine stocks, each stock ten thousand branches, each branch ten thousand shoots, each shoot ten thousand bunches, and each bunch ten thousand grapes, each grape yielding twenty-five measures of wine —adding a similar story about wheat. ("Wonderful vine! Wonderful wheat!" Adams rejoiced.) Undoubtedly these Fathers, Middleton protests, are full of gross absurdities; and as to the question of their veracity . . . Here Adams could not contain himself: "Veracity! Veracity! Veracity!" he exclaimed. "To vindicate the veracity of politicians, philosophers or theologians in any age would not be an easy task. It would be easier to show that in general they adopted another rule: 'When it is to combat evil 'Tis lawful to employ the devil.' Or Cato's 'Corruptâ civitate corruptio est licita.' "

His last book, *An Examination of the Bishop of London's Discourses,* carried Middleton back a full quarter of a century. In 1724 Anthony Collins, a famous freethinker, caused great excitement by a book claiming that Christianity has no just foundation if it cannot be based upon the prophecies of the Old Testament, arguing at the same time that the fulfillment of these prophecies can be proved only by twisting the facts.[34] Among the innumerable answers, the book called forth a collection of six sermons by Thomas Sherlock, later Bishop of London, maintaining that the prophecies were not independent of each other but formed a series leading up to the appearance of the Messiah.[35] Middleton ridiculed the Bishop's "antediluvian chain," maintaining that he had not properly met the "free-thinking author," that in fact he had strengthened his position. Sherlock wanted to find out the identity of the serpent whom Moses represented as the tempter of Eve. By subtle and precise reasoning he came to the conclusion that it was the devil—a hypothesis which always infuriated Middleton. Yet in his last paragraph the old warrior quietly meditated:

"Happy would it be for them all, if dropping those vain contests and wrangling about questions wholly speculative, fruitless, and inexplicable . . . men would apply their pains and zeal to promote and inculcate those practical, social, and real duties which our reason and senses prescribe in common to all as the chief good of our nature, the foundation of all religion, the source of all our happiness in this life, and of all our hopes in that which is to come." [36]

Most of Adams's comments heartily endorse Middleton. Why this unusually good humor? Evidently, like Jefferson, he was impressed by Middleton's logic. In any case, he could not be abusive toward a writer whom his friend recognized as his mentor. He had assured Jefferson in his most affable manner: "I agree with you as far as you go, most cordially, and, I think, solidly. How much farther I go, how much more I believe than you, I may explain in a future letter. This much will I say at present: I have found so many difficulties that I am not astonished at your stopping where you are; and, so far from sentencing you to perdition, I hope soon to meet you in another country." [37]

5

Arthur Ashley Sykes, who studied at Cambridge about the same time as Middleton, was another famous polemist. He won his spurs in the Bangorian controversy, one of the most acrimonious struggles in the history of the Church of England.

On March 3, 1717, Benjamin Hoadly, Bishop of Bangor, delivered a sermon before the King on *The Nature of the Kingdom or Church of Christ*, denying that there was such a thing as a visible church of Christ. He was attacked at once by Andrew Snape, Provost of Eton, and soon afterwards a committee of the convocation of Canterbury recommended the condemnation of the sermon. Dr. Sykes, who as rector of Dry Drayton had preached a similar sermon at Cambridge only three months before, came to Hoadly's defense with several pamphlets. The fight was in full swing long after Hoadly ceased to be Bishop of Bangor. Translated first to Hereford and then to Salisbury, he was finally appointed to the rich see of Winchester. But the tracts were still pouring from the press. It has been estimated that more than two hundred pamphlets—*Enquiries* and *Answers*, *Defences* and *Vindications*—were published from the pens of some fifty contestants. Sykes's fortunes meanwhile followed those of Hoadly. Soon after the Bishop of Bangor advanced to Salisbury, the rector of Dry Drayton became a prebendary at the great cathedral there; and when the Bishop of Salisbury was made Bishop of Winchester, he also exchanged his prebendal stall at Salisbury for one at Winchester.

Sykes had been dead for nearly thirty years when John Disney published the *Memoirs* of his life and writings in 1785. Adams received a copy from the author while still in London. He must have known Disney from his attendance at the services in Essex Street Chapel where Disney, together with Dr. Lindsey, served as pastor. Adams enjoyed reading Sykes's discourses, passages of which were reproduced in Disney's book. "I wish I owned or could purchase Sykes's works!" he sighed. Some of his comments were made upon these texts and the rest upon Disney's narrative. The debate thus assumed a triangular form.

The first notes appear in the chapter on Sykes's *Brief Discourse on Miracles,* which was published in 1742.[38] Sykes believed that the Gospel miracles were all credible, but that the later ones were fictitious. He treated the subject again in an analysis of Middleton's work, raising two questions: "What are the grounds upon which the credulity of miracles, in general, is founded?" and "Upon what grounds are the miracles of the Gospel, in particular, credible?"[39] Adams saw the point. "Two very pertinent questions," he remarked. Dr. Dodwell in his reply to Middleton was disposed to agree with Sykes's arguments but for their bearing-ultimately against the ascription of miracles to the first three centuries.[40] Adams appreciated his doubts too. "If miracles did not cease with the Apostles," he wrote, "if miracles continued for the three first centuries, how can it be proved that they have yet ceased? Even Chateaubriand will claim credit and Abbé Paris."[41]

Sykes's collision with William Warburton, the most pugnacious of all the theologians, was of course inevitable. Fighting everyone (except Pope, whose friend he was), Warburton did not take criticism kindly. So when Sykes objected to the fundamental argument of his *Divine Legation of Moses,* namely that such a legation was proved by the fact that Moses had never inculcated the doctrine of a future state of rewards and punishments, he flared up and violently berated him. Adams, however, took Sykes's side: "I am glad to find," he stated, "Sykes acknowledges the truth that Jews and Gentiles believed a future state of rewards and punishments." Although an enemy of popery, Sykes stood firmly for toleration. In 1746 he issued two pamphlets in which he pleaded for the treatment of Catholics as good citizens. "What is seated in the will," he wrote, "is not the object of force, but of reason and persuasion; and the instant religion ceases to be voluntary, it loses its existence." Adams found this "a noble apothegm." And when Sykes demanded that this rule should be applied to "every religious opinion not inimical to the constitutional rights and civil liberties of our country," he was wholeheartedly with him: "A generous and just principle!"

He was especially fascinated with the chapter on Sykes's *Paraphrase and Notes upon the Epistle to the Hebrews,*[42] covering every one of its twenty-five pages with notes. Sykes and Disney believed that Saint Paul was the author of the Epistle as it exists in Greek. Adams, who from Middleton had acquired a good deal of information about the state of the Apostle's learning, argued strenuously against both:

Disney: That the Epistle to the Hebrews was *received* by the Latin churches is shown by the citations made from it by Clemens in his Epistle to the Church of Corinth.

Adams: What is meant by *"received* in churches?" The Gospel of St. Thomas and the Acts of Paul and Thekla were *received*, and so was the prophecy of Enoch. The truth is that nothing was canonical till the Council of Nicaea. Then and not till then was settled the norma of canonicality. And by whom?

Sykes: The similitude of sentiments, and even phrases and words, between the writer of this Epistle and St. Paul is certainly surprisingly remarkable.

A.: If Luke wrote it, the simility of his sentiments, phrases and words with his Gospel and Acts was not surprising.

S.: Whatever difficulty has ever been started about the author of this Epistle has been in order to account for the difference of style between this and the rest of St. Paul's Epistles . . .

A.: If some of his Epistles were written by Luke, some by Titus, some by Tertius, some by Timothy, and some by Onesimus, the difference of style is not surprizing.

S.: Even those who conjectured a translation agree that St. Paul was the author of the Hebrew Epistle, and they never *object* to its being a true or just version.

A.: How can they object? When the Hebrew is destroyed?

D.: Mr. Peirce believes that the Epistle was written in Hebrew, and that it was probably translated into Greek by St. Luke.[43]

A.: This is the most candid and the most plausible opinion. But the question recurs, why was the original destroyed? What suspicions of interpolation, and indeed of fabrication, might be confuted if we had the originals! In an age or in ages when fraud, forgery, and perjury were considered as lawful means of propagating truth by philosophers, legislators, and theologians, what may not be suspected?

S.: All those who allege that this Epistle was not St. Paul's have done it only to account for the style and manner of writing, and not from any one single evidence.

A.: Does the burthen of proof rest upon the infidel to prove a negative? The believer, the assertor, should prove his affirmation.

D.: Mr. Peirce examines the testimonies of Clement, Origen, Eusebius, Athanasius, Cyril, Augustine, etc.

A.: And he might as well add Chateaubriand in 1814.[44] And the whole Acta Sanctorum.[45] When homousianity was established and

Christianity totally corrupted,[46] no doubt authorities enough might be accumulated.

To the end Adams, once the best trial lawyer in Massachusetts, stuck to his own opinions: "If St. Paul ever wrote anything in Greek except his name and a concluding sentence or two, the most eminent Fathers are not competent witnesses." But soon he found common ground again with Sykes. The Doctor emphasized that the Epistle to the Hebrews was written to persons who had been "illuminated," that is, to Jews who had already become Christians:

S.: The arguments are such as prove Christianity to be an institution in every respect superior to the law of Moses . . .

A.: That the superiority of Christ to Moses was the point of this Epistle need not be doubted.

S.: It is usually affirmed that "the legal sacrifices of the Old Testament derived all their efficacy from Christ, that great sacrifice slain from the foundations of the world."

A.: Christ, the great Sacrifice. "Slain from the foundations." What a figure!

S.: Lord Bolingbroke in more than one place treats Moses and St. Paul as arrant impostors . . .

A.: The rake would not have said this of Brama, Confucius, Zoroaster, Pythagoras, Numa, Mahomet, Loyola, or Swedenburg.

Sykes refuted Bolingbroke's charge that the Apostle's doctrines of grace, predestination, reprobation, etc. were unworthy of God; however, Disney gives only a brief summary of his arguments. Adams, left in the dark, complained: "My Friend Disney! I wish you had been more explicit in this place!"

In interpreting St. Paul's meaning, Sykes at times ascribed to Jesus powers which belong only to God. ("There are some," Adams noted, "who conceive St. Paul to have been a Calvinist: not a Socinian nor an Arian.") So Disney makes a strong plea for his own Unitarianism:

D.: The union of all Christians is anticipated, as it has been demonstrated to be the doctrine of Christ, his apostles and evangelists, as also of Moses and the prophets. Nor is it less the language of the religion of nature than of revelation . . .

A.: The human understanding is the first revelation from its maker. From God; from Heaven. Can prophecies, can miracles repeal, annul

or contradict that original revelation? Can God himself prove that
three are one and one three? The supposition is destructive of the
foundation of all human knowledge, and of all distinction between
truth and falsehood.

D.: It is nothing but a fondness for established formularies, a fear of
forsaking the trammels and prejudices of education, and an apprehension of imaginary consequences that men are backward to declare that
God is essentially and numerically one, without equal . . . and that
Jesus Christ is no other than a man divinely commissioned by God as
his messenger.

A.: Aye! Dr. Disney! Fondness, fear, apprehension, not of imaginary
but very real, very serious, and very dangerous consequences make
men "backward" to declare many other truths, as well as those that
you believe so sincerely and devoutly.

It was with great curiosity—and good humor—that Adams read
about Sykes's *Resurrection of the Body*,[47] supposedly composed from
memoranda left behind by Sir Isaac Newton. ("Papers of the great
Knight," he took note.) Dr. Sykes pointed out that there was no such
expression as "the resurrection of the body" or "flesh" in the New
Testament, and that nothing of the kind appeared even in the creed
"fabricated" at the Council of Nicaea.

S.: If vain curiosity had not led people to a particular explication of
the article, how many disputes had been avoided!

A.: Tucker's vision and vehicular state is an entertaining commentary on this subject.[48]

S.: So long as we are taught to believe that "all are to be judged,
quick and dead," is it not an idle question, with what bodies shall we
come?

A.: I should rather have a purer vehicle than this flesh! And better
eyes, and steadier fingers.

S.: May the true cause of infidelity not lie among those who profess
a faith which they call Christian, and which is found inconsistent with
reason, and even common sense?

A.: Here is the great secret.

S.: How many additions were made to what the Gospel of Christ
has said concerning the Son and the Holy Ghost, in the several creeds
framed in the fourth century?

A.: Aye! and additions the most monstrous, the most absurd, the
most corrupt!

S.: Till Christianity is professed pure and uncorrupted, it must have its enemies; and if offences arise, "woe unto him by whom the offence cometh."

A.: Against whom is this woe pronounced? How shall we know what is pure and uncorrupted but by the first revelation? Is Sykes pure? Is the great Knight pure? Love God and man! that is pure. Do as you would be done by! that is pure. Three units are three times one! that is pure. All this can be understood by men, women, and children, rich and poor, without the study of three-score years in a million volumes of philosophers, divines, and historians in Hebrew, Greek, Latin, Sanskrit, English, French, German, Spanish, Italian and Russian.

On the last pages Disney draws a pleasing portrait of Dr. Sykes. In his final eulogy he speaks of the high esteem in which Thomas Hollis held him, sending a complete set of his works to Harvard College.[49] The testimony of Mr. Hollis, he writes, will bring more reputation to the writings of Dr. Sykes than it was in the power of the committee of convocation in 1717 to take away by either indirect reflection or threat.[50] Adams was reminded of developments in America: "Are there not convocations, synods, general assemblies, conventions, and oecumenical councils, spiritual, theological and ecclesiastical, now in embryo or foetus, or already born, in our United States? Both Presbyterian and Episcopalian?" [51]

The Constant Reader

Besides those books with which Adams grappled in earnest, there are dozens of others which contain substantial comments. These notes, too, are valuable, because they throw additional light on episodes in Adams's career and reveal the wide variety of his interests. Many of them have been mentioned in the various chapters of this volume; and, for the sake of the special student, a few more are listed here.

Adams made his earliest notes in John Winthrop's *A Lecture on Earthquakes,* published in connection with the earthquake which shook New England in November 1755. A lively controversy arose between Professor Winthrop and the Reverend Thomas Prince about the use of lightning rods, which had recently been invented by Benjamin Franklin. The pastor of the Old South Church in Boston wondered whether the vehemence of the visitation could not be attributed to the fact that more "iron points" had been erected in Boston than anywhere else. Adams took the side of the Harvard scientist. In his later years he disagreed with Franklin on many points: it is pleasant to know that the iron points were not among them.[1]

Jean-Jacques Burlamaqui's *Principles of Natural and Political Law* was widely read in the Colonies. Adams acquired his copy in the 1763 edition. He took issue with the Swiss jurist in many cases. Once he raised the question: "What is the law of nature as to intercourse between the sexes, and what is the *morality* of it?" Burlamaqui stated that some nations had cautiously inserted in their constitution a clause by which the King was declared to have forfeited his crown if he broke the laws. "It admits of question," Adams believed, "whether these clauses are not as dangerous to the peace of the kingdom as any unconditional submission." This note proves that he read the work before the Stamp Act and his writing of the "Dissertation on the Canon and Feudal Law."[2]

In *The Importance of the American Revolution*, Dr. Richard Price, the English dissenting minister, discussed among other things the national debt of America, recommending the establishment of a sinking fund for its liquidation. Adams vehemently opposed the idea, feeling that the money thus saved would be diverted for political uses. "As public funds cannot be guarded against misapplication, they are always evils, they always introduce corruption . . .," he remarked.[3]

William Gordon, the author of the *History of the Rise, Progress, and Establishment of the Independence of the United States of America*, Adams thoroughly distrusted. "In spirit," he wrote, "he was an English Protestant Dissenter, and a Presbyterian parson." He accused the historian of having changed his manuscript at the bookseller's request, softening his praises of America. For a long time Gordon was held in high repute in this country, only his style being condemned as "meagre and jejune." However, it is known today that he had plagiarized three-fourths of his book, mainly from Edmund Burke's articles in the London *Annual Register*—which shows that critics should think twice before they abuse an author for his style.[4]

John Bristed's *Hints on the National Bankruptcy of Britain*, 1809, was in the nature of a reply to *L'État de France* by Alexandre d'Hauterive, Napoleon's Under Secretary for Foreign Affairs, and was addressed primarily to the American public in order to offset the effects of the Embargo Act of 1808. The writer praised British agriculture, but Adams, the *gourmet* and connoisseur, had his own opinion: "The general superiority of Britain in agriculture is admitted; yet their wheat is not equal. The clover is not equal to French lucerne. Their best cheese is not to be compared to the fromage de Roquefort, nor their best butter to beurre de Brittany. No nor the most exquisite roast beef of Old England to roast beef that I have eaten in France: any more than that English china is to be compared to the porcelaine de Sèvres, or their tapestry to that of Gobelin. Some of the French broadcloths are superior to any in England, and their nankeens bear no comparison."[5]

His opinion of William Godwin's *Political Justice* Adams tersely summed up on the flyleaf. "This book," he wrote, "exceeds in deliberate intentional falsehood whatever of Pharisaical, Jesuitical, Machiavellian or fanatical is to be found in the Universal Library." And a little below he added: "Wilkes studied long, so comes near as possible to treason without committing it. Godwin has studied longer, to see how much like truth he could dress a lie."

After reading Madame de Staël's *L'Influence des passions*, Adams expressed his desire: "I should like to see a treatise on the influence of emulation on the happiness and on the misery of individuals and of nations." The author's exaggerated eulogies on Baron Necker he treated tolerantly as "a fine compliment from a daughter to her father." However, when Madame de Staël went off into a rapturous passage on the love of glory which "ought to fill the soul with pride," he sternly rebuked her: "Vain woman! The soul ought to fill itself with a meek and humble anxiety!" [6]

Adams's library includes scores of presentation copies, many of them with revealing inscriptions. Characteristic is the first volume of the *Political Disquisitions* by James Burgh, the noted English reformer, who in 1774 offered his book "as a small token of his regard for the political character of that gentleman who had distinguished himself as a patriot, and the true friend of civil and religious liberty." Adams regarded the book as "the best service that a citizen could render to his country" in a great crisis.

In view of the decisive part which Adams played in securing the American claims to the fisheries off Canada and Newfoundland, special interest attaches to the little volume *Observations sur le traité de paix conclu à Paris,* published at the French government's inspiration in 1780. As if to memorize the contents, Adams repeated whole sentences on the margins, copied out the names of all the towns, capes, and harbors, and heavily underscored no less then two hundred lines. The book shows that he was, as he had stated, well prepared for the peace negotiations.[7] In Thomas Whateley's *Observations on Modern Gardening* he jotted down the names of some twenty country places, adding in many cases: ". . . which I saw in April 1786 with Mr. Jefferson." In his set of the *Œuvres* of Buffon the section on the birds of America particularly attracted him. He marked the pages about the "degeneration" of animals in the Western hemisphere—a theory which, as may be remembered, aroused Jefferson's indignation in his *Notes on the State of Virginia.*

The *Golden Verses* of Pythagoras, the great mathematician and founder of a religious brotherhood, Adams examined point by point. He was pleased with some of the maxims, such as those on the sanctity of oath, the respect due to parents, affection to friends, and benevolence to mankind. But many of the injunctions appeared to him "mad." At the end he proudly asserted—the conclusion of all his philosophy: "How dark, mean, and meagre are these Golden Verses, however celebrated and really curious, in comparison with the Sermon on the Mount, and the Psalms of David or the Decalogue!" [8]

NOTES

[1]
No Statues or Monuments

1. Theodore Parker, *Historic Americans* (Boston, 1870), 200–201. The four essays in the volume—on Franklin, Washington, Adams, and Jefferson —were written in 1858.

2. Letters to Benjamin Rush, March 23 and April 12, 1809, *Old Family Letters: Copied from the Originals for Alexander Biddle* (Philadelphia, 1892), 226. (Of the two volumes published, only the first contains letters by Adams; the volume number, therefore, will be not cited in these references.) *The Works of John Adams*, edited by Charles Francis Adams (Boston, 1850–56), IX, 616–619. (Hereafter references will be given only to the volume and page numbers.) When Adams's letters appear in both the *Old Family Letters* and in his *Works*, only the latter source is quoted.

3. August 28, 1811, IX, 635–640.

4. January 8, 1812, *Old Family Letters*, 369.

5. II, 51, 110, 54, 134, 68, 67, 163, 357, 379, 401, 411; III, 137.

6. December 4, 1758, II, 52.

7. Correspondence between John Adams and Mrs. Mercy Warren, in *Collections of the Massachusetts Historical Society*, Fifth Series, IV (Boston, 1878), 315–511. At eighty-two—one reads with astonishment—in a letter to Jefferson, Adams called Pickering, his former Secretary of State, a "rogue," whom he "wanted to whip . . . till the blood came." April 19, 1817, X, 253.

8. April 4, 1790, *Old Family Letters*, 55.

9. November 11, 1807, *ibid.*, 168–170. The letters of March 19 and April 22, 1812, further discuss Washington's shortcomings. "The great Character was a Character of Convention," Adams wrote; there was a time when all statesmen and officers "expressly agreed to blow the trumpet of panegyric in concert, to cover and dissemble all faults and errors . . ." And then: "That Washington was not a scholar is certain. That he was too illiterate, unlearned, unread for his station and reputation is equally past dispute." (*Old Family Letters*, 372, 373, 377.)

10. Article published in the October 23, 1811, issue of the *Boston Patriot*; reprinted in *Works*, I, 663–664. Also letters to Mrs. Mercy Warren, in 5 *Coll. of Mass. Hist. Soc.*, IV, 413–414, 431.

11. Letter to Robert R. Livingston, July 22, 1783. *The Writings of Benjamin Franklin*, edited by Albert Henry Smyth (New York, 1905–06), IX, 62. Adams, of course, knew this letter too; he mentioned it in his *Boston Patriot* article, which, however, was devoted to the refutation of an earlier letter by Franklin.

12. July 23, 1806, *Old Family Letters*, 106–107.

13. II, 55–56; III, 197.

14. July 23, 1806, *Old Family Letters,* 107.

15. In the same letter he claimed having done "more labor, run through more and greater dangers, and made greater sacrifices" than any man among his contemporaries. (*5 Coll. of Mass. Hist. Soc.,* IV, 470.)

16. February 26, 1812, *Old Family Letters,* 297.

17. April 18, June 20, 1808, and March 23, 1809. (*Old Family Letters,* 181, 186, 224.) The Quids, or Quiddists—so-called as being a *tertium quid* to the Federalists and the administration Republicans—were the followers of John Randolph, who advocated extreme states' rights. They favored Monroe rather than Madison as successor to Jefferson. Regarding the later party developments, it should be noted that the followers of Andrew Jackson (the left wing of the party started by Jefferson) assumed the name of "Democrats," while Jackson's opponents (mainly the remnants of the old Federalist party) called themselves "National Republicans." The third Republican party—the direct ancestor of the one which bears that name today—was formed in 1856.

18. August 7, 1809, *Old Family Letters,* 237.

19. July 31, 1809, *Correspondence between John Adams and William Cunningham* (Boston, 1823), 151.

20. December 27, 1810, *Old Family Letters,* 272. See also Adams's letters of January 17, June 21, and August 28, 1811, *op. cit.,* 276, 288; IX, 638.

21. October 23, 1809, *Cunningham Correspondence,* 181.

22. "I do not consider little flirts and spats and miffs and piques," he wrote on January 8, 1812, "forgotten by me in a moment as enmities . . ." *Old Family Letters,* 369–370.

23. July 20, 1807, *5 Coll. of Mass. Hist. Soc.,* IV, 334.

24. *Letter from Alexander Hamilton Concerning the Public Conduct and Character of John Adams* . . . (New York, 1800). See Chapter XIII, 263.

25. IX, 303.

26. *Cunningham Correspondence,* 160; August 23, 1805, *Old Family Letters,* 75.

27. I, 616–619. Jefferson's letter was first published in 1836. (*The Writings of George Washington,* edited by Jared Sparks, Boston, 1834–37; X, 159–160.) Had Adams known about the letter, he would hardly have kept silent about it. (See also note 4 to Chapter X.)

28. *The Life of Thomas Jefferson* (New York, 1858), I, 187.

29. Letter to Timothy Pickering, August 6, 1822, II, 514.

30. Letter to Madison, August 30, 1823. *The Works of Thomas Jefferson,* edited by Paul Leicester Ford (New York, 1904–05), XII, 308. (Hereafter it will be noted as Jefferson's *Works.*)

31. Adams expressed their relationship in his own way. "You should remember," he wrote to Dr. Rush, "that Jefferson was but a boy to me. I was at least ten years older than him in age and more than twenty years older than him in politics." (October 25, 1809, *Old Family Letters,* 246.)

32. Letter to Madison, January 30, 1787, *The Works of Jefferson* (New York, 1884), II, 107. (The passage is missing from the 1904–05 edition of Jefferson's *Works,* to which references in the present volume are given.)

33. December 17, 1796, January 22 and 30, 1797, Jefferson's *Works,* VIII, 255, 271–274, 279.

34. December 5, 1811, Jefferson's *Works*, XI, 174. Jefferson, who once at least had quoted Franklin's remark about Adams with approval, in this letter suggested a correction: "Changing a single word only in Dr. Franklin's character of him, I knew him to be always an honest man, often a great one, but sometimes incorrect and precipitate in his judgments . . ."

35. October 12, 1823, Jefferson's *Works*, XII, 314.

36. *Correspondence of John Adams and Thomas Jefferson*, edited by Paul Wilstach (Indianapolis, 1925), 189–190. The letter, at Adams's request, was actually printed and circulated, and exerted some influence upon the election of John Quincy Adams to the Presidency. (Gilbert Chinard, *Honest John Adams*, Boston, 1933, 343.) It should be noted that neither Jefferson's letter nor Adams's reply is included in Adams's collected *Works*.

37. January 22, 1825, X, 414. During his first year in Paris, Jefferson stayed at the Hôtel Tête-Bout, Cul-de-sac Tête-Bout, and afterwards moved to a house at the corner of the Grande Route des Champs Elysées and Rue Neuve de Berry.

38. February 25, 1825, Jefferson Papers, Library of Congress. (Quoted by Chinard, *op. cit.*, 344.)

39. July 13, 1813, X, 52.

40. IX, 331.

41. *The Education of Henry Adams* (New York, 1942), 24–25; *Charles Francis Adams* by his son Charles Francis Adams (Boston, 1900), 46.

42. *Cunningham Correspondence*, 43.

43. *Historic Americans*, 213, 220, 210.

44. "I have received none of your favors since I begin to write," he stated in his last letter, although Mrs. Warren had answered him promptly. (*5 Coll. Mass. Hist. Soc.*, IV, 478.)

45. The letters were dispersed at a public sale in 1943 in New York. The Boston Public Library acquired a considerable number of them.

46. *The Political Science of John Adams* (New York, 1915). See note 20. It may be noted that in 1790 there were only three local banks; in 1800 there were 28; in 1811 no less than 88; and by 1816, 246. As Calhoun stated in the debate over the second United States Bank in 1816, the local banks circulated 170 million dollars of bank notes on not more than 15 million dollars of specie.

47. Vernon Louis Parrington, *The Colonial Mind, 1680–1800* (New York, 1927), 308.

48. Henry Adams, *op. cit.*, 25.

49. In a remarkable letter, written to his wife in 1780 from Paris, Adams stated his case clearly: "I could fill volumes with descriptions of temples and palaces, paintings, sculptures, tapestry, porcelain, etc., etc., etc., if I could have time; but I could not do this without neglecting my duty. The science of government, it is my duty to study, more than all other sciences; the arts of legislation and administration and negotiation, ought to take place of, indeed to exclude, in a manner, all other arts." And then he prophesied: "I must study politics and war that my sons may have liberty to study mathematics and philosophy. My sons ought to study mathematics and philosophy, geography, natural history and naval architecture, navigation, commerce and agriculture; in order to give their children a right to study painting,

poetry, music, architecture, statuary, tapestry, and porcelain." (*Letters of John Adams, Addressed to His Wife*, Boston, 1841, II, 68.)

50. IX, 331.

51. June 7, 1809, *Cunningham Correspondence*, 124.

52. *The Letters of Benjamin Rush*, superbly edited by L. H. Butterfield and recently published in two volumes by the American Philosophical Society, contains many letters to John Adams, thus indirectly throwing considerable light on his thought in 1805–1813. "To the deepest and finest of all of Rush's friendships, that with John Adams," the editor aptly writes, "this collection is a monument." It is a pleasure to learn from the editor's acknowledgment that Mr. Henry Adams, 2nd, acting on behalf of the trustees of the Adams Manuscript Trust, gave permission to microfilm the entire series of Rush's letters to John Adams.

In an article, "The Dream of Benjamin Rush: the Reconciliation of John Adams and Thomas Jefferson," printed in the Winter 1951 issue of *The Yale Review*, Mr. Butterfield also made the important announcement that the whole of Adams's and Jefferson's correspondence in their old age was "soon to be published in full."

[II]

John Adams among His Books

1. Letter to Samuel Dexter, March 23, 1801, IX, 580–581; letter to Christopher Gadsden, April 16, 1801, IX, 585. (Adams also quoted in Latin the line from Horace's fifth satire: "Et genus et virtus, nisi cum re, vilior alga est.")

2. January 30, 1768, II, 208–209.

3. Letter to William Tudor, January 24, 1817, X, 239.

4. *Deed and Other Documents . . . by President Adams* (Cambridge, 1823), 4, 13.

5. December 27, 1810, *Old Family Letters*, 269.

6. July 18 and September 14, 1813, X, 56, 67–68, 57.

7. Letter to Dr. Rush, April 21, 1803, Jefferson's *Works*, IX, 457; *ibid.*, 457–563.

8. X, 66.

9. Letter to John Adams, October 12, 1813. (See also note 10.)

10. The work was first reproduced in facsimile in 1904, with an introduction by Cyrus Adler. Jefferson's letter of October 12, 1813, is quoted by Adler, *op. cit.*, 14–15.

11. April 17, 1817, X, 254.

12. On June 26, 1760, Adams noted in his Diary: "I have begun to read the Spirit of Laws, and have resolved to read that work through in order and with attention, I have hit upon a project that will secure my attention to it, which is to write, in the margin, a sort of index to every paragraph." (II, 93.) The volume is not now in the Adams library.

13. The first twenty pages of d'Alembert's *Discours préliminaire* was translated or paraphrased by John Quincy Adams on the margins.

14. Letters of September 19 and December 22, 1806, and February 2, 1807, *Old Family Letters,* 111–113, 114–116, 120–121, 126.

15. *Rousseau* (London, 1873), Preliminary.

16. Lewis Rosenthal, "Rousseau in Philadelphia," *Magazine of American History,* July 1884, 54. "The works, diaries, and correspondence of the fathers of the American Revolution attest . . . clearly, by their silence, that Rousseau and his coterie had no influence in America . . ."

17. Chapter VII, "Colonial Newspapers and Magazines," by Elizabeth Christine Cook, *op. cit.,* I, 119.

18. Howard Mumford Jones, whose *America and French Culture, 1750–1848* (University of North Carolina Press, 1927) examines a vast number of sources, particularly felt the absence of first-hand information. He himself prepared later "The Importation of French Literature in New York City, 1750–1800" (*Studies in Philology,* October 1931) and "The Importation of French Books in Philadelphia, 1750–1800" (*Modern Philology,* November 1934).

19. *Early Proceedings of the American Philosophical Society* (Philadelphia, 1884). Professor Jones quotes several entries of the arrival of such books, *America and French Culture,* 404.

20. III, 189–190.

21. "Mr. Turgot, the Duke de la Rochefoucauld, and Mr. Condorcet and others, admired Mr. Franklin's Constitution and reprobated mine." (IX, 623.)

22. *Old Family Letters,* 54. Adams's letter to Dr. Richard Price, the English dissenting minister, usually regarded as his first censure of the French Revolution, is dated April 19, 1790. (IX, 563–564.)

23. *The Works of Edmund Burke* (Boston, 1869), III, 218, 221.

24. *Ibid.,* 380, 345.

25. Chateaubriand, *Essais historiques sur la Révolution* (Paris, 1836), II, 130; Taine, *L'Ancien régime* (Paris, 1876), 221–222; Albert Sorel, *L'Europe et la Révolution française* (Paris, 1885), 234; Félix Rocquain, *L'Esprit révolutionnaire avant la Révolution* (Paris, 1878); Marius Roustan, *Les philosophes et la société française au XVIIIᵉ siècle* (Paris, 1911).

26. *Voyage dans les États-Unis d'Amérique,* Paris, l'an VII, III, 13–14. The Duc de la Rochefoucauld-Liancourt (1747–1827) was a first cousin of the Duc de la Rochefoucauld d'Enville. It was he who on July 12, 1789, reported the restlessness in Paris to the King. "But this is a revolt!" Louis exclaimed. "No, Sire," the Duke answered, "this is a revolution."

One may note that Adams bought his mansion, originally that of the Vassall family, in 1787. At the time of the Duke's visit, the house had only four rooms. It was in 1800 that Adams enlarged it. (That part of Braintree was set off in 1792 as the town of Quincy.)

27. "The fields of grain, the vineyards, the castles, the cities, the parks, the gardens, everything is beautiful, yet every place swarms with beggars," he wrote in his Diary on arriving in France. (III, 121.) *Twenty-Six Letters Respecting the Revolution in America,* written in Holland in 1780, VII, 272–275, 302–304.

28. November 13, 1815, X, 174.

29. Letter to Charles Holt, September 4, 1820, X, 391. "Perhaps this is too general a statement," Charles Francis Adams comments.

30. Letter to John Adams, October 28, 1813, Jefferson's *Works*, XI, 348, 349.
31. Letter to John Adams, September 4, 1823, *ibid.*, XII, 310–311.
32. *The Literary History of the American Revolution, 1763–1783* (New York, 1897), I, 94.
33. April 5, 1817, X, 251.
34. *Letters of Benjamin Rush* (Princeton University Press, 1951), II, 1090; *Old Family Letters*, 344.

[III]

Adams's Political Philosophy

1. Letter to Jefferson, November 13, 1815, X, 174.
2. Letter to Richard Henry Lee, November 15, 1775, IV, 186.
3. IV, 181.
4. IV, 284; VI, 128.
5. IV, 230. Benjamin F. Wright, Jr. seems to have overlooked this fact. After quoting Article XXX, he writes: "John Adams was the principal author of this constitution . . ."; and then, still referring to the Article, he continues: "It was primarily in defense of this principle that Adams wrote his *Defence of the Constitutions of Government of the United States of America*" (*American Interpretations of Natural Law*, Harvard University Press, 1931, 120–121). The work was written, the present writer contends, to advocate the division of the legislative power into three branches, and not in defense of the separation of powers.
6. Locke's *Treatise on Civil Government*, §149, §152. Adams's *Works*, IV, 358.
7. Paul M. Spurlin, *Montesquieu in America, 1760–1801* (Louisiana State University Press, 1940).
8. *The Spirit of the Laws*, Book XI, Chapter 6. (Vol. I, p. 171, in the London, 1914, edition.)
9. Walter Bagehot, *The English Constitution* (New York, 1930), 78–79, 295.
10. Adams himself testified to this. Referring to Massachusetts, New York, and Maryland, he wrote in 1814 to John Taylor: "It was not an affected imitation of the English government, so much as an attachment to their old colonial forms . . . which . . . induced the legislators of those three states to adopt their new constitutions." (VI, 487.)
11. Jefferson wrote in his *Summarie View* of 1774: "His majesty . . . and his ancestors, conscious of the impropriety of opposing their single opinion to the united wisdom of two houses of parliament . . . for several ages past have modestly declined the exercise of this power [veto] in that part of his empire called Great Britain . . . It is now, therefore, the great office of his majesty to resume exercise of his negative power . . ." (*Works*, II, 78–79.)
12. Josef Redlich, *The Procedure of the House of Commons*, Preface by Sir Courtenay Ilbert (London, 1908), xii. It is pertinent to quote here Roger Sherman's letter to John Adams. "The negative vested in the crown of Great

Britain," he wrote on July 20, 1789, "has never been exercised since the Revolution [of 1688] . . . so that the nation is in fact governed by the cabinet council, who are the creatures of the crown." Charles Francis Adams added (in 1851) the footnote: "This seems but a superficial view at best. The negative of the crown has gone out of use, because the custom has grown up of conceding the control of the administrative power to the majority which controls the legislature." (VI, 439.)

13. *A Dissertation on Parties*, in *The Works of Lord Bolingbroke* (London, 1754), II, 176.

14. *Book of Fallacies*, in *The Works of Jeremy Bentham* (Edinburgh, 1843), II, 445. Quoted by Correa M. Walsh in *The Political Science of John Adams*, 142.

15. IV, 579; VI, 219.

16. *The Records of the Federal Convention of 1787*, edited by Max Farrand (Yale University Press, 1911), III, 452; II, 204; III, 454.

17. Letter to John W. Campbell, September 3, 1809. *Works*, XI, 117. In 1814 Adams wrote to John Taylor: "This correspondence is intended for your amusement and mine . . . I am confident that if my letters were printed, there would not be found six people in the world who would read them with attention." (VI, 463.)

There was no new edition of the *Federalist* between 1802 and 1810 or between 1810 and 1818. In all, fourteen editions, out of a total of about sixty, appeared in the first half of the nineteenth century. Jonathan Elliot's *Debates on the Adoption of the Federal Constitution*, first published in 1830, were, however, several times reprinted.

18. Joseph Story, *Commentaries on the Constitution of the United States* (Boston, 1833), II, 63–65.

19. George Bancroft, *History of the Formation of the Constitution* (New York, 1883), II, 125–128.

20. Jefferson's *Works*, I, XIV. The five essays in the 1945 edition of *The Economic Basis of Politics*, the first four written in 1916 and the fifth in 1945, present most clearly Professor Beard's ideas on the subject. The essay on "The Doctrine of Political Equality," discussing Rousseau's influence, is especially valuable.

21. Letter to Georg Wedemeyer, March 5, 1852, in *Marx and Engels, Correspondence, 1846–1895* (New York, 1934), 57. "What I did that was new," Marx continued, "was to prove: 1., that the existence of classes is only bound up with particular, historic phases in the development of production; 2., that the class struggle necessarily leads to the dictatorship of the proletariat; 3., that this dictatorship itself only constitutes the transition to the abolition of all classes and to a classless society."

Engels in his late years protested against the idea that either Marx or he regarded the economic element as the only determining factor in society. There are "innumerable intersecting forces," he wrote, and admitted his and Marx's "guilt" in not having sufficiently emphasized this point in their writings. (*Ibid.*, 472, 475, 481, 510, 517.)

22. January 3, 1759, II, 59.

23. *The Oceana and Other Works of James Harrington* (London, 1747), 101, 42, 253, 55, etc.

24. Theodore W. Dwight, "Harrington and His Influence upon American Political Institutions and Political Thought," in the March 1887 issue of the *Political Science Quarterly*, contains useful suggestions.

25. VI, 280; IX, 217.

26. IV, 290; VI, 65.

27. Walsh, *op. cit.*, 143.

28. Letter to James Sullivan, May 26, 1776, IX, 376.

29. V, 457.

30. VI, 495, 456.

31. According to Charles Francis Adams, John Adams's estate at the time of his death was worth about a hundred thousand dollars. (I, 639.) However, in his letter of September 12, 1811, written to Dr. Rush, Adams had estimated his fortune, with the "depreciated currency," at only fifty thousand dollars. (*Old Family Letters*, 362.) This was after he had satirically reflected on the "sacrifices" made for the public by Franklin, who had left his grandson a fortune of five hundred and thirty thousand dollars, and of Washington, who had left his nephews four or five hundred thousand dollars. (*Ibid.*, 345.)

32. Jefferson's correspondence and Anas contain countless passages about the "monarchists."

33. Farrand, *Records*, I, 282–311. Hamilton's outline of his speech contains the statement: "The monarch must have proportional strength. He ought to be hereditary, and to have so much power, that it will not be to his interest to risk much to acquire more." However, this may have been only a theoretical suggestion.

34. "It was morally certain," Hamilton wrote later, ". . . that Madison must have concurred in the vote of Virginia. Thus, if I sinned against Republicanism, Mr. Madison was not less guilty." (Letter to Timothy Pickering, September 16, 1803. Farrand, *Records*, III, 398.)

35. February 23, 1787, IV, 579.

36. Letter of June 11, 1787. *Proceedings of the Mass. Hist. Soc.*, Second Series, XVII, 465.

37. This was already a concession on his part. On July 24, 1789, he wrote to Dr. Rush: "The most modest title you can give him, in any reasonable proportion to the wealth, power and population of this country, and to the constitutional authority and dignity of his office is 'His Majesty, the President.'" (*Old Family Letters*, 46.)

38. *Journal of William Maclay*, edited by Edgar S. Maclay (New York, 1890), 30; Letter to Madison, July 29, 1789. Jefferson's *Works*, V, 485.

There is a passage in Adams's *Novanglus* which, humorous though it sounds, could not have been written by anyone else. To his contention that the Colonies were "distinct states" or "realms" connected with England only by the person of the King, his opponent, "Massachusettensis," replied that in that case the King "appears in a new capacity, of King of America, or rather in several new capacities, of King of Massachusetts, King of Rhode Island, King of Connecticut, etc." Adams remained undaunted. "This is no absurdity at all," he thought. "He will appear in this light, and does appear so, whether parliament has authority over us or not. He is King of Ireland, I suppose, although parliament is allowed to have authority there. As to giving his majesty those titles, I have no objection at all; I wish he would be graciously pleased to assume them." (IV, 114–115.)

39. *Gazette of the United States*, April 27, 1791, VI, 272.

40. Jefferson's *Works*, VI, 283, 259.

41. VIII, 506, 507.

42. *Old Family Letters*, 37–38.

43. Letter of April 18, 1790, IX, 566.

44. Charles D. Hazen, *Contemporary American Opinion of the French Revolution* (Johns Hopkins University Press, 1897), is still the best book on the subject.

45. April 24, 1796, Jefferson's *Works*, VIII, 240. Jefferson's letter to Mazzei was published in a Florentine paper; from the Italian text it was translated into French and printed in the *Moniteur;* and from that it was retranslated into English, first appearing in America in *The Minerva* of May 14, 1796. Jefferson did not repudiate the letter, but to friends he blamed the translator for the stronger expressions.

Philip Mazzei (1730–1816), a native of Italy, was an agent of Virginia in Europe during the American Revolution. In 1785 he returned to Europe. In 1788 he published in Paris his *Recherches historiques et politiques sur les États-Unis de l'Amérique septentrionale*, in four volumes. Soon after, he entered the service of the King of Poland, residing for several years at Warsaw. After the division of Poland, he became a pensioner of the Emperor of Russia. In 1813 he published his *Memorie.*

46. IX, 109.

47. Letter to Jefferson, June 14, 1813, X, 42. Frank M. Anderson, "The Enforcement of the Alien and Sedition Laws" in *Annual Report of the American Historical Association* (Washington, 1914), 115–126.

48. Repeated by Adams in his letter of July 11, 1807, to Mrs. Warren. 5 *Coll. of Mass. Hist. Soc.*, IV, 324.

49. *Ibid.*, 325.

50. July 28, 1807, *ibid.*, 360–361.

51. August 19, 1807, *ibid.*, 477. The "personal motives" refer to Adams's disapproval of James Warren's alleged sympathy with Shays's Rebellion, and his own refusal to use his influence as Vice-President in the interests of Mrs. Warren's son. Soon after his election, on May 29, 1789, Adams had written to Mrs. Warren: "No doubt there have been many and great exaggerations and misrepresentations. But one thing is indubitable, that G[eneral] Warren did differ for a time from all his friends and did countenance measures that appear to me, as they did to those friends, extremely pernicious:" In the same letter, he told her rather curtly: "You are pleased to say, Madam, that you are sure of our patronage for certain purposes. In the first place, I have no patronage; in the next, neither your children nor my own would be sure of it if I had it." (*Warren-Adams Letters*, II, Boston, 1925, 313–314.) Now the situation was the reverse. In 1804, at the age of seventy-eight, General Warren was chosen one of the presidential electors for Massachusetts, while John Adams was still under the umbrage of accusations of monarchism.

52. Walsh, *op. cit.*, 283. Merriam, *A History of American Political Theories* (New York, 1926), 129.

53. Vernon Louis Parrington, *The Colonial Mind, 1680–1800* (New York, 1927), 311. Madison, too, had changed his opinion. "Mr. Madison," Adams wrote to Dr. Rush in 1806, "you say . . . acquitted me of any intention to change the Constitution of the Union or the individual States, and I solemnly assure you, I never had a wish in my heart or a thought in my head of attempting any alteration in this respect." (*Old Family Letters*, 96.)

54. VI, 220. Jefferson's *Works*, I, 236; Letter to Gouverneur Morris, February 27, 1802, in Hamilton's *Works*, edited by Henry Cabot Lodge (New York, 1885–86), VIII, 591–592.

55. VI, 67. Jefferson's *Works*, I, 184–185. However, on the same occasion —August 13, 1791—Hamilton made also the remark: "That mind must be really depraved which would not prefer the equality of political rights which is the foundation of pure republicanism, if it can be obtained consistently with order."

56. Letter of March 26, 1806, *Old Family Letters*, 97.

57. Letter to Roger Sherman, July 17, 1789, VI, 428; Letters to John Taylor, April 15, 1814, VI, 470, 473.

58. In her *A Study of "Monarchical" Tendencies in the United States, from 1776 to 1801* (University of Illinois, 1923 [?]) page 128, Louise Burnham Dunbar concludes: "There is reason to believe that several plans of monarchical character received serious consideration in the United States between 1776 and 1787"; that ". . . the existence of monarchical purposes in the Constitutional Convention is largely a matter of definition"; that "the exigencies of practical politics after 1787 account for much but not all of the current suspicion regarding monarchical tendencies from 1787 to 1801"; and that ". . . the people of the United States were essentially antimonarchical in the period studied."

59. Letter to H. Niles, January 14, 1818, X, 276. See also William Tudor, *Life of James Otis* (Boston, 1823), 61.

60. III, 449, 463.

61. II, 370–377, 537.

62. *The Works of James Wilson* (Philadelphia, 1804), III, 204, 206, 225, etc.

63. IV, 23, 75, 99, 104, 122, 149, 157, etc.

64. IV, 57, 79.

65. Calvin's *Institutio Christiana* was widely read in England by Anglican and Puritan divines alike, and became especially influential through the writings of Thomas Cartwright and John Knox.

66. The doctrine of the Laws of Nature was congenial to English legal thinking; the English Common Law, although it developed independently of the Roman Law, had assimilated the doctrine through the Canon Law. "On the whole," Sir Frederick Pollock wrote, "the natural justice or 'reason of the thing' which the Common Law recognizes and applies does not appear to differ from the Law of Nature . . ." He defined the latter as "a living embodiment of the collective reason of civilized mankind." (*The Expansion of the Common Law*, Boston, 1894, III, 128.)

67. *Studies in History and Jurisprudence* (New York, 1901), II, 599.

68. VI, 237, 245, 250, 271, 395, etc.

69. In his ninetieth year, Adams advised Jefferson not to bring European

scholars to the University of Virginia. "They are all infected with episcopal and presbyterian creeds, and confessions of faith," he wrote. "They all believe that great Principle which has produced this boundless universe, Newton's universe and Herschel's universe, came down to this little ball, to be spit upon by Jews. And until this awful blasphemy is got rid of, there never will be any liberal science in the world." (Letter of January 22, 1825, X, 415.) One may note that in his letters to Jefferson, Adams, almost instinctively, tried to minimize the differences in their religious views.

70. Parrington, *op. cit.,* 320.

71. The name is variously spelt as Nedham and Needham. Adams used the first form, which is adopted here.

72. August 28, 1811, *Old Family Letters,* 357.

73. Letters to John Taylor, VI, 515. It was just like Adams to want to compose "An Essay on Method." In early 1806 he submitted such a piece to the *Monthly Anthology* in Boston. The young editors were puzzled as to whether the paper was original or a translation. One of them, William Smith Shaw, undertook to find out, but his report is not known. (*The Anthology Society,* edited by M. A. DeWolfe Howe, Boston, 1910, 68.) At any rate, the March 1806 issue of the magazine published the article, unsigned, a brief note expressing the editors' hope that readers would find in it "much of that unadorned, manly, and dignified sense which we see in the philosophical writings of the ages of Anne and the first George." The allusion sounds as if the editors had thought that the paper was a translation after all. But the style is later than that of the ages of Anne and the first George. Professor George W. Sherburn, of Harvard, whose opinion the present writer sought in the matter, promptly suggested Hugh Blair's *Lectures on Rhetoric,* Chapter XXXV on historical writing, as the probable source of Adams's article. To be sure, a subsequent comparison of the texts showed that Adams copied several sentences from Blair, and followed the latter's ideas fairly closely. (At the crucial passage, between pages 40 and 41 of the third volume of Adams's copy of Blair's *Lectures,* Basel, 1789, there is a bookmark, a bill sent to him for "2 Barrels of Superfine Vine.")

[IV]

Bolingbroke, the Ishmael of His Age

1. Adams's *Works,* I, 43. David Mallet, Bolingbroke's literary executor, published in 1754 *The Works of Lord Bolingbroke* in five quarto volumes. These were the political and historical studies which had appeared previously. In the same year Mallet also published *The Philosophical Works of Lord Bolingbroke,* in five octavo volumes, none of which had been printed before.

2. II, 24, 23, 28, 105, 117, 125; X, 82.

3. Letter to Francis Eppes, January 9, 1821, Jefferson's *Works,* XII, 195; Gilbert Chinard, *The Literary Bible of Thomas Jefferson* (Johns Hopkins University Press, 1928), 19.

4. Walter Bagehot, *Biographical Studies* (London, 1907), 169.

5. The first St. John received his title "Earl of Bolingbroke" in 1624 from a manor that had belonged to the family of his ancestor Margaret Beauchamp, through whom the St. Johns were connected with the Tudors.

6. *The Works of Jonathan Swift,* edited by Temple Scott (London, 1897–1910), II, 273.

7. October 15, 1725. *The Works of Alexander Pope* (London, 1871), VII, 58.

8. *The Works of Lord Bolingbroke* (Philadelphia, 1841), IV, 111. "The germ of almost every doctrine and of almost every idea in the *Essay on Man,* more or less developed, will, on careful inspection, be found in the Minutes." John Churton Collins, *Bolingbroke* (New York, 1886), 161. Also Leslie Stephen, *Alexander Pope* (London, 1880), 164–170; Walter Sichel, *Bolingbroke and His Times* (New York, 1902), II, 326–330.

9. Bolingbroke's *Works,* III, 34, 49, 56, 188, 427, etc.

10. Sichel agrees that Bolingbroke's ethical system tallies with Spinoza's *intellectualis amor,* yet he thinks that Bolingbroke "probably" never read Spinoza. The two references to Spinoza in the *Philosophical Essays* (III, 202, 380) seem to show that he did, although Shaftesbury undoubtedly served as an intermediary. The latter's indebtedness to Spinoza has been minutely shown by John M. Robertson in his edition of the *Characteristics* (London, 1900). "It is morally certain that Shaftesbury's main ideas were given to him; and as a matter of fact they are nearly all explicit or implicit in Spinoza, whose teaching Shaftesbury was sure to hear of in his sojourn in Holland in 1698, if he had not studied it before." (xxxii.) It is interesting to note that Louis Racine, son of the great dramatist, complained that Pope's *Essay on Man* was Spinozistic! (*La Religion,* Paris, 1742, 34, 69, 150.)

11. Bolingbroke's *Works,* I, 205.

12. *The Minister's Answer to the Occasional Writer.* In the second number of *The Occasional Writer* Bolingbroke reprinted some passages from the *Answer* (Bolingbroke's *Works,* I, 228–230), but his irony was lost against the insults.

13. Beginning on September 5, 1730, it continued through May 22, 1731.

14. This, too, was published in *The Craftsman.* The first letter appeared on October 27, 1733, and the last on December 28, 1734.

15. Joseph Spence, *Anecdotes of Books and Men* (London, 1820), 320–321. *Letters on the Spirit of Patriotism: On the Idea of a Patriot King* (London, 1749), "Advertisement."

16. *Life of Johnson,* I, 311. Bolingbroke predicted in his "Letters to Pope": "You will have less to apprehend from their malice and resentment than a writer in prose on the same subjects would have . . ." *Works,* III, 41.

17. *A View of Lord Bolingbroke's Philosophy* (London, 1754). Also A. W. Evans, *Warburton* (Oxford, 1932), 179–180.

18. The literary relationship of Voltaire and Bolingbroke has received, of course, a good deal of attention on the part of their biographers—Charles de Rémusat, Lord Morley, John Churton Collins, Robert Harrop, Archibald Ballantyne, Walter Sichel, and others. A special study of the subject is Arthur-Sydney Hurn's *Voltaire et Bolingbroke* (Paris, 1915). A sharp dissent from the prevailing opinion has been voiced by Norman L. Torrey in "Bolingbroke and Voltaire—a Fictitious Influence," in the September 1927

issue of the *Publications of the Modern Language Association of America*.

That Voltaire's professed opinion of Bolingbroke was insincere is obvious from his letter to Madame du Deffand, written after the appearance of Bolingbroke's posthumous works. "I cannot understand," he wrote, "how a man who appeared to take such large views could produce such trivialities . . ." (April 23, 1754, *Oeuvres complètes*, LV, 95–96.) Nor could his admiration prevent him from calmly remarking to an English visitor in his eighty-third year: "Bolingbroke had a striking figure and voice; in his works there are many leaves and little fruit . . . (*beaucoup de feuilles et peu de fruits*)." Martin Sherlock, *Lettres d'un voyageur anglois* (London, 1779), 141.

19. Boswell's *Life of Johnson*, I, 312. Leslie Stephen, *History of English Thought in the Eighteenth Century* (London, 1902), I, 177–184, II, 168–179. (The first edition appeared in 1876.) William E. H. Lecky, *The History of England in the Eighteenth Century* (London, 1878–1890), I, 130.

20. Disraeli, *Vindication of the English Constitution* (London, 1835), 185–186.

21. I, 41. John Adams owned a set of the five octavo volumes of the *Philosophical Works* (London, 1754). The first volume bears his signature and the date "Paris, March 6, 1780." The political works he had in separate editions, published in London in 1770, 1773, 1775, and without date.

22. *Remarks on the History of England*. A new edition. London, T. Davies (n.d.), p. xiii; the Philadelphia 1841 edition of Bolingbroke's *Works* omits the dedication and the preface as "written by another and a very inferior hand"—an assumption which does not seem justified. (References to the excerpts from Bolingbroke's *Works* given here will be to the editions which Adams owned and also to the Philadelphia edition of 1841 which may be more easily accessible.)

23. The best-known (some of them the most notorious) editors of the Republican gazettes of the day. The *Dictionary of American Biography* contains notices on each of them.

24. Davies ed. (n.d.), 10; Philadelphia ed., I, 294.

25. In the spring of 1783 Charles James Fox (1749–1806), one of the Whig leaders, and Lord North (1732–1792), the arch-Tory, formed a coalition cabinet under the leadership of the Duke of Portland. Fox took the post of foreign secretary and North that of home secretary. It was Fox's purpose to give "a good stout blow" to the influence of the King, while North, known until then as the King's man, wished to assert his independence. The cabinet introduced many bills curtailing the King's prerogatives in appointments, patronage, etc., but before the end of the year it fell.

26. See Chapter XI.

27. The unflattering reference—coupling his name with that of Thomas Paine, whom Adams despised—is evidently to John Lawrence (Lawrance, Laurance), 1750–1810, judge advocate general during the Revolutionary War, and afterwards Congressman and Senator from New York. An ardent Federalist, he was a director of the Bank of the United States. Adams's dislike of banks may account for his remark.

28. Tenth London ed. of 1775, 108; Phil. ed., II, 73.

29. Cadell ed. of 1770, 15–16; Phil. ed., II, 178.

30. Joseph Butler (1692–1752), Bishop of Durham, whose *Analogy of Religion,* with its doctrine of probability, was directed against the deists.

31. Conyers Middleton (1683–1750), the famous theologian, was the author of a *Life of Cicero,* published in two volumes in 1741. See Chapter XIV, 290–294.

32. Davies ed. of 1775, 2; Phil. ed., II, 352.

33. In his *Remarks on the Life and Writings of Dr. Jonathan Swift* (London, 1752), the Earl of Orrery drew a eulogistic sketch of Bolingbroke: "The wisdom of Socrates, the dignity and care of Pliny, and the wit of Horace appeared in all his writings and conversation . . ."

34. London, 1678. Adams had a copy of this enormous folio. The first three chapters, extending to f. 150, are covered with his marginal notes—summaries of what he read.

35. Bolingbroke's *Works,* III, 66.

36. At the foot of the page a note, evidently by David Mallet, ascribes the verses to John Philips. The present writer, in going through Philips's *Poems* (London, 1776), has been unable to find the lines.

37. *Philosophical Works* (London, 1754), I, 248; Phil. ed., III, 192.

38. *Ph. W.,* II, 236; Phil. ed., III, 371.

39. *Ph. W.,* III, 1; Phil. ed., III, 461.

40. *Ph. W.,* II, 334; Phil. ed., IV, 111.

41. *Ph. W.,* IV, 3; Phil. ed., IV, 161.

42. Constantin-François Volney was the author of *Les Ruines,* 1791, and the *Catechisme du citoyen français,* 1793, works in which he advocated a morality independent of all revealed religions. Being a Girondist, he was imprisoned in 1793; regaining his freedom, he came to America, where he became a friend of Jefferson. During the tension with France he was suspected of intrigues aiming at the delivery of Louisiana to the Directory, and under the Alien Act was obliged to leave the country. However, he kept up his friendship with Jefferson, who in 1798–99 made a new translation of the first twenty chapters of *Les Ruines.* The translation, completed by Joel Barlow in Paris, was published there in 1802. In 1803 Volney published his *Tableau du climat et du sol des Etats-Unis d'Amérique,* in the preface of which he made a harsh attack against John Adams, whom he accused of revengefulness because of his unfavorable review of the *Defence of the Constitutions of the United States.* Professor Gilbert Chinard, who believes that Volney was an agent of the French government, has found no traces of Adams's animosity against him. (*Volney et Amérique,* Johns Hopkins University Press, 1923.)

43. *Ph. W.,* IV, 383; Phil. ed., IV, 365.

44. Spence, *Anecdotes,* 369. Thomas Macknight, *Life of Bolingbroke* (London, 1863), 689.

45. Samuel Hopkins was, next to Jonathan Edwards, the most important American theologian of the eighteenth century. His *System of Doctrines,* 1793, teaches that God does all things for his own glory, and that every one should gladly take his place in the divine plan. His doctrine has been called "willingness-to-be-damned."

46. Samuel Clarke (1675–1729) was the founder of the so-called "intellectual" school in religion. In 1712 he published his *Scripture Doctrine of*

the Trinity, which led to accusations of Arianism. He was a close friend of Isaac Newton and Bishop Hoadly. Price, Lindsey, Sykes, and other Unitarian ministers were among his followers.

47. This short treatise, written in 1716, was frankly an imitation of Seneca.

48. A reference to Cicero's *De natura deorum*, in which Gaius Aurelius Cotta (ca. 124–73 B.C.) is introduced as an interlocutor who supports the principles of the New Academy.

49. *Ph. W.*, V, 29; Phil. ed., IV, 389.

50. Charles Blount (1654–1693) and Thomas Morgan (d. 1743) were prominent English deists. Blount, the author of *Anima mundi*, of *Diana of the Ephesians*, etc., was a follower of Hobbes; Morgan, who described himself as a "Christian deist," wrote *The Moral Philosopher*.

51. William Vassall was one of the outstanding loyalists in Boston, who fled early to England, where he died in 1800, at the age of eighty-five.

[V]

Rousseau and the Man of Nature

1. Adams's *Works*, II, 148–149.
2. III, 454.
3. Quoted by Charles Francis Adams, IV, 216.
4. The Convention, which opened at Cambridge on September 1, 1779, chose a committee of thirty for the framing of the Constitution. This committee asked Adams to prepare a Declaration of Rights, and named a sub-committee of three—James Bowdoin, Samuel Adams, and John Adams—for the drafting of the Constitution itself. However, the sub-committee delegated this task, too, to John Adams. (IV, 215–216.)

It should be noted that William V. Wells, the biographer of Samuel Adams, contests John Adams's claim to the sole authorship of the Massachusetts Constitution. "So exactly did this form of government," he writes, "represent the known theories of Samuel Adams, that for a long time in Boston he was reputed to have been its originator, though afterwards, in public estimation the authorship was divided between the two kinsmen." (William V. Wells, *The Life and Public Services of Samuel Adams*, Boston, 1865, III, 80–87.)

5. IX, 563–564.
6. Letter of July 13, 1813, X, 53.
7. Voltaire's marginal notes on Rousseau were first published by Edouard Gardet in 1860, and were reprinted by Louis Moland in his edition of Voltaire's *Oeuvres complètes*.
8. However, Rousseau's development had many phases. The doctrine of the "innate goodness" of man—he first merely denied the existence of original sin—was so often attributed to him that he finally accepted it. In the same way, primitive man became the "noble savage."
9. Already in 1791 there had appeared *De J.-J. Rousseau considéré comme l'un des premiers auteurs de la Révolution*, in two volumes, by A. Mercier.

Since then there has been hardly a book in the immense literature on Rousseau without a chapter about his influence on the Revolution. "Wherever, during the last century and a half," C. E. Vaughan writes, "man has revolted against injustice and oppression, there we may be sure that the leaven of the second *Discourse* has been working; there the spirit of the great liberator has without doubt contributed to the result." (*The Political Writings of Jean-Jacques Rousseau*, Cambridge, 1915, I, 5.)

10. The *Mondain*, which consists of about one hundred twenty-five verses, declares at the outset:

> "J'aime le luxe, et même la mollesse,
> Tous les plaisirs, les Arts de toute espèce,
> La propreté, le goût, les ornemens:
> Tout honnête homme a de tels sentimens."

It has no great respect for the state of nature:

> "La Soye et L'Or ne brilloient point chez eux:
> Admirez-vous pour cela nos Ayeux?
> Il leur manquoit l'industrie et l'aisance:
> Est-ce vertu? C'étoit pure ignorance."

Familiarly addressing "Mon cher Adam, mon vieux et triste père," Voltaire drew a repulsive picture of him as well as of "Madame Eve," a pair more hideous than "two green apes" or "two cloven-footed goats." (The *Mondain* and its sources are discussed by André Morize, *L'Apologie du luxe au XVIIIᵉ siècle*, Paris, 1909.)

11. Jean-Louis Chouet to Rousseau, 18 June, 1755. (*Correspondance générale de J.-J. Rousseau*, Paris, 1924–34, II, 192–193.) Rousseau's Genevan citizenship lasted only for eight years. After the condemnation of his *Émile* by Archbishop Beaumont, the Parlement of Paris issued an order for his arrest and the burning of his books—and the Little Council of Geneva followed the example. A year later, Rousseau, having fled to Neuchâtel, a territory of the King of Prussia, informed the Republic of his resigning "forever" from his citizenship.

12. Only a part of Adams's notes on the dedication is included here. He also read the preface with close attention, as his numerous underlinings show.

13. The English translation was published in London in 1761 as *A Discourse upon the Origin and Foundation of the Inequality among Mankind.* (The excerpts are given here, with some modifications, from this translation; the page references are to both this translation and the Hachette edition of the *Oeuvres complètes*.) *Discourse*, 37; *Oeuvres*, I, 90.

14. The passage has been often quoted and misquoted. Leaving out the introductory words "it would be horrible . . . ," it is presented as Rousseau's approval of the state of imbecility. Adams had read it in the same spirit.

15. This most revolutionary of Rousseau's statements was derived from Pascal: " 'This dog is mine,' said the poor boy; 'that is my place under the sun'—here is the beginning and symbol of the usurpation of the whole earth." (*Pensées*, Première partie, IX, #53.)

16. *Discourse*, 99; *Oeuvres complètes*, I, 105.

17. Adams read the *Économie politique* in the third volume of the 1764 edition of the *Oeuvres de Rousseau*, published in nine volumes with a Neuchâtel imprint.

18. The consequences of the doctrine of political equality are stated with great clarity by Charles A. Beard in *The Economic Basis of Politics* (New York, 1945 edition), 46–70. See Chapter III, 33.

19. *Oeuvres de Rousseau* (1764), III, 322; *Oeuvres complètes*, III, 283.

20. "Two lines of thought meet and cross in the politics of Rousseau. He is the champion of individual liberty. He is the champion also of the sovereignty of the State. He is the heir of Locke. He is the disciple also of Plato and, in this point though in no other, of Hobbes." (Vaughan, *op. cit.*, 4.)

21. The excerpts from the text here given are from the first English translation, *Social Compact* (London, 1764). *Social Compact*, 83; *Oeuvres complètes*, III, 334.

22. He had the 1764 edition, in four volumes, with a Neuchâtel and Paris imprint, and twelve engravings by Gravelot. Adams's notes in the book were published by Gilbert Chinard in the January 1931 issue of *Modern Language Notes*.

23. The late Irving Babbitt's attitude towards Rousseau had a striking resemblance to that of John Adams. As readers of his *Rousseau and Romanticism, Democracy and Leadership*, etc., and as his former students at Harvard will well remember, Professor Babbitt never tired of insisting on standards and checks to safeguard the golden mean, the humanistic ideal. He had evidently made a study of Adams's works. In one of his books he approvingly quotes Adams's saying that man is a reasoning but not a reasonable animal; and he used Adams's statement about his political creed (which begins the second paragraph of the third chapter of the present volume) as an epigraph for one of his books.

Rousseauistic "romanticism" was the object of Babbitt's fear and hate; and this was the word for which Adams was groping. However, although "romantic" and "romantical" were already introduced in the seventeenth century, "romanticism," according to the Oxford Dictionary, was not invented until 1803 and came into vogue only some fifty years later. So Adams had to satisfy himself with approximations like "fanciful," "impractical," "chimerical," etc. In the exclamation "This is romance!" he came closest to what he wanted to say.

[VI]

Frederick, Voltaire, and d'Alembert

1. The son of John Quincy Adams, then in London with his father. George Washington Adams was born in Berlin in 1801. Having graduated from Harvard in 1821, he became a lawyer, and was elected to the legislature for Quincy. As John Quincy Adams records in his Diary, George was with John Adams when the latter died on the Fourth of July, 1826. He was

drowned on April 30, 1829, in a fall from a steamer on Long Island Sound.

2. X, 169. Jean-Baptiste de Boyer, Marquis d'Argens (1704–1771), was a scholar and an adventurer. It was his *Lettres juives, chinoises, et cabalistiques,* published at The Hague in twenty volumes, which attracted Frederick's attention. For more than twenty-five years he lived at the Prussian court. Then, at sixty, he offended the King by marrying a Berlin actress. He returned to his native Aix-en-Provence, where two years later he died.

3. The commission of Silas Deane (1737–1789) was to purchase supplies —especially clothing and arms, munitions and artillery—in Europe to be paid for by cargoes shipped from America. With the help of the playwright Beaumarchais, author of *Le Mariage de Figaro,* who formed the imaginary house of Roderique, Hortalez & Company, Deane succeeded in securing eight shiploads of military supplies.

4. *Diplomatic Correspondence of the American Revolution,* edited by Jared Sparks (Boston, 1829–30), I, 20, 32, 47; II, 78.

5. The subject has been comprehensively treated by Frïedrich Kapp in his *Friedrich der Grosse und die Vereinigten Staaten* (Leipzig, 1871).

6. VII, 99, 107.

7. March 9, 1784, VIII, 189–190.

8. October 27, 1786, VIII, 415.

9. The *Oeuvres posthumes,* in fifteen volumes, were published in Berlin in 1788–89. In 1789 a *Supplément* and the four volumes of the *Oeuvres* appeared.

10. "Frederick's deepest passion, the one which entitles him to a place among the *philosophes,* was 'son goût pour l'étude.'" (G. Rigollot, *Frédéric II, philosophe,* Paris, 1875, 218–219.)

11. The first Berlin edition of Frederick's works contains one hundred sixty-six letters to Voltaire, most of these dating from 1736–40 and 1770–78. The *Briefwechsel Friedrich's des Grossen mit Voltaire,* 1908–11, includes double that number. D'Alembert's first published letter to the King is from 1760; that of Frederick to him, from 1765. The *Oeuvres posthumes* includes both sides of the correspondence, 110 letters by the King and 126 by d'Alembert.

The excerpts from the letters here published have been translated from the French (Adams's copy) by Miss Margaret Munsterberg. References to them will be given by the date of the letters.

12. VIII, 627–IX, 37.

13. Indignant over the two Treaties of Vienna whereby France, in exchange for the whole of Lorraine, recognized the Austrian female succession and yielded to Austria on the Polish question, Frederick wrote a burning essay, *Considérations sur l'état présent du corps politique de l'Europe,* urging that the just balance between Austria and France required a third power—which must be Prussia. Adams, with Napoleon's campaigns uppermost in his mind, followed with interest the exposure of the French desire for conquest. (His comments are omitted from the present volume.) The *Considérations,* calculated to arouse the maritime powers and the German princes, was meant to be published anonymously in London, and then in French as if it were a translation from the English. However, it remained unprinted during Frederick's life.

14. Letter of May 8, 1737.

15. May 20, 1737.

16. August 16, 1737.

17. December 14, 1737.

18. August 3, 1740.

19. November 28, 1740.

20. October 24, 1766.

21. The *Philosophie de l'histoire*, which Voltaire later used as an introduction to his *Essai sur les mœurs*, is generally regarded as the beginning of modern historical writing. The *Traité sur la tolérance*, written in vindication of Jean Calas, shows Voltaire the humanitarian at his best. (Adams's comments, omitted from the present volume, were published by Gilbert Chinard in *Modern Language Notes*, 1931, 26–29.)

22. December 25, 1813, X, 82.

23. Written originally in Latin, the *Réflexions sur la cause générale des vents* was published in 1747 in Paris. D'Alembert was not yet thirty.

24. The valley of Jehoshaphat has been identified by tradition with the valley between Jerusalem and the Mount of Olives. ("Let the heathen be weakened, and come up to the valley of Jehoshaphat: for there I will sit to judge all the heathen round about." Joel 3:12.)

25. October 18, 1770.

26. August 13, 1777.

27. Johann Georg Zimmerman, a physician of Hanover, attended the King during his last illness. In 1788 he published *Ueber Friedrich den Grossen und meine Unterredungen mit ihm kurz vor seinem Tode*. Frederick died in a different manner than one may guess from Adams's comment. "Je vais me reposer" were supposed to be his last words. The King had requested in his will that he be buried along with his dogs; his desire, however, was not fulfilled.

28. August 17, 1771.

29. III, 147.

30. Sir Andrew Mitchell, whom Carlyle described as "by far the best Excellency England ever had in the Prussian court," stayed at his post, with the exception of short intervals, from 1756 till his death in 1771, at the age of sixty-three. In his youth he had a lively interest in the *philosophes;* while studying in Paris, he had formed an acquaintance with Montesquieu. *Memoirs and Papers of Sir Andrew Mitchell*, by Andrew Bisset (London, 1850).

31. Pyrrho of Elis (ca. 360–270 B.C.), a Greek skeptic philosopher, was the founder of the school known as Pyrrhonism. The main principle of his thought is *acatalepsia*, the impossibility of knowing things in their own nature. Pyrrho regarded *ataraxia*, or imperturbability, as the only proper attitude.

32. Adams was quoting from the first epistle of Pope's *Essay on Man:*

> "Hope humbly then; with trembling pinions soar;
> Wait the great teacher Death, and God adore!"

[VII]

The Communism of the Abbé de Mably

1. "Montesquieu, Rousseau, and Mably were the great authorities of the time . . . The politicians of the Revolution were raised on their works! They read and reread them every day; they found in them inexhaustible evidence, in the way Pascal and Bossuet found it in St. Augustine." Alfred Espinas, *La Philosophie sociale du XVIIIe siècle et la Révolution* (Paris, 1898), 110.

2. *Oeuvres de Maximilien Robespierre*, edited by Laponneraye (Paris, 1840), III, 607–642.

3. *Oeuvres de Mably* (Paris, 1794–95), I, 6.

4. "Our poor writings about real equality and the system of communistic administration are but reminiscences of the famous publicists who discussed these great questions before us . . ." (Victor Advielle, *Histoire de Gracchus Babeuf et du babouvisme*, Paris, 1884, II, 51.) André Lichtenberger, *Le Socialisme et la Révolution française* (Paris, 1899), 221.

5. "Mably was a conspirator of an altogether different hue than the Genevan," Babeuf said at his trial. "One should hear him declaim against the property owners; and then judge whether it is edifying to prosecute his disciples, when, under the government of the Capets, the masters themselves loudly professed the same doctrine." Advielle, *Babeuf*, II, 48.

6. "He represents certain aspects of the eighteenth century in France with a clarity to which no other person can pretend. He shows the result of that union of high ethical idealism with *a priori* deduction better than any of the other *philosophes* of the century." Harold J. Laski, Introduction to Ernest A. Whitfield, *Gabriel Bonnot de Mably* (London, 1930), xi.

7. "Éloge historique" by the Abbé Brizard, pronounced in 1787, in *Oeuvres de Mably*, I, 117.

8. III, 350, 354.

9. Adams's explanatory note appeared as a Postscript to the first volume of the original edition of the *Defence*. His letter to Mably was written in December 1782, after their first meeting. (V, 491–496.)

10. To John Webb, September 25, 1785, IX, 544.

11. See Note 10 in Chapter V.

12. Pierre Bayle, *Oeuvres diverses* (The Hague, 1737), III, 361. (Quoted by Morize, *op. cit.*, 67.) Bernard de Mandeville, *Fable of the Bees*, was first published in 1705, and Jean-François Melon, *Essai politique sur le commerce*, in 1734.

13. *De la législation*, Première partie, 13. Since there is no modern edition of Mably's works, references to the excerpts given here will be to the first edition of 1776. The excerpts have been translated by Miss Margaret Munsterberg. Adams's notes in this volume are written in pencil, and many of them are blurred and difficult to read.

14. *De la législation*, Première partie, 64.

15. *Ibid.*, 122.

16. *Ibid.*, 129.

17. Refers to the bribery charges current during the French Revolution.

William Cobbett (writing under the pseudonym of Peter Porcupine) stated: "The Mother Club in America met at Philadelphia on the 3rd of July, 1793, about six or seven weeks after Genêt's arrival in the city, during which space . . . more than *twenty thousand* Louis d'ors had been distributed." He also quoted from one of Fauchet's letters: "Two or three days before the proclamation [against the Whisky Rebellion] was published, and of course before the cabinet has resolved on its measures, Mr. Randolph came to see me with an air of eagerness, and made to me the overtures, of which I have given you an account in my No. 6. Thus, with some thousands of dollars, the Republic could have decided on civil war or peace! Thus the consciences of the pretended patriots of America have already their prices! . . ." ("History of the American Jacobins" in William Playfair, *The History of Jacobinism*, Philadelphia, 1796, II, 18, 35.) Adams had a copy of Cobbett's pamphlet, and he repeated many names and dates on the margins.

As is well known, Edmund Randolph, Jefferson's successor as Secretary of State, resigned on August 19, 1795, when Washington confronted him with Fauchet's dispatch which the English had intercepted. In spite of his *Vindication*, which included a certificate by Fauchet exonerating him, Randolph's conduct has been considered suspicious by most historians. In a paper entitled "Edmund Randolph, Not Guilty!" published in the April 1950 issue of *The William and Mary Quarterly* (Third Series, Vol. VII, No. 2, 179–198) Irving Brant examines the case anew.

18. *De la législation*, I, 143.

19. *Ibid.*, 194.

20. The new constitution of Sweden, which curbed the power of the nobility, was promulgated by Gustavus III in 1772. It proved very popular; and Mably's work reflects his optimism over the liberal reforms. However, the King, one of the great enlightened monarchs of the century, was murdered in 1792, and during his successor's reign both the domestic and foreign affairs of the country fell into chaos.

21. A reference to Article XXIV of the Treaty, insuring the humane treatment of prisoners of war. *Diplomatic Correspondence*, Second Series, II, 230–231.

22. *De la législation*, I, 237.

23. *Ibid.*, 261.

24. *Op. cit.*, Deuxième partie, 8.

25. In his early twenties, Gustavus Vasa was the leader of the Swedes' war of liberation against the Danes. The revolt started among the peasants of Dalicarlia, a west midland region of Sweden. In 1523 Gustavus was crowned King. During his long and memorable reign Sweden was converted to Lutheranism.

26. *De la législation*, Deuxième partie, 138.

27. It would be a mistake to conclude from Adams's comment that the Abbé had become a voluptuary in his old age. His *Principes de morale*, published in 1784 and written probably ten years earlier, exalts virtue even more than his other works (if that is possible). The nearest Mably came to license in it was his denial of Malebranche's doctrine that "all dispositions to love corrupt the soul and deserve God's hatred if their object is anyone

but God." To be sure, he speaks of the *châleur de sang* of adolescence, but only to advise young people how to direct their energies toward study. Indeed, the book preaches an austere self-control: "If one can escape the seductions of love," Mably writes, "one can escape also those of avarice and ambition."

28. "Rohilla" is the name of an Afghan tribe, the word meaning "mountaineers." One of the charges which Burke raised against Warren Hastings was that he had entered into an engagement with the Nabob of Oude for "extirpating the nation of the Rohillas." Adams probably remembered the word from Hastings's trial.

[VIII]
Turgot's Attack on the American Constitutions

1. Adams's *Works*, III, 122. The duchess was the widow of Nicolas de la Rochefoucauld, duc d'Enville, who in 1745 led the ill-fated expedition against Annapolis. Her palace in Paris and her country home at Roche-Guyon were centers for the radical intellectuals. Her son Louis-Alexandre, duc de la Rochefoucauld, early distinguished himself by his interest in reform. An earnest patriot, he took an active part in the Revolution, but by the summer of 1792 was sharply opposed to the Jacobins. On September 14 of that year he was stoned to death by a mob at Gisors, in the presence of his mother and wife.

2. The Comte de Vergennes, Minister of Foreign Affairs, must have encouraged the enterprise, for the royal censor, Jean-Baptiste Robinet, was one of the editors. However, secrecy had to be maintained; no editor's name was given, and the fictitious imprint "À Anvers" was used. (For a bibliography of the periodical, compiled by Paul Leicester Ford, see the July 1889 issue of *The Pennsylvania Magazine of History and Biography*.) Adams, too, supplied later information and wrote anonymous articles for the *Affaires*. (VII, 60.) He was a diligent reader of the magazine; whenever he saw his name mentioned, he copied it on the margin.

3. The first edition appeared with a fictitious Philadelphia imprint. (Adams had no less than five copies.) The compiler was supposed to have been Claude-Ambroise Régnier, a lawyer from Nancy, who became Minister of Justice and Duc de Marsa under Napoleon. Gilbert Chinard, however, found a letter in which the compiler signed himself as "Directeur des Hopitaux Militaires rue des Francs Bourgeois," which disproves the earlier identification. (*Year Book of the American Philosophical Society*, Philadelphia, 1943, 96.)

4. Lewis Rosenthal, *America and France* (New York, 1882), 67–68.

5. See Chapter II.

6. The physiocrats regarded agriculture as the sole source of wealth, and thought that any other kind of work was unproductive. Quesnay's *Tableau économique*, printed in 1758, was the manifesto of the group. Turgot's chief contribution to political economy was the *Réflexions sur la formation des richesses*, published in 1765.

7. Alphonse Jobez, *La France sous Louis XVI* (Paris, 1871), I, 337.

8. In the Parliament the King seated himself on a throne when wishing to make a proclamation which he regarded as final.

9. Épître CIX, *Oeuvres complètes* ([Kehl], 1784), XIII, 283.

10. In the same year, the book was reissued in Boston, and in the next in New Haven, Trenton, and Philadelphia. Within a few months, Mirabeau issued a French translation of Dr. Price's essay, together with Turgot's letter and a pamphlet of his own. "What is suitable for England, is not for you," the orator harangued the American republics. "No balance of powers, no complicated constitutions! Are your governors, who are removable, kings? Are your executive councils so many houses of lords? Do you, can you, have a representation other than the assemblies of citizens who are equal by nature and law?"

11. In September 1783 Adams moved to Auteuil, where in the following August his wife and daughter joined him. "Distant from the putrid streets of Paris," he enjoyed the place.

12. VIII, 232.

13. On board the *Sensible*, on his return trip to America after his first stay in France, Adams had many conversations with Barbé-Marbois, the secretary of the French mission to Philadelphia. Turgot figured prominently in their talks. "I said," Adams noted in his Diary, "that I had the pleasure to dine often with M. Turgot at his house and at ours; that Mr. Franklin was very intimate with M. Turgot, who I thought was a very good man." Marbois judged the fallen minister "a little too systematical, and a little too enthusiastical." Adams defended him by insisting that "enthusiasm was sometimes a very good quality, at least very useful." Marbois, however, remained convinced that enthusiasm would not do "when opposed by millions of people of great weight," and Adams thought that the agent was "one of the best informed and most reflecting men" he had known in France. (III, 216.) A few years later he had good reason to revise his opinion about Marbois.

14. Correa M. Walsh, *The Political Science of John Adams*, 14.

15. *Catalogue of Books, Tracts, Autographs of the Late Mr. E. B. Corwin Which Will Be Sold at Auction Commencing November 10, 1856.* Price's *Importance of the American Revolution* (London, 1785), bound together with his *Essay on the Population of England*, was no. 3607. The authenticity of Adams's notes was attested by Joseph Sabin, editor of the *Bibliotheca Americana* who compiled the Corwin catalogue, and also by contemporary notes in the volume itself. The volume is now in the Boston Athenaeum.

16. Price, *Additional Observations on Civil Liberty* (London, 1777), 151. In a letter, Condorcet expressed Turgot's difficulties in a different way: "Vous n'êtes point du tout *charlatan* et c'est un defaut, vu ce qu'on est à Paris ou à Versailles!" *Correspondance de Condorcet et de Turgot*, edited by Charles Henry (Paris, 1892), 250.

17. The excerpts from Turgot's letter are given in the translation published by Dr. Price. Page references are to both Dr. Price's pamphlet and Gustave Schelle's definitive *Oeuvres de Turgot* (Paris, 1913-23), in five volumes. (*Observations*, 108; *Oeuvres*, V, 533.)

18. Adam Smith, then tutor of the young Duke of Buccleugh, spent the

better part of 1766 in Paris, where he frequented the society of Quesnay, Turgot, Helvetius, Morellet, and others. "Turgot thought very highly of his talents," Morellet wrote. "We discussed the theory of commerce, banking, public credit, and many points of his great work, the *Wealth of Nations*, which he was meditating." (*Oeuvres de Turgot*, I, 32.) Smith agrees in most fundamentals with the physiocrats; and Turgot's *Réflexions* left its imprint on his work. Josiah Tucker, Dean of Gloucester (1712–1799), was held in great esteem by the French economists. Turgot translated into French two of his books—his *Reflections on the Naturalization of Foreign Protestants*, in 1755, and *The Case of Going to War for the Sake of Trade*. The latter, entitled *Guerres de commerce*, remained unpublished and the manuscript is lost.

19. The allusion is to Edmund Burke's *Letter to the Sherrifs of Bristol*, 1777, a criticism of the British government's war measures against America. In spite of its good intentions, the *Letter* made a scornful reference to "certain recent discussions" of liberty, evidently Dr. Price's *Observations on the Nature of Civil Liberty*, 1777. "There are people," Burke wrote, "who have split and anatomized the doctrine of free government, as if it were an abstract question concerning metaphysical liberty and necessity . . ." (P. 188.) Here is the phrase to which Turgot took exception. He must have read the French translation of Burke's *Letter* which appeared in the *Affaires de l'Angleterre et de l'Amérique*. (Nos. XXII, 81–89, XXIII, 131–156.)

20. Turgot was evidently thinking of the inviolability of natural rights. However, in the section of his *Defence* devoted to Dr. Price, Adams gave a new twist to Turgot's idea, using it as an argument against the infallibility of majority rule. "I shall cheerfully agree with M. Turgot," he wrote, "that it is very possible that laws, and even equal laws, made by common consent, may deprive the minority of the citizens of their rights . . . To take in M. Turgot's idea, then, we must add to Dr. Price's ideas of *equal laws* by *common consent*, this other—for the *general'interest* or the *public good*." (IV, 402.)

21. The baccalaureate oration of the young Turgot (the Abbé de l'Aulne, as he was then known), *Tableau philosophique des progrès successifs de l'esprit humain*, which is regarded as the first formulation of the doctrine of progress, contains a prediction of the American Revolution: "The Colonies are like fruit which cling to the tree until they are ripe; becoming self-sufficient, they do what Carthage did and what America will do some day." (*Oeuvres*, I, 222.)

22. The Constitution of Pennsylvania established a single assembly and an executive council of twelve, and abolished the office of governor. The Constitution of South Carolina established a general assembly and a legislative council. In his copy of the *Recueil* Adams compared the preambles of the Constitutions of Virginia and Pennsylvania, noting the similarity or identity of the articles. Finally he wrote on a blank leaf:

"The following Constitution of Pennsylvania was well known by such as were in the secret to have been principally prepared by Timothy Matlack, James Cameron, Thomas Paine, and Thomas Young, all ingenious men, but none of them deeply read in the science of legislation. The Bill of Rights is taken almost verbatim from that of Virginia which was made and published before the other was begun, as may be seen by a comparison of the two and their dates. The frame of government is the worst that has been established in America, and will be found so in experience. It has weakened that state, divided it, and by that means embarrassed and obstructed the American cause more than any other thing."

The second Constitution of Pennsylvania, adopted in 1790, introduced the bicameral system, restored the office of governor, and abolished the executive council. The second Constitution of South Carolina, of 1778, divided the general assembly into two distinct bodies, a senate and a house of representatives.

23. It was the Constitution of Delaware which demanded such an oath. New Jersey proclaimed that "all persons, professing a belief in the faith of any Protestant sect . . . shall be capable of being elected into any office of profit or trust."

24. Adams was not responsible for the third article of the Massachusetts Declaration of Rights, which, by compulsory taxation, provided only "for the support and maintenance of public Protestant teachers of piety, religion, and morality," giving equal protection of the law to "every denomination of Christians." This article was prepared by a special committee, after Adams's draft had been rejected. At the Convention of 1820, Adams proposed that "all men of all religions" be substituted for "men of every denomination of Christians," but in vain. The state support from the churches was finally withdrawn and the protection of the law extended to "all religious sects and denominations" by the 11th Amendment adopted in 1833. (IV, 221–224; Samuel E. Morison, *A History of the Constitution of Massachusetts*, Boston, 1917, 23–24, 32, 38.)

25. *Oeuvres*, IV, 568–628.

26. Condorcet, *op. cit.*, 137–151. An edition of Turgot's *Mémoire sur les municipalités* was prepared by Du Pont de Nemours for the Assembly of Notables in 1787 (*Oeuvres*, IV, 570); thus by the time of writing his *Defence*, Adams *may* have read about Turgot's plan. (Cf. C. M. Walsh, *op. cit.*, 14–15.)

27. Under the date of January 7, 1777 (erroneously printed 1776).

28. In no. XVII, under the date of February 24, 1777.

29. "The 'Lettres d'un Banquier,'" Paul Leicester Ford says, "were written, so I have seen stated, by Dr. Edward Bancroft." (*Pennsylvania Magazine*, 1889, 222.) However, Professor Chinard, in a letter to the present writer, doubts the correctness of the statement. "The Banquier," he writes, "is in my opinion an entirely fictitious person, or rather a composite person. That Bancroft contributed something is very likely, but so did many others, possibly Benjamin Vaughan among them. The letters of the Banquier include a great deal of the correspondence received from various sources by the man who subscribed himself 'the writer of the *Affaires de l'Angleterre et de l'Amérique*' and who was simply Genet, Sr."

Bancroft's contributions to the *Affaires*, if they really existed, were only part of his many-sided activities. A native of Westfield, Massachusetts, he served as Secretary to the American Commissioners in Paris, living in Franklin's house—and also was a British spy. Besides his frequent trips to London, he had an ingenious way of supplying information to the British. He placed his letters, written in invisible ink, in a sealed bottle which he deposited in a hollow tree near the Tuileries, to be collected there every Tuesday evening by a messenger, who in turn left another bottle with instructions for him. In 1784 Bancroft made a proposal to the British Cabinet for the "recovery of the sovereignty of the new United States." He died, as a respected scientist, in 1821. His treachery was not discovered until some seventy years later. (Samuel F. Bemis, "British Secret Service and the French-American Alliance" in *The American Historical Review*, 1923–24, 474–495.)

30. The *first* draft of a Confederacy, or "League of Friendship," was presented by Franklin to Congress on July 21, 1775. This was shelved, and it was only a year later that Congress appointed a committee to prepare a *second* draft, which was submitted, in the handwriting of John Dickinson of Pennsylvania, on July 12, 1776. Yielding to the demand of the small states, it recommended a system in which each state had one vote, instead of the proportional representation suggested by Franklin. But even this draft appeared to some members as one which invested Congress with too strong a power, and on August 20 a *third* draft was substituted. In the fall of 1777 an agreement was reached, and the Articles passed Congress on November 15.

31. The error of the *Affaires* is remarkable, considering the magazine's connection with Franklin, who had received a copy of the draft on August 20 while still in America. It was retained in the *Recueil*, published many months after the Articles of Confederation had been adopted.

32. Evidently Turgot regarded the union of Canada with the United States as inevitable. To be sure, the Articles of Confederation left the door open for Canada.

33. The formation of the Society of the Cincinnati in 1783 was received with alarm by the people and by many leading statesmen. Aedanus Burke, one of the associate judges of South Carolina, published a pamphlet to prove that the Society "creates a race of hereditary patricians." His work was reprinted in every state (and was translated by Mirabeau into French). Many lampoons and broadsides denounced the Society in violent terms. Franklin ridiculed it as an attempt to set up an "hereditary knighthood," Samuel Adams saw in it a stride toward an "hereditary military nobility," and John Adams condemned it as "an order of chivalry," as "the first step taken to deface the beauty of our temple of liberty." He replied tartly to Lafayette, who, as one of the members, tried to explain their purposes to him: "It is against our confederation, and against the constitutions of several States . . . It is against the spirit of our governments and the genius of our people."

Later, however, his opinion changed. In the third volume of his *Defence*, he criticized the Society solely on the ground that it was established without consulting the people. "If these gentlemen had been of opinion that titles and ribbons were necessary in society," he thought by then, "they should have taken measures for calling conventions of the people, where it should have been determined, first, whether any such distinctions should be introduced; secondly, how many such orders; thirdly, what number of individuals of each; and, lastly, there should have been in convention a general election of noblemen for each of the thirteen states." (IX, 524; VIII, 192; V, 489.)

It may not be irrelevant to note here that Colonel William Stephens Smith, Secretary of the American Legation in London, who in June 1786 married John Adams's daughter Abigail, was one of the founders of the Society of the Cincinnati, later serving three terms as its president. He was a great admirer of Baron Friedrich Wilhelm Steuben; his eldest son was named after the General, and the second after John Adams. In his letter of November 11, 1788, Adams assured his daughter that he was "completely initiated into the order of Cincinnatus, without any vote of the Society."

34. *Observations*, 122; *Oeuvres*, V, 538.

35. Excerpts were first printed in Jean-Louis Favier's *Politique de tous les cabinets de l'Europe* (II, 394–420), published in 1793.

36. *Oeuvres*, V, 390, 406.

37. I, 306.

38. *Oeuvres*, V, 510–519.

39. Du Pont de Nemours, *Oeuvres de M. Turgot* (Paris, 1809–11), I, 415. In 1798 Du Pont wished to come to America, hoping to found "an agricultural and commercial establishment" in Western Virginia. His request for a passport was, however, refused. "I shall not be guilty of so much affectation of regard to science," President Adams wrote to Secretary of State Pickering, "as to be very willing to grant passports to Du Pont de Nemours or any other French philosophers, in the present situation of our country. We have had too many French philosophers already, and I really begin to think, or rather to suspect, that learned academies, not under the immediate inspection and control of government, have disorganized the world, and are incompatible with social order." (VIII, 596.) It was only a year later that the author of the *Philosophie de l'univers* could sail for America. His plan for the colony failed, and within two years he returned to France. In 1815 he came to America again, and here he died in 1817. His sons founded the ammunition factory at Wilmington, Delaware—an institution of truly universal design.

40. General Lincoln's surrender at Charleston on May 12, 1780, particularly depressed him. "What is one to think," he asked Du Pont, "of these Americans who allowed themselves to be captured with 16,000 men, 400 pieces of cannon, good fortifications, and a promontory defended by a dozen bastions which let pass under their guns a fleet with its arms in the holds of the ships? And these people claim the honor of defending liberty!" (*Oeuvres*, V, 627.) The news of the defeat, as it reached Paris, was of course exaggerated. The army which capitulated to Clinton consisted of 2,000 Continentals and 2,000 militiamen.

41. William Morgan, *Memoirs of the Life of the Rev. Richard Price* (London, 1815), 73–74.

[IX]

The Composition of Adams's Defence

1. Chapter III, p. 46.

2. Adams's *Works*, IV, 342. (Charles Francis Adams transposed the paragraph, in the form of a footnote, to the section on St. Gall.)

3. IV, 318–319.

4. IV, 339.

5. IV, 322.

6. IV, 371.

7. Of King Stanislaus's book he writes: "It would be a pleasure to translate the whole; but it is too long . . ." (IV, 373.)

8. It is surprising that Adams did not include any selection from Aristotle, who regarded the compounding of power as an indispensable safeguard of the stability of the state. Perhaps he thought that the writings of Machiavelli and Montesquieu embodied the teachings of the *Politics*. In any case, he quoted Aristotle only once, and then to censure him for excluding the farmers, artisans, and merchants from the ranks of citizenry. His notes in the English translation of the *Politics*, published by William Ellis in 1776 under the title *A Treatise on Government*, show that he read the volume carefully. On the margin of the pages in which Aristotle tries to justify slavery, he wrote:

"It must be granted that the ideas of nobility among the Greeks were more ingenious and consistent than those of the modern nations. When the ancients worshipped Venus in her temples according to their religion established, they reasoned justly when they concluded that all the families among them who were descended by natural generation from that Goddess were entitled to more respect than the rest. It was natural to believe that she would be pleased to see something like adoration paid to her posterity, tho' mortal. No wonder then that all the descendants of Anhisis by this Goddess were respected, and so many of them at last deified among the Romans. Hercules, too, as the son of Jupiter and Alcmena, must have left a divine posterity. This nobility was indeed iure divino."

9. IV, 569.

10. IV, 572. The French translator gives only a brief *résumé* of this section, wryly remarking that "a large number of our readers, although perhaps wrongly, would be little inclined to recognize Homer's authority in politics." (*Défense des constitutions américaines*, Paris, 1792, I, 356.)

11. IV, 521.

12. V, 11.

13. V, 22.

14. *The Works of Nicholas Machiavel* (London, 1763), I, 107.

15. V, 107.

16. V, 9, 206.

17. V, 332.

18. IV, 275.

19. V, 45, 112, 121.

20. V, 288–289, 322.

21. V, 426.

22. V, 489.

23. *Défense*, II, 1–3. Charles Francis Adams merely states that the Italian history was omitted "on the ground of the facility had by Europeans of access to the original authorities." (IV, 276.) He also made some slighting remarks about the translator, the jurist Delacroix.

24. August 25, 1787, VIII, 448.

25. One should note that when the first volume of the *Defence* was published in February 1787 Adams had no intention of continuing the work, and yet by August of the same year the second volume had appeared in print. His main part in the preparation of these translations, the present writer believes, may have consisted only in the occasional deletion and summarizing of sentences. The location of the corresponding passages in the Italian is made difficult by Adams's habit of starting and finishing his paragraphs in an arbitrary manner: often he sets off a block of straight translation with a phrase of his own, or cuts it short by omitting the last line. One should also note that for the *Davila* translation, which was much shorter, Adams had a full year, working in a more familiar language.

26. Charles Francis Adams thought it "not improbable" that the volume occasioned Adams's review. (VI, 6.) The book contains a few marginal notes.

27. IV, 194.

28. VI, 6. Turgot was in correspondence with John Tuberville Needham (1713–1781), the Catholic divine and scientist, but there is no evidence that he ever heard of Marchamont Nedham.

29. He includes many quotations from Livy. These passages in Latin are impressive, yet they would have served just as well in English, as many actually did in *The Universal History*.

30. VI, 45–46, 90, 109.

31. VI, 155, 193.

32. VI, 171.

33. Anthony à Wood, *Athenae Oxonienses*. III (London, 1817), 1183.

34. David Masson, *The Life of John Milton* (London, 1877), IV, 334. In an article "Milton, Needham, and *Mercurius Politicus*," in the April 1936 issue of *Studies in Philology*, J. Milton French has called attention to the fact that the first half of the series of editorials was largely a reprint of *The Case of the Commonwealth of England Stated . . . with a Discourse of the Excellencie of a Free-State above a Kingly Government*, a book published under Nedham's own name in 1649 and republished in 1650; and he has suggested that if Nedham was able to write these papers, he could also have written those included in *The Excellencie of a Free State* of 1656. There is however, a chance that Milton had collaborated with Nedham on his first book, too. "Many of these articles," Mr. French writes, "are rich in examples from the history of many European nations, which we know Milton had studied exhaustively ten years or so before, and which he had been working over shortly before in connection with his *History of Britain*." *The Excellencie of a Free State* is not only "rich in examples," but the examples are its very essence; and if these had originated with Milton, he must have had a considerable share in the work.

35. VI, 217.

36. May 20, 1789, IX, 558–559.

37. He wrote to Dr. Rush: "I know not whether you have ever seen a boudoir. I never heard of one in Great Britain or America. I had two of them in my house at Auteuil, which was nothing less than the magnificent Hôtel de Rohan. A boudoir is a pouting room. The idea is, when the lady has the vapors, and is a little out of health or humor, she may retire to a bath

in the center of this apartment and contemplate her own face and figure in every possible direction and position, till the sight of her own irresistible charms shall restore her good opinion of herself, and her usual gaiety and good humor. The room is an octagon. Eight entire and immaculate French mirrors extending from the floor to the ceiling compose the eight sides. The ceiling too is one entire mirror. So that the lady cannot turn to any point of the compass without seeing herself multiplied an hundred times, indeed ad infinitum. My boudoir is such a room; in which our dear United States may contemplate themselves and see their own defects as well as beauties. I hope it will never be used to teach wanton experiments, as it is easy to see the ladies' bathing room may be . . ." (June 12, 1812, *Old Family Letters*, 394–395.)

[X]

Lessons from the Civil Wars of France

1. Davila was born at Padua in 1576, and was named Enrico Caterino in honor of Henri III and Catherine de Medici, in whose court his elder brothers served. As a boy of seven he was taken to France, and after a few years of schooling became a page to Catherine. In his youth he joined the French army and fought in many of the battles of Henri IV. Soon he conceived the idea of writing a history of the civil wars. Some of it, he states, he wrote as an eyewitness; in addition, he visited battlefields and interviewed people who had taken part in the events. After the restoration of peace he returned to Italy and, although not yet twenty-five, became commander of the forces of the Venetian Republic. For years he served as captain of various fortresses in Lombardy and later as governor of Zara in Dalmatia, meanwhile working steadily on his book. Without much hope of its success, the Venetian printer Thomas Beglione published the *Historia* in 1630. A few months later Davila was killed by a ruffian at Brescia.

2. In preparing his *Discourses*, Adams made many marginal notes in his copy of the *Histoire des guerres civiles de France*. First of all, he copied out the names of the *dramatis personae* in the order of their appearance. His *Discourses on Davila* cover only the first five books of Davila's *Histoire*; yet his comments were far more numerous in the next five. What rich material there would have been for another series of articles! All these notes are omitted from the present volume.

3. Etienne de la Boëtie (1530–1563) was one of the noblest figures of the French Renaissance. How is it possible, he asks in his *Servitude volontaire* (later called *Contr'un*), that millions of people subject themselves to a single individual, often to a completely worthless one? "I firmly believe," he writes, "that there is nothing more contrary to God than tyranny, and that He reserves some special punishment for tyrants and their accomplices." The treatise became especially influential during the civil wars; forgotten in the seventeenth century, it was read again with enthusiasm in the eighteenth.

One should note here that on April 30, 1791, following the last article of the *Discourses on Davila*, the *Gazette of the United States* began the publication of *A Discourse of Stephen Boethius*, "Concerning Voluntary Servitude: Or the Anti-One," as translated for the paper. Eight installments appeared, the last in the issue for July 9, 1791, reproducing the treatise up to about the middle. There the series abruptly broke off. The translator's name is not given; it seems, however, certain that he was none other than John Adams. In fact, at the end of the *Discourses on Davila* he himself had announced the translation.

4. The Adams-Jefferson controversy became embittered by the publication of the articles of Publicola in the Boston *Columbian Centinel*, the first appearing on June 8, 1791, and ten more following. They took Jefferson to task for his charge of "political heresies" and trenchantly criticized Thomas Paine's *Rights of Man*, finding its praise of the French Revolution "as undistinguishing as was the censure of Mr. Burke." The articles, at first attributed to John Adams but actually written by John Quincy Adams, provoked rough answers from "Brutus," "Agricola," "The Ploughman," and others. Jefferson, fearful of the effect which his letter to the American publisher of the *Rights of Man* (see Chapter I, p. 7) may have produced on Adams, apologized to him, declaring "in the presence of the Almighty" that nothing was further from his intention than to have their political differences brought before the public. (Jefferson's *Works*, VI, 298, 284.) Adams was pleased. "The friendship," he replied, "that has subsisted for fifteen years without the smallest interruption, and, until this occasion without the slightest suspicion, ever has been and still is very dear to my heart." Nevertheless, he rehearsed all the trouble which Jefferson's recommendation of Paine's pamphlet had caused him. "The question everywhere was," he wrote, "what heresies are intended by the Secretary of State? The answer in the newspapers was, 'The Vice-President's notions of a limited monarchy, an hereditary government of King and Lords, with only elective Commons.'" (VIII, 508–509.)

Jefferson's defense took a curious turn. Answering Adams on August 20, he asserted that his note to the printer "really had no effect" and that if Publicola had not attacked Paine's principles "not a word on the subject would ever have been said." And then he penned this painful denial: "Indeed, it was impossible that my note should occasion your name to be brought into question; for, so far from naming you, I had not even in view any writing which I might suppose to be yours . . ." (*Works*, VI, 315.) What had prompted him to contradict so flagrantly his letters to Washington, Madison, and Paine when at the same time he did not hesitate to affirm to Adams that "Paine's principles were the principles of the citizens of the United States"? The reason must be sought in the delicate relationship—friendship without intimacy—which existed between the two men. By his disclaimer Jefferson evidently wanted to spare Adams's feelings. (See also Chapter III, 39.)

5. It is worth noting that the last installment of the *Discourses*, which had perhaps given the greatest offense, was not included in the volume. A mild postscript was added instead—a final exhortation that unless balance is preserved liberty will be lost forever.

6. I, 454.

7. VI, 232.

8. Rereading his volume, Adams noticed the slip: "How it happened I know not; but this first Number ought to have been succeeded by the fourth," he wrote on the margin. In editing the *Works*, Charles Francis Adams corrected the mistake.

9. VI, 393.

10. Yet Adams took some liberties with the text. For example: "People say," Davila writes, "that in the last years of his life this monarch [François I] recommended to Prince Henri, his son, to distrust the excessive power of his subjects." After the word "monarch" Adams inserted: "If we may call by that name a prince who was, in effect, nothing more than the first individual in a miserable oligarchy"—a statement which Davila would never have made.

11. See Chapter III, p. 47.

12. *The Works of Adam Smith* (London, 1812), I, 81, 82, 95; Adams's *Works*, VI, 237, 239, 234.

13. He appended in his copy the names "Young," "Shakespear," "Johnson," etc., without, however, mentioning the works themselves.

14. It should be noted that in reprinting the *Discourses on Davila*, C. F. Adams inserted these marginal notes—or rather, "such of them as are in any way interesting." However, he left out some very interesting ones, notably those which refer to the American scene. Besides, some of the notes are linked to wrong passages in the reprint, so that their meaning is lost.

15. No page references will be given to the first edition of the *Discourses on Davila*, since the volume is now very rare.

16. The review appeared in the April 1805 issue of the *Monthly Anthology* of Boston. It was seven pages long, two columns to a page. The writer, Arthur Maynard Walter (1780–1807), like most of his associates, was really a young man—twenty-five. To be sure, he argued with "the great author of the *Discourses*" on several points, the origin of the Salic laws being only one. At the end he criticized the style as "rough and unpolished." Anger at the review did not prevent Adams from submitting an article to the *Monthly Anthology*. (See Chapter III, note 74.)

17. A reference to the speech of Logan, a Mingo chief, as given by Thomas Jefferson in his *Notes on the State of Virginia* (Richmond, 1853), 67–69. The authenticity of the account is discussed *ibid.*, 240–269.

18. VI, 272. See Chapter III, p. 39.

19. This is a mistake. James Otis, as chairman of the meeting of November 20, 1772, read the pamphlet aloud; but everybody knew that Otis, declared *non compos mentis* the year before, was by then an ill and broken man. The first and most important part of the pamphlet on the Rights of the Colonies was written by Samuel Adams; and the second and third parts, on the violations of these rights and a solicitation of the support of other towns, were by Joseph Warren and Benjamin Church respectively.

Ten years later John Adams repeated the error. Remembering the circumstances of the writing of the Declaration of Independence, he wrote to Timothy Pickering: ". . . the essence of it is contained in a pamphlet, voted and printed by the town of Boston, before the first Congress met, composed by James Otis, as I suppose, in one of his lucid intervals, and pruned and polished by Samuel Adams." (II, 514.) The statement, made public by Pickering on July 4, 1823, caused a good deal of confusion. Jefferson accepted the allegation that Otis wrote the pamphlet (Jefferson to Madison, August 30, 1823). Today, however, Samuel Adams's authorship of the "Rights of the Colonies" is firmly established, since a complete draft in his handwriting has been discovered among the Committee of Correspondence Papers, now in the New York Public Library.

20. In his Autobiography, written in 1805, Adams records that he was appointed a member of the subcommittee "in which a set of articles were drawn and debated one by one." After several days of deliberation, they agreed upon all the articles except the one defining the authority of Parliament "which was indeed the essence of the whole controversy." Adams took a sheet and drew up the article—the fourth—which was accepted. (II, 374–375.) It should be noted, however, that Adams's Diary makes no mention of these proceedings in Congress; and that, according to C. F. Adams, there is among the papers of John Adams "in handwriting somewhat resembling that of Major Sullivan [the New Hampshire delegate] a draft of the articles as they were first submitted to the committee." (II, 375–377, 535–542.)

21. An allusion to Jean François de la Harpe's *De la guerre déclarée par nos derniers tyrans à la raison, à la morale, aux lettres et aux arts,* published in 1796. La Harpe, a disciple of Voltaire, hailed the Revolution with enthusiasm, but during his imprisonment at the time of the Terror he became a fervent Catholic and Loyalist.

22. Alexander McGillivray, the half-breed chief of the Creek Indians, opposed the Americans during the Revolution, and, supported by both Spain and England, tried afterwards to establish a confederation of the Southern Indians. Washington, soon after his election to the Presidency, prevailed upon him to come to New York. On August 7, 1790, a treaty was concluded which settled the Creek boundary and trade, and granted McGillivray the rank of brigadier general with a yearly pension of twelve hundred dollars. Returning home, however, McGillivray found the Indians dissatisfied, and when the Spanish offered him a pension of thirty-five hundred dollars he repudiated the treaty of New York. He died in 1793, at the age of thirty-four.

23. An examination of the 1805–07 issues of the *Gentleman's Magazine, Monthly Review, Monthly Repository, Universal Magazine, European Magazine,* and a number of lesser known English periodicals has failed to discover the "silly review" which provoked Adams's protest.

24. Michel (Miguel) Servetus was burnt alive at Champel, a suburb of Geneva, for his "heretical" views, on October 27, 1553. Inclined toward Arianism, he denied the dogma of the Trinity and the eternity of the Son. His chief accuser was Calvin.

25. In his *Life of Oliver Ellsworth* (New York, 1905), 183, William Garrott Brown calls Adams's note "curious," considering the fact that Ellsworth, like Adams himself, took a very conservative view of the French Revolution. Maclay's Journal does not mention the incident.

26. Daniel 3: 8–30.

27. With the exception of Johnson's romance, these are all novels by Voltaire.

28. From the first satire of Horace (which reads "ridentem" instead of "ridendo")—"What is to prevent one from telling the truth laughingly?"

[XI]

The French Revolution

1. *On the Love of Our Country* (London, 1790), 23, 49.
2. *A Vindication of the Rights of Men* (London, 1790), 102–103.
3. *A Vindication of the Rights of Woman* (London, 1792), 342, 7.
4. The *Rights of Woman* must have been on the press when the *Projets de décrets sur l'instruction publique*, together with Talleyrand's *Rapport sur l'instruction publique*, appeared in Paris. This may explain why Mary Wollstonecraft discussed the educational provisions of the new French constitution in a preface rather than in the body of her work. The bill allows girls to attend primary schools until their eighth year, but provides only for the establishment of institutions where they may learn some handiwork "suitable to their sex." Talleyrand's report, after stating it as a self-evident principle that education must be made equally available for both sexes, goes on to say that "for the sake of the common happiness, and particularly that of women, the latter should not aspire at all to exercise their political rights and functions."
5. *The Letters of Horace Walpole* (London, 1859), IX, 385.
6. Letter of December 26, 1792. Kegan Paul, *William Godwin: His Friends and Contemporaries* (London, 1876), I, 210.
7. Ralph Leslie Rusk, "The Adventures of Gilbert Imlay," in *Indiana University Studies* (March 1923).
8. Paul, *Godwin*, I, 218.
9. Letter of July 8, 1794. William Godwin, *Memoirs* (first published in 1798), reprinted by W. Clark Durant in 1927. P. 263. References will be to this edition.
10. Thomas Hardy (1752–1832) was one of the founders of the London Corresponding Society, the aim of which was to promote parliamentary reform. Horne Tooke (1736–1812) and Thomas Holcroft (1745–1800) were active in the Constitutional Society. Both societies were sympathizers of the French Revolution. In 1794 Hardy and Tooke, with several others, were tried for high treason but were acquitted.
11. Quoted in C. B. Roylance Kent, *The English Radicals* (London, 1894), 141.
12. Letter to Hannah More, January 24, 1795; Walpole, *Letters*, IX, 452.
13. "Advertisement" to Wollstonecraft's *The French Revolution*.
14. Godwin, *Memoirs*, 100.
15. Issue for October 1797.
16. That Mary Wollstonecraft was religious is obvious from many passages of *The Rights of Woman* as well as of *The French Revolution*. "As far down as the year 1787," Godwin writes, "she regularly frequented public worship, for the most part according to the forms of the Church of England." Later, she attended some of the sermons of Dr. Price. (Godwin, *Memoirs*, 27–28.)

17. Wollstonecraft, *The French Revolution*, 15.

18. On June 7, 1778, Adams watched the King and the Queen at the grand procession of the Knights of the Blue Ribbon at Versailles. Nearly thirty years later, he added to the entry in his Diary: "She was an object too sublime and beautiful for my dull pen to describe. I leave this enterprise to Mr. Burke. But, in his description, there is more of the orator than of the philosopher." He somewhat boastfully adds that Burke probably saw the Queen only once, whereas he has seen her perhaps fifty times. (III, 172–173.)

19. The statement is from Étienne de la Boëtie's *Servitude volontaire*. (See Chapter X, p. 166, and note 3.)

20. Wollstonecraft, *The French Revolution*, 178.

21. As a member of the Committee of Public Safety, Jean-Marie Collot d'Herbois was sent in October 1793 to Lyons to punish the city for its revolt. With Fouché's help, he instituted the *fusillades*—or *mitraillades*—there, executing more than sixteen thousand people. During the Thermidorian reaction, he was first acquitted; after a second trial, however, he was deported to Cayenne, where he died in January 1796. (See also note 26.)

22. Wollstonecraft, *The French Revolution*, 232.

23. William Murray, Earl of Mansfield, was Chief Justice of England from 1756 until 1788. His interpretation of libel gave rise to some stormy debates. The occasion was the prosecution of the publisher of Junius's "Letter to the King." In trying the bookseller Almon, who pleaded that his name had been substituted on *The London Museum* by another publisher, and that copies had been sold in his shop without his knowledge, Mansfield ruled that "proof of the sale was *prima facie* sufficient and must stand till exculpated by some other evidence."

24. Jean-Sylvain Bailly, the great astronomer, was president of the National Assembly. The day after the storming of the Bastille he was made mayor of Paris by acclamation. For two years he attended to his difficult duties with enormous industry, but the "massacre" of the Champ de Mars on July 17, 1791 made him odious to the extremists. He retired to Nantes, writing his *Mémoires d'un témoin*. In May 1793 he was arrested and on November 12 was guillotined in Paris.

25. Wollstonecraft, *The French Revolution*, 245.

26. This refers to the *noyades* perpetrated by Jean-Baptiste Carrier at Nantes, the *fusillades* of Joseph Fouché (Minister of Police under Napoleon, who gave him the title of Duke of Otranto) and of Collot d'Herbois at Lyons, and the countless other atrocities carried out during the Terror. The word "Langridge"—or "Langrage" or "Langrel"—means a kind of shot formerly used in sea battles for tearing sails or rigging. It is similar to the *mitraille*, or grapeshot.

27. The Count of Artois, youngest brother of Louis XVI, was the chief of the reactionary party. In July 1789 he left France, carrying on his intrigues from various courts abroad. During the reign of his brother, Louis XVIII, he became the leader of the ultra-royalists. Succeeding to the throne in 1824 as Charles X, he set up, to quote Wellington, "a government by priests, through priests, for priests." After the revolution of 1830 he fled to England, where he died in 1836.

Victor François, Duc de Broglie, was made Marshal of France in 1759 after his victory over the Prussians at Berghen. His defeat at Wellinghausen in 1761 brought him into disgrace, but he was recalled to service by Louis XVI. Minister of War in 1789, he was violently opposed to the Revolution. At the head of an army of *émigrés*, he invaded the Champagne in 1792.

The Duchesse de Polignac, the former Gabrielle de Polastron, fled France with her husband two days after the taking of the Bastille. They went first to Switzerland, and then to Vienna, where she died in December 1793. Marie Antoinette's *vif attachement* to Madame de Polignac is discussed by all her biographers.

28. Charles Alexandre de Calonne, former intendant of Metz and Lille, was named Comptroller General in 1783. To win the support of the Queen, the Count of Artois, and the courtiers, he. allowed the squandering of enormous sums. Then, to remedy the desperate financial situation, he had the assembly of notables convoked and proposed the levying of taxes on all property. The notables were furious, and demanded the accounts of his spending. In April 1787 he was dismissed and exiled to Lorraine, from where he escaped to England. In October 1802 he returned to France, and died there in the following month.

29. See note 30 to Chapter IV.

30. Evidently neither Mary Wollstonecraft nor Adams knew that only seven prisoners (one feeble-minded) had been found in the whole fortress at the time of its capture. The garrison consisted of eighty-two *invalides* and thirty-two Swiss guards.

31. Refers to the French civil wars. The League of the Catholics, headed by the Guises, was formed to prevent the accession of Henri de Navarre to the throne. (See Chapter X.) The Fronde, a revolt against Cardinal Mazarin, lasted from 1648 till 1652.

32. Barnave (Antoine-Pierre-Joseph-Marie), a young lawyer from the Dauphiné, was one of the greatest orators of the National Assembly. In January 1792 he retired to Grenoble, but six months later, after a memorandum of his discussing measures for the stemming of the Revolution had been found in the King's cabinet, he was arrested, and in November 1793 guillotined in Paris.

33. Louis-Marie, Vicomte de Noailles, fought in the American war. His speech of August 4, 1789, led to his election to the presidency of the Assembly. Discouraged by the excesses of the Revolution, he escaped to England and finally to America. He became a general in Napoleon's army, and was killed at Havana by cannon-shot from an English corvette. The Duc d'Aiguillon served with distinction in the war against the Austrians. A letter of his addressed to Barnave, denouncing the Legislative Assembly, was intercepted and he barely had time to escape to London. The Duc de Châtelet-Lomont—the son of the Marquise du Châtelet, Voltaire's "divine Émilie"—became suspect soon. He was guillotined in December 1793.

34. Wollstonecraft, *The French Revolution*, 282.

35. The Abbé Maury, an extreme royalist, made a vow that he would "either perish in the Revolution or, fighting it, would gain the Cardinal's hat." He fled France in the fall of 1790; was named Archbishop *in partibus* in 1792; and two years later became Cardinal. In 1806 he made his peace with Napoleon, returned to Paris, and in 1810 was appointed Archbishop

of Paris. On the restoration of the Bourbons he was expelled from France, and retiring to Rome he was imprisoned there by the Pope.

Jean-Joseph Mounier proposed the oath to the third estate that they should not adjourn "until they had established the Constitution of France on a solid foundation." His motive, however, was less dramatic than is generally supposed. He made his recommendation to counteract the Abbé Sieyès's radical motion that the deputies go to Paris and there declare themselves an assembly.

36. Wollstonecraft, *The French Revolution*, 297.

37. For a discussion of Marchamont Nedham's *The Excellencie of a Free-State*, published in 1658, see Chapter IX, pp. 162–164.

38. The Marquis de Lally-Tollendal (1751–1830) voted for union with the third estate; after the October riots, however, he emigrated, returning only during the Consulate. He was the son of the Irish Jacobite Sir Gerard O'Lally, the commander of an unsuccessful French expedition to India, who was tried and executed for treason in 1766. The Marquis devoted many years to the vindication of his father's memory. It is to these activities of his that Adams refers.

39. Wollstonecraft, *The French Revolution*, 329.

40. A few pages after his paean on Marie Antoinette, Burke reminds men of learning of their debt to the nobility and the clergy: "Along with its natural protectors and guardians, learning will be cast into the mire, and trodden down under the hoofs of a swinish multitude." (*Reflections on the French Revolution*, London, 1890, 88.)

41. Wollstonecraft, *The French Revolution*, 344.

42. The final vote was taken on September 10, 1789; 849 deputies voted for a single assembly, 89 voted for two chambers, and 122 declared themselves "insufficiently informed."

43. The *Reflections on the French Revolution* found great good in the "venerable bodies" of the parliaments. "I must think," Burke wrote, "such a government well deserved to have its excellencies heightened, its faults corrected, and its capacities improved into a British constitution." (London, 1890, 145–146.)

44. Wollstonecraft, *The French Revolution*, 355.

45. Adams discusses Hume's "Idea of a Perfect Commonwealth" in his *Defence*, describing Hume's plan of representation as "an ingenious device to get rid of the people and their representatives." (IV, 466–468.) Hume's opinion of Locke appears in the last chapter of *The History of England*.

46. The Kings of France were consecrated at Rheims with the oil of the holy phial (*la sainte ampoule*), which was believed to have been brought from heaven by a dove for the baptism of Clovis, and was preserved in the abbey of St. Remi. During the Revolution the abbey was ransacked and the holy phial was broken. Only a fragment of it is preserved, in the treasury of the cathedral of Nôtre-Dame at Rheims. (Like his predecessors, Louis XVI was crowned at Rheims, in spite of opposition by Turgot who, as Comptroller General, wanted to save the expense incurred by the festivities.)

47. In February 1794 revolution broke out in Geneva, transferring much of the power of the Little Council to the General Assembly. In July the government gave way to the Revolutionary Tribunal. After the overthrow

of the Terror in Paris, the French Convention promised to respect the independence of the city. However, in 1798 Geneva was annexed to France, and became the capital of the French department of Léman. Holland was conquered by the armies of Dumouriez and Pichegru by 1795, and transformed into the Batavian Republic, in close alliance with France.

48. A bitter critic of Lord Bute's foreign policy, John Wilkes founded the magazine *The North Briton*, in which he lampooned the government. Prosecuted for seditious libel, he was committed to prison, but as a member of Parliament he had to be discharged. For two years he traveled in France and Italy, making friends with some of the *philosophes*. On his return to England, his wrangle with the government continued; elected to and expelled from Parliament, a war of pamphlets raged around him. An idol of the populace, in 1772 he was elected Lord Mayor of London.

49. Wollstonecraft, *The French Revolution*, 393.

50. *Ibid.*, 399.

51. *Ibid.*, 407.

52. An aria from Grétry's *Richard Coeur de Lion*, first presented at the Comédie-Italienne on October 21, 1784. In 1792 the opera was banned; the composer, however, was made inspector of the Conservatoire.

53. Wollstonecraft, *The French Revolution*, 472–473.

54. In 1784 Calonne began the building of a customs wall, with sixty elaborate gates, around Paris. The work, suspended for a while, was nearly finished by the time of the Revolution. The architect Le Doux also erected many monuments and rotundas, and laid out several impressive avenues.

55. In the summer of 1788 Brissot de Warville came to America. Spending a large part of his six months in Boston and the vicinity, he visited John Adams, whom he had previously met in London. "I don't know whether he has an ill opinion of our character, of our constancy, or of our understanding," he wrote later, "but he does not believe that we can establish freedom even such as the English enjoy; he does not believe that, according to our ancient States-General, we even have the right to demand that no tax should be imposed without the consent of the people." His *Nouveau voyage dans les États-Unis* was published, in three volumes, in 1791.

Editor of the *Patriote français* and a member of the Assembly, Brissot played an important part in the Revolution. He wielded a great influence especially over foreign policy, and the declarations of war against Austria and England were largely due to him. He voted for the death of the King, but on condition that the condemnation must be ratified by the people. Together with Vergniaud, the great orator, and nineteen other Girondists, he was guillotined on October 31, 1793.

56. Writing during the winter of 1793, Miss Wollstonecraft undoubtedly refers to Condorcet's educational plan, submitted to the Legislative Assembly on April 20 and 21, 1792. (See also note 4.) Condorcet's chief objective was civic education—the inculcation of republican ideals and aids for the increase of prosperity. However, by 1796, when Adams first read *The French Revolution*, Condorcet's plan, which had never become law, was discarded, and the Convention enacted an educational reform of its own. Adams, apparently, overlooked the change.

57. John Adams must have had in mind the four letters which he ex-

changed with his cousin in the fall of 1790 and which were published in pamphlet form in 1802. In one of his letters John Adams gave his interpretation of the word "republic"; he meant by it "a government in which the people have collectively, or by representation, an essential share in the sovereignty." Samuel Adams's answer was rebuking: "Is not the *whole* sovereignty, my friend, essentially in the people? . . . That the sovereignty resides in the people, is a political doctrine which I have never heard an American politician seriously deny . . . *We, the people*, is the style of the federal constitution." (VI, 415, 421.)

58. Wollstonecraft, *The French Revolution*, 494.

59. Adams also read, and here and there annotated, a number of other books on the French Revolution: William Playfair's *History of Jacobinism*, 1796, including William Cobbett's *History of the American Jacobins;* the four volumes of Necker's *De la Révolution française*, 1796; the three volumes of Christophe-Félix Montjoie's *Histoire de la conjuration de Louis-Philippe-Joseph d'Orléans*, 1796; and the four volumes of the Abbé Barruel's *Memoirs Illustrating the History of Jacobinism*, 1799. These marginal notes are omitted from the present volume.

[XII]

Condorcet and the Idea of Progress

1. Adams's *Works*, III, 137.
2. *Oeuvres de Condorcet*, edited by A. C. O'Connor (Paris, 1847–49), VIII, 13.
3. *Ibid.*, 49.
4. *Ibid.*, 94.
5. For notes on Mazzei see Chapter III, note 45.
6. See note 4 to Chapter X.
7. "Aux citoyens français sur la nouvelle constitution," June 1793. *Oeuvres*, XII, 672.
8. The best book on Condorcet's career is *Condorcet et la Révolution française* by Léon Cahen (Paris, 1904), which also contains a vast amount of biographical information.
9. *Oeuvres*, VI, 1.
10. The report was written by Pierre-Claude Daunou (1761–1840), who later became editor of the monumental *Histoire littéraire de la France*.
11. *Oeuvres*, VI, 244.
12. The belief, repeated even by J. B. Bury in *The Idea of Progress*, that Condorcet wrote his work without recourse to source material has been proved incorrect. His visitors, among them his secretary, supplied him with books. (Cahen, *Condorcet*, 528–529.)
13. Comte, *Cours de philosophie positive*, 200–201.
14. *Oeuvres*, VI, 281.
15. *Ibid.*, 273.
16. *Ibid.*, 262, 265, 236.

17. *Theory and History of Historiography*, translated by Douglas Ainslie (London, 1921), 245.

18. See Chapter I, 6–7; XIII, 262–263, and notes 9–13.

19. Letter to Samuel Perley, June 19, 1809, IX, 624.

20. April 22, 1817, X, 256.

21. Condorcet, *Outlines of an Historical View of the Progress of the Human Mind* (London, 1795), 3; *Oeuvres*, VI, 13. The page references to Condorcet's work given here are to the English translation which Adams read and to the O'Connor edition of 1847–1849. "I regret," Adams wrote to Jefferson on June 20, 1815, "that I have only an English translation of Condorcet's 'Outlines of an Historical View of the Progress of the Human Mind.'" Paul Wilstach, ed., *Correspondence of John Adams and Thomas Jefferson* (Indianapolis, 1925), 113.

22. *Outline*, 27; *Oeuvres*, VI, 30.

23. *Outline*, 53; *Oeuvres*, VI, 48–49.

24. Charles Churchill (1731–1764), the English poet and satirist, a collaborator of John Wilkes on *The North Briton*, is meant. A caricature by Hogarth depicts him as a bear hugging a pot of porter.

25. *Outline*, 71; *Oeuvres*, VI, 61.

26. *Outline*, 113; *Oeuvres*, VI, 92.

27. *Outline*, 156; *Oeuvres*, VI, 123.

28. On that day (18 Fouctidor) Bonaparte overthrew the royalist and clerical groups of the Legislative Assembly; of the Directory, Barthélemy was deported while Carnot escaped to Switzerland.

29. *Outline*, 234; *Oeuvres*, VI, 178.

30. Algernon Sidney, author of the *Discourses Concerning Government*, which vindicates the right of resistance to kingly oppression, was implicated in the so-called Rye House Plot and, charged with high treason, was beheaded on December 7, 1683.

31. John De Witt, the friend of Spinoza, was made Grand Pensionary of Holland in 1653, at the age of twenty-eight. He restored the finances of the country and conducted foreign affairs with great sagacity. After the French invasion of 1672 William III of Orange seized power, and John De Witt and his brother Cornelius were atrociously murdered by the mob.

32. *The Sophiometer, or Regulator of Mental Power* was one of the countless works of John Stewart, called the "Walking Stewart" (1749–1822). Stewart traveled on foot through Persia, Arabia, and Ethiopia and, on his return, walked through France and Spain. Twice he visited America. He lectured extensively, and was the author of an *Opus Maximum* and of such works as *The Apocalypse of Nature; The Revolution of Reason; The Conquest of the Moral World*.

33. Marcus Manilius (Manlius), of the time of Augustus and Tiberius, was the author of the *Astronomicon*, a poem in five books, written under the influence of Lucretius. But whereas Lucretius considers the universe as a work of chance, Manilius saw everywhere *ratio* in its order.

34. *Outline*, 357; *Oeuvres*, VI, 265.

35. Reading the *Lettres d'un bourgeois de New-Heaven*, Adams recorded on the flyleaf: "The following four letters were written by the Marquis of Condorcet, a man of science, but little acquainted with history; ignorant,

totally ignorant of all writings on the science of government, with very little knowledge of the human heart, and still less of the world. The letters themselves are a demonstration of all this. They are plainly written as an answer to my Defence: but it is plain that he had not read it. His enthusiasm for Turgot provoked him to write an answer to my book without reading it. It should be recollected that he has written a Life of Turgot, and that that Life is a rhetorical panegyric." The rest of Adams's marginal notes are omitted from the present volume.

[XIII]

Napoleon's Bid for a Continental Alliance

1. At this time Napoleon was, of course, still "Bonaparte." It was on May 10, 1802, that his given name was first used, and even then together with his surname. On that day the Council of State decided on the question to be put to referendum: "Is Napoleon Bonaparte to be made Consul for life?"

2. Less than two months after he ascended the throne in 1796, Paul embarked upon his patronage of the Knights of St. John—a less quixotic enterprise than it appears to most historians. The Tsar's interest in Malta was probably due not so much to a crazed infatuation with a medieval crusading Order as to a desire to obtain a foothold in the Mediterranean.

3. Artaud de Montor, *Histoire de la vie et des travaux politiques du Comte d'Hauterive*, second edition (Paris, 1839), 103.

4. The Treaty of Campo Formio, concluded on October 17, 1797, gave Venice, the whole of Venetia, Dalmatia, and Istria to Austria; in turn, the Emperor renounced all claims to the Netherland Provinces, recognized the Cisalpine Republic (formed from Lombardy), and promised to help France acquire the left bank of the Rhine. However, within a few months Austria was organizing a second coalition against France. The new war, lasting for over two years, ended with the Treaty of Lunéville, through which France acquired Belgium and Luxembourg, in addition to the left bank of the Rhine.

5. In his *Mémoires*, dictated to his secretary at St. Helena, Napoleon gave a detailed account· of the rise and fall of the Northern League, and of the relations of France with the neutral powers, including America.

6. Montor, *Hauterive*, 74.

7. Hauterive had his share in all the diplomatic affairs of the time. He did most of the groundwork for the Treaty of Amiens, with which the English "appeased" Napoleon; and he drew up the first draft of the Concordat with the Vatican, which further enhanced Napoleon's power and prestige. In 1809, upon the conclusion of the peace with Austria, the Emperor made him a Count. The Restoration caused little change in his activities; instead of preparing documents for Napoleon, he prepared them for Louis XVIII. Not until his last years could he find time for his cherished archaeological interests. Yet, as a member of the Académie des Inscriptions, he was helpful in sending Champollion to Egypt.

8. He also noted that the June 27 issue of the *Port Folio* had a review of

the book. In fact, not one but five articles appeared in the Philadelphia weekly—in the issues for June 11, July 11, 18, 25, and August 15—written by "an American resident abroad."

9. The X Y Z episode is one of the most curious incidents in American diplomatic history. The American envoys—John Marshall, Elbridge Gerry, and Charles C. Pinckney—arriving in Paris on October 4, 1797, were soon visited by three political agents who made their demands for a bribe and a loan. In their dispatches, the envoys gave their names as Bellamy, Hottinguer, and Hauteval; it was Secretary of State Pickering who substituted the letters X Y Z in his report to Congress. There was also a fourth agent, designated as W—Madame de Villette, the widow of a Royalist colonel, who "made herself particularly agreeable to the American envoys." After the publication of the intrigue and the resulting excitement in America, Talleyrand disclaimed any connection with the affair, which he represented as a hoax perpetrated upon the Americans. To Gerry, however, he acknowledged that the agents were his confidence men.

Napoleon's memoirs contain illuminating passages about the episode— the "intriguing agents" of the French ministry; the "money to be divided between the Director B[arras] and the Minister T[alleyrand]"; the effects of the defeats in Italy upon the Directory's attitude towards America; John Adams's speech in Congress; and his own order to the Army for the mourning of Washington's death. (*Mémoires*, III, 312–318.)

10. *The Public Conduct and Character of John Adams.* Aaron Burr obtained a copy and lengthy extracts were published in the Republican press. Thereupon Hamilton abandoned all pretense of secrecy and presented the copyright to John Lang, who printed three editions within a year. Another edition was issued by William Duane, editor of the Republican *Aurora.* "This pamphlet has done more mischief to the parties concerned, than all the labors of the Aurora," Duane wrote on a copy. (Paul Leicester Ford, *Bibliotheca Hamiltoniana*, New York, 1886, 57.)

11. Noah Webster wrote under the pseudonym of "Aristides"; William Pinckney's *Remarks* appeared under the name of "Caius"; and Uzal Ogden signed his *Letter* as "A Citizen of These States."

12. IX, 281. See also Chapter I, 7.

13. X, 113. He returned to the subject in several other letters to Lloyd. On February 6, 1815, he wrote: "My own 'missions to France,' which you call the 'great shade in my Presidential escutcheon,' I esteem the most splendid diamond in my crown; or, if any one thinks this expression too monarchical, I will say the most brilliant feather in my cap." (*Ibid.*, 115.) And he insisted that "the soundest statesmen of the ruling party in both houses" were "highly pleased" with his missions to France. (*Ibid.*, 118.)

History has certainly endorsed Adams's estimate of the French negotiations. Some writers, however, have drawn an unwarranted conclusion from his actions. Thomas A. Bailey, for instance, believes: "Adams knew perfectly well that he would dig his political grave if he averted the war that his party so ardently desired. The inflated popularity of the Federalists would collapse, and he himself would probably not be reelected in 1800 . . ." (*A Diplomatic History of the American People*, New York, 1940, 87.) This was not Adams's opinion. In his first letter to Lloyd he protested: "Had the administration persevered in the war against France, it would have been turned out at the election of 1800 by two votes to one . . ." Hamilton himself knew how unpopular the idea of war with France was. On December 22, 1800, he wrote to Theodore Sedgwick: "I am of opinion the treaty [with France] must be ratified. The contrary condition would, I think, utterly ruin the federal party and endanger the internal tranquility." It is obvious, therefore, that Adams attributed his defeat to Hamilton's machinations, not to the popular reaction to the averting of war with France. (Napoleon thought that Adams "had yielded to the general opinion" when he had decided to send a new mission to France. *Op. cit.*, 318.)

14. The framing of the new constitution began at once after the *coup d'état* of Brumaire and was completed by December 13, 1799.

15. *État de la France*, 18. An English translation of Hauterive's book by Lewis Goldsmith, *State of the French Republic at the End of the Year VIII*, was published in London in 1801. Its style, however, is heavy and involved; and since little use of it has been made here, references are given only to the French original.

16. In his Report of December 13, 1790, Hamilton saw the principal advantage of a National Bank in "the augmentation of the active or productive capital of a country." But this did not mean "thesaurisation," that is, the hoarding of gold. On the contrary, Hamilton stated that "gold and silver, where they are employed merely as the instruments of exchange and alienation have been, not improperly, denominated dead stock . . . ," and he urged that gold and silver should serve only as "the basis of a paper circulation."

Adams's charge of "recruitement" refers, of course, to Hamilton's role during the war scare. After his appointment as Inspector General of the army-to-be (twelve regiments, including six companies of cavalry), Hamilton was busy with plans for organizing a force of fifty thousand. However, only three thousand men volunteered for the ranks, while no less than fifteen thousand applied for commissions. Hamilton's military ambitions included vast schemes for the conquest of Louisiana and the Floridas—and even "the detachment of South America from Spain." He was in touch with General Miranda, the Venezuelan revolutionist and adventurer, to whom he explained (in a letter of August 22, 1798) that Great Britain should furnish the fleet and the United States the army for the enterprise. On the same day, he advised Rufus King, the American ambassador to England, that "the command in this case would very naturally fall upon me." He was even more explicit in his letter of January 26, 1799, to Harrison Gray Otis.

17. Passed on October 9, 1651, the Navigation Act prohibited the importation of goods into England in any but English ships, or else in the ships of the country in which the goods were produced. The Act struck a blow at the Dutch carrying trade, and war became inevitable. Through the victories of Blake, Deane, and Monck in 1652–53 the maritime ascendance of England was secured.

18. Barras (Paul-François-Jean-Nicolas de) was one of the most corrupt figures of the Revolution. A violent Jacobin, in October 1793 he crushed the counterrevolution in the South; later, allying himself with the moderates, he helped to overthrow Robespierre. As a member of the Directory, he was

involved in scandalous financial transactions. He helped to bring about Napoleon's marriage to Joséphine de Beauharnais, one of his own mistresses. His political career ended with the Consulate.

19. *État de la France*, 97.

20. See Chapter III, 38. Adams had no mean opinion of the influence of his work!

21. The quarrels were due to the dynastic ambitions of Elizabeth Farnese, the wife of Philip V of Spain. Elizabeth claimed the succession of the Duchy of Parma for her sons, should the ruling Duke, her uncle and stepfather, die without issue. The western powers recognized her claim, and the Emperor gave his consent in the Treaty of Vienna in 1731.

22. In the first half of 1799 the Russian general Suvaroff repeatedly defeated the French armies in Italy; and there were insurrections and disorders throughout the country.

23. Virgil's *Aeneid*, Book VI, lines 726–727. In Dryden's translation:

> "This active mind, infused through all the space,
> Unites and mingles with the mighty mass."

24. *État de la France*, 124.

25. After the fall of the Greek empire in 1204, Venice acquired the Cyclades, the Sporades, Crete, the islands and the eastern shores of the Adriatic, the shores of the Propontis and the Euxine, and the littoral of Thessaly, thus commanding the trade route between Asia Minor and Europe and becoming a European power.

26. Refers to the spectacular embassy which George III sent to the Emperor Chien-Lung in 1793, under the leadership of the Earl of Macartney. The British sovereign's presents to his Oriental cousin consisted of "specimens of the best British manufactures, and all the late inventions for adding to the conveniences and comforts of social life"—with the purpose, of course, of "exciting a more general demand for the purchase of similar articles." There were also toy machines, a planetarium, and two magnificent chandeliers among the gifts. (George Staunton, *An Embassy from the King of Great Britain to the Emperor of China*, London, 1798, II, 114–115.)

27. In June 1792 the Legislative Assembly sent commissioners to San Domingo, who on August 29, 1793, proclaimed the emancipation of the slaves. The whites staged a riot and appealed for help to the English in Jamaica. Sonthonax, one of the commissioners, relying solely upon the former slaves, suppressed the rebellion with vigor.

28. *État de la France*, 175.

29. In the spring of 1794 Victor Hugues led an expedition of eight hundred men to the Windward Islands, which had surrendered to the British. Arriving at Guadaloupe, he defeated Generals Graham and Prescott and reconquered the islands, with the exception of Martinique and Dominique. On February 3, 1797, he issued an order authorizing the ships of the Republic as well as the French pirates to take possession of any neutral vessel headed for the Windward or the Leeward Islands that were manned by the British and occupied by *émigrés*.

30. An allusion to the convention which the American envoys were to sign in Paris on September 30, 1800. The document was signed again on

October 3 in Joseph Bonaparte's *château* at Morfontaine (or Mortefontaine) in the presence of the three consuls. At the banquet Napoleon gave a toast: "To the memory of the French and Americans who died on the battlefield for the independence of the New World." Cambacérès drank "to the successes of Washington," and Lebrun "to the union of America with the northern powers to enforce respect for the freedom of the seas." (*Mémoires de Napoléon*, III, 329.)

31. Friedrich von Gentz, author of the *Essai sur l'état de•l'administration des finances de la Grande-Bretagne*, was entrusted by the English government with answering Hauterive: he did so in his *Von dem Politischen Zustande von Europa vor und nach der Französischen Revolution*, published in 1801. A brilliant and cynical writer, who from a liberal became the chief spokesman of reaction, he was a confidential adviser of Metternich and served as secretary of the Congress of Vienna. François d'Ivernois fled from Geneva to England before the Revolution engulfed his native city. An economist, he exposed the financial weaknesses of France, extolling England's strength. Hauterive discussed his *Pertes que la Révolution et la guerre ont causées au peuple français*, published in London in 1799.

32. The Maginot Line had its predecessors. The most important fortifications on the northern borders were erected by Vauban from 1655, when he was appointed *ingénieur du roi*, till his death in 1707. Stretching from Dunkirk to Verdun, this *enceinture* included a hundred and sixty fortresses built or rebuilt by the great military architect.

33. *État de la France*, 289.

34. The style of Gilbert Burnet, Bishop of Salisbury (1643–1715), author of the *History of the Reformation in England*, is full of reservations. Glancing at a page in any of his books, one is struck by the swarms of "buts."

35. Jean-Baptiste Colbert, Comptroller General and Minister of Marine during the 1660's and 1670's, wished to imitate the Navigation Act of the British, but his trading companies, in spite of their monopolies, failed.

36. Addington's peace policy was upheld by a huge majority in the House. With the renewal of the war, however, his mediocrity became evident; he resigned, and entered the new Pitt ministry as president of the council.

[XIV]

Dr. Priestley and Other English Divines

1. Adams to Jefferson, August 15, 1823, X, 409.

2. March 13, 1796, I, 488.

3. Letter to Thomas Belsham, January 11, 1798. John T. Rutt, *Life and Correspondence of Joseph Priestley* (London, 1832), II, 391.

4. Letter to George Thatcher. Manuscript in the Boston Public Library.

5. Letter to John Adams, August 1, 1799, IX, 6.

6. August 13, 1799, IX, 14.

7. *Memoirs of Dr. Joseph Priestley* (London, 1806), 201–202.

8. "Trial of Thomas Cooper for a Seditious Libel," in Francis Wharton, *State Trials of the United States* (Philadelphia, 1849), 659–681. Cooper was

thirty-five when he came to America. Two years before, he drew Burke's attack upon himself for having instituted correspondence between the Manchester Constitutional Society and the Jacobins. From 1811 on he taught chemistry at Carlisle, at the University of Pennsylvania, and finally at South Carolina College, of which he became president. In his later years he renounced his radical views and ardently defended slavery.

9. Jefferson's *Works*, IX, 217–218.

10. *Ibid.*, 458–459.

11. Thomas Belsham, *Memoirs of Theophilus Lindsey* (London, 1812), Appendix.

12. June 14, 1813, X, 42.

13. June 25, 1813, Wilstach, *Correspondence*, 71.

14. July 18, 1813, X, 57.

15. Dr. Samuel Clarke (1675–1729), English divine, was the founder of the so-called "intellectual" school, which deduced the moral law from a logical necessity. His chief work is *The Scripture Doctrine of the Trinity* (London, 1712), which brought upon him the accusation of Arianism. Daniel Waterland (1683–1740), Vice-Chancellor of the University of Cambridge, was inclined toward orthodoxy. He replied to Dr. Clarke's *Scripture Doctrine* by his *Vindication of Christ's Divinity* (London, 1719). Thomas Emlyn (1663–1741) was the first preacher who described himself as a Unitarian. After the publication of his *An Humble Inquiry into the Scripture Account of Jesus Christ* (1702), he was tried and imprisoned. John Leland (1691–1766) was a bitter foe of the deists. His chief work is *A View of the Principal Deistical Writers*, published in 1754–56.

16. August 12, 1813, Jefferson's *Works*, XI, 333.

17. J. T. Rutt, *Life and Correspondence*, II, 381.

18. *Historical Eulogium* (Paris, 1807), 39.

19. July 22, 1813, Wilstach, *Correspondence*, 71; X, 83.

20. *Early Opinions*, I, xxii.

21. Count Nicolaus Ludwig Zinzendorf (1700–1760) was a German religious and social reformer. He was the chief patron of the Bohemian or Moravian Brethren, for whom he built a village on his estate and whose missionary work he promoted. Emanuel Swedenborg (1688–1772), the Swedish scientist and mystic, was the founder of the New Church based on his *Divine Love and Wisdom*. Joseph Lomas Towers (1767–1831) was the son of Joseph Towers, the coadjutor of Dr. Richard Price. Himself a Unitarian minister, the younger Towers in 1796 published his *Illustrations of Prophecy*. George Stanley Faber (1773–1854), a learned theologian, published a number of books on Revelations, the Mosaic records, the mysteries of the Cabiri, the Arminian controversy, and similar subjects.

22. Pope, *Essay on Man*, I, 23–24.

23. *Institutions of Moses*, 167.

24. X, 83. Ocellus Lucanus (fifth century B.C.) was perhaps a pupil of Pythagoras himself. The treatise *On the Nature of the Universe* has been attributed to him—wrongly. Timaeus (fourth century B.C.) was a Greek historian; he introduced the system of reckoning by Olympiads. In 1815 Adams acquired both volumes, in the French translation of the Marquis d'Argens.

25. Priestley, *Doctrines*, 121.

26. William Enfield (1741–1797) published his work in 1791, in two volumes. It was reprinted in 1819 and in 1840.

27. Johann Jacob Brucker's *Historia critica philosophiae* was published at Leipzig in 1742–44.

28. Joseph Stevens Buckminster (1774–1812), a member of the Anthology Society, was minister of the church in Brattle Street, Cambridge. William Smith Shaw (1778–1826) was treasurer of the Anthology Society. From his devotion to the library which the Society founded he became known as "Athenaeum Shaw."

29. Middleton's *Works*, II, 138–177.

30. *Ibid.*, 23–75.

31. *Ibid.*, 79–103.

32. *Ibid.*, 123–134.

33. *Essays: Moral, Political and Literary* (London, 1875), 3.

34. *Discourse on the Grounds and Reasons of the Christian Religion.*

35. *The Use and Intent of Prophecy* (London, 1725).

36. *Works*, III, 226.

37. July 18, 1813, X, 58.

38. Disney, *Memoirs*, 241–285.

39. *Two Questions, Previous to Dr. Middleton's Free Inquiry.*

40. William Dodwell, archdeacon of Berks, published his *Free Answer to Dr. Middleton's Free Inquiry into the Miraculous Powers of the Primitive Church* in 1749. Middleton replied with a *Vindication.* (*Works*, I, 287–369.)

41. François de Paris (1690–1727), an ascetic Jansenist, became famous because of the cures wrought at his tomb in the cemetery of Saint-Médard.

42. Disney, *Memoirs*, 310–335.

43. James Peirce (1674–1726) was deprived of his pulpit at Exeter under the charge of Arianism. In his retirement he composed his *Paraphrases of St. Paul's Epistles.* The one on the Epistle to the Hebrews was published in 1727.

44. Adams must have been thinking of the *Génie du christianisme*, 1802, and the *Martyrs*, 1809.

45. The publication of the *Acta sanctorum* was begun by the Bollandist Fathers of Belgium in 1643 and completed with the sixty-third volume in 1902.

46. The Council of Nicaea, 325, condemned the teaching of Arius and declared that the Son of God was of the same nature or substance with the Father. *Homoüsian* (from *homos*, the same, and *ousia*, essence) means *of the same substance.*

47. Disney, *Memoirs*, 345–352.

48. Abraham Tucker (1705–1774), English moralist and metaphysician, was the author of *The Light of Nature Pursued*, in seven volumes. In a letter to Jefferson (December 2, 1816, X, 232) Adams mentions having read the work "in the last year or two."

49. Thomas Hollis (1720–1774), like his great-uncle of the same name, was a benefactor of Harvard College. After the fire of 1764, which destroyed the library in old Harvard Hall, he sent over a remarkable collection of books on political theory. He was called "the republican" because of his in-

terest in seventeenth-century republican literature. He left his property to Thomas Brand, who in turn was the benefactor of Disney, bequeating him a fortune worth about £5,000 a year.

50. In censuring the Bishop of Bangor, the committee of the convocation of 1717 promised to make public its "animadversions" also against several other "offensive books"—including the works of Dr. Sykes.

51. In reading these works, Adams copied out thousands of names and dates on the margins—a sign of his eagerness to absorb all the information. They are, of course, omitted from this volume. In addition, it should be noted that Adams's comments in all these theological books have been severely pruned; and that those in Dr. Middleton's *The Dispute between the Apostles Peter and Paul* and *A Treatise on the Roman Senate* have not been discussed.

[XV]

The Constant Reader

1. Adams's notes on the pamphlet have been published in their entirety by the present writer in the March 1950 issue of *Isis*, Vol. XLI, Pt. 1, 11–14.

2. For the complete text of Adams's notes see the April 1951 issue of *The Boston Public Library Quarterly*, Vol. III, No. 2, 113–117.

3. See *Ibid.*, 109–112.

4. See *Ibid.*, 119–122.

5. See *Ibid.*, 122–125.

6. For the complete text of the notes see the January 1926 issue of *More Books*, Vol. I, No. 1, 101–105.

7. See *The Boston Public Library Quarterly, loc. cit.*, 106–110.

8. See *More Books, loc. cit.*, 106–110.

INDEX

Index